A CENTURY OF VOTES FOR WOMEN

How have American women voted in the first 100 years since the ratification of the Nineteenth Amendment? How have popular understandings of women as voters both persisted and changed over time? In *A Century of Votes for Women*, Christina Wolbrecht and J. Kevin Corder offer the first comprehensive account of women voters in American politics over the last ten decades. Bringing together a wide range of data, the book provides unique insight into women's (and men's) voting behavior and traces how women's turnout and vote choice evolved over a century of enormous transformation overall and for women in particular. Wolbrecht and Corder show that there is no such thing as "the woman voter;" instead they reveal considerable variation in how different groups of women voted in response to changing political, social, and economic realities. The book also demonstrates how assumptions about women as voters influenced politicians, the press, and scholars.

Christina Wolbrecht is Professor of Political Science and Director of the Rooney Center for the Study of American Democracy at the University of Notre Dame. She is author of the award-winning books *Counting Women's Ballots* (with J. Kevin Corder) and *The Politics of Women's Rights*.

J. Kevin Corder is Professor of Political Science at Western Michigan University. His books include *Counting Women's Ballots* (with Christina Wolbrecht), which received the 2017 Victoria Schuck Award, and *The Fed and the Credit Crisis*.

D0802428

A CENTURY OF VOTES FOR WOMEN

American Elections since Suffrage

Christina Wolbrecht

University of Notre Dame

J. Kevin Corder

Western Michigan University

CAMBRIDGE
UNIVERSITY PRESS

CAMBRIDGE
UNIVERSITY PRESS

University Printing House, Cambridge CB2 8BS, United Kingdom

One Liberty Plaza, 20th Floor, New York, NY 10006, USA

477 Williamstown Road, Port Melbourne, VIC 3207, Australia

314–321, 3rd Floor, Plot 3, Splendor Forum, Jasola District Centre, New Delhi – 110025, India

79 Anson Road, #06-04/06, Singapore 079906

Cambridge University Press is part of the University of Cambridge.

It furthers the University's mission by disseminating knowledge in the pursuit of education, learning, and research at the highest international levels of excellence.

www.cambridge.org
Information on this title: www.cambridge.org/9781107187498
DOI: 10.1017/9781316941331

First published 2020

Printed in the United Kingdom by TJ International Ltd., Padstow, Cornwall

A catalogue record for this publication is available from the British Library.

ISBN 978-1-107-18749-8 Hardback
ISBN 978-1-316-63807-1 Paperback

Contents

Figures

Acknowledgments

In May of 2015, we met for lunch at Purple Porch Co-op in South Bend, Indiana to celebrate signing the contract for our book, *Counting Women's Ballots: Female Voters from Suffrage Through the New Deal*. Our research into women voters immediately after suffrage had commenced in the Fall of 1998, so we were thrilled and more than a little relieved to be closing in on the completion of that project. We were, however, still in the midst of finishing the final revisions before the manuscript went into production. On the last page of the last chapter, printed for mark-up for the last time, Wolbrecht had scribbled an outline for a new book, describing and analyzing women voters, not just immediately after suffrage, but throughout the first 100 years following the ratification of the Nineteenth Amendment. Maybe we weren't completely done with women voters, after all? The book in your hands (or on your screen) is the answer to that question.

We are grateful for the support and feedback which made this book possible. Conversations with Lisa Baldez, Karen Beckwith, Adam Berinsky, Barry Burden, Nancy Burns, Erin Cassese, Devin Caughey, Sara Chatfield, Michael Coppedge, Jane Junn, Philip Klinkler, Corrine McConnaughy, Melissa Michelson, Heather Ondercin, Virginia Sapiro, Eric Schickler, and Maya Sen – as well as others we are surely but regretfully forgetting – enriched and improved our work. Presentations at the American, British, and Canadian Political Development workshop (Oxford University, UK), the Historical Women's Movements conference (University of Pennsylvania), and the Political Parties in Comparative Perspective conference (Georgetown University, Firenze, Italy) helped us refine and improve our arguments. Talks on *Counting Women's Ballots* at Northwestern University, University of California-Berkeley, the Ohio State University, Cornell University, University of Denver, University of Texas-Austin, and Western Michigan University aided us in drawing out the implications of that work for later elections. Public presentations to the Kalamazoo Public Library and Kalamazoo Ladies' Library Association and to Notre Dame alumni at the National Women's Rights Historical Park in Seneca Falls helped us learn to convey our research in ways that we hope are clear and compelling for those who do not look at voting data for a living.

We also benefited from excellent research assistance. At Western Michigan, graduate student Vilitcia Barghouti, and at Notre Dame, undergraduates Casey Baker, Katelyn Berens, Ceramontana Crowell, Madeline Doctor, Kathryn Doyle, Zachary Herford, Kate Lenahan, Joseph McKenna, Lisa Michelini, Avery Naylor, Caitlyn O'Connell, Rachel O'Grady, Ryan Schaffler, MacKenzie Thurman, Allison Towey, Jenna Wilson, Zachary Yim, and especially Katie O'Sullivan, helped us with a range of tasks, most notably tracking down many of the newspaper stories we use to help illuminate public discourse about women voters over time. We are grateful for financial support from the Department of Political Science at Western Michigan University, made possible by Chet Rogers and John Clark. At Notre Dame, Wolbrecht is thankful for the support of collaborator and chair David Campbell, as well as Kathy Cummings, Karen Graubart, and Karrie Koesel. We are especially indebted to editor Sara Doskow at Cambridge University Press for her enthusiasm and guidance from start to finish, and to the anonymous reviewers for their cogent and generous feedback.

As always, we are grateful to our families, who did not riot when we told them we were going to write another book. Corder appreciates the willingness of his wife, Susan Hoffmann, to remain enthusiastic about each new iteration of every figure. Wolbrecht thanks her husband, Matt Doppke, whose support remains constant and essential (and only occasionally sardonic), and her daughters, Ella and Jane, who will cast their first ballots in the second century of women's enfranchisement, helping to ensure that the future is indeed female.

CHAPTER 1

Women at the Polls

The right of citizens of the United States to vote shall not be denied or abridged by the United States or by any State on account of sex.

Congress shall have power to enforce this article by appropriate legislation.

Nineteenth Amendment to the US Constitution

THE NINETEENTH AMENDMENT TO THE US CONSTITUTION WAS RATIFIED IN August 1920, setting off a flurry of speculation about how newly enfranchised women would vote in the upcoming presidential election. Although women in fifteen states already enjoyed the right to vote by 1920, politicians and observers nonetheless expressed uncertainty about what to expect. "Women's Vote Baffles Politicians' Efforts to Forecast Election" claimed one newspaper.[1] Another reported that "anxious politicians of both parties are sitting up nights worrying about [women's votes]."[2] Appeals to new women voters emphasized issues specific to women, such as equal pay and maternity care, and issues related to women's roles as mothers, such as child labor and education.[3] In the aftermath of the election, many claimed that women had handed the election to Republican Warren G. Harding, for reasons ranging from his good looks to the Republican party's support of women's suffrage.[4] Others attributed the Republican advantage to specific groups of women; the women many considered most likely to turn out to vote in 1920 – suffrage activists – tended to be native-born white women, who like native-born white men, were expected to vote Republican.[5]

Almost a century later, the presidential election of 2016 – with Tweets, Russian meddling, and the first-ever woman major party nominee – differed dramatically from the presidential election of 1920. And yet, there are striking similarities between the two when it comes to women voters. Interest in the potential impact of women was again pervasive: "The Trump-Clinton Gender Gap Could be the Largest in More Than 60 Years," predicted NPR.[6] "Women May Decide the Election," claimed *The Atlantic*.[7] Parties and candidates continued to target women voters, defined as women, and especially as mothers: Hillary Clinton highlighted her famous declaration that "women's rights are human rights" in an "appeal to female voters," explained NPR.[8] Donald Trump was "Targeting 'Security Moms,'" according to *Time* magazine.[9] As in 1920, post-election analysis focused on the distinct contributions of different groups of women to the Republican victory: "Clinton Couldn't Win Over White Women," emphasized popular election website, FiveThiryEight. "Why Hillary Clinton lost the white women's vote," echoed the *Christian Science Monitor*.[10]

The presidential elections of 1920 and 2016 both featured widespread speculation about the impact of women voters. In both elections, appeals to and analysis of women voters often were grounded in assumptions and stereotypes about women's interests *as women*, and particularly as mothers. In both elections, the Republican candidate won. Yet, the actual political behavior of women in these two elections was quite different. In 1920, our best estimates are that about one-third of eligible women turned out to vote. In 2016, 63% of women cast ballots in the presidential election. Women were much *less* likely to turn out than were men in 1920 (a nearly 35 point gap, on average), but women were slightly *more* likely to turn out to vote than were men in 2016 (4 point gap). Women's partisan preferences also shifted. Republicans had a slight advantage, at most, among women in 1920, but by 2016, it was Democrats who maintained a consistent advantage among women. Both women (63%) and men (60%) overwhelmingly supported Harding in 1920. Exit polls conducted in 2016 indicated that only 41% of women voted for Trump compared to 52% of men.[11]

A Century of Votes for Women describes and explains how women voted in presidential elections from the ratification of the Nineteenth Amendment until the present day. Our brief discussion of women voters in the first (1920) and last (2016) elections covered here highlights four key arguments of this book. First, the actual voting behavior of women – both the extent to which they turn out to vote and the parties and candidates they tend to support – has varied considerably over time. We trace the evolution of women's turnout and vote choice across the past century briefly below and in detail in the chapters that follow. Second, popular discourse about "the woman voter" varies but also is characterized by remarkably consistent themes and assumptions over these ten decades, despite extraordinary changes in women's lives. Third, women (like men) are not a monolithic group and other identities and experiences are often as or more important than gender for women's voting behavior. Fourth, history matters. Women's (and men's) electoral behavior must be understood within the unique political, social, and economic context in which it takes place.

Women Voters Over Time

Women's voting behavior has evolved since the ratification of the Nineteenth Amendment. The story of voter *turnout* is largely one of women becoming increasingly similar to men. In terms of *vote choice*, however, women have become more distinct. The first women voters lagged considerably behind men in their tendency to enter polling places, although the extent to which women and men turned out (and the size of the turnout gender gap) varied from state to state depending on the political context.[12] By 1964, women's increasingly high turnout combined with women's greater numbers in the eligible electorate translated into more women than men casting ballots for president. Since 1980 women have been more likely than men to turn out in presidential elections.[13]

The historical trajectory of women's vote choice – which parties and candidates women tend to support at the polls – is a more complicated story. In the main, the ebbs and flows of women's vote choice have reflected the broader electoral trends of the nation as a whole: Republicans were the majority party, consistently winning presidential elections, in the period immediately after extension of the suffrage. Women, like men, voted overwhelmingly Republican. In a dramatic shift, Democrats wrested majority status from the GOP during the New Deal period of the 1930s, and would maintain that status for at least the next 50 years. Women, like men, contributed to the emerging and persistent Democratic majority. As that majority status eroded across the second half of the twentieth century and into the twenty-first, both men and women shifted toward the Republican party. These shared shifts are significant. Despite women's historic exclusion from the electorate, differences in gender socialization, and women's distinct position in the social and economic structure, women and men generally cast ballots for the same parties and candidates.

Yet, in some places and in some times, women's vote choice diverged from that of men. Women voters were slightly more likely than men to cast Republican ballots in some elections prior to 1964. Women voters have become consistently more likely than men to support Democratic candidates, and men to support Republicans, since at least 1980.[14] This does *not* mean that a majority of women cast Democratic ballots in every election since 1980; Republicans won majorities of women's votes in 1984 and 1988. But the percentage of men casting Republican ballots is larger than the percentage of women doing so in every presidential election from 1980 on, even when Republicans captured a majority of the votes of both women and men. In some recent elections – 2000, 2004, 2012, and 2016 – a majority of women favor the Democratic candidate, while a majority of men favor the Republican.[15]

Framing Women Voters

Women voters have been the subject of considerable interest and speculation across these ten decades. Observers and campaigns have often assumed women's gender per se is the key to understanding women's political behavior and interests. Women's presumed natural disinterest in the rough-and-tumble world of politics explains their relatively low turnout in early presidential elections, for example.[16] Women's interest in issues specific to women – suffrage, equal pay, abortion – have been invoked to explain their choice of party and candidates.[17] Fundamental personality and values differences, such as women's greater compassion, are assumed to explain women's support for social welfare programs and the parties associated with them.[18] The interests of women voters have been repeatedly understood in terms of their roles as wives and mothers: Women oppose war (ranging from Korea to Iraq) because they fear their husbands and sons being sent off to fight. Women are concerned with inflation and high prices because they manage the household finances. Women prioritize education and health care because of their maternal concern for the well-being of children. These beliefs about the interests and behavior of women as voters has shaped women's political influence, the creation of public policy, and the ways in which candidates and parties appealed to female voters. We seek to

4

not only describe how women voted, but how women voters were understood by contemporaries and scholars.

Women are Not a Voting Bloc

American women are diverse. Not all women turn out to vote or vote the same way. Gender is not the most salient political identity shaping electoral behavior for most women (or men). Factors such as race, ethnicity, class, religion, employment, education, and marital status all shape women's (and men's) electoral behavior in important ways. Women's experiences also are shaped by their location; where women exercise their electoral rights is often as important as the fact that they are women. Among the most important aspects of women's diversity is race. The Nineteenth Amendment prohibited the denial of voting rights on the basis of sex. It left in place, however, legal and extra-legal practices which denied voting rights on other bases, most notably on the basis of race in the American South.[19] As a result, most women of color continued to be excluded from the suffrage until the passage of the Voting Rights Act in 1965 and face unique challenges today.[20]

Diversity means that it is impossible to speak of "the woman's vote." There is no one stereotypical woman, but rather as many "kinds" of women voters as there are kinds of men voters. Multiple factors determine women's decision to turn out to vote and who to vote for, many of which trump the impact of being a woman. Women also vary in their political views, generally and specifically related to women's rights. Women have both opposed and supported suffrage, equal pay, abortion rights, the Equal Rights Amendment, and family leave policies. Women are capable of holding and expressing sexist beliefs – both benevolent and hostile – with consequences for their electoral behavior.[21] We describe women's rates of turnout and party vote share in a general sense, but our further analysis emphasizes the considerable variability of electoral behavior across different groups of women.

The Importance of Historical Context

Finally, voters do not cast ballots in a vacuum. Rather, the decision to turn out to vote and for whom to cast a ballot is made within a specific moment, characterized by events, issues, conditions, and candidates that shape and frame decisions in particular ways. For that reason, we have organized our discussion of women voters historically, which allows us to highlight the specific issues and candidates, as well as the social, economic, and political developments, that shaped electoral choices for women and men, and how those actions were understood, in each election and era.

Major political developments ranging from the New Deal and the Cold War to the civil rights movement and 9/11 have transformed American politics for citizens in general and often for women in particular. Technological and economic developments, such as the expansion of mass-produced clothing and food and the shift from an industrial to a post-industrial economy, have had social and political impacts broadly, as well as specifically for women. Significant changes in the conditions of women's lives – the increasing participation of women in the paid workforce, the expansion of occupations open to women, changes in marital practice and stability, and shifting patterns of pregnancy and child-rearing – have always had political consequences.[22]

The chapters that follow provide ample support for these arguments and observations, and we return to them again in the conclusion. In this introductory chapter, we prepare readers for our discussion of women voters across the past century in three ways: First, we identify and discuss some of the key issues involved in thinking about and examining women as voters in American politics across 100 years. Next, we briefly review the many monumental developments in the lived experience of women's lives across this ten-decade period. Finally, we describe, in the most general sense, the turnout and vote choice of women voters from 1920 through 2016, highlighting general trends that are explored in greater detail throughout the book. We conclude the chapter with a preview of the chapters which follow.

THE STUDY OF WOMEN VOTERS

This is a book about women voters. Specifically, it is a book about the turnout and vote choice of American women in presidential elections from the ratification of the Nineteenth Amendment in 1920 through the election of 2016. We seek to understand how women used the vote – and how political observers and scholars explained women's use of the vote – across the past 100 years.

In this section, we review a number of the key issues that arise when we examine women as voters.

Women Voters and the Gender Gap

To understand women voters as women, we must be attentive to the voting behavior of the rest of the voting age population – that is, to men. In other words, if we want to understand how, if at all, women as a group employ their right to vote in a distinctive manner, we need to compare their turnout and vote choice to that of men. The difference between the political behavior of women and men is known in both popular and scholarly parlance as the gender gap. The term "gender gap" was coined by feminist activists seeking to gain political leverage from the fact that women were less likely than men to cast ballots for Republican Ronald Reagan in 1980. Activists argued that the gender gap was a reaction to Reagan's anti-feminist positions; by revealing the electoral costs of those actions, they hoped to create political pressure in favor of women's rights.[23] The size, consequences, and reasons for the gender gap remain politically contested; Republicans, for example, have an incentive to highlight the problems Democrats seem to have in attracting men's votes, while Democrats frame their advantage among women as a seal of approval for their policy positions. Despite its political origins, the term gender gap is now in widespread use to describe any and all differences between women and men ranging from economics and health to movie dialogue and celebrity chefs.[24]

The divergent voting preferences of women and men remain the original definition and prevailing use of the term gender gap. For the sake of clarity, we use the term "turnout gender gap" when speaking of differences between the percentage of eligible women turning out to vote versus the percentage of men doing so. Differences between the percentage of women voting for a candidate or party (usually the winning one) and the percentage of men who do so are described as the "gender gap" or the "partisan gender gap." Measurement of the gender gap is contested, but our measure is the standard approach used by activists, the press, and scholars since the gender gap was "named" after the 1980 election.[25]

We are cognizant that the gender gap can obscure as much as it reveals, particularly when considering change over time. A change in the size of the partisan gender gap, for example, can result from dramatic shifts in men's preferences while women remain steadfast for one party, shifts among women but not men, or shifts in the party preferences of both women and men. Each has different implications for our understanding of the political behavior of women and of the impact of gender on electoral politics.[26] For this reason, our practice is to present women's and men's turnout and vote choice separately, rather than the gender gap alone, in most cases.

The Male Standard

While useful, comparisons of women's and men's voting behavior can be problematic.[27] In voting, as in other areas, the behavior of men is often presented as the standard; that is, male turnout and vote choice are understood as *normal* and any divergence from the male standard by women is viewed as a puzzle to be solved. Women's turnout is considered high or low relative to male turnout. Women's support for particular parties is only presented as notable when it diverges from the partisan preferences of men.

The focus on comparison with men can lead to distorted and inaccurate understandings of women's political behavior. In recent decades, popular and scholarly discussions of the gender gap gave the impression that women were strong supporters of the Democratic party. Women of all racial and ethnic groups have been more supportive of Democrats than similar men since at least 1980, but in the case of white women that does not always, or even usually, mean that women supported Democrats more than they supported Republicans. Indeed, a majority of white women supported the Republican candidate in every presidential election since 1950, save two. Black women, on the other hand, have consistently given a majority of their votes to Democratic candidates to an even greater extent than have black men during this period. A focus on the gender gap combined with a failure to recognize diversity among women gives the mistaken impression that all women vote Democratic.[28]

The male standard hampers our understanding of women as voters in other ways as well. When political activists identified the partisan gender gap in favor of Democrats in 1980, popular discourse focused on women as the cause of any divergence in party preference between women and men. Men's choice of candidates was presumed to be the norm; women's a deviation. Not surprisingly, then, explanations for the gender gap (discussed in Chapter 3) have tended to focus on women per se – women's growing autonomy from men, women's reaction to the parties' changing positions on women's rights issues, the impact of women's increased education and employment, and so on. Yet, in reality, the emergence of the current gender gap was as much or more due to the behavior of men as it was women: Men shifted to the GOP after the 1960s, while women remained Democrats or shifted toward the Republican party to a lesser extent than men (see Chapter 7).[29]

The male standard also is problematic when men's political behavior is treated as not just normal, but as normatively ideal. For example, one of the key findings of early voting research was that women were less likely to express a sense that they personally can influence the political world; that is, they were less likely to express political efficacy. This shortcoming was viewed as key to understanding why women lagged behind men in voter turnout but also as a failure of women as citizens.[30] Yet, later scholars noted that framing women as deficient for not expressing more personal efficacy assumes that men's tendency to view themselves as effective political agents was a reasonable and even laudable belief. But is it? Political scientists Sandra Baxter and Marjorie Lansing explain:

> Instead of interpreting the difference as an inadequacy in women, we suggest that given the very limited number of issues that citizens can affect, the lower sense of political efficacy expressed by women may be a perceptive assessment of the political process. Men, on the other hand, express irrationally high rates of efficacy.[31]

We compare women's and men's voting behavior throughout this book, as one way of determining when gender is, and is not, meaningful for electoral behavior. We avoid claiming that one group's behavior is the standard against which the other's behavior should be judged or offering conclusions than how one group measures up normatively against the other.

While our focus is on the specific, political act of voting, we also are aware that the male standard can shape even our understanding of what is political. When we judge women by whether they vote, donate to political campaigns, know national political figures, or run for office, we are holding women to a standard of political activity that is defined by things men have traditionally done. When we turn to other behaviors, such as working with community organizations, volunteering on civic and political campaigns, and knowing everyday economic information (like prices) – all of which are absolutely political – a very different picture of women's engagement emerges.[32] In this book, our concern is with traditional electoral participation, but we remain cognizant of the diverse other ways in which women engage in political activity.

One Hundred Years?

We begin our examination of women voters with the presidential election of 1920, held just weeks after the ratification of the Nineteenth Amendment. For the study of women voters, the election of 1920 is both "too late and too early."[33] The election of 1920 is too late because women had been voting in American elections for decades prior to the ratification of the Nineteenth Amendment. Indeed, a few propertied women cast ballots in several New England states in the late eighteenth century. As states expanded voting rights for men without property in the early decades of the nineteenth century, they closed those state-level loopholes for women.[34] As a result of the determined work of suffragists in state campaigns in the second half of the nineteenth century, women in fifteen states had secured the right to vote in most elections prior to 1920 (see Chapter 2).[35] The national woman suffrage amendment was the culmination of a long-term process of expanding, and sometimes constricting, voting rights for women in the United States.

At the same time, the election of 1920 is much too early to declare universal female suffrage accomplished. There were short-term delays for women; four Southern states refused to let women vote in 1920 due to their failure to meet registration deadlines that occurred months before the Nineteenth Amendment was ratified. (Other states with similar deadlines adjusted their rules to accommodate new women voters.)[36] Women in those states were unable to vote in a presidential election until 1924.

In the longer term, Jim Crow practices in the South meant most black women continued to be disenfranchised on the basis of their race for decades following the presidential election of 1920.[37] The continuing disenfranchisement of black women after suffrage occurs in a broader context in which suffragists, especially in the final decades of the struggle, often adopted racist and ethnocentric arguments in favor of giving women the right to vote, claiming that native-born white women would counter the votes of black and immigrant men. How could such men, suffragists explicitly argued, deserve the right to vote when respectable white, middle-class women did not? Prominent suffragists engaged in overtly racist language and behavior and excluded black suffragists from white suffrage organizations and activism. The woman suffrage cause was linked to racism and Jim Crow long before the Nineteenth Amendment was ratified.[38]

Just as the Fifteenth Amendment (on which the Nineteenth is expressly modeled) forbade the denial of voting rights on the basis of "race, color, or previous condition of servitude," the Nineteenth Amendment similarly prohibited the denial of voting rights "on account of sex." However, neither the Fifteenth nor the Nineteenth Amendment established an affirmative right to vote, akin to the rights to speech, assembly, due process, and so on enshrined elsewhere in the US Constitution. Indeed, the Constitution itself says little about voting and does not guarantee the right to vote to anyone (see Chapter 2). The Nineteenth Amendment thus did not directly confront legal or extra-legal practices that denied people of color, including women of color, the right to vote in the South.[39]

The impact of Jim Crow on access to the vote for black women was enormous. Nationwide, women of color comprised only about 5% of the total female electorate in any election before 1964, despite black women being 11% of the population (see Figure 1.1).[40] Nonetheless, some black women were able to vote prior to the 1965 Voting Rights Act. Historian Suzanne Lebsock details the considerable lengths to which local governments and the Democratic party went to keep black women from registering (and to encourage white women to register in order to counteract black women at the polls) in 1920s Virginia. These efforts were not entirely successful, however; Lebsock concludes: "By the end of 1920 Virginia was still a bastion of white supremacy, but several thousand black women had achieved the dignity of citizenship," often as a result of great individual and collective effort and cost.[41] The implementation of Jim Crow varied, in part based on the relative size of the black community; the larger the African American population, the greater the efforts were to suppress their votes. In their study of black and white Southerners (see Chapter 5), Donald R. Matthews and James W. Prothro report African American registration rates varying from zero to more than 60% across Southern counties in 1960. On the whole, however, the reality was that while the Nineteenth Amendment prohibited the denial of voting rights on the basis of sex, Jim

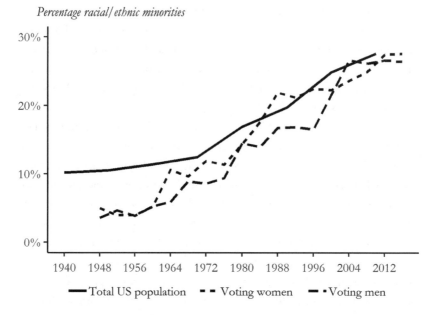

Percentage racial/ethnic minorities

Figure 1.1 Racial composition of US voters shows women of color generally lacked access to the ballot until the 1960s (ANES and US Census), 1948–2016

Crow and other practices kept the vast majority of African American women from exercising their voting rights for decades.

While the ratification of the Nineteenth Amendment did not mean that all women had access to the ballot, it is nonetheless a landmark for women in American politics. The amendment transformed women's relationship to the political sphere, as well as the "boundaries between male and female."[42] Politics as the sole province of men and the home as women's natural place were considered fundamental aspects of masculinity and femininity. By prohibiting discrimination in access to the ballot on the basis of sex, the Nineteenth Amendment recognized women as political actors in their own, independent right, challenging long-held norms about women, men, and the nature of politics itself.[43] The installation of those principles into the US Constitution represented a profound challenge to traditional political structures that excluded and disparaged women. The Nineteenth Amendment thus was a key step in a long, not always straightforward, process of expanding political equality and access to power for women. The centennial of that achievement provides an opportunity to take stock of how American women have used their hard-won right to vote and how women voters have been understood by contemporary observers and later scholars.

Identifying Periods of Analysis

In the chapters that follow, we divide the past ten decades into five time periods to facilitate our understanding of women voters. How did we select these periods? We are focused in this book on (1) the voting rights of women, (2) the shifting political, economic, and social context, especially with regards to women, and (3) the actual voting behavior of women. All three of these dynamics have experienced considerable change during the past 100 years. All three are clearly interrelated. Yet, each has followed a unique trajectory. The empirical chapters are structured around key shifts in all three.[44]

Legal order. In terms of legal suffrage rights, the period 1920 to the present day might be described as a single period in which women enjoyed voting rights post-Nineteenth Amendment. That amendment prohibited discrimination in access to the vote on the basis of sex.[45] Unlike the prohibition on race and previous servitude as voting qualifications in the Fifteenth Amendment, there was no state-implemented, aided, and endorsed retraction of suffrage rights for women qua women after 1920.

Yet, the right to vote is not a constant for all American women across this period, as we have discussed. Most notably, the same formal and informal institutions that denied the vast majority of African American men access to the ballot in the first half of the twentieth century applied with equal force to African American women. Despite the concerns of white Southerners that the repression of black voters would be more difficult in the case of black women, the Jim Crow South found ways, including violence, to deny women of color the vote. For the vast majority of black women, the Voting Rights Act of 1965 is a transformative moment as or more central to voting rights than is the Nineteenth Amendment in 1920. There are therefore at least two important shifts in women's voting rights across this century.

Gender order. Both the expectations for and reality of women's political, economic, and social lives – what we term gender orders – is a second dynamic that organizes our analysis. Gender orders describe the actual practice and structure of society and institutions, but also are ideational in the sense of a set of culturally shared, idealized feminine and masculine roles, characteristics, behaviors, and stereotypes, as well as conscious and unconscious biases related to sex and gender.[46] Traditional views of gender (or what we term traditional gender orders) are characterized by distinct and conservative sex roles and norms, and greater male power and status relative to women. Egalitarian gender orders, on the other hand, institute or propose a view of women and men as fundamentally equal in capacity, opportunity, and rights. These are of course ideals, with most periods characterized by a mix of both traditional and egalitarian gender norms.

While the Nineteenth Amendment certainly represents a challenge to a key aspect of traditional gender norms, it did not necessarily disrupt other types of gender traditionalism which were consequential for women's use of the ballot. For example, continuing (and legally enforced) sex segregation in the workforce and sex role differentiation in the family have significant consequences for women's use of the vote.[47] At the same time, while the expansion of suffrage to women was likely both an expression of and helped to bring about shifts in widely held views about women and gender (i.e., ideation), the passage of the Nineteenth Amendment did not necessarily change assumptions about women's political capacities or interests, as we show.

The previous 100 years have been characterized by dramatic and successful challenges to traditional gender order and shifts toward egalitarian gender order. Progress is not linear, however, but characterized by the undermining of some aspects of traditional gender order and the reconfiguring and reassertion of others. The challenging of sexual mores in the "Roaring Twenties" followed by the opening up of opportunities for women in the workforce made possible by the Great Depression, and especially the Second World War, created a period of shifting gender roles and norms in the 1920s through the early 1940s, although most sex-based legal structures remained unchanged. On the other hand, the 1940s through the early 1960s are generally understood as a period in which traditional femininity and gender roles were reasserted in culture and institutions. The late 1960s and 1970s witnessed the emergence of the second wave of the women's movement, dramatic shifts in women's participation in the paid workforce and in the structure of families, and significant transformations in gender roles in the United States and throughout the world.

A conservative backlash against those changes contributed to the emergence of the modern culture war in the 1980s and 1990s. Understanding the evolving framing of and rhetoric surrounding women as voters requires attention to the dynamics of gender orders in the United States over time.[48]

Electoral behavior. Women's voting behavior shifts over time, as does our capacity to observe it. With very few exceptions, official vote records do not and cannot distinguish between the turnout and vote choice of women and men. Reliable mass surveys did not begin to appear until the mid-1930s, and were not widely available until the 1950s. Exit polls did not come into wide use until the 1970s. Thus while commentators and scholars make claims about how women voted from the 1920 election onwards, the quality and quantity of the available evidence varies considerably over time. Even when reliable public opinion data are available, the degree to which informed analysis of *how* and *why* women voted as they did is disseminated through the press and to the public varies as well.[49]

We trace stability and change in the two key aspects of women's electoral behavior: turnout and vote choice. Women remained less likely to turn out than men until 1980, although due to the greater numbers of women in the population and their eligibility to vote, there were more women than men in the active presidential electorate from 1964 onwards.[50] The story for vote choice is more complicated. Conventional wisdom (and some data analysis) has long described women voters as favoring the Republican party, but only to a very small degree, before the early 1960s. Women and men were then largely indistinguishable in their party preference until 1980. From that time on, women have been consistently more likely to favor Democratic candidates, although the presence and extent of that advantage varies across groups and over time.[51]

Organizing the century. Focusing on these three dimensions – the status of legal voting rights relevant to women (legal order), gender roles, norms, and structures (gender order), and the actual voting behavior of women (electoral behavior) – we divide the century into five periods: the first women voters (1920–36); feminine mystique and the American voter (1940–64); feminism resurgent (1968–76); the discovery of the gender gap (1980–96); and the new millennium (2000–16). In each empirical chapter, we specify key aspects of the political context, with special attention to shifting gender norms and practices as well as relevant shifts in the legal environment in which women cast their votes. The ultimate goal of each chapter is then to describe and review trends in, and explanations for, the turnout and vote choice of women voters.

Our first period (1920–36), for example, kicks off with a dramatic shift in women's legal access to the franchise with the ratification of the Nineteenth Amendment (legal order). Restrictions on voting by people of color and immigrants, however, continue to bar some women from the vote. We highlight important changes in gender roles (gender order), as sexual mores were loosened during the "Roaring Twenties" and technological changes – electricity, indoor plumbing, mass-produced food and clothing – were transforming the domestic obligations of women. Yet views about women's political interests remained rooted in motherhood and domesticity, and assumptions about women's essentially apolitical nature remained strong.[52] Until recently, information about the actual turnout and vote choice of women (electoral behavior) has been virtually nonexistent as public opinion surveys were unavailable or unreliable during this period. Nonetheless, both contemporary and later observers made rather definitive claims about how women used their votes.[53] In this period, we use recent research to inform our description of the turnout and vote choice of the first women to enter polling places after the Nineteenth Amendment was ratified. Each empirical chapter offers a similar overview of a key period for women as voters in American politics.

Turnout and Vote Choice in Presidential Elections

When we examine women voters we are interested in two distinct, but related political choices. First, the choice of whether to exercise the right to vote – the participation decision. Second, the choice of candidates – the vote choice decision. These choices are intertwined: People turn out to vote largely in order to cast ballots for particular parties and candidates.[54]

A number of scholars interested in the electoral behavior of women have focused on gender differences in party identification, rather than actual vote. These two behaviors are closely related; the most powerful predictor of vote choice is the party with which a citizen identifies. Not surprisingly, respondents who say they identify as Republicans tend to vote for Republican candidates, and respondents who claim Democratic identification tend to vote for Democratic nominees.[55] The strength of the association between party identification and vote choice shifts over time, but it is usually quite strong.[56]

Party identification is generally more stable than vote choice over the lifetime, so focusing on vote choice allows us to observe more clearly the way women respond to specific electoral contests and contexts. Gender differences in vote choice tend to be associated with gender differences in party identification, and the arguments for why women tend to be more or less likely than men to identify with specific parties are largely indistinguishable from the arguments for why women tend to be more or less likely to vote for each party's candidates. In our discussion of the causes of gender differences we highlight explanations offered for both vote choice and party identification.

Our focus is on women voters in presidential elections. Certainly presidential elections have been the focus of much of the rhetoric and analysis around women voters. As the most prominent and salient of American elections, presidential contests provide an ideal opportunity to trace the electoral behavior of women and men. In other races, most notably for the US House and US Senate, the powerful impact of incumbency can overwhelm other effects, including gender. While the patterns we identify, such as women's increasing propensity to turn out and the recent relative Democratic advantage among women voters, characterize elections for other offices, those races are characterized by their own unique dynamics as well.[57]

Sex and Gender

We are cognizant of our use of the terms sex and gender. It has become commonplace to treat sex as a biological marker distinguishing females from males, while gender is understood as the social meaning we give to sex; gender is the set of stereotypes, norms, and expectations that society assigns to the biological categories of women and men. Importantly, gender characterizes, shapes, and defines not only human beings but also institutions, social organization, and the state.[58]

Some would argue that the two broad categories we examine here – women and men – are examples of simple sex difference. In a strict sense, the vast majority of the research we describe and present distinguishes between women and men, but does not measure gender (in terms of femininity and masculinity) or gender identity. However, we choose to use the term gender in this book to highlight that our focus is on "men and women as social groups rather than biological groups."[59] Our analysis of the turnout and vote choice of women and men relies on observations of the reported (or assumed) gender identity of citizens in census reports, exit polls, and public opinion surveys. Explanations for how and why women vote and vote the way they do are deeply rooted in gender role expectations and norms that are sustained and reproduced through social, economic, and political interactions, institutions, and practices. And perhaps most simply, the widespread adoption of the term "gender gap" has generated a strong association between the term gender and the political behavior of women and men. We recognize that gender is a far more complicated concept than the simple difference in women's and men's observed electoral behavior that we examine here. Recent work, for example, has begun to explore non-binary gender identification and voting behavior as well as the impact of masculinity and femininity distinct from sex. One benefit of our use of the term gender is that it emphasizes the complexity of how gender roles and stereotypes operate, and thus captures the complexity of the electoral behavior we seek to understand.

THE EVOLVING LIVES OF WOMEN VOTERS

It would be difficult to overstate the extent of social, economic, and political change across the last century. The Great Depression, postwar boom, oil crisis, inflation, tech boom, and real estate crash. American's rise as a global power and recurring struggles on the world stage. Social and racial progress and backlash. These developments and many more provide the backdrop for the electoral contests of this age in general, and for women voters in specific ways.

The 100-year period we examine here also is characterized by dramatic changes in the lived experiences of American women. In this section, we highlight three developments since 1920 that are particularly consequential for women and politics: Women have become more likely to complete college; more likely to delay marriage and families; and more likely to participate in the labor force. The combination of these factors implies a fairly radical change in the social and economic status of women relative to men, as well as absolute gains in economic security and educational attainment. The implications of these changes in status are clear for women's turnout: Each change should increase turnout. The impact of these changes on women's ties to the major political parties is more complicated. While we explore the political implications in more detail in later chapters, we set the stage here by describing the three major changes in broad strokes.

Education

Both women and men realized major gains in educational attainment after 1940, but the timing of those gains was quite different for the two groups, as data from the US Census demonstrates in Figure 1.2. College completion rates for men rose faster than for women before 1983. In that year, women were a third less likely to have four years of college or more than men. At the same time, younger women began to graduate college at higher rates than younger men, narrowing the overall gap between men and women each year. While generational differences remain, the educational attainment advantage among women in younger cohorts is now large enough to make the rate of college completion similar between women and men overall. Today, women are more likely than men to have completed four years of college and this educational advantage is likely to persist and grow over time.

Work

Women had increasingly entered the paid workforce since the nineteenth century, particularly poor, African American, and immigrant women. In the 1920s, increasing numbers of young and unmarried white women joined the labor force as well. The Second World War famously witnessed a sharp expansion in women's labor force participation; while the rate of women engaged in paid work declined after 1945, it did not return to prewar levels, and continued to rise thereafter. Labor force participation rates after the Second World War reveal very different trajectories for men and women (see Figure 1.3).[60] Men had nearly universal labor force participation in 1948, but the proportion of men aged 16 and over engaged with work dropped to nearly 70% by 2016. The percentage of women in the paid workforce, on the other hand, increased dramatically after 1948 (when it was barely over 30%) and plateaued after 2000 at about 60%.

Percentage of any age with a college degree

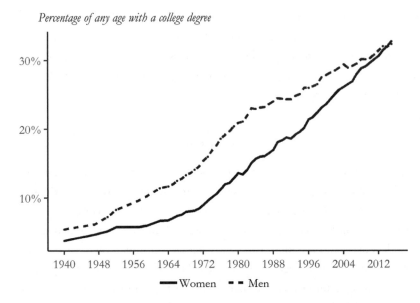

Figure 1.2 Women catch up to men in college attainment by 2015 (US Census), 1940–2016

Labor force participation rate, percentage

Figure 1.3 Women's labor force participation grows sharply, while men's declines, in the postwar era (Bureau of Labor Statistics), 1948–2016

Live births per 1,000 women aged 15–44

Figure 1.4 Baby boom and bust across the twentieth century (National Center for Health Statistics), 1920–2016

Marriage and Family

Finally, a combination of economic transformations, shifting social norms, legal changes, and wider access to effective contraception transformed patterns of marriage and childbearing in the United States. The change in the fertility rate (number of children born per 1,000 women aged 15–44) is clearly the most dramatic of the changes we identify; see Figure 1.4.[61] The average number of children born to women fell across the nineteenth century and into the twentieth, with a particularly rapid decrease during the Great Depression. Fertility rates famously "boom" after the Second World War, as women had more children and at a younger age. The Baby Boom crested in 1960, as fertility rates fell to levels lower than before the war and then largely stabilized from the mid-1970s onward. All of these shifts in childbearing would have consequences for the opportunities, constraints, and interests of women.

There is a related but distinct pattern for marriage. According to the US Census, the percentage of women over 15 who were unmarried was fairly stable

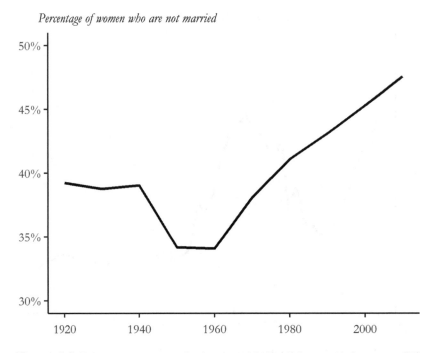

Percentage of women who are not married

Figure 1.5 Fewer women marry in the second half of the twentieth century (US Census), 1920–2016

at just under 40% before the Second World War (see Figure 1.5). The postwar period also witnesses a marriage boom as the age of first marriage declines and the percentage of unmarried women plummets. After 1960, however, legal and social changes contribute to rising divorce rates, delayed marriage, and eventually expanding rates of cohabitation. By 2020, fully one-half of women will be unmarried.

Women's Changing Lives

By the twenty-first century, American women were more likely to obtain a higher education, to work outside of the home, to be unmarried, and to have fewer children than at any previous point in American history. The political impacts of these developments are both enormous and contested. Many have highlighted the ways in which these changes have increased women's independence, power, and control over their own lives. That autonomy, Susan Carroll has argued, permits women to develop and recognize their own, independent, and gendered political interests, as well as the opportunity (due to declining dependence on patriarchal security) to act on those distinct preferences as political actors.[62]

Others have emphasized how these developments have resulted in a more precarious position for many American women. Due to less opportunity to develop resources (including experience), as well as sex (and race) discrimination, women were more likely to hold less stable and less well-compensated jobs. Increasing marital instability and changing fertility patterns generated more female-headed households dependent solely on women's income. The "second shift" that most women performed in their own homes created a substantial burden for women, however well-educated or well-compensated.[63]

Both of these effects – greater autonomy and greater precariousness – are clearly at work in many American women's lives today. More generally, shifting roles and experiences shaped women's expectations and perspectives in multiple ways. In the chapters that follow, we explore how these dynamics contributed to how women voters have been understood by candidates and the press, how women have identified and prioritized their own interests, and how women's political power and influence has shifted.

WOMEN VOTERS

We turn, finally, to reviewing in broad strokes the electoral behavior of women as a whole. In these figures, we use American National Election Studies data (described in Chapter 5) to trace women's turnout and vote choice from 1948 (when these surveys were first conducted) through 2016. (In the empirical chapters, we use other data to observe women voters in elections before 1948.) Self-reported turnout data in Figure 1.6 show that women's turnout lagged men's by an average of over 10 percentage points prior to 1964, but that gap had narrowed to zero by the early 1980s. In recent decades, women are consistently more likely than men to turn out to vote in presidential elections.

Who women voted for is a more complicated story. The first thing to notice about Figure 1.7 is that women and men overwhelmingly voted the same way. As the parties' fortunes rose and fell across the twentieth and into the twenty-first century, women and men move in the same direction from election to election. When women swung to Republicans, so did men. When men voted

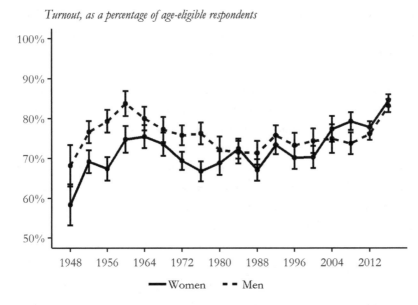

Turnout, as a percentage of age-eligible respondents

Figure 1.6 Women's turnout initially lags, but eventually exceeds, men's turnout (ANES), 1948–2016

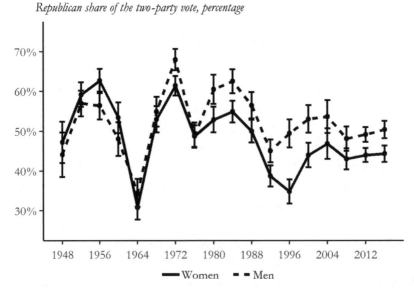

Republican share of the two-party vote, percentage

Figure 1.7 Women and men vote similarly, but gender gaps emerge after 1980 (ANES), 1948–2016

for Democrats, so did women. For all our talk of gender differences, women and men were consistently more similar in their electoral choices than they were different.

That said, gender differences are apparent, especially since the 1980 presidential election. Women were more likely than men to vote for the Republican presidential candidate prior to 1964 but differences were small and largely insignificant. This pattern reversed in 1964, but differences remained too small to be meaningful. From 1980 on, men were more likely than women to vote for Republican presidential candidates. In the chapters that follow we delve more deeply into the turnout and vote choice of women and men across these ten decades, putting the electoral behavior of women within the shifting legal, social, and economic context.

PLAN OF THIS BOOK

When Hillary Rodham Clinton accepted the Democratic party's nomination in 2016, she wore a white pantsuit, consciously invoking the white dresses worn by suffragists more than a century before she became the first female major party nominee for president. Women have cast ballots in presidential elections for more than 100 years because other women both confronted and adapted gender role expectations to fight for women's right to vote. Since women first entered polling places, popular discourse and social scientific research has sought to understand women voters.

In this book, we trace how women have used their right to vote in presidential elections from 1920 – the first presidential election after the suffrage amendment was ratified – through to the historic presidential election of 2016. In Chapter 2, we provide further context for understanding women voters by examining why women were excluded from the franchise for so long and how women finally won the vote. In Chapter 3 we review and organize major explanations for women's voting behavior promoted by political observers, politicians, and scholars since suffrage. This discussion informs our discussion of women voters in the chapters which follow.

Chapters 4 to 8 represent the core of this book as we examine how and why women turned out to vote and for which candidates in periods spanning the nearly 100 years since the Nineteenth Amendment was ratified. We start with the first women voters, whose entrance into the electorate was shaped by two world wars, the Great Depression, and the most significant partisan realignment in American history. We turn next to the period of the 1940s and 1950s when traditional gender norms and attitudes both shaped women's voting and the analysis of it. We then trace the shifting electoral behavior of women as a broad set of disruptions – most notably the second wave of the women's movement – transformed American politics in the late 1960s and 1970s. With the discovery of the gender gap in 1980, female voters attracted unprecedented attention – and scrutiny – from political observers and from the candidates who sought their votes in the decades that followed. Finally, we consider the ways in which women employed their votes at the dawn of a new millennium, as women's issues and women's political representation remained as central to politics as ever. We conclude by summarizing the various trends in women's electoral behavior across the entire century of enfranchisement.

The Nineteenth Amendment transformed the political status of American women. How did women use their hard-won political rights? In the chapters that follow we trace not only the actual behavior of women voters, but how that behavior has been understood within both popular discourse and scholarship.

CHAPTER 2

Women Without the Vote

O N JULY 19, 1848, SOME 300 WOMEN AND MEN GATHERED AT Wesleyan Chapel in Seneca Falls, New York. They had traveled from as far as fifty miles away in response to an advertisement Elizabeth Cady Stanton, Lucretia Mott, and three other women had placed in the *Seneca County Courier* just five days earlier, inviting the public to a "women's rights convention." After two days of speeches and deliberations, sixty-eight women and thirty-two men (one-third of those in attendance) signed the Declaration of Sentiments, modeled after the Declaration of Independence. The document identified grievances related to employment, marriage, and property, and directly critiqued women's place in society, religion, and the home.[1]

Of the dozen resolutions in the Declaration of Sentiments, only one failed to garner unanimous support: Women's right to vote. The idea of women voting was so outlandish that many in attendance believed a suffrage resolution would discredit the whole event. Only after an appeal from Stanton and famed abolitionist Frederick Douglass, insisting that the vote was the key to securing all other goals, did the resolution narrowly pass. Reaction to the convention was swift, as the event and its demands were ridiculed and denounced in the press and from the pulpit. Many signatories subsequently requested their names be removed from the document. The quest for voting rights for women appeared over before it had begun.[2]

Despite a rocky beginning, the woman suffrage movement had indeed been launched. In fits and starts over the next seven decades, women organized, campaigned, and lobbied for the right to vote. Both the demand for the ballot and the very fact that women entered the political sphere to request it challenged long-standing and widely held beliefs about women's place in politics. Why was the right to vote for women so controversial? Why did it take so long for women to secure that right?

The belief that women should be excluded from politics can be traced throughout the long history of Western political thought, and particularly to the liberal and republican political philosophies that informed the American Revolution and US Constitution. The new form of government envisioned in the Declaration of Independence and established by the Constitution even inspired the articulation of a new political role for women – the Republican Mother. Positive influence over husbands and sons and nurturing future generations of citizens and soldiers were understood as women's contribution to this new nation. The view that women should not have direct influence in politics was so strongly held that the demands for women's suffrage articulated in the Declaration of Sentiments encountered extensive and enduring opposition; the goal of universal woman suffrage would not be realized for more than 70 years after Seneca Falls.

Of the 300 or so attendees at the Seneca Falls women's rights convention, only one, then-nineteen-year-old Charlotte Woodward, lived to vote in the presidential election of 1920.[3] Before we examine the voting behavior of Charlotte and the other women who would eventually join her at the polls, we answer the question of why it took so long to give Charlotte, and other American women, the right to vote.

A WOMAN'S PLACE

The fact that many women were denied the vote until a mere century ago strikes many twenty-first-century Americans as absurd. Yet the exclusion of women from political life has a long history and deep roots in the public philosophies on which the American political system is based. For these reasons, opposition was widespread and intense. Suffrage was long in coming. Across the nineteenth and into the twentieth century, evolving gender roles and ideology, liberalizing political pressures around the world, and the efforts of suffrage activists themselves helped make women's suffrage possible.

Women in the American Constitutional System

The authors of the US Constitution spent little time discussing the right to vote during the Constitutional Convention of 1787. The regulation of voting was left almost entirely to the states; the Constitution contains only a few, mostly indirect, references to voting rights. Article I, Section 2 states that in elections to the House of Representatives "the Electors in each State shall have the Qualifications requisite for the Electors of the most numerous Branch of the State Legislature." Article II, Section 1 grants states power over presidential voting, allowing that presidential electors will be chosen "in such Manner as the Legislature thereof may direct." Indeed, Article II does not even require the direct election of the electors who select the president and vice president, and in some early elections, presidential electors were chosen directly by state legislatures.[4] In 1874, in a case brought by women's suffrage advocates, the US Supreme Court unanimously confirmed that "the Constitution of the United States does not confer the right of suffrage upon anyone."[5] For women to secure the right to vote required either action by states or a constitutional amendment.

While the original Constitution was largely silent on the right to vote, it is clear that the Framers did not expect women to vote. Women were considered citizens, but to the Framers, citizenship did not necessarily include voting rights.[6] Specific language disenfranchising women was unnecessary as it was widely understood that only (white, propertied) men would vote. At least one delegate to the Constitutional Convention heard an appeal for greater rights for women, however. In a now famous exchange of letters, Abigail Adams implored her husband John to "Remember the Ladies," suggesting only partially in jest that

> If particular care and attention is not paid to the Ladies, we are determined to foment a Rebellion, and will not hold ourselves bound by any laws in which we have no voice, or representation.

John Adams' response indicates the views of the Framers and their contemporaries regarding women's participation in politics:

> I cannot but laugh … We know better than to repeal our Masculine systems … We are obliged to go fair, and softly, and in Practice you know We are the subjects. We have only the name of Masters, and rather than give up this, which would compleatly [sic] subject Us to the Despotism of the Petticoat, I hope General Washington, and all our brave Heroes would fight.[7]

The Original Rationale for Suffrage Exclusion

The Constitution's Framers were deeply influenced by liberal and republican theories which inspired challenges to traditional monarchies and the spread of democracy in the seventeenth and eighteenth centuries. While these two strands of political theory differ in important ways, they shared an assumption that women were to be excluded from political life. Both liberal and republican thinkers considered independence a crucial prerequisite for citizenship, particularly voting. Property-owning requirements, for example, were often justified by the claim that the dependence of the poor renders them unable to express an independent will.[8] Yet, even men who did not own property were considered independent heads of their households, and thus could be viewed as capable of voting.[9] Women, on the other hand, were "dependent on men almost by definition" – that is, dependence was a key aspect of what it meant to be female – and the idea that women would cast ballots was unthinkable.[10]

Women also were assumed to be naturally delicate and physically weak. The ability to contribute to the defense of the republic was a critical aspect of citizenship. The perception that women were unable or unwilling (due to their moral qualms about the use of force) to fulfill the obligations of citizens by taking up arms meant they should also be denied certain privileges of citizenship, such as casting a ballot. This emphasis on physical strength reinforced men's independence, and women's dependence. A man's ability to engage in physical combat was evidence of, and served to protect, his independence.[11]

These arguments were important but mostly employed to bolster the more fundamental belief at the time of the founding of the United States: Politics was simply outside of women's sphere of interest and ability. To be removed from the hurly burly of politics was a central aspect of what it meant to be a woman. Ideas about citizenship and political activity were inherently masculine: Strong men were good citizens, and good citizens were strong men.[12]

Republican Motherhood: Women's Place in Politics

The US Constitution created a new political order premised on a contract between citizens who gave their consent and the state which governed them. If women could not cast ballots, then what was their place in this system? As we have seen, political thought of the time offered little guidance other

than the widely accepted proposition that women lacked the qualities necessary for direct engagement with politics. Historian Linda Kerber argues that
to solve this problem, early Americans developed an ideology of "Republican
Motherhood" to bridge the gap between ideals of democracy and the
perceived inability of women to participate directly in politics. The concept
of Republican Motherhood suggested that women's natural role in the private
sphere had a public dimension. As women were inherently more pious and
moral, a woman's contribution was to educate and encourage civic virtue in
her sons and husband. In doing so, women helped to temper the passions of
men, a grave threat to democracy. Women made it possible for men to perform
the duties of citizenship. As Republican Mothers, women used their natural
attributes to contribute indirectly to the republic within the confines of house
and home.[13]

Exclusion from politics protected women and their feminine qualities from
degradation. In the home, women were free from ambition and corruption,
preserving the purity and morality that was central to their role. Because
women were inherently unselfish, they did not desire political power, status, or
influence. Prohibiting women from participating in politics helped guarantee
that women would not develop such egotistical and unfeminine goals. Since
women were not directly involved in politics, their support of their husbands
and sons was believed to be motivated solely by moral virtue. The concept of
Republican Motherhood thus both justified the continued exclusion of women
from the political arena, while identifying a means by which women might
make unique contributions to the Republic.[14]

The Changing Meaning of the Vote

At the time of the Founding, citizens understood the political role of women
to be limited to a specific set of duties and obligations within the home. Yet,
despite the prevalence of these views, some women did vote in the early days
of the Republic and before. A few women who owned property, especially
single women and widows without husbands to represent the interests of their
households, cast ballots in New Jersey, New York, Connecticut, and several
towns in Massachusetts in the late eighteenth century. For example, immediately after the Revolutionary War, the New Jersey state constitution provided
suffrage rights to "all inhabitants" of particular means, and a 1790 legislative

act confirmed that female inhabitants were included in the provision. As states began to remove property requirements in the early decades of the nation's history, they simultaneously moved to exclude women. When the New Jersey constitution was rewritten after the elections of 1807, women were specifically disenfranchised.[15]

As the changing requirements for voting suggest, Americans' ideas about the meaning of the ballot, as well as the laws governing its use, evolved over time. The Framers' relative silence on the topic reflects the fact that they viewed voting and voting rights to be relatively minor and unimportant aspects of the political system they had created. In the first decades of the nineteenth century, however, property restrictions were eliminated or considerably scaled back, creating a system in which virtually all white men could vote, a landmark in world history. Voting began to emerge as a central symbol of American democracy. Andrew Jackson's successful populist campaign in 1828 helped elevate elections and mass participation to a core feature of democratic politics. As the primary way in which most Americans interacted with their government, elections became rituals of democracy and voting was increasingly viewed as the foremost act of citizenship.[16]

Expanding the Rationale for Suffrage Exclusion

The woman suffrage movement emerged at a time when voting was viewed as increasingly important. This brought new urgency to the rationale for women's exclusion from politics. In the more than 70 years between the first demand for women's suffrage at Seneca Falls in 1848 and the ratification of the Nineteenth Amendment in 1920, opponents of voting rights for women developed and articulated both new and old arguments against suffrage expansion. Indeed, the challenge to traditional gender roles offered by the suffrage movement, as well as by other developments such as industrialization, led opponents to express even greater reverence for traditional femininity and limited female roles.[17]

The nineteenth century witnessed the development of a widespread ideology about women's unique character known as the Cult of True Womanhood.[18] Women were believed to be naturally characterized by piety, purity, submissiveness, and domesticity. Inherently devout, women were responsible for passing on religious values and practices to their husbands and children.

Purity, especially sexual purity, was essential to female virtue. In particular, women's purity provided a check against the natural sexual aggressiveness of men. As with female piety, the purpose of women's purity was to encourage men to lead more virtuous and moral lives. While women provided religious and moral guidance, their proper position still required submission to their husbands or fathers. A woman's role clearly required her to stay within the confines of the home, where she was naturally suited to the responsibilities of the household, above all motherhood. True Womanhood represented a broad understanding of women's place and women's nature which did not replace but rather integrated the ideology of Republican Motherhood into a gender role worldview. Both emphasized that motherhood was a woman's natural occupation; via Republican Motherhood, that role included raising virtuous sons and encouraging husbands to be good citizens, her contribution to civic society at large.[19]

Men and women thus occupied "separate spheres," with men's domain the public sphere of business and politics, and women's place the private sphere of home and family.[20] While belief in natural gender difference and distinct roles precedes the nineteenth century, the ideal of separate spheres gained particular power during this period.[21] Industrialization and urbanization contributed to an increasing disconnect between men's and women's work and lives. In a rural, agricultural society, men and women labored, often side by side, on the shared project of maintaining a farm and home. With industrialization and urbanization, the work of men and of working-class women increasingly shifted to the factory and office, leaving the home the domain of middle- and upper-class white women. Women of color continued to work in agriculture as well as in domestic service in this period.[22] Glorifying the home and domestic responsibilities as the natural and divine order for women not only separated men from women, but middle- and upper-class white women from their poorer sisters and sisters of color as well. Historian Gerda Lerner concluded it was "no accident that the slogan 'woman's place is in the home' took on a certain aggressiveness and shrillness precisely at the time when increasing numbers of poorer women *left* their homes to become factory workers."[23] The capacity to fulfill the feminine ideal was a demarcation of elevated social class.

Excluding women from politics continued to be advocated as a means to protect women from debasement and corruption, and to maintain their innate purity and grace. It was, suffrage opponents explained, because they held women in such high esteem that they denied them the vote. Women who entered politics relinquished any right to chivalry and the protection of men.[24] An anti-suffrage cartoon presented women with a choice: Reject the right to vote and retain the safety and happiness of the home, or obtain the vote and accept the degradation of the "street corner."[25]

Arguments about biological differences between the sexes also animated the debate. Innate physical weakness made white women unfit for the rigors of the electoral competition and unable to defend the republic against threats, foreign or internal, including perceived threats from African Americans and immigrants. Women were naturally emotional (and thus unstable and impulsive), while logic – necessary for sound political judgment – was the province of men. On the whole, the intellectual and physical demands of voting were simply too taxing for white women's weaker constitutions.[26] Opponents even appealed to a higher power, arguing that "God has ordained man and woman to perform different functions in the state as well as in the home."[27]

Evolving Arguments for Women's Suffrage

Advocates for women's suffrage critiqued the Cult of True Womanhood and emphasized the essential equality of men and women. Many early suffrage proponents had been active in the movement to end slavery, and abolition rhetoric helped shape their arguments about the unjustness of the unequal treatment of women. Early suffragists declared women human beings and citizens first and foremost. They emphasized women's common humanity and essential equality with men, and adapted the ideals on which the American republic had been founded, such as natural rights and popular sovereignty, to argue for the extension of the right to vote to women.[28]

However, when women's suffrage failed to materialize after the Civil War, and in the face of an entrenched opposition, later suffragists increasingly adopted arguments that did not challenge, but instead accepted, the Cult of True Womanhood. Rather than assert that women should have the vote because they were equal to men, suffragists increasingly argued that women should be given the right to vote *because* of their differences. Women, they agreed, were innately different from men – more moral, self-sacrificing, and domestically minded. Unlike opponents, however, suffrage activists asserted that these differences were a compelling reason to include women in politics.

In the context of widespread concern about corruption and scandal, women's votes could inject much-needed morality.[29]

This shift in argument and strategy has been criticized on several fronts. Arguing that women merit enfranchisement on the basis of their unique qualities fails to challenge the fundamentally unequal position of women. While the 1848 Declaration of Sentiments offered a broad critique of women's unequal status in religion, industry, marriage, and the family, many later suffragists sought the vote alone, not broader liberation and equality for women.

Moreover, difference rhetoric was often racist and nativist: If "lower" elements (people of color, immigrants) were allowed to vote, some suffrage activists argued, why should pious and respectable (that is, native-born and white) women not be allowed to do the same? Women voters, supporters claimed, would effectively counter the dangerous and destabilizing influence of immigrants and racial minorities. Prominent suffragists made clearly racist claims and arguments. In adopting such rhetoric, and excluding women of color from white suffrage organizations, many white suffragists pursued a narrow victory for some women, rather than a broader campaign to realize the rights and dignity of all women, including their immigrant, indigenous, Latina, and African American sisters.[30]

The shift away from arguments about suffrage grounded in women's essential equality with men, and toward arguments that highlighted women's difference, also demonstrate how the Cult of True Womanhood contained "the seeds of its own destruction."[31] The denial of voting rights to women was based in part on the idea that men's and women's political interests were one and the same. A woman did not need a vote because her husband cast his ballot on behalf of the household as a whole.[32] By emphasizing women's difference, the Cult of True Womanhood raised the possibility that husbands may be incapable of adequately representing the interests of wives. In the words of suffrage leader Carrie Chapman Catt in 1897, "If women are like men, then they certainly possess the same brain and that should entitle them to the ballot; if they are not like men, then they certainly need the ballot, for no man can understand what they want."[33]

Should we understand women as essentially the same or fundamentally different than men? The debate about equality versus difference persists to this day. Debates over the Equal Rights Amendment, women in combat, and pornography, to name a few, have directly engaged the question of whether treating women the same as men or recognizing dissimilarity (in particular, differences in power and position) are the most just ways for the law to address women as women. Feminist legal scholars such as Catharine A. MacKinnon place what she calls "sameness versus difference" at the center of debates over issues ranging from sexual harassment to statutory rape. To treat women and men as equals, she argues, is to reproduce structural inequality and bias in the law.[34]

The sameness versus difference tension enters into our understanding of women as voters as well: Contemporary debates about the gender gap have often assumed women's greater support for Democrats stemmed from a uniquely female propensity to nurture and care (distinctive gender), which leads women to favor social welfare programs supported by the Democratic party. Others, however, have challenged this interpretation, suggesting that women are motivated by the same self-interest as men; it is their economic position (vulnerability), not their nature, that makes women distinct in their policy preferences and partisanship (resource inequality).[35] We discuss these lines of argument in greater detail in Chapter 3.

The "Domestication of Politics"

Women's place may have been in the home, but many women left their homes to engage in politics long before the right to vote was won. Women were active and visible in American politics in a number of ways, including within the abolition movement and the temperance movement, and in other social reform, labor, consumer protection, good government, and moral purity campaigns.[36] Activists often invoked moral and religious arguments – that slavery was immoral and drinking a sin, for example. Temperance, in particular, directly confronted concerns about protecting and preserving the family and home. As a result, women's particular qualities and supposed expertise provided a rationale, even requirement, for women's political voice on these questions.[37]

Through these reform efforts, women expanded the sphere of acceptable activity for women.[38] The line between the public (men's sphere) and the private (women's) became increasingly blurred, as women rationalized activity outside of the home on the basis of the very qualities – moral purity, selflessness, dedication to home and family – that had been used to justify women's restriction to the private sphere. Women's participation was framed as "municipal housekeeping." Women had long been held responsible for cleaning their own homes, both literally and in terms of ensuring moral and ethical standards. Now women also could be tasked with cleaning the public square by attacking such problems as political corruption, alcohol abuse, and the exploitation of children.[39]

These reform campaigns had widespread impact. The state and federal government adopted an increasingly broad set of responsibilities for the care and welfare of its citizens in the late nineteenth and early twentieth century. While the greatest expansion of government responsibility would come with the New Deal in the 1930s, the roots of that transformation can be traced to the preceding decades, and in many cases, to the activism of women.[40] Many of the new tasks of government involved objects and arenas understood to be the primary jurisdiction of women – the food and medicine women purchased for their families, the children women were responsible for educating, and the moral norms women were expected to guard and transmit.

The ultimate effect was what historian Paula Baker has called the "domestication of politics."[41] Women activists helped change the nature of politics by expanding the definition of political to include the economic, and more importantly, social welfare of citizens, areas in which women were believed to have particular expertise. Politics thus increasingly infringed on women's sphere, and women were increasingly entering the male sphere of politics. Female activists had an impact on society's willingness to accept political activity by women, as well as an impact on the nature of political activity itself.

THE STRUGGLE FOR WOMEN'S SUFFRAGE

In 1840, abolitionists from around the world gathered in London for the World Anti-Slavery Convention. Lucretia Mott, founder of the first Female Anti-Slavery Society, and Elizabeth Cady Stanton, the wife of a prominent abolitionist, were among the American delegation. After some debate, the convention ruled that only male delegates would be seated. Frustrated, Mott and Stanton spent several days walking around London, discussing and analyzing the unequal status of women. Activism in the abolitionist movement armed them with the rhetoric, ideas, and most importantly, the knowledge and skills to organize for social change. Eight years later, Mott, Stanton, and others issued their call for what would be the first women's rights convention.[42]

In the early nineteenth century, the legal concept of coverture, inherited from English common law, specified that married women were legally "covered" by their husbands and ceased to possess a separate legal identity. Under coverture, women could not inherit property, testify in court, or sign enforceable contracts. In the first decades after the American Founding, both women and men increasingly challenged these laws as unfair and a source of considerable hardship for women and children. These legal structures also made it difficult for men to pass down wealth and capital to daughters, and hampered the development of property rights and the commercial economy in the new United States. By the time of the Seneca Falls women's rights convention in 1848, a number of state legislatures were beginning to legislate expanded legal rights for women through various Married Women's Acts.[43]

Despite these legislative efforts, women's social, political, and economic position remained starkly unequal. Modeled after the Declaration of Independence, the Seneca Falls Declaration of Sentiments cataloged women's grievances, including injustice in marriage and divorce, lack of access to education and professional careers, higher moral standards, and religious discrimination. As we have seen, the resolution for voting rights was controversial; many attendees believed the demand so outrageous that it would taint the rest of the document. And indeed, the overwhelmingly negative response to the convention and the Declaration of Sentiments made it clear that traditional views were widespread and deeply held.[44]

While the Seneca Falls organizers are rightfully credited with launching the suffrage movement, there was very little suffrage organization or activism between Seneca Falls and the Civil War. A series of annual women's rights conventions were held and a loose network of women lobbied state legislatures for various reforms, including women's suffrage. However, no women's rights or suffrage organizations were created and few proposals received legislative consideration.[45]

The Civil War and the reforms that followed raised the hopes of women's rights activists, many of whom had been active in the abolition movement. If slavery could be ended, albeit at an enormous cost, then surely the equally unthinkable demand for women's political rights could be achieved as well. Women's hopes were quickly dashed. Republicans, the party that saved the Union, made it clear that they intended to limit the extension of the suffrage to black men. Not only did the three amendments added to the US Constitution (known as the Reconstruction Amendments) fail to enfranchise women, but Section 2 of the Fourteenth Amendment connected, if indirectly, the word male to voting rights in the Constitution for the first time.[46]

The impact of the Civil War and the Reconstruction Amendments on the woman suffrage movement was enormous. First, the emphasis on voting as a central aspect of African American citizenship in the Reconstruction Amendments encouraged women's rights advocates to focus their attention on suffrage as a goal. Before the Civil War, activists and observers referred to the women's rights movement, but after the War, the term woman suffrage movement came into wide usage. The second effect was to divide suffragists strategically and organizationally. Many activists, including Lucy Stone, Henry Blackwell, and Frederick Douglass, argued that "this hour belongs to the negro" and supported the Republican Party's decision to enact suffrage for black men, rather than universal suffrage for men and women regardless of race and previous servitude. Despite also having been active in the abolition movement for many years, Elizabeth Cady Stanton, Susan B. Anthony, Sojourner Truth, and others refused to support amendments that failed to include suffrage for women.[47]

In 1869, the two camps established separate woman suffrage organizations. The American Woman Suffrage Association (AWSA), headed by Stone and Blackwell, generally supported and worked within existing institutions, including the nationally dominant Republican party. The National Woman Suffrage Association (NWSA), founded several months earlier by Stanton and Anthony, tended to take a more radical approach and offered a more wide-ranging critique of social and political institutions.[48] Both were overwhelmingly white organizations. A few black women were active in either AWSA or NWSA, but white suffrage organizers repeatedly rebuffed the membership or participation of black women, fearing they would alienate white male legislators who opposed black enfranchisement and often reflecting their own racist views. African American women responded by organizing their own suffrage organizations at the state and local levels throughout the late nineteenth century.[49]

Despite splits and controversies, the cause of women's suffrage gained momentum and achieved a few early successes. For a variety of reasons, frontier states led the way.[50] Kentucky had allowed school suffrage (voting only for school boards) to white widows with children as early as 1838, a full ten years before Seneca Falls.[51] In 1869, the newly organized territory of Wyoming granted full suffrage to women, a provision it kept when becoming a state in

1890. The official record of the State of Wyoming claims that one delegate to the state constitutional convention put an end to debate over women's suffrage by declaring, "if consideration is given to disfranchise half of our people, it should not be the better half."[52] Colorado gave women the right to vote in 1893, followed by Utah and Idaho in 1896.[53] The enfranchisement of women received extensive consideration in states outside of the South; between 1870 and 1890, an average of more than four states per year took up the issue of women's suffrage through state legislative votes or public referendum.[54]

In 1890, the NWSA and AWSA merged into the National American Woman Suffrage Association (NAWSA). Yet unification accompanied a period activists referred to as "the doldrums." No new states adopted women's suffrage between 1896 and 1910. Suffragists were similarly stalled at the national level, where suffrage bills failed to be reported out of congressional committees. Despite the lack of advance, the suffrage movement grew dramatically during this period, drawing in an increasingly wide range of women. At the same time, the first generation of suffragists were gradually replaced by a second generation of leadership, who adopted new strategies and arguments for women's suffrage.[55]

The doldrums came to an end in 1910 when Washington state enfranchised women. Over the next ten years, more than twenty states enacted some form of women's suffrage, via public referendum or legislation. Success of the state efforts, as well as of other Progressive reforms, further energized the movement. However, differences over tactics and priorities once again divided suffragists. Alice Paul took over leadership of NAWSA's Congressional Committee in 1913, eventually founding a separate suffrage organization, the Congressional Union. Paul and others were influenced by the growing international movement for woman suffrage, including the militant strategies – mass demonstrations, hunger strikes, and jail protests – practiced by English suffragists. Paul sought to adopt the British strategy of holding the party in power responsible for failing to achieve women's suffrage. Since Democrats controlled Congress, Paul mobilized her supporters to campaign against Democrats around the country, despite strong opposition from other suffrage leaders who considered the strategy unwise and counterproductive.[56]

While both the Democratic and Republican parties endorsed women's suffrage in their 1916 platforms, the national effort remained stalled. Paul's Congressional Union staged an ongoing picket of the White House in 1917, chaining themselves to public property and risking arrest and jail. At the same time, the second generation of leadership at NAWSA, most notably Carrie Chapman Catt, developed the "Winning Plan," designed to capitalize on the threat of women's votes in states where women already had the ballot to push for both national and state-level suffrage for women. By 1917, the Plan had yielded important suffrage victories, particularly in New York, which increased pressure for federal action.[57]

The stage was set for the accomplishment of the woman suffrage movement's ultimate goal. In 1918, the House of Representatives passed the Nineteenth Amendment, but it was voted down in the Senate. Both chambers passed the Nineteenth Amendment in 1919.[58] The campaign shifted to the battle to achieve ratification in the states before the next election. By August of 1920, suffragists were just one state short. Tennessee was viewed as the last chance for victory. As the final vote approached, suffragists expected to lose narrowly, but at the last minute, Representative Harry Burn (at twenty-four, the youngest member of the Tennessee House) switched his vote from nay to yea in response to an appeal from his mother. The proclamation certifying the ratification of the Nineteenth Amendment was signed on August 26, 1920.[59]

Why was national women's suffrage achieved in 1920? As we have seen, various American states enfranchised women in the late nineteenth and early twentieth century, but national enfranchisement required more than 70 years of activism. Worldwide, the United States is part of a wave of countries that enfranchised women in the first decades of the twentieth century, but the United States was by no means the first to do so; the first self-governing country to grant women the right to vote in national elections was New Zealand in 1893.[60] Others trailed behind; Greece did not enfranchise women nationally until 1952 and Switzerland only provided universal suffrage to women in 1971.[61]

In the United States, resistance to women's suffrage is attributed to the resilience of traditional gender role ideology, which glorified gender differences and constrained women's political role. Racism – specifically, fear that the enfranchisement of women might embolden and facilitate African American electoral participation in the South – also created an important barrier to suffrage expansion in the US. Federalism and the structure of representation in the US Congress gave Southern representatives significant veto power over national suffrage legislation. The powerful liquor industry, fearing that women voters would support Prohibition, committed significant resources to opposing state and national level efforts to enfranchise women. Urban political machines, powerful organizations in many states, generally opposed women's suffrage as they feared it would disrupt the patronage system that underpinned their regime.[62]

Nearly 100 years after the fact, scholars continue to debate what made the ultimate success of women's suffrage possible in the United States. The increasing participation of women in the workplace and public sphere challenged traditional ideas about gender roles. Threats to democracy and the spread of revolutions helped foster the expansion of suffrage rights throughout the world as a way for those in power to encourage popular commitment to democratic government. Politicians saw a strategic opportunity to mobilize women voters where competition was high and the woman suffrage movement was strong. The First World War provided opportunities for women to demonstrate their patriotism and capacity to contribute as citizens. The strategic choices of the woman suffrage movement are often recognized as key, although there is less consensus as to whether credit belongs to traditional suffrage activists, such as represented by Carrie Chapman Catt's "Winning Plan," or radical militancy, which included White House protests and hunger strikes in prison spearheaded by Alice Paul. The success of the woman suffrage movement in leveraging its organizational resources to establish effective coalitions with influential third-party movements and other organizations in various states both helped pass state-level suffrage and put pressure on members of Congress.[63]

Even with the achievement of the Nineteenth Amendment, important limitations to women's access to the ballot remained in both the short- and long-term. In four Southern states – Arkansas, Georgia, Mississippi, and South Carolina – officials declared that since women had failed to register six months in advance of the election as required by law, they were unable to vote in the presidential election of 1920.[64] This was not the only possible way for states to handle such procedural challenges to incorporating women voters. In a number of other states, legislatures and state officials extended registration deadlines, altered procedures, or allowed women's more limited previous registration (such as for school suffrage in states like Connecticut and Massachusetts) to carry over into general election registration.[65]

More importantly, the same formal and informal institutions which effectively disenfranchised black men and others in Southern states were employed to effectively deny black women the right to vote, regardless of the Nineteenth Amendment. The discriminatory application of literacy tests, poll taxes, and registration requirements, the threat of violence, job loss, and other penalties, and anti-democratic state regimes successfully combined to create extremely low rates of voter turnout among African American women and men in the first half of the twentieth century. White Southerners had feared that the threat of backlash would make it difficult to use the same violent tactics to disenfranchise black women as black men, but this problem did not materialize. A 1920 headline from the *Chicago Defender*, the leading black newspaper in the country, made it clear how violent tactics were employed to discourage black women from voting: "Drive Women From Polls in South: Southerners Threaten to Use Gun and Rope on Race [black] Leaders."[66] It would take the concerted efforts of the civil rights movement to register black voters and the passage of the Voting Rights Act in 1965 – some 45 years later – to make the Nineteenth Amendment's enfranchisement of women a reality for most African American women.[67]

CONCLUSION

The passage of the Nineteenth Amendment transformed women's place in American politics. Suffrage is a central right of democratic citizenship, and in gaining that right, women's relationship to the political system was made more direct, equal, and influential. Beyond the ability to cast a ballot, enfranchisement reconfigured power relations between men and women "because it exposed and challenged the assumption of male authority over women."[68] Rather than the Republican Mother affecting politics through husbands and sons, women were now American voters with a direct voice in the choice of representatives and the composition of government.

Yet, many of the key ideas underpinning the Republican Mother ideal and the Cult of True Womanhood did not disappear entirely after the ratification of the Nineteenth Amendment. Rather these beliefs and expectations about women were reworked and reimagined for a new political context. The persistent claim that women voted as their husband in the first decades after suffrage can be traced to the presumption that women are fundamentally uninterested in politics and incapable of independent political judgment. Similarly, contemporary explanations for women's political preferences that emphasize women's natural inclination to care and nurture are grounded in a view of women as having distinct moral values and qualities. Categorizing female voters as "soccer moms" or "security moms" is another way to say that motherhood is the central identity through which women experience and affect politics.

In the chapters that follow, we trace both the popular understandings of women as voters, and the actual turnout and vote choice of women, across the ten decades since the ratification of the Nineteenth Amendment. The transformation of women's economic, social, and political status in the twentieth century stands as "one of the biggest social changes of our times."[69] Yet much of the popular rhetoric describing and explaining women's choices as voters still echoes the fundamental ideas that justified women's exclusion from the electorate for so long.

CHAPTER 3

Explaining Women Voters

CONSIDER THE PRESIDENTIAL ELECTIONS OF 1932 AND 1980. THESE two contests occurred less than 50 years apart but represent distinctly different moments for the political fortunes of the major parties. The historic election of 1932 ushered in a new Democratic majority that would persist for decades. In that election, slightly fewer than 50% of eligible women turned out to vote, compared to three-quarters of men, a more than 25-point difference. Despite differences in turnout, both women and men gave a large majority of their votes to the political party that promised to work aggressively to alleviate the suffering of the Great Depression: 60% of women and 57% of men cast their ballots for Democrat Franklin Roosevelt.[1]

The election of 1980 was similarly historic, marking the ascendancy of a conservative Republican party in modern American politics. Women's political behavior in that election was notably different from 1932, however. While in 1932 women lagged behind men in voter turnout, the presidential election of 1980 was the first in which a larger percentage of women (61.9%) turned out to vote than men (61.5%). While both women and men voted overwhelmingly Democratic in 1932, the election of 1980 drew considerable attention for the fact that men and women favored different candidates: Only 47% of women cast their ballots for Republican Ronald Reagan compared to 55% of men.[2]

What explains the behavior of women voters? Why were women so much less likely to turn out to vote than men in the first decades after suffrage but more likely than men to exercise their voting rights today? Why did women eventually become more likely than men to vote for Democrats? Politicians, the press, scholars, and even the public all have been interested in the answers to these questions. A central goal of this book is to identify the key ways in which women's voting has been understood since suffrage was broadly extended to women in 1920. Both popular accounts and scholarly work are rife with various competing and complementary explanations for the voting behavior of women, ranging from women's natural compassion to women's greater economic vulnerability.

In this chapter, we review the major arguments and hypotheses that have been put forward to explain women's voting behavior across these ten decades. We argue that most approaches to women's voting behavior fall into one of two broad categories: **distinctive gender** or **resource inequality**.[3] Distinctive gender explanations assume women are in some way a unique social group whose electoral behavior requires group-specific explanations. Whether due to innate differences or gender role socialization, women's personalities, values, and interests are simply different from men's, and those differences explain women's political participation and choice.

Resource inequality explanations, on the other hand, attribute distinctive electoral behavior to differences in women's and men's social and economic resources, and the political opportunities and constraints those resources provide. We know that resources and characteristics ranging from educational attainment to religiosity shape political behavior. In the logic of resource inequality, gender differences in political behavior emerge because women are more or less likely to possess various politically relevant resources.

In this chapter, we show how popular and scholarly perspectives on women voters fit within these two broad categories, distinctive gender and resource inequality. We discuss the evidence that supports these perspectives, as well as the shortcomings and challenges with both. With these conceptual tools, we then turn to the first women voters in the chapter that follows.

DISTINCTIVE GENDER

Distinctive gender explanations share an emphasis on the uniqueness of women *as women*. Underlying these explanations are more general assumptions – that basic dispositions explain political engagement, that personal interest motivates political preferences – but the basic claim of distinctive gender explanations is what makes women's voting behavior distinct are factors specific to women. The nature of the types of gender differences viewed as consequential for electoral behavior ranges from innate personality traits to fundamental political interests and values.

Essentialism

An important form of distinctive gender is essentialism, the assumption that women are naturally or inherently different than men; that is, that gender differences in personality, role, values, and so on are a function of natural, biological differences between the sexes. This idea has ancient roots and gained the status of a core legal doctrine in the nineteenth century.[4] In *Bradwell* v. *Illinois* (1873) the Supreme Court explained the self-evident nature of women:

> The *natural* and proper timidity and delicacy which belongs to the female sex evidently unfits it for many of the occupations of civil life. The constitution of the family organization, which is founded in the divine ordinance, as well as *in the nature of things*, indicates the domestic sphere as that which properly belongs to the domain and functions of womanhood (emphasis ours).[5]

Such conceptions of women remain widespread in many circles. Prominent feminist critic Phyllis Schlafly, for example, emphasized the "fundamental *inherent* differences between men and women," arguing women are naturally and instinctively drawn to maternal concerns.[6] Importantly, however, this is not a perspective limited to conservative or antifeminist voices. Advocates for greater equality and opportunity often suggest that women in politics are inherently less corrupt, more collaborative, and more compassionate. In debates over issues ranging from abortion and sexual harassment to childcare and the glass ceiling, the idea that men and women remain essentially different in their predispositions and qualities, particularly related to public roles and private responsibilities, remains a central theme.

Distinguishing the effects of nature (essentialism) from nurture (socialization) remains an empirical challenge across disciplines. Psychological research shows that X and Y chromosomes are linked to differences in brain processing and activity, but those differences are neither as broad nor as specific as popular stereotypes suggest.[7] Few studies of women voters have directly addressed the question of whether gender differences in electoral behavior are "natural"; rather, studies which control for a myriad of measurable factors and still find gender differences often attribute such findings to the independent impact of gender without distinguishing between nature and nurture as the cause.[8] Recent twin studies, the gold standard for identifying inherited rather than learned behaviors in the biological sciences, suggest that genetics may indeed play a role in generating gender gaps in political attitudes, but not in ways that map simply onto traditional expectations about women and emotion, care, or domesticity.[9]

Gender Role Socialization

More common are distinctive gender explanations rooted in the concept of gender role socialization, a life-long process in which distinct gender roles are produced and reproduced through norms, parenting, social and economic segregation and practices, family structure, and other social forces. Gender role socialization creates expectations and incentives for distinct qualities and behaviors for women and men.[10] Experiences deemed central to womanhood, such as mothering, may further encourage distinctive values and attitudes among women.[11] The effects can multiply. When social norms encourage women to embody certain values such as care and empathy, women may assume greater responsibility for childcare and be more likely to seek employment in care-giving occupations. Those experiences may in turn lead women to develop greater care and empathy.[12] Moreover, given women's place in the social and economic structure, there are strong incentives for girls and women to be sensitive to relationships, compassionate, and collaborative.[13] Kindness and agreeableness, for example, might be learned (and taught) responses to a world where women have less economic, social, and physical power, and thus rely on the goodwill of men for their safety and security. Evidence of the varying ways in which gender roles are produced and reproduced throughout life is clear. How gender socialization shapes political behavior remains contested.

Values and Traits

A common characteristic of distinctive gender explanations is the presumption that women – due to biology or to gender role socialization – differ from men across a range of fundamental personality traits, values, and perspectives. Women are expected to be more communal, men more agentic. Women are generally viewed as, among other things, more nurturing, moral, and honest. Men are assumed to be more assertive, strong, and independent, while women are believed to be more timid, fragile, and dependent. While expectations about the implications of those presumed gender differences for political behavior vary, the basic qualities associated with women and men remain remarkably consistent over time and place.[14]

Femininity. Traits associated with femininity include the tendency to be warm, expressive, loving, tender, graceful, sociable, thoughtful, sympathetic, and soothing. Masculinity, on the other hand, is associated with assertiveness, leadership, confidence, ambition, and energy. Research in psychology has demonstrated that women are in fact more likely to exhibit feminine traits and less likely to exhibit masculine traits than are men, although there are considerable variations in both sets of traits across both groups and over time.

These gendered personality traits shape political behavior. Today, masculinity predicts political engagement (discussing and knowing about politics), while femininity predicts Democratic – and masculinity predicts Republican – identification and vote choice. When measures of gendered personality traits are included in statistical models of political behavior, sex (whether the respondent is female or male) is no longer a clear predictor; in other words, it is femininity and masculinity that are associated with engagement, partisanship, and vote choice, not whether someone is female or male. Evidence of different patterns of behavior between women and men may actually be capturing different distributions of femininity and masculinity across women and men, rather than the effects of sex per se.[15]

Compassion. One of the most persistent and popular distinctive gender explanations focuses on women's tendency for compassion. The psychologist Carol Gilligan famously argued that women's morality tends to be based on an "ethic of care" due to women's greater connectedness and relational bonds. Men, on the other hand, are characterized by an "ethic of rights or justice."[16] While research has since disputed aspects of Gilligan's claims, her arguments have had a significant impact on social science scholarship, including work on the gender gap.[17] Most notably, gender gap research has long highlighted women's greater support for so-called "compassion issues," such as social welfare, education, health, and programs for the poor, and expected that those divergent issue preferences contribute to the gender gap in partisanship and vote choice.[18]

Research indicates that, on average, women are indeed more compassionate than men. It is far less clear that more compassionate citizens support particular policies or identify with a particular party. Analysis of the few surveys which included direct, valid measures of compassion and separate measures of political attitudes finds little association between the two. Indeed, the compassion hypothesis may be viewed as an example of how gender role stereotypes shape both popular and scholarly expectations for women's political behavior. Studies of the gender gap often refer to health, education, and poverty programs as "compassion issues"; gender gaps in attitudes toward those policies are offered as evidence of women's greater compassion (as scholars often lack more direct measures of compassion) and then used to explain the partisan gender gap. The framing of these policies as "compassion issues" assigns a gendered value (compassion) to specific policy debates. The term "compassion issues" is rarely found outside of gender gap research. For instance, union members, African Americans, and white working-class voters all are more supportive of spending on education, health, and poverty programs, but this tendency is generally attributed to self-interest rather than a greater propensity to compassion among those groups.[19]

A Woman's Place is in the House (and Senate)

As we have seen, the idea of "separate spheres" – that women's place is in the private world of the home and family while men's domain is the public arena of business and politics – has a long history in American political thought.[20] Today, few people agree with the statement "a woman's place is in the home." Yet, in many different ways, the idea that politics is not an appropriate arena for women continues to be communicated and the idea that women are generally less inclined to politics remains popular.[21] Women indeed express less confidence in their political skills and qualifications and are more reluctant to engage in competition and advocacy, with varying political consequences, including for voting.[22]

Here again, however, we should be mindful of the male standard problem. Rather than solely attribute gaps in political participation to women's lack of confidence and assertiveness in the political arena, we might also ask if men overestimate their abilities and knowledge, leading to "artificially high" political interest, and thus participation.[23] Research suggests the presence of female candidates and office-holders may challenge the stereotypes of politics as men's business with positive effects on women's political engagement. The presence of female role models – prominent women politicians – is associated with greater political engagement among women, especially young women.[24]

Historically, women's perceived political disinterest has been used to justify both the exclusion and the inclusion of women in politics, as well as to both belittle and promote women's political choices. Once women received the vote, for example, the assumption that women were naturally concerned with the home and family and thus uninterested in politics did not disappear. Instead, women's low turnout became evidence to support the idea that women were naturally apolitical.[25]

Similarly, women's natural aptitude for the home (and not the political arena) has been used to justify the exclusion of women from the corrupt and cruel world of politics since the Founding.[26] On the other hand, observers and suffragists also used those stereotypes to justify women's inclusion: For example, suffrage activists claimed that women would engage in "Municipal Housekeeping" and clean up politics.[27] The claim that women are in a sense above the dirty world of politics continues to characterize discourse about women as political actors. In a recent Pew survey, respondents were more likely to expect women in political leadership (rather than men) to exhibit traits such as compassion and empathy (especially) as well as honesty and ethics, an ability to solve problems through compromise, and a willingness to stand up for values.[28]

Women's Interests

Other distinctive gender explanations emphasize gender-specific political self-interest rather than women's unique values and traits. One strand of argument defines women's interests narrowly, as issues that apply particularly to women, such as reproductive rights, equal pay, or women's suffrage. Some argued, for instance, that the first women voters supported the Republican party as a reward for granting women the vote.[29] The modern pro-Democratic gender gap has been attributed to the Republican party's abandonment of the ERA, pro-life shift on abortion, and general rejection of the modern women's movement.[30] Expressions of shock over the 52% of white women who voted for Donald Trump in 2016 – despite his many offensive actions and statements regarding women – is another example of the assumption that gendered self-interest overwhelms other political identities and attitudes.[31]

Research offers little reason to expect that women's interests as defined here explain the gender gap in vote choice. Women and men differ little in their attitudes toward women's rights issues such as equal pay and abortion.[32] Women may weight those issues more heavily in their vote choice than do men, but both women and men give far greater weight to issues such as the economy, civil rights, and social welfare. Evidence suggests that social issues have played a larger role in shaping women's vote choice and expanding the partisan gender gap in recent years, but the most relevant culture war debates for women have been gay rights, not women's rights.[33]

Another definition of women's self-interest emphasizes women's traditional role as caregivers and traditional spheres of expertise, such as the home and the family. In the nineteenth century, women's activism on issues such as child labor, temperance, and moral purity was framed, including by activists themselves, as an essential female impulse toward caregiving and protection of home and children. In the twentieth and early twenty-first century, the continuing presence of women in roles that include caring for children and others has informed definitions of "women's issues" that include education, health care, and social welfare policy. This, in turn, has been used to explain women's greater identification with the post-New Deal Democratic party which "owns" those issues.[34] As we discuss below, social welfare attitudes indeed appear key to understanding the gender gap, but it is less clear that these attitudes can be attributed to women's traditional concern for the family.

Women's interests as mothers also are invoked to explain women's political behavior. From the time of the Founding through the nineteenth century, "Republican Motherhood" defined (and limited) women's place in politics as encouraging civic virtue in her sons and husband (see Chapter 2).[35] In the twentieth century, the experience of motherhood has been a popular explanation for women's aversion to the use of force and war (concern for threats to husbands and sons) and support for social welfare, health care, and education programs. In popular discourse, soccer moms, waitress moms, security moms, and even hockey moms represent modern renderings of the expectation that motherhood is the dominant experience directing women's political choices.

A number of theorists have argued for mothering as central to women's worldview. Even women who do not mother, some have argued, are naturally and/or socialized to be nurturing, supportive, and concerned with the well-being of others.[36] Recognizing that motherhood is only one of many factors that shape women's political engagement, social scientists note the potential for motherhood to affect political behavior, given how the experience shapes social networks, invokes strong gender role expectations, and may shift conceptions of self-interest. Empirical evidence suggests that motherhood matters for political beliefs and practices but in conflicting ways: Motherhood has been found to both facilitate and constrain women's political engagement and to push women in various ideological directions on policy issues. Mothers have been shown to be more conservative on gay rights, legalized marijuana, and support for the military and police, but more liberal on health care and child care. At the same time, men's political views also are (but less consistently or strongly) shaped by fatherhood.[37] The rhetorical emphasis on women as mothers is not without cost, however. When politicians and the media frame women as mothers they necessarily narrow the span of interests associated with women, excluding key concerns from political debate. Perhaps most importantly, mothers in politics are often implicitly, and even explicitly, portrayed as white and suburban, ignoring the political interests of other women and other mothers.[38]

RESOURCE INEQUALITY

We term the second set of approaches to understanding women's electoral behavior resource inequality. The central assumption of resource inequality explanations is that women's electoral participation and choices are shaped by their resources, just as men's political behavior is.[39] Gender differences in voting behavior arise because women tend to have different resources than do men. Importantly, the word "resource" refers not only to material resources such as income and wealth (although both are certainly politically consequential) but also to non-material resources, such as access to networks (which can provide exposure to political norms, information, and opportunity); experiences (such as interaction with government or on-the-job leadership roles); and opportunity (e.g., invitation, encouragement, and access to political arenas).

In the first decades following women's enfranchisement, for example, women were less likely to have access to higher education and paid employment. The resource inequality claim is that it is those demographic differences, and not something about women as women, that explain women's lower turnout.[40] Similarly, since women were less likely than men to work outside the home, they had narrower social networks that exposed them to fewer cross-cutting cleavages; as a result, women were more loyal partisans than men.[41] As women's roles were transformed across the twentieth century, so was their turnout and vote choice. Women's greater participation in the paid work-force, lower relative pay, and declining marriage stability helped make women more sympathetic to a social safety net and thus, the argument goes, more supportive of Democrats.[42] While the salient factors and their impact may shift with the times, disparate access to resources remains key.

The resource inequality approach is defined by the basic presumption that gender differences in political behavior are the consequence of differences between men and women in the level and distribution of social, political, and economic resources. Women's turnout is lower because women have access to fewer politically mobilizing networks or are less likely to work outside the home. Women vote Democratic because they are, on average, poorer than men. Yet, in some cases and at some times, key determinants of turnout and vote choice appear to function differently for women than they do for men. For example, while employment was a significant predictor of turnout among men, studies of voters in the 1940s and 1950s suggested that it was a less powerful predictor for women; housewives and women who were employed outside the home turned out at similar rates.[43] One interpretation is that the impact of employment is different for women and men because of some fundamental gender difference (distinctive gender). It seems more likely that employment was related to other politically relevant factors in different ways in one period compared to the other. In the immediate postwar period, many housewives enjoyed high household incomes, status, and social networks due to their spouses (factors facilitating turnout), while it was largely poor women and women of color who worked outside the home,[44] and may have faced other barriers to voter turnout. While a distinctive gender approach might focus on the different impact of employment in this period, the resource inequality approach directs attention to the association between employment and other relevant characteristics.[45]

Socioeconomic Status

Gender differences in socioeconomic status are central to resource inequality explanations for women's political behavior. Socioeconomic status (SES) is one of the most consistent and strongest predictors of both turning out to vote and partisan preference. Women tend to have fewer socioeconomic resources: Historically they are less likely to have attained higher education, although that is no longer the case. Historically and today, women are less likely to work outside the home or in professional and managerial occupations, and earn less money than men.[46] If women have lower SES than men, we would expect women to turn out at lower rates and to lean Democratic.

An important, and more nuanced, version of the SES resource inequality narrative focuses on women's economic vulnerability more generally to explain the modern pro-Democratic gender gap. The vulnerability hypothesis emphasizes women's more precarious position in the economic and social structure. As women entered the paid workforce in the twentieth century, they often did so from a position of disadvantage. Last hired, they were first fired. Sex discrimination and sexual harassment further contributed to women's insecurity in the workplace. Marital instability and changing fertility patterns generated more female-headed households in which women's contributions to household income were primary. The mid-century growth of the social welfare state both provided a much-needed safety net to vulnerable women, as well as an important source of employment, since women were significantly over-represented among human services workers. By one estimate from the 1990s, a quarter of American women worked in jobs closely associated with the government, compared to fewer than 10% of men. Almost half of women lived in families that receive government payments compared to a third of men. Women's support for the social welfare state and for the party most strongly associated with it, the Democrats, is thus attributed to both economic self-interest in a social safety net (as both provider and beneficiary) and a capacity to identify with the disadvantaged due to one's own vulnerability.[47]

In contrast to the vulnerability hypothesis, the autonomy hypothesis focuses on how some of these same changes as well as others created greater independence for women. Employment outside the home, Susan Carroll famously argued, exposes women to non-traditional gender roles and to gender-based discrimination, as well as provides an opportunity for women to develop politically relevant skills and gain political knowledge through social interactions.[48]

By making women less (or not at all) dependent on men, Carroll argues, higher-status employment and higher incomes in particular permit women to identify their independent, gendered interests. Those interests are typically understood to include non-discrimination policies, government programs (due to women's tendency for employment in the public sector), and assistance to working parents, all policies associated with the modern Democratic party. Whereas the vulnerability hypothesis predicts greater Democratic support among poorer women in particular, the autonomy hypothesis predicts greater Democratic support especially among professional and upper-income women.[49]

Empirical support for these perspectives has been mixed. Those in occupations related to redistribution are more likely to favor social welfare programs[50] and vulnerability related to divorce has been associated with support for the Democratic party.[51] On the other hand, cross-national research indicates that women who are in the weakest positions economically are actually the most similar to men in their political preferences. Scholars argue that women with little economic power are necessarily more dependent on men and thus have reason to vote consistent with men's self-interest. Women with better labor market opportunities are both less vulnerable and free to vote in their own self-interest; when women have the option of supporting themselves outside of marriage "spouses will have conflicting preferences over who receives family benefits, and they will differ over any policies that affect their outside options."[52] Others find little difference in the gender gap across economic groups.[53]

The vulnerability and autonomy hypotheses also demonstrate how the two types of explanations – distinctive gender and resource inequality – interact. Women's greater economic vulnerability (resource inequality), for example, stems in large part from childbearing and childrearing responsibilities which are intimately tied to gender role expectations and differences (distinctive gender). The over-representation of women in public care professions, such as social work, education, and health (resource inequality), may similarly be a function of gender role socialization or essential gender differences (distinctive gender). Gender-based power imbalances within the home and workplace make women less likely to attain valuable skills and resources which in turn have consequences for women's political engagement.[54] Complicating all of this, proponents of the autonomy hypothesis propose that (material) independence from men permits women to discover and act on their interest *as women*, suggesting that alleviating resource inequality may help facilitate the realization of distinctive gender.[55]

NEW DIRECTIONS: SOCIAL IDENTITY THEORY

Distinctive gender and resource inequality approaches share a key assumption: Preferences – either due to the specific traits and interests of women or due to women's social and economic characteristics and resources – explain choice of candidate and party. This assumption is entirely consistent with basic theories of representative democracy: Citizens have preferences over policies and outcomes and they cast their ballots for the candidates and parties who best represent those preferences. And indeed, there is substantial evidence that policy preferences predict vote choice and party identification, particularly on highly salient issues.[56]

Yet the expectation that policy preferences drive partisan choice is highly contested. Beginning with the influential early vote studies, scholars have consistently found that partisanship has a large impact on vote choice, and that partisanship is a long-standing stable identification rooted in other social identifications.[57] Issue attitudes are less likely to shape partisanship than to be shaped by it, as citizens align their policy preferences with their partisanship (and the positions advocated by prominent party politicians) rather than the reverse. There is certainly no dearth of evidence that citizens do just that.

Why might that be? In this view, party identification is understood as a form of social identity. Citizens develop mental images of each party and the kinds of people associated with them. Party identification is less a process of selecting the party which shares your policy views, but rather a process of associating with the party whose supporters are closest to your own conception of self. As with social identity in general, individuals are more sympathetic toward, trusting of, and positive about in-group, rather than out-group, members. This conception of partisanship is consistent with research showing that partisanship develops at an early age (before policy knowledge or preferences) via socialization, that most citizens have little policy knowledge, that policy preferences shift more easily than party identification, and that people hold clear party images in their minds.[58]

This perspective is central to the study of party identification but largely absent from dominant approaches to the gender gap. In an important exception, recent research by political scientist Heather Ondercin uses the increasing variation in the representation of women in each party's congressional delegations over time as a measure of the parties' gender images in the late twentieth and early twenty-first century. The increasing relative presence of women among Democratic (but not Republican) congressional delegations is hypothesized to have helped link women as a group to the Democratic party, and in doing so, contributed to an increase in Democratic identification among women, and a decrease among men.[59]

Political scientists Leonie Huddy and Johanna Wilman also adopt a social identity conception of partisanship in their work on the gender gap. Recognizing variation in subjective gender identity and group consciousness among women, they focus on feminist identity as a form of politicized gender identity and find that feminist identity increases Democratic identification among women above and beyond ideology, issue preferences, and demographic characteristics.[60] While there is little evidence that attitudes on women's rights issues (such as abortion and the ERA) explain the gender gap, the evolving positions of the two major parties on these issues – with Democrats establishing themselves as the party linked to feminism and the women's movement and Republicans as the party opposed by 1980 – may have shaped the parties' images in the public mind in a way that had consequences for women's and men's party identification, and thus their vote choice.[61]

CONCLUSION

Why do women (and men) vote as they do? Observers and scholars have approached this question from a range of perspectives. The expectation that social and economic characteristics at least shape and possibly determine political behavior and attitudes – the assumption at the heart of the resource inequality perspective – is foundational to the social sciences and has been repeatedly and extensively confirmed by empirical research. A significant body of scholarship demonstrates that women's differential access to and experience with politically relevant resources and opportunities helps explain differences in the turnout and vote choice of women and men.

Research also supports a distinctive gender approach. Some of the evidence comes from the limits of resource inequality explanations: Differences in the electoral behavior of women and men often persist after key economic and social characteristics are well accounted for.[62] More generally, the expectation that women are characterized by distinctive traits, values, and capacities is both widely held and often supported by empirical research. In recent years, new survey instruments and experimental research designs have offered insights into the ways in which women's distinctive qualities shape political behavior and attitudes.[63]

There is good reason to expect that both distinctive gender and resource inequality factors contribute to gender gaps in political engagement and preferences.[64] In the chapters that follow, we review how women voted in specific periods, and trace the evolving popular and scholarly understanding of why and how women vote. Across these ten decades, women were at times less likely and at other times more likely to turn out than men. Women were at times more likely to vote Republican and at other times more likely to vote Democratic than men. Resource inequality and distinctive gender explanations shape our expectations and understanding of women's voting behavior in each period, but also highlight the challenges to making broad generalizations about women and politics across a nearly 100-year period.

CHAPTER 4

Enter the Women Voters

WITH THE RATIFICATION OF THE NINETEENTH AMENDMENT IN 1920, those who had fought to accomplish women's suffrage throughout the nation had high hopes for new women voters. "Let the politicians keep in mind the fact that the women's vote is going to be a tremendous factor in this election," warned one suffrage activist.[1] Another predicted a "marked change because of women's entrance into the electorate."[2]

Yet almost as soon as women gained the right to vote, observers began to claim that women's suffrage was a failure. Women did not turn out to vote. When they did vote, they did not transform politics, but rather voted like – or even as directed by – men. In his popular treatise on America in the 1920s, *Only Yesterday*, journalist Frederick Lew Allen described the "American woman": "She won the suffrage in 1920. She seemed, it is true, to be very little interested in it once she had it; she voted, but mostly as the unregenerate men about her did."[3]

Despite the confident claims of contemporary observers, we actually know very little about the first women voters. With few exceptions, official records report only the total number of votes cast overall and for each candidate. Whether women cast ballots and for which candidates cannot be directly determined from the vote record alone. Reliable public opinion polls – the modern solution to this problem – are virtually nonexistent during this period.

In this chapter, we take advantage of our recent research which offers new insight into how women voted immediately after suffrage. In previous work, we combined election and census data and exploited recent methodological innovations to estimate the turnout and vote choice of new female voters in presidential elections following suffrage for a larger and more diverse set of places – a sample of ten American states – than had previously been possible.

Each of our historical chapters follow a similar structure: an overview of electoral history; examination of women's changing lives and the efforts of politicians, the press, and scholars to understand and appeal to them; discussion of challenges and opportunities for observing women voters; and a careful review of whether and for whom women voted in presidential elections of the period. In this chapter, then, we first cover American electoral politics between the First and Second World War to understand the historical context and dominant lines of partisan cleavage at the time when women entered the electorate nationwide. Next, we highlight major developments for women during this era, focusing on the changing conditions of women's lives from the Roaring Twenties through the Great Depression, and the political appeals directed at new women voters by uncertain parties and candidates. We discuss the challenges to observing the behavior of women voters during the period immediately following suffrage, and briefly review our approach to overcoming those obstacles.

We then examine what we know about women's turnout and vote choice during the five presidential elections from 1920 to 1936. Women initially failed to turn out to vote at the same levels as men, sparking claims that women's suffrage was a failure. A closer look reveals that where women were first enfranchised was as important as the fact that they were women: In places where the election was competitive and barriers to voting were low, women's turnout was quite high, overall and relative to men. Women who did vote generally supported the same candidates as men – Republicans in the 1920s and Democrats in the 1930s – which many interpreted as evidence that women voted as their husbands directed – another conventional wisdom complicated by a closer look at available evidence.

AMERICAN ELECTORAL POLITICS, 1920–1936

The two decades between the end of the First World War and America's entrance into the Second World War were periods of both stability and change. The 1920s was in many ways a conservative decade, characterized by ardent patriotism, nativism, and anti-communism. The economy was generally strong, prosperity was widespread, and economic interests were ascendant, particularly in politics. On the other hand, social norms – or at least, women's skirt lengths – were famously liberalized during the "Roaring Twenties," and Progressive reform, while largely marginalized within both of the major parties, remained an important social and political force.[4]

In the first elections of the 1920s, both parties' nominees reflected the conservative mood of the period. Republicans selected Ohio Senator Warren G. Harding in 1920 and his vice president (who ascended to the presidency in 1923) Calvin Coolidge in 1924. Both represented the conservative, business-oriented wing of the GOP rather than its reformist Progressive branch. Democrats similarly chose candidates from the more conservative wing of their party: Ohio governor James M. Cox in 1920 and John W. Davis, a fairly unknown compromise candidate, in 1924. In response to the conservative options offered by the major parties, reform groups united behind the candidacy of Wisconsin Senator Robert M. La Follette in 1924. La Follette and the Progressive party received about 17% of the vote, a strong showing for a third-party candidate. Republicans nonetheless maintained their dominance in presidential elections, capturing a whopping 60% of the popular vote in 1920 and 54% in 1924.[5]

These electoral patterns began to unravel in 1928. The Republican nominee, Commerce Secretary Herbert Hoover, represented a fairly standard GOP choice. On the Democratic side, however, the party's nominee, New York governor Al Smith, embodied the emerging face of the Democratic party: urban, immigrant, and Catholic. The parties' nominees differed only slightly on most issues, but offered a stark choice on the defining issues of the campaign: "rum and religion."[6] Smith, the first Catholic major party nominee, was widely understood to oppose Prohibition, a touchstone issue in the long-standing ethno-cultural conflict over religion, values, and social class in American politics.[7] As with other 1920s presidential elections, Republicans won easily. However, the Smith candidacy generated an increase of nearly 7 million voters nationwide and disrupted established voting patterns. Democrats made significant inroads into the Republican-dominated North, particularly in counties with large Catholic and immigrant populations.[8] Republicans, on the other hand, performed unusually well in the South in 1928. The Republican surge in the South was fleeting, but in the 1930s Roosevelt built on Smith's mobilization of immigrant, urban, and Catholic voters in the North to permanently reshape the Democratic party coalition.[9]

The Great Depression, beginning with the stock market crash in 1929, reordered American politics. In 1932, Democratic nominee Franklin D. Roosevelt, governor of New York, promised new leadership and a "New Deal" for the American people. Incumbent Republican president Herbert

Hoover faced the nearly impossible electoral challenge of presiding over an unprecedented economic catastrophe. Roosevelt garnered a decisive 57% of the vote in 1932.[10]

Under Roosevelt, Democrats forged a new majority – the New Deal coalition – of those most harmed by the economic downturn, including workers, immigrants, Catholics, Jews, Southern whites, and African Americans. Disagreement about the appropriate size and role of the federal government led to a sharper ideological and policy contrast between the parties. In 1936, the popularity of New Deal programs gave Roosevelt almost 61% of the vote, the largest recorded landslide at that point in American history.[11]

AMERICAN WOMEN IN THE 1920s AND 1930s

Women's Lives

From the Jazz Age to the Great Depression, women's lives were transformed in the two decades between the world wars. The decade of the 1920s is remembered for the loosening of sexual mores, shortened skirt lengths, and the rise of the carefree single working woman. Marriage was increasingly defined in terms of romantic love and companionship, providing both opportunities for personal fulfillment but also new pressures for women. By the 1920s, electricity, indoor plumbing, and factory-produced food and clothing were easing the burden of women's traditional work. The number of children in the average family had dropped across the nineteenth century and continued to decline in the early twentieth. Women of color and immigrant women continued to work outside the home in industry, agriculture, and domestic service. Increasing numbers of white women, especially those unmarried and young, joined the paid workforce, many in growing, sex-segregated occupations like secretary, telephone operator, and social worker; most white women still did not work after marriage, however. These experiences, along with broadening access to education, challenged and changed traditional ideas about the nature and capacity of women.[12]

The dominant image of women in the 1920s – the flapper – was explicitly non-political. Consumed with parties, fashion, dancing, and music, the stereotypical young woman of the 1920s was having too much fun to care about the social reform agitation of their mothers and grandmothers. In reality, women remained active in politics. The National American Women's Suffrage Association reorganized itself as the League of Women Voters (LWV) a few months before the ratification of the Nineteenth Amendment. The LWV offered voter education and mobilization and made policy recommendations, but did not endorse candidates or parties. The National Women's Party (NWP) turned to advocacy for the ERA, an issue that divided reformed-oriented activist women and gained little traction in the 1920s and 1930s. An increasingly hostile conservative backlash meant that the Progressive Movement in general was in defense and decline in the 1920s, including women's reform organizations such as the National Women's Trade Union League (WTUL) and the National Consumers League (NCL). Many women's groups nonetheless persisted after suffrage, and new ones were founded. These groups were active in US politics, if largely out of public view, testifying before Congress and lobbying for policy change.[13]

Just as it upended politics, the Great Depression also upended American women's lives. Fertility rates, declining since the nineteenth century, dropped precipitously (see Figure 1.4). Women increasingly sought paid employment to alleviate the financial crises in their families. While women were accused of taking urgently needed jobs from men, sex segregation in the workforce meant women largely participated in separate, woman-dominated labor markets. Smaller families and changing economic demands meant many women increasingly spent a significant portion of their adult lives engaged in activities other than mothering. The idea of an adult woman in a role other than, or in addition to, motherhood represented a significant social transformation.[14]

The Quest for Women Voters

What did women voters want? The ratification of the Nineteenth Amendment required parties and candidates, as well as the press, to confront this question directly and immediately. In 1922, Democratic National Committee chair Cordell Hull told the *Washington Post* that "it is not our policy to recognize much difference in the issues which will appeal to the men and women voters." In the same breath, however, Hull highlighted the appeal to women of the party's efforts to ensure equal gender representation of women. Although there were certainly instances of politicians and observers highlighting the essential similarity of women's and men's political interests, this latter approach – assuming women are mobilized by issues of specific concern to them, such as the representation of women or women's suffrage – was more common. In that same article, Republican leaders asserted that "there is a woman's point of view which is to be welcomed and encouraged. Therefore, certain policies of the Harding administration will be emphasized to win the support of women voters."[15]

Echoing the nineteenth-century view of True Womanhood, women's interests were often defined in terms of their roles in the home, as mothers and as wives. Looking forward to the entrance of women into elections, the *Washington Post* explained:

> The ballot is more than a fad to most women. It is the means to the end of better government, better homes and town in which to raise children, better schools and in general a better world in which to live. Women think of politics in terms of the home and family.

In 1920, both parties' platforms included planks advocated by the new League of Women Voters. Harding issued a long litany of campaign pledges meant to appeal to women, including equal pay for equal work, a ban on child labor, strong Prohibition enforcement, and maternity and infant protection. Democrats emphasized the fact that the Nineteenth Amendment passed under a Democratic president, Wilson's appointments of women, and their support of the League of Nations (appealing to women's presumed aversion to violence and war).[16] Both parties highlighted women at their conventions, established greater representation of women on party committees, and expanded their separate women's organizations.[17]

Parties, candidates, and the press sometimes expanded the view of women's interests to include women's independent (economic) roles as well. For example, in a debate over import tariffs (which Democrats opposed, and Republicans supported) in 1922, both parties sought to appeal to women:

> The Democrats are proceeding with the theory that women are primarily housewives, and not farmers or manufacturers, and are therefore … interested in the cost of things they must buy, and not in the price of things they have to sell. The Republicans contend that, no matter how cheap things may be, if the husbands or the women themselves are out of jobs, they will be unable to buy things. They point out the fact that more than half of the people employed in the textile industry, which would be chiefly affected by the flood of cheap clothing from Europe, are women.[18]

Efforts to appeal to and train female voters continued in 1924.[19] Both Democrats and Republicans, for example, organized women's clubs, and at the local level, candidate and party clubs held teas, presented speakers, and made the case for the appeal of the candidate on the issues that they believed mattered most to female voters.[20] These issues were largely defined in terms of traditional, domestic roles; for example, the 146-page Women's Democratic Campaign Manual highlighted the party's positions on issues relating to children and family.[21] Progressive party nominee La Follette had been a strong advocate of women's suffrage and his wife, Belle, a popular suffragist speaker. The Women's Division of the La Follette campaign featured speeches by well-known women activists, such as Hull House founder Jane Addams and suffragist Harriet Stanton Blatch.[22]

Both parties once again exerted considerable effort to appeal to female voters specifically in 1928. The organization and activity of the Republican campaign was described as "unusually segregated on gender lines."[23] The party highlighted Hoover's work on behalf of housewives, his support for Prohibition, and his commitment to peace.[24] Gender, ethnicity, and religion intersected in important ways. The *New York Times* described a prominent Republican addressing a local Women's Republican Club as saying, "I cannot say very much of Mrs. Smith, but if the contest were between Mrs. Hoover and Mrs. Smith ..." The writer noted that "There, [the speaker] adroitly left his hearers to draw their own inferences."[25] "The implication was that [Irish Catholic] Mrs. Smith lacked the essential Nordic background, and was somewhat deficient in those social graces and intellectual attainments which characterized the wife of the Republican nominee."[26]

As with the Republicans, the Democratic campaign emphasized women's traditional roles and appealed to women through women's offices and campaign committees, female speakers, and gender-specific appeals. Democratic nominee Al Smith hailed mothers as "one of our greatest national assets,"[27] and highlighted his stances on such issues as protective labor laws. Even his controversial stance on Prohibition was reframed to appeal to women, with Democrats imploring women to "Think clearly on the Prohibition issue."[28]

The women's divisions of both parties continued to be well-organized and active in seeking women's vote in the 1930s, but direct appeals to women tended to be less prominent than in the 1920s.[29] The content of those appeals shifted as well. Republicans continued to emphasize women's traditional, domestic roles. Democrats, on the other hand, shifted toward greater emphasis on the economy and work, consistent with their broader message. In contrast to the Democrat's emphasis on women as wives, mothers, and consumers in the 1920s, the party explicitly reached out to women as workers. Democratic women's organizations were organized around occupations and other interests. Eleanor Roosevelt was an active speaker on the campaign trail, but unlike previous (potential) First Ladies, she did not particularly emphasize her role as a mother or housewife.[30]

Women were front and center in the New Deal more broadly. Leading up to the Great Depression, many women had entered social work, education, and health occupations, gaining skills and expertise relevant to both their careers and their political activism. The remarkable expansion of the role of the federal government in just those areas during the New Deal offered unprecedented opportunities for women. Prominent women including Eleanor Roosevelt (redefining the role of First Lady), Secretary of Labor Frances Perkins (the first woman to sit in the cabinet), Molly Dewson (head of the Women's Division of the Democratic National Committee), and Mary McLeod Bethune (Negro Affairs Director of the National Youth Administration) provided new models of politically active women. Dewson in particular successfully urged President Roosevelt to appoint women throughout the government.[31] The New Deal itself owed a great deal to the work of women:

> Indeed, the entire concept of social security, government-sponsored insurance for the unemployed, the elderly, and fatherless children, as well as expanded public health programs, could be traced not only to innovations in western Europe but also to the earlier activities of female-led private charities, settlement houses, and the provisions of the Sheppard-Towner Act in the 1920s.[32]

The New Deal elevated the visibility of issues that tapped into the expertise and interests of women, as the state increasingly inserted itself into women's traditional sphere of family, children, health, and education. The influence and role of women in the New Deal is a reminder of how women shaped politics beyond the voting booth as well.[33]

OBSERVING WOMEN VOTERS

The first two decades following the ratification of the Nineteenth Amendment pose a particular challenge for observing the voting behavior of women and men. With a few notable exceptions, the official voting record cannot tell us whether or for whom women and men voted. As the social scientists William Ogburn and Inez Goltra lamented in 1919: "women's ballots are not distinguished from those of men but are deposited in the same ballot box."[34] As a result, the *New York Times* concluded in 1932, "No one will ever know exactly what part the women played in the final result since voting machines tell no tales on them."[35]

The modern solution to this problem is the public opinion poll. However, reliable mass surveys covering politics and elections were simply not administered in the first presidential elections following national suffrage. For the five presidential elections from 1920 through 1936, we rely on the best data available to us: In previous research, we combined census records (number of age-eligible women and men) and election returns (number of votes cast for each presidential candidate) in ten states in the five presidential elections following suffrage. We then applied a statistical technique known as ecological inference to estimate the turnout and vote choice of women and men in each state. These ten states are not representative of the United States as a whole; rather, they were selected to provide the greatest possible diversity in context (such as region, political competitiveness, and election restrictions) within the constraints of available data. The ten states in the sample under-represent the West and South, but the sample population is comparable to the United States as a whole in terms of vote share and the proportion of white, foreign-born, and urban. These data cover a wider span of places across a longer time period than any other available data about women voters after suffrage, and thus represent our best available resource for examining the voting behavior of the first women voters.[36]

While ecological inference provides insight into the turnout and vote choice of women and men in presidential elections after suffrage, without public opinion polls we are unable to further subdivide voters by other politically relevant characteristics, such as race and education, as we do in later chapters. The estimates we use do not reveal anything, for example, about how black women voted compared to white women or how less-educated men voted compared to less-educated women. As the vast majority of people of color still lived in the Jim Crow South during this period, we can assume that most black women were systematically denied the right to vote, and any conclusions we make about women who actually voted should be understood to describe white women almost exclusively. We can observe other aspects of these racial dynamics, however. These data do permit us to examine how women and men turned out and voted in different kinds of places (for example, those in and out of the Jim Crow South) and indeed, remind us of the importance of context in shaping electoral behavior.[37]

How would women vote? While at first uncertain and even optimistic, political observers quickly and confidently reached largely pessimistic conclusions about the role of women in US elections. Yet the lack of appropriate survey data has meant that most of the conventional wisdom on the first women voters is based on little or no reliable empirical evidence. In the sections that follow, we describe what recent research can tell us about women voters immediately after suffrage.

TURNOUT

The Nineteenth Amendment to the US Constitution was ratified near the end of August 1920, a mere ten weeks – give or take – before Election Day. Various organizations, in particular the new League of Women Voters (LWV), sought to educate and mobilize women voters, offering both substantive advice as well as practical demonstrations on the concrete skills – lever-pulling, ballot-filling – necessary to exercise the right to vote.[38] Prior to ratification, the major political parties created women's committees charged most centrally with mobilizing new women voters as partisans.[39] However, even in the North party organizations focused exclusively on mobilizing white women; efforts to mobilize black women were limited to churches and other organizations.[40] Both the LWV and the parties continued to mobilize women voters throughout the 1920s and 1930s even as the novelty of women's suffrage passed and coverage of their efforts declined.[41]

In the decades immediately following suffrage, women were less likely to turn out to vote than were long-enfranchised men. Figure 4.1 shows the rate of turnout for women and men among the age-eligible population in our ten-state sample from 1920 through 1936. In 1920, women's turnout averages just 36% compared to the 68% of men who turned out to vote, a 32-point turnout gender gap. Both women's and men's turnout increases over time, but women's at a sharper rate than men's. By 1936, more than half of all eligible women turn out to vote and the turnout gender gap has narrowed to 24 points.

Explaining Women's Turnout

These recent estimates permit us to examine a number of long-standing claims about the turnout of the first women voters.

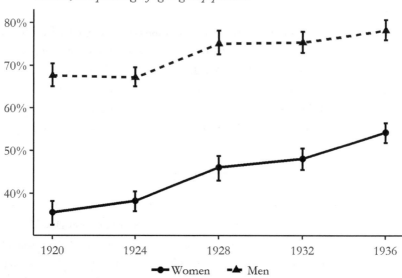

Turnout, as a percentage of age-eligible population

Figure 4.1 Women's turnout lags behind men's in the first elections after suffrage, but the turnout gender gap slowly narrows over time, 1920–36

Are women voters responsible for declining turnout? Beginning in the 1880s, turnout in American elections began its long, infamous decline from the historic highs of the Reconstruction Era. Much of the deterioration can be attributed to declining turnout in the South as Reconstruction ended and systematic disenfranchisement of African American and poor white citizens was enacted and enforced. The gradual enfranchisement of women in the decades leading up to and following 1920 also has been identified as a factor.[42] Figure 4.2 shows overall turnout from 1880 through 1948 in the ten states in the sample, as well as estimates for male and female turnout in those ten states in the five presidential elections between 1920 and 1936.

As we can see, the most significant declines in turnout precede the national enfranchisement of women, suggesting other factors were at work. That said, the addition of women to the national electorate did dampen overall turnout in 1920. These estimates suggest that, had women continued to be excluded from the electorate, overall turnout would have increased in 1920 and may well have returned to nineteenth-century levels by 1936. With the inclusion of women, overall turnout reaches a high of 66% after 1920 in these ten states, a

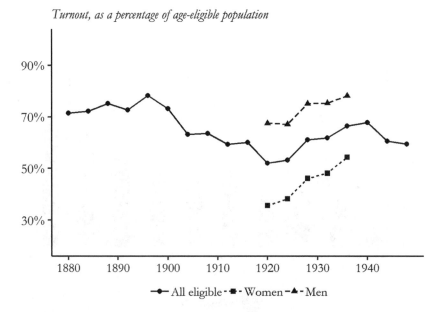

Figure 4.2 By 1936, men's turnout was at or near levels not seen before 1900 (US Census, CQ Press), 1880–1948

figure which would be considered quite respectable today but that represented a significant decline from the 1880s and before.

Was women's suffrage a failure? That women generally failed to take advantage of their new right quickly emerged as conventional wisdom about suffrage, calling into question the entire suffrage cause. By 1924, multiple headlines, in outlets ranging from *Harper's Weekly* to *Good Housekeeping*, asked "Is woman's suffrage a failure?"[43] Many long-time suffrage activists were gravely disappointed that their grand victory had not translated into more widespread turnout among women and a greater perceived impact on elections.[44]

Most scholars echoed this pessimistic assessment. An early study titled "American women's ineffective use of the vote" was widely cited at the time and in later research.[45] Early, often impressionistic accounts shaped views of the first women voters for decades to come as "[m]any conclusions drawn in the 1920s were incorporated into standard histories of the impact of the adoption of the Nineteenth Amendment."[46] Dominant conceptions of women

Turnout, as a percentage of age-eligible population

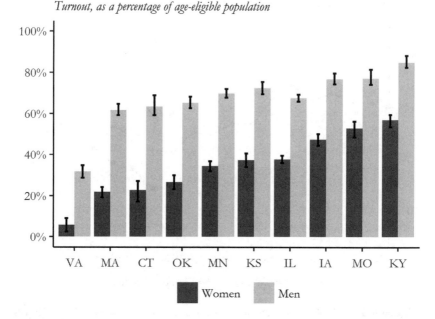

Figure 4.3 Turnout of women and the size of the turnout gender gap vary considerably across states, 1920

as inherently apolitical (distinctive gender) contributed to the acceptance of this negative characterization of the first women voters, as observers assumed that low rates of turnout solely reflected women's disinterest in politics.

A closer look at women's turnout in the 1920s and early 1930s complicates the view of women as inherently less interested in politics than men. Figure 4.3 shows the turnout of women and men in each of the ten states in the sample in 1920 (the pattern of turnout across states looks similar in 1924 and 1928). Both the rate at which women turn out and the size of the gender gap varies considerably across states. In Missouri and Kentucky, more than half of women turned out to vote in the first election in which they were eligible to do so. The turnout gap in Missouri, the smallest state-level gap, was just 24 points. In Virginia, on the other hand, fewer than 10% of women turned out in 1920, and in Massachusetts and Connecticut the turnout gender gap was 40 points.

If women were generally or inherently disinterested in politics, why was women's turnout so high in some states and so low in others? One answer has to do with the political context that women confronted. Close elections have long been identified as a spur to turnout. Competition induces parties and candidates to expend greater effort on voter mobilization, encourages heightened press coverage, generates excitement and greater interest in the election, and increases the perceived value of any one vote.[47] During the 1910s and 1920s, most American states were highly one-partisan, dominated by one or the other major political party. Among the ten states examined here, the two exceptions to this rule are Missouri and Kentucky, the two states where women's turnout is highest. The level of competition is reflected in the presidential election results; Democrats won Kentucky by just 0.4 points in 1920. At the other end of the figure, Democrats held a 23-point advantage in Virginia in 1920, and Republicans took Massachusetts by a margin of more than 40 points.

Competition mattered. Figure 4.4 shows women's and men's turnout, on average, in one-party Democratic states, one-party Republican states, and competitive states in 1920. Both women and men were affected by differences in the level of competition in their own states, with turnout lower where there was less competition and higher where there was more. The impact of competition on women, however, was greater. Women's turnout in competitive states is 39 points higher than in one-party Democratic states, compared to a 32-point gain for men, and 20 percentage points higher than in one-party Republican states, compared to a 12-point gain for men. As a result, the turnout gender gap is smallest in the competitive states (about 26 points) compared to either kind of one-party state (about 33–34 points).

The states also differed in the ease with which citizens could exercise their voting rights. Some states erected significant barriers to voting. The three states in our sample with the most stringent voting laws also had the lowest levels of turnout among women. Massachusetts and Connecticut required voters to take literacy tests. Connecticut and Virginia had long residency requirements. Virginia levied a poll tax, among other discriminatory practices directed at African Americans and poor whites. In Virginia, these restrictive voting laws were part of a broader anti-democratic Southern political system and hierarchical and deferential social structure which further depressed political participation, and led to distinctively low turnout rates in general elections. This set of states is not an accident; the imposition of restrictive state election laws were directed particularly at African Americans in the South and immigrants in the Northeast.[48]

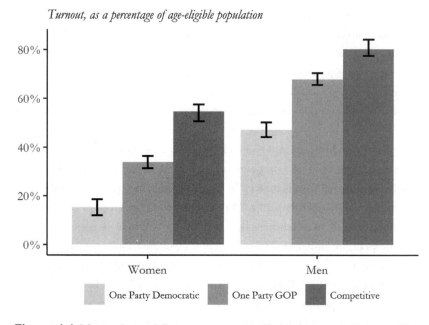

Turnout, as a percentage of age-eligible population

Figure 4.4 Men and especially women are most likely to turn out in competitive states, 1920

In the South, segregationists had opposed women's suffrage in part because they feared they would not be able to suppress turnout among women of color with the same tactics as they did men. They need not have worried, as white supremacists found plenty of ways, including those long employed against black men, to suppress the voting rights of black women. For example, historian Suzanne Lebsock recounts how separate registration offices were set up for black and white women in Richmond, Virginia in 1920. Fewer registrars were assigned to black women and black women were more likely to have their registration challenged. To further add to the inequality, newspapers ran photos of the resulting long lines outside of the black registration offices, suggesting that white citizens should be sure to register to counter this supposed surge in the registration of black women.[49] Extra-legal tactics were employed as well. An October 1920 *Chicago Defender* headline explained how violence and intimidation were used to "Drive Women from Polls in South; Southerners Threaten to Use Gun and Rope on Race Leaders."[50] These practices discouraged the nearly 30% of the Virginia population that was African American (as well as low-income whites) from voting. Similarly more than 60% of the population of Connecticut and Massachusetts was first- or second-generation immigrant, so the impact of these legal barriers on turnout was substantial as well.[51]

These practices were directed at and by far the most consequential for African American women and men. Legal barriers and an anti-democratic context likely suppressed the votes of Southern white women as well. Historian Sarah Wilkerson-Freeman has shown how scholars and activists of the time recognized the poll tax in particular as a barrier to white women; when family budgets were tight, poll taxes were often paid for the male head-of-household (who might also benefit from veterans' exceptions) but not for the wife. While Wilkerson-Freeman demonstrates how this phenomenon, and the role of women in particular, was downplayed by future scholars of Southern politics, evidence of the impact can be found in the various groups – from the Women's Division of the Democratic National Committee to local white women's clubs – who organized against the poll tax in the decades after the Nineteenth Amendment was ratified.[52]

These practices also reduced turnout among men, but suppressed the votes of newly enfranchised women in these states even more. Figure 4.5 shows the turnout of women and men in states with restrictive election laws versus those which only required residency. Female turnout declines by 24 points (a drop of 56%) between less restrictive and restrictive states, compared to a 17-point decline (about a 23% decline) for male turnout. As a result, the gap between male and female turnout is larger in states with multiple suffrage restrictions (a 37-point gap) compared to states with only the residency requirement (a 30-point gap).

In sum, any conclusion about women's turnout after suffrage depends a great deal on where you look. The difference between the turnout of women in Virginia, where fewer than 10% of women turned out to vote, and Kentucky, with 57% of women voting, is more than 50 points, exceeding the turnout gender gap overall and in any one state. Clearly location and context mattered as much as gender for explaining women's turnout. In places where competition was high and barriers to voting were low, an impressive percentage of women turned out to vote in the first elections in which they were eligible.

Did rum and religion mobilize new women voters? Both observers and scholars expected that the presidential election of 1928 was especially mobilizing

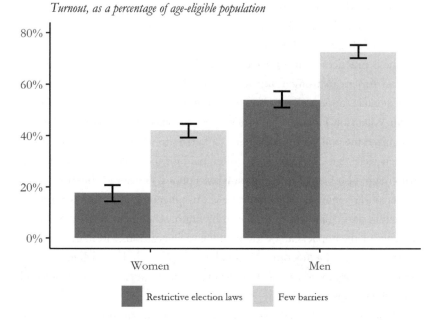

Turnout, as a percentage of age-eligible population

Figure 4.5 Men and women are more likely to turn out in states without legal barriers to voting, 1920

for women.[53] Headlines such as "Forecasts Big Vote by Women of State" and "This Year's Woman Vote to Set a High Record" were common.[54] The *New York Times* went so far as to claim that "This year the President of the United States will probably be chosen by women."[55] Many states reported increases in female registration.[56] From a distinctive gender point of view, the central issues of that campaign – Prohibition and religion – were seen as natural interests of women. Women were leaders and activists in the temperance movement, consistent with women's traditional role as family protector. Women were likewise viewed as the keepers of moral and religious traditions, and thus expected to be mobilized by threats to their religious identities. In particular, urban, immigrant women were believed to have been slow to mobilize initially (compared to native-born white rural women) but enthusiastic in support of Smith in 1928.[57] At the same time, many expected that native-born and rural women would turn out in even higher numbers in defense of Prohibition and Protestantism in 1928.[58]

The expansion of the active electorate in 1928 is indeed spectacular – in our ten-state sample, more than 25% more people cast ballots in 1928 compared to

1924. Women's turnout in 1928 was 8 points higher than in 1924. But women were not unique in responding to the contest between Hoover and Smith; men's turnout also increased by 8 percentage points in 1928. Because more men were already turning out to vote in 1924, these similar percentage point increases for women and men translate into more new male voters in 1928 than female.[59] The presidential election of 1928 was highly charged and mobilizing, but not uniquely so for women, despite widespread assumptions about their particular affinity for the issues of Prohibition and religion.

Explaining the first women voters. Even in states and elections where women's turnout was high in the 1920s and 1930s, women's turnout still lags behind men's and women's turnout was discouraged by lack of competition and barriers to voting to a greater extent than men's. Why? Resource inequality is surely part of the answer. While we cannot explore the impact of these factors directly, we know that in the 1920s and 1930s, women remained less likely than men to be well-educated and less likely to work outside the home, both factors associated with a greater propensity to turnout.

Perhaps the most important resource women lacked was experience.[60] Voting is habit forming; turnout in the past increases the probability of turnout in the future.[61] Those who have been systematically denied the opportunity to develop the habit due to disenfranchisement are disadvantaged in the future. The effects were long-lasting. Women who were older at the time of enfranchisement (that is, who had been denied the opportunity to develop the habit when they were younger) were less likely to turn out to vote throughout their lives than women born after the ratification of the Nineteenth Amendment.[62] Data reported in Chapter 7 suggests that these effects persist into the 1980s.

Surely inexperience hampered new women voters. However, other newly enfranchised groups have acclimated quickly, turning out at nearly equal rates and in much the same manner as those already in the electorate.[63] New female voters, however, confronted unique conditions; political scientist Kristi Andersen writes, "viewing women as simply one instance of the class of 'newly enfranchised voters' is inadequate" because women were not only denied the vote, but had been taught to understand themselves as "*by nature unsuited* to politics" (italics original).[64] In other words, and consistent with a distinctive gender perspective, women were socialized differently. In particular, women entering the electorate in the 1920s had been socialized during a period of widespread female disenfranchisement and norms against women's political engagement.[65]

We have reason to expect that attitudes about appropriate roles for women continued to discourage some women from voting after 1920. For example, in a study of non-voting in 1920s Chicago nearly 8% of respondents (one-ninth of all female non-voters) gave "disbelief in women's voting" as a reason and another 1% cited "objections of husband."[66] Almost 20 years later, researchers conducting voter surveys in Eric County, New York, during the 1940 presidential election reported that "remarks such as these are not infrequent" in their surveys:

> I don't care to vote. Voting is for the men.
>
> I think men should do the voting and the women should stay home and take care of their work.
>
> I have never voted. I never will … A woman's place is in the home … Leave politics to the men.[67]

The authors emphasize that the impact of such views is broader than simply those who express them. By creating a context in which political activity is expected of men but not of women, men will feel compelled to vote even when not particularly interested in politics, while women who lack political interest will feel less social pressure to participate.

Both the variation in women's turnout and the persistent turnout gender gap can be attributed, then, to both resource inequality and distinctive gender, as well as to the interaction between them. Women lacked some resources available to men, most notably experience with the ballot. Importantly, women lacked that resource in large part due to distinctive gender norms that justified women's long disenfranchisement and discouraged women from voting after suffrage was won.

VOTE CHOICE

While turning out at lower rates that men, many women entered polling places for the first time in the presidential elections of the 1920s and 1930s. How did these women cast their first ballots? Figure 4.6 shows the Republican share of the major party vote for women and men in the five presidential elections from

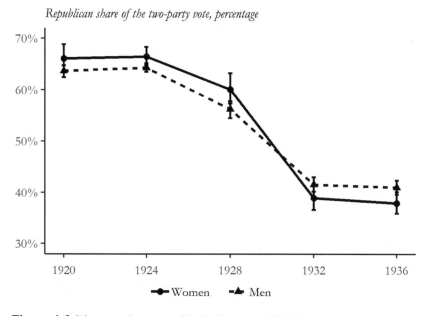

Republican share of the two-party vote, percentage

●— Women   ▲ Men

Figure 4.6 Women and men voted in similar ways, 1920–36

1920 to 1936. Overall, women in the ten-state sample voted quite similarly to men, both in each election and in the pattern of shifting party advantage. Despite the burden of historic disenfranchisement, women were capable of integrating into the electorate and casting ballots that looked remarkably like those of long-enfranchised men.

Explaining Women's Vote Choice

The conventional (and scholarly) wisdom about the first women voters ranges from "voted like their husbands" to "made the Republican landslide possible." What do we know about the choices of women voters in the period immediately following suffrage?

Was women's suffrage a failure (redux)? The "woman suffrage as failure" conventional wisdom held that not only did women fail to use their new right (as we have discussed), but when they did, they simply voted as their husbands instructed.[68] This expectation was repeated often in the press and popular discourse. "American women vote as their husbands, brothers, or fathers indicate," claimed journalist Charles Edward Russell in 1924.[69] "Most of the women I know … vote as their husbands vote," echoed writer Katharine Fullerton Gerould.[70] The assumption that women followed their husband's direction is consistent with a distinctive gender approach which assumes political disinterest among women as well as traditional notions about authority and power within the family.

With access to only census data and election returns, we cannot determine whether or not women simply voted like their husbands. Given the general similarity of the patterns of partisan vote choice for women and men it is likely that many married couples cast ballots for the same candidate. The Republican-dominated era preceding the election of Roosevelt in 1932 was characterized by strong mass partisanship, in part because partisan, ethnic, religious, and class identities tended to overlap and reinforce each other. As most people married within their ethnic, religious, and class in-group, most married couples likely shared perceived interests and party preferences, even without one partner directly influencing the other.[71]

Were the first women voters Republicans? An alternative narrative holds that women's suffrage initially benefited the GOP. In particular, both contemporary observers and later scholars have attributed the 1920 Republican landslide in large part to new female voters.[72] The main explanations take a distinctive gender approach: Women were voting on the basis of their gendered self-interest. Despite the conservative presidential nominees of the 1920s, the Republican party was the major party most associated with Progressivism (considered consistent with women's values of care and honesty). It was also a Republican Congress that passed the Nineteenth Amendment. On the other hand, a partisan gender gap in favor of the GOP may have reflected variation in the tendency of different groups of women to turn out, consistent with a resource inequality approach. Suffragists were overwhelmingly middle-class Protestant white women, characteristics associated with Republican identification in the mass electorate. If suffragists were more likely to turn out than other women, that might help to explain a Republican advantage among women.[73]

There does indeed appear to be a slight Republican advantage among women in the ten-state sample as a whole in the first three elections after suffrage. As with turnout, however, a closer look at the data in each state complicates our conclusions about the partisan leanings of the first women

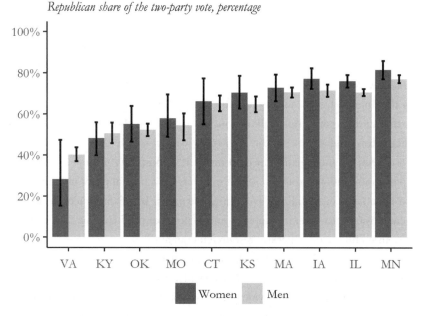

Republican share of the two-party vote, percentage

Figure 4.7 Women more likely to support Democrats in Democratic-leaning states, more likely to support Republicans in Republican-leaning states, 1920

voters. Figure 4.7 shows the Republican share of the ballot cast by women and men in each of the ten states in the sample in 1920. In half of the states, the difference in vote choice between women and men is small enough that we can only conclude that the two groups probably voted similarly in that presidential election. Despite the uncertainty associated with the estimates, it is likely that women in Virginia were less likely than men to vote for the Republican party. Kansas, Iowa, Minnesota, and Illinois also are exceptions, but in the opposite direction; in these four states, women are clearly more likely to vote Republican than are men. Both 1924 and 1928 show similar patterns, both in terms of the exceptional states and the direction of the advantage among women.

What explains this pattern? Democrats had been the dominant party in Virginia since the end of Reconstruction, while Republicans had been the majority party in the Midwestern states of Kansas, Iowa, Minnesota, and Illinois for decades. Newly enfranchised women voters may have been particularly loyal to the locally dominant party in their state. Both parties and interest groups (such as labor unions and professional organizations) worked to mobilize and persuade men. Women's interest groups, on the other hand, had little experience in mobilizing women as voters. Parties were better prepared than independent women's groups to influence the vote choice of new women voters.[74] As a result, political scientist Anna Harvey has argued, early women voters were more loyal than men to the dominant local party organizations best equipped to successfully mobilize them. Unlike most gender gap scholarship and rhetoric, this explanation focuses less on the qualities of women themselves and more on the structures within which they act politically. Disenfranchisement had denied women the opportunity to develop effective voter mobilization resources, which may have given local party organizations an advantage in mobilizing women as partisans. In this instance, distinctive gender (pervasive norms against women's political participation that underlie disenfranchisement) generates resource inequalities.

Gender role ideology may have interacted with social and economic structures in another way as well. The period preceding 1920 was characterized by strong partisanship and widespread one-partyism. Even when denied the right to vote, women lived in communities where in most cases one political party controlled political office and enjoyed broad loyalty among the mass electorate. Partisan messages were likely strong and consistently in favor of the dominant party with consequences for political socialization, social pressure, and information in the community. While both women and men would have been exposed to these strong partisan messages, women may have experienced more homogenous and reinforcing partisan cues. Men were more likely than women (particularly middle-class white women) to work outside of the home or venture beyond their immediate neighborhood, thus exposing them to a greater diversity of partisan cues. Presented with conflicting messages, we might expect men to less consistently favor one party in their vote choice. The partisan cues women received, on the other hand, may have been more uniform, resulting in more consistent and stable vote choice for the dominant local party.[75]

Did women support the Progressive party? Many expected women to be particular supporters of Progressives. Women (and women's organizations) had been active and prominent in the Progressive movement, and Progressive ideals, such as moral reform, were consistent with the qualities associated with women.[76] Concern that women would use the vote to achieve Progressive goals,

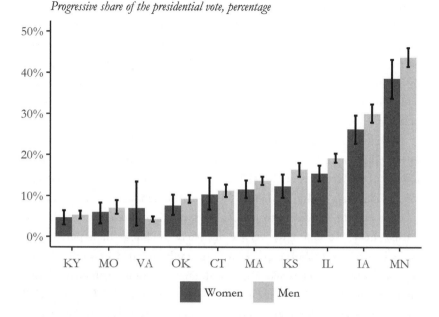

Progressive share of the presidential vote, percentage

Figure 4.8 Men, not women, were more likely to support Progressive La Follette in Illinois and Kansas, 1924

particularly Prohibition, galvanized a number of active opponents to women's suffrage, most notably the liquor industry.[77]

The candidacy of Progressive party candidate Robert M. La Follette in 1924 offers a unique opportunity to evaluate this expectation. A close look at the state-level estimates for women's and men's support for the Progressive party[78] fails to uncover any evidence that women were uniquely supportive of the Progressive party (see Figure 4.8). In only one state – Virginia – does the point estimate for women's vote share for the Progressive party exceed men's vote share, but, since turnout in Virginia is so low, we cannot be confident that the estimated difference is meaningful. In most states, we can only conclude with any confidence that women's and men's Progressive party vote share did not differ. However, in two states – Illinois and Kansas – the estimates indicate that men were more supportive than women of La Follette. In these states, Progressives would have done better had women not been enfranchised, an ironic outcome for a movement which benefited from the dedicated activism of so many women.

Did women contribute to New Deal realignment? The presidential elections of the 1930s were among the most transformative and consequential in American history, as the decades-long dominance of the Republican party gave way to a new majority Democratic coalition. This change was generated by both massive mobilization (new voters entering the electorate as Democrats) and conversion (previous Republican voters switching to the Democratic party).[79]

We have reason to expect that women did play a distinctive role in New Deal realignment. Since women had been less likely than men to turn out to vote in the elections of the 1920s, more women than men were available for mobilization – that is, there were more women who were not already members of the active electorate. At the same time, women who *had* voted during the 1920s may have been more likely to change their party choice since their relatively short experience at the polls provided less opportunity to reinforce partisan preferences.[80] Yet, with few exceptions, women are largely absent from scholarly analysis of the New Deal elections.[81] Many (especially early) New Deal realignment scholars appear to have accepted the suffrage-as-failure narrative and did not view women as a distinctive group worth investigating.

Overall, the ten-state estimates show that men and women contributed in roughly equal numbers, but in different ways, to New Deal realignment. With many women not yet participating in elections in the 1920s, more women than men were mobilized into the electorate for the first time as Democrats in both 1932 and 1936. At the same time, women who were already voting by 1928 were somewhat more likely than men to defect from Republican to Democratic support in the 1930s.

While there continued to be more men in the active electorate overall in the 1930s, the significant new mobilization of women combined with the greater rate of defection among women who previously voted Republican generated as many new women voters for Democrats as new men voters: In the ten sample states Democrats gained approximately 1.6 million additional votes from women and approximately 1.4 million additional votes from men by 1936. Democrats attracted an impressive 95% more female voters over 1928 compared to about 50% more male voters. One possible reason: Later scholarship on the modern gender gap finds women are particularly hard hit by and politically responsive to economic hardship, the engine of partisan change during this period.[82] Only 16 years after the extension of suffrage to women and after early accounts dismissed women's suffrage as a failure, women were a large and important source of electoral support for the emerging Democratic majority.

Explaining the first women voters. The dearth of survey data during these two decades makes it difficult to observe *how* women voted, much less explain *why* women voted the way they did. The nature of the available data – state-level estimates, but no individual-level measures of characteristics or attitudes – also makes it difficult for us to evaluate popular explanations focused on factors such as social class or immigration or the distinctive attitudes or values of women. On the other hand, the availability of state-level estimates focuses our attention on contextual and structural factors which are often under-appreciated in survey-based analysis and in the study of women voters.

Despite women's long disenfranchisement, the generally similar patterns of vote choice for women and men, both across place and time, suggests that for the most part, women's votes were determined by the same individual and contextual factors which shaped men's votes. As no less an authority on women and politics than Eleanor Roosevelt wrote in 1940,

> I think it is fairly obvious that women have voted on most questions as individuals and not as a group, in much the same way that men do, and that they are influenced by their environment and their experience and background, just as men are.[83]

CONCLUSION

Each of the historical eras examined in each chapter represents a distinct period for women in terms of legal order (laws and practice related to women's rights, especially in the electoral arena); gender order (the norms and practices related to gender roles); and the actual electoral behavior of women. The period from 1920 to 1936 begins with a major change in women's legal status: a constitutional amendment giving women the right to vote. This legal shift is accompanied by substantial changes in gender norms: shorter skirts, changing family responsibilities, and more women in the workforce. Yet the underlying presumption that politics is fundamentally men's work does not fade as quickly as laws change. Women were indeed less likely to cast ballots than men in this period – with meaningful variation across states – and those who did largely voted as men did, although not necessarily at men's direction.

Women enfranchised by the Nineteenth Amendment entered a political system characterized by entrenched parties and strong partisan attachments. The New Deal elections of the 1930s permanently disrupted long-standing political loyalties and ushered in a new dominant economic cleavage in American politics. Despite the legacy of disenfranchisement, women voters responded to these tumultuous events in much the same way as long-enfranchised men. Turnout among both women and men rose as presidential elections became increasingly salient and competitive. Women, like men, tended to favor Republicans in the 1920s and Democrats in the 1930s.

There was considerable interest in how women would use their hard-fought right. Conclusions quickly drawn at the time soon became a conventional wisdom that found its way into textbooks and social science research. Few women took advantage of their new right. Those who did voted like their husband did, or perhaps supported the Republican party. By the New Deal, women voters were judged to have failed to form an effective voting bloc and are largely absent from most elections and voting scholarship of the period.

This conventional wisdom was accepted because it was consistent with dominant assumptions about women as political actors. Women were inherently disinterested in politics, so their reluctance to enter polling places and their willingness to follow the guidance of their husbands was unsurprising. Women were naturally concerned with the home and family, sympathetic to the reforms advocated by the Progressive Movement, and thus likely to favor traditionally Progressive-leaning Republicans at first. These explanations also were consistent with an expectation that the women who had supported suffrage would be those most likely to use their new right. Suffrage leaders tended be native-born white Protestants, a group who tended to vote Republican.

Women were indeed substantially less likely to turn out to vote than long-enfranchised men. Yet a closer look reveals that where legal barriers were low and competition was high, women overcame their supposed natural disinterest in politics and a significant percentage made use of their new right. Women did, in the main, vote like men, although whether this was because they voted as their husbands instructed is not something we can determine from available data. It seems likely that at least some women came to similar voting decisions as their husbands due to shared backgrounds, attitudes, and interests, rather than command or direction. In the first elections after suffrage there is evidence of women being mobilized into locally dominant parties. Once realignment was underway, women were both more likely to be newly mobilized and to convert from previous Republican support. As a result, women were responsible for a significant share of the new Democratic majority in the 1930s.

The gap between the reality and the image of women voters is understandable during this period when so little good data on the sex of voters are available. In the next chapter, the emergence of modern survey research in the postwar era opens up new opportunities to observe and understand voters. The first scholars to analyze these data directed a limited part of their attention to women and gender, but the basic conclusions they reached would shape views of women as voters for decades to come.

CHAPTER 5

Feminine Mystique and the American Voter

THE DECADES OF THE 1940s AND 1950s CONJURE CONFLICTING IMAGES of American women. The strong and independent Rosie the Riveter of the Second World War soon gave way to June Cleaver, the perfect suburban mother. Betty Friedan would later describe this aggressive reassertion of traditional gender roles as "the feminine mystique." For women and politics, this era is usually cast – if discussed at all – as one of relative political quiescence, sandwiched between impassioned Progressive and suffrage activism and the second wave of the women's movement. While the view that women were absent from politics in the immediate postwar period has been challenged on several grounds,[1] our understanding of women as voters during this period remains limited and often characterized more by stereotypes than evidence.

Unlike the initial decades after women's suffrage, those interested in women voters were not without data during this era. Pioneering public opinion polling, including the early Gallup surveys and the American National Election Studies (ANES), offered unprecedented opportunities to observe voting behavior. The classic voting studies – including *The American Voter*, referenced in the chapter title – relied on these data and continue to shape how scholars and the public understand the American electorate to this day.

"The American voter" was largely understood to be a white man. Women received some attention from scholars, but were judged – and usually not favorably – against the standard of white male behavior. Women are described as less politically engaged and active than men in the 1940s and 1950s. This deficit was consistently attributed to gender role norms: "Some women do not believe that voting is part of their duty … voting is considered 'man's work.'"[2] The dominant narrative held that women who did vote were strongly influenced by their husbands, or by their roles as wives or mothers.

Yet, by the first decade after the Second World War, a variety of surveys revealed the difference between women's and men's rate of turnout had narrowed to less than 10 percentage points. Politics may have been men's work, but nearly as many women as men participated in presidential elections. The same surveys indicated that women's votes were in fact quite similar to men's, perhaps due to their husband's persuasion or perhaps because women were influenced by the same factors that influenced men, challenging expectations that women's votes reflected distinctive political preferences.

We again begin by examining electoral politics, women, and women in electoral politics during this era. We then discuss the new public opinion polling data which revolutionized the study of American elections and offered a more robust empirical understanding of women voters, among other groups. Our fundamental conclusions are generally the same for this period as for the period immediately preceding it: Women lagged men in participation and women's preferences for candidates were very similar to men's. What the early survey data permits us to see is that politically relevant demographic characteristics – education, working outside of the home, having children – often have larger and even different effects for women than men.

AMERICAN ELECTORAL POLITICS, 1940–1960

By 1940, the Democratic party had consolidated its position as the majority party in the United States, a status Democrats would maintain for at least the next 30 years. Democrat Franklin Roosevelt secured unprecedented third and fourth terms in 1940 and 1944. These contests were dominated by debate over the war abroad and the New Deal at home. Roosevelt died just three months into his fourth term, elevating Harry Truman to the presidency. With the end of the war in 1945, the Cold War with the Soviet Union and the on-going conflict in Korea continued to raise questions about America's role in the world and the conditions under which American soldiers should be put at risk.[3]

It did not take long for cracks in the Democrats' New Deal coalition to emerge. Sidestepping civil rights had been one key to the success of the New Deal and to Roosevelt's ability to preserve unity between the Northern and Southern wings of his party. Once both economic crisis and the war had passed, civil rights became increasingly difficult to avoid. When Democrats adopted several pro-civil rights planks at their 1948 convention, Southern Democrats bolted and formed a third party, the States' Rights Democrats (better known as the Dixiecrats) with South Carolina Senator Strom Thurmond as their standard bearer. Truman narrowly won the 1948 election, but Alabama, Mississippi, Louisiana, and South Carolina failed to cast Electoral College votes for the Democratic nominee for the first time since Reconstruction. The damage was permanent; after 1948, no Democratic presidential candidate would again receive super-majorities from Southern white voters.[4]

Faced with Democratic ascendancy, Republicans in the 1940s and 1950s clashed internally over whether they should accept the major changes in the role of the federal government represented by the New Deal (the moderate position) or stake out a strong conservative alternative. In the 1950s, moderates generally held sway, in large part due to their success in recruiting World War II hero General Dwight D. Eisenhower as their party's standard bearer. Eisenhower's personal appeal helped Republicans win the presidency against the Democratic nominee, Illinois Governor Adlai Stevenson, in both 1952 and 1956. In 1960, Democrats selected Massachusetts Senator John F. Kennedy to lead their party. As only the second Catholic nominee in American history, religion was a central issue, as was foreign policy – the Cold War, Cuba, and China, in particular – and civil rights. In one of the closest contests in American history, Kennedy narrowly defeated Eisenhower's vice president, Richard M. Nixon, returning Democrats to the White House.[5]

In retrospect, political debate in this period was far more tempered and the parties were far less polarized in the 1940s and 1950s than in the years to come. While the parties differed in their positions on the appropriate size of the federal government, social welfare, and labor rights, such issue differences were not particularly sharp or salient, in part because perceived moderates tended to represent the Republican party nationally and both parties were diverse ideologically. The parties were not sharply divided on civil rights, and the national Democratic party had not yet remade itself as the champion of those rights, although a realignment reflecting that division was already underway at the state level.[6]

AMERICAN WOMEN IN THE 1940s AND 1950s

Women's Lives

The Second World War had a profound impact on American women's lives. The war effort encouraged many women to join the paid workforce and upended patterns of marriage and motherhood. With the resolution of the war, many called for a return to traditional gender roles, and indeed, the decade of the 1950s is strongly associated with the feminine ideal of the white stay-at-home mother in the suburbs.[7]

During the war, employers in desperate need of labor employed not only single women, but married women with children as well. The US War Production Board mounted an ambitious campaign to encourage women to enter the workforce, ranging from the famous Rosie the Riveter poster to the commitment of the War Labor Board to enforcing equal pay for women. The military created women's auxiliaries in the various branches of the armed services. In both the civilian and military workforce, work remained largely segregated by sex and race. More than six million women joined the paid workforce for the first time during the war, while many others left traditional female service occupations for factories.[8]

The end of the war in 1945 reversed or slowed nearly all of these trends. With the return of men from war, the United States experienced a spike in marriage and an unprecedented Baby Boom that would last until 1960 (far longer than similar booms in Europe), reversing the decades-long decline in fertility. In every class, racial, and social group, women had children earlier, more often, and closer together; the number of children per family averaged 3.5 in the 1950s, a figure not seen since the turn of the century. The result was a dramatic increase in births in the United States and a long-lasting demographic impact. Figure 5.1 summarizes the way that work, marriage, and family evolved in the 1940s and 1950s (for sources, see Figures 1.2 through 1.5).[9]

Some women resisted the movement to return home, preferring to keep their jobs and protesting the less-attractive, less-well-paid employment opportunities now available to them. Other women joined, or reentered, the workforce in expanding occupational sectors like education, social work, retail, and service. The tendency for paid work to be the province of poor women and women of color decreased, as middle- and upper-income white women increasingly

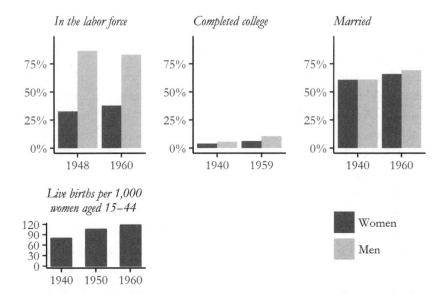

Figure 5.1 Women marry, have children, and enter the labor force in the 1940s and 1950s

entered the workforce as well. Most women continued to stop working for a period in their 20s and 30s, when their children were young. While female labor force participation did decline immediately after the war from its dramatic wartime surge, it did not entirely return to prewar levels and the longer-term upward trend of women in the paid workforce continued in the 1950s. In 1940, the year before the US entered the Second World World War, a quarter of all women were in the workforce; by 1960, that figure would be nearly 40%. The result was a disconnect between the resilient feminine ideal of the white suburban full-time mother and homemaker and the increasing participation of women in the paid workforce in the 1950s.

Women in Politics

This disconnect carried over into politics. Representation of women voters in the press continued to be characterized by two competing narratives – women are independent political actors who evaluate candidates much like men and women remain tied to children and home in ways that both makes them unlikely to vote and requires the parties tailor specific appeals to women.

Despite the prominence of the feminine mystique, it was not uncommon for politicians and the press to frame women as independent political actors unrelated to their gender during this period.[10] As one columnist suggested, at least partially in jest, in 1944, "It is never certain, furthermore, that a housewife, reputedly so busy all day with her domestic chores, has not been surreptitiously spending her mornings with her newspaper. For policy reasons she may not be able to admit this."[11] When asked about women voters, party leaders and campaign advisers often stressed the importance of appealing to women in the same way as they appealed to men. Argued one party operative, "There is no women's vote; there are no women's issues – women are people." Another political columnist agreed, "Never talk down to them. Don't ask what women are interested in as distinct from men. They are interested in good government, peace, and in what they've got to spend – taxes and prices – the same as men."[12]

More commonly, campaign strategies and press coverage emphasized women's status as wives and mothers, and their traditional roles in the home.[13] Woman and mother were often treated as synonymous. Asked about Eisenhower's supposed advantage among women, for example, his opponent Adlai Stevenson replied, "It would be said that as Mom goes so goes the nation."[14] According to a Democratic Women's Division official in 1960: "This is one of our major efforts, getting that wife to get out and vote. Many of the women are confused by the voting machine, or they let the husband do the voting, or they can't get away from the house and the kids."[15] Women's interests also were framed in terms of their traditional roles. An advocate for women voters explained why women should vote:

> When a woman turns on a faucet in her kitchen, politics comes into that kitchen with the water. When she takes her automobile out of the garage, politics rides with her on the public road! When she sends her children off to school, politics goes along with that child.[16]

Traditional gender stereotypes appeared in many forms: A 1944 story describing a Brooklyn representative who used his franking privilege to send 10,000 cookbooks to women in his district.[17] Harry Truman explaining that "A politician's work, like a woman's, is never done."[18] A 1956 RNC assistant chair asserting, "I certainly don't believe women vote their emotions wholly, but I can imagine a woman not voting for a candidate because of the way he parts his hair. I cannot imagine a man doing that."[19] A story about women candidates in

1960 titled, "Six Throw Bonnets in the Ring."[20] Similarly, coverage of women in politics emphasized their clothing, hair, age, and demeanor, often at great length. A 1944 story titled "Increased Governmental Activity by Women Urged for Postwar Era" features an activist described as an "attractive woman industrialist" and "one of the nation's best-dressed women."[21] In an item about Rep. Clare Booth Luce (R, CT), the writer explains that Luce "honestly admits being 40 years of age. She looks about 22!" and her hair and clothing (from her dress to her "black alligator oxfords") are described in detail.[22] A 1960 story on the candidates' wives not only characterizes Lady Bird Johnson as "trim" but lists her actual height and weight.[23] A long story on women voters that same year concludes that "Today women of voting age outnumber men. Yet, offsetting this to some extent has been the fact that women have generally stayed in the kitchen in unhealthy numbers on Election Day."[24]

OBSERVING WOMEN VOTERS: THE SURVEY REVOLUTION

How did women vote in the 1940s and 1950s? The emergence of reliable public opinion polling in the late 1930s, the community voting studies pioneered by researchers at Columbia University in the 1940s, and the establishment of the American National Election Studies (ANES) at the University of Michigan in 1952 made reliable answers to these questions available for the first time. The initial reports on these data established the field of voting research in the United States and set the parameters, both theoretical and empirical, for the study of American voters for decades to come.

Private polling companies such as Gallup and Roper began regularly surveying American opinion on a variety of topics, including politics, in the 1930s. Put to many uses, these data appear in influential analyses of elections of this period, such as pollster Louis Harris' 1954 book, *Is There a Republican Majority?* (1952 election), and political scientist Robert Lane's 1959 volume, *Political Life* (elections through 1952).[25] Beginning in 1936, George Gallup wrote a syndicated column describing his survey findings for dozens of major American newspapers.[26]

Scholars primarily at Columbia University conducted pioneering in-depth surveys in specific communities (Erie County, Ohio in 1940 and Elmira, New York in 1948) to understand the dynamics of public opinion and vote choice during presidential campaigns. *The People's Choice* and *Voting* (respectively) offer valuable insight into the processes that produce election outcomes. Lazarsfeld, Berelson, and their collaborators emphasized the social nature of voting, with interactions within families, neighborhoods, and workplaces shaping political knowledge, attitudes, and identity.[27]

Beginning with a small exploratory survey in 1948, researchers at the University of Michigan developed the ANES into a regular, large, and nationally representative public opinion election survey, measuring everything from political interest and knowledge to views on parties, candidates, and issues.[28] The first major report on the ANES data, *The American Voter* (covering elections from 1948 to 1956), provided unprecedented insight into the American electorate. Among many influential contributions to the study of voting behavior, authors Campbell, Converse, Miller, and Stokes highlighted the stability and impact of partisan identification, a political predisposition developed largely through socialization.

These surveys and associated published research can tell us a great deal about women voters in the elections of the 1940s and 1950s. The Gallup and Harris polls revolutionized our understanding of public opinion with both consistent questions and timely polls on contemporary issues and debates. The ANES provided, and continues to provide, invaluable information about a multitude of political attitudes and behaviors on which much of our understanding of American voting behavior is built.

These surveys also reveal a great deal about common assumptions and expectations about women as political actors during this period, beginning with the construction of the surveys themselves. The Gallup polls, for example, were designed primarily to understand voters – the active electorate – rather than the American populations as a whole. As a consequence, from the mid-1930s to the mid-1940s, the Gallup samples were comprised of 65–70% men by design as the survey protocol directed interviewers to always sample men first. Gallup also assumed there was no need to explain how women voted; in his own words: "How will [women] vote on election day? Just exactly as they were told the night before."[29]

The new surveys defined political action and knowledge in terms of traditionally male activities and interests. The early polls generally failed to query citizens about attitudes toward gender equality and roles – a "women's place is in the home" – both because such attitudes were accepted as normal rather than questioned, and presumably because women and gender were not considered political.[30] Importantly, the Gallup poll asked whether respondents would be willing to vote for a qualified woman for president as early as 1937, but most items about gender roles and women in politics do not appear in mass surveys until the early 1970s.[31] As a result, determining the impact of these attitudes on political behavior is difficult to impossible prior to that time. In this period (and every period), the interpretation of the data scholars did have available for analysis often reflects contemporaneous stereotypes about women and gender, as we discuss below.

These surveys are limited in other ways. In particular, observing the electoral behavior of African Americans was a challenge, in large part due to the research design priorities of the major election surveys. Since the Gallup polls targeted the active electorate, not only women, but Southerners and African Americans were deliberately under-represented in their surveys in the 1930s and 1940s.[32] The investigators responsible for the early community studies in the 1940s chose northern suburbs (Eric County, Ohio, and Elmira, New York) as their representative American places at a time when the vast majority of African Americans lived south of the Mason-Dixon line. The selected communities had small to nonexistent African American populations; as a result there are either no (1940) or very few (originally just 17 in 1948) African American respondents in the Columbia community voting studies.

The nationally representative random samples featured in *The American Voter* and other ANES-based work were designed to provide an accurate estimate of the voting behavior of the nation as a whole. A sample of fewer than 2000 respondents was sufficient to achieve that goal. Since racial minorities were a small share of the population, each survey included only a small number of African American respondents (typically fewer than two hundred in early ANES surveys). Any inference about African American voters is uncertain or imprecise.[33] Further subdividing the population to examine women and men separately only adds to the problem. To address exactly this challenge, Donald Matthews and James Prothro conducted a survey of a nearly equal number of African American and white Southerners in the summer of 1961. These data, which we discuss below, provide a rare opportunity to observe gender and African American political engagement during this period.[34]

We rely in this chapter on the ground-breaking ANES, as well as recently improved Gallup survey data. Gallup surveys were collected and published by the American Institute for Public Opinion beginning in 1936 and branded the "Gallup poll" by 1952. The surveys conducted after 1953 are random samples of the US population and administered at least monthly. Surveys administered before 1953 were not random, but "quota-controlled" samples, as we suggest above. While modern opinion polls use probability sampling methods in which respondents are chosen at random (or something approaching random), in quota-controlled sampling researchers seek to create a sample with a predetermined proportion of different groups of people, such as the active electorate.[35] For that reason, the 1944, 1948, and 1952 survey responses employed here are weighted so as to be more representative of the American public as a whole.[36] We rely on the two surveys immediately after each election to gauge turnout, vote choice, and a limited number of demographic characteristics (gender, race, age, education level, marital and parenthood status, employment, and region). Since the Gallup surveys are large and we use multiple surveys, the total number of respondents is larger than a typical ANES survey. The ANES includes a wider variety of questions but early iterations of the ANES were small (662 respondents in 1948, for instance). In comparison, the 1940–60 Gallup data includes over 31,000 respondents across twelve polls.[37] We also present data from the ANES, the bedrock on which so much of our knowledge about voting in the United States is built, as well as other published reports.

TURNOUT

In the 1940s and 1950s, women weighed entering into electoral politics in an environment that encouraged women's participation while also reinforcing stereotypes about the inappropriateness of the political arena for women. How likely were women to turn out to vote during those decades? What factors influenced their political participation?

The Gallup surveys, summarized in Figure 5.2, reveal a gender gap in turnout of 7–8 points in the six elections from 1940 to 1960. This is similar, but perhaps slightly smaller, to turnout gaps reported in the ANES data, which put the gender gap in turnout at about 10 percentage points.[38] Both surveys rely on self-reports of voting, and reported turnout is exaggerated by about 20 percentage points above actual turnout. By 1960, both surveys indicate that women's self-reported turnout was about 75%, while men's turnout was about 80%. Note as well that the Gallup polls appear to show more stable turnout

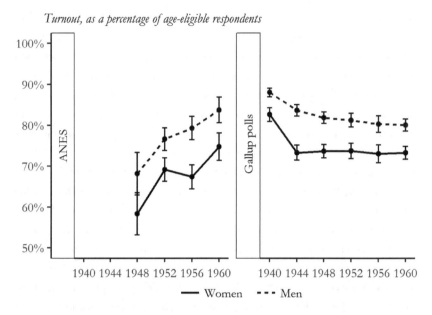

Figure 5.2 Women less likely to turn out than men, but typically the gap is less than 10 percentage points, 1940–60

than the ANES, but this is largely driven by the 1948 ANES data, which was an unusual survey.

Women Are Not a Voting Bloc

As we highlighted in Chapter 1, women voters are not a single, cohesive group. A multitude of factors and identities other than gender help explain women's turnout and vote choice, and the way that gender operates on electoral behavior can change across social groups as well. The innovative public opinion polls of this period were the first to permit researchers to examine subsets of women and investigate the different impact of characteristics and context on the electoral behavior of women and men. We focus here and in later chapters on five specific demographic characteristics: race, age, education, household type (a combination of marital status, presence of children, and labor force participation), and geographic region. The choice of these demographic variables is based on analysis of ANES data, specifically statistical models of both turnout and vote choice (Republican versus Democrat) for men and women. The statistical models – estimated separately for men and women – permit us to isolate the effects of each of these characteristics. While the figures summarize the simple relationship between each demographic variable and turnout or vote choice, our discussion and conclusions are informed by the statistical models.

Race. Not all groups of women (or men) were equally likely to turn out to vote. The *active* electorate was overwhelmingly white during this period. While the Great Migration was diversifying northern constituencies, more than 60% of African Americans continued to live in the authoritarian South as late as 1960 where, as a result of both legal and extra-legal barriers, black turnout was extremely low.[39]

Importantly, these potential black voters in the South were largely left out of the early Gallup surveys. As we discuss above, Gallup sought a picture of the active electorate, which provided little reason to interview black Southerners who were generally disenfranchised during the 1930s and 1940s, when Gallup polling began. In Gallup polls conducted near the 1940 election, for example, only one black respondent – out of 200 total black respondents – was from the South. In the typical Gallup survey in the 1940s and 1950s, 80–90% of African American respondents were from the Northeast (Middle Atlantic) and the Midwest, and thus not representative of the black population as a whole, most of whom lived in the South.[40]

The failure of the Gallup organization to survey substantial numbers of black citizens in the South has consequences for our ability to observe trends in black voting in this period. Figure 5.3 reports the average across Gallup polls for the presidential elections of the 1940s and 1950s – twelve surveys spanning six elections. Since the data are samples from a larger population, we also include the margin of error, an indicator of the confidence we have in each estimate, in this and all survey-based figures. In these surveys, about 80% of whites reported voting, compared to an estimated 70% of African Americans (even with weighting for the actual regional distribution of the black population). That 70% of African Americans cast ballots at a time when a significant majority lived in the Jim Crow South is clearly an inaccurate estimate. The shortcomings of these data also affect our

Turnout, as a percentage of age-eligible respondents

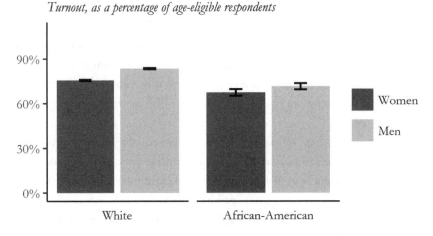

Figure 5.3 Self-reported turnout appears slightly lower for women among both whites and African Americans (Gallup), 1940–60

conclusions about gender: The small turnout gender gap appears consistent across racial groups, but without valid information about black Southerners, our confidence is limited.

Even with the overrepresentation of black respondents outside of the South, African American respondents never account for more than 5% of those reporting having voted in any of the Gallup polls from 1940 through 1956, despite comprising at least 9 to 10% of the national population.[41] Only after the 1965 Voting Rights Act and changes in polling practices do we observe a level of racial diversity in the electorate, and in surveys, which permits us to offer reliable estimates of the voting behavior of women and men of color in individual elections.

We are not entirely without information about Southern black voters, however. Matthews and Prothro's unique survey of black and white Southerners in 1961, designed in large part to overcome the problem of small samples of black respondents, is an important exception which provides insight into racial differences in political participation in the Jim Crow South. The study highlights the key role of context in determining political behavior: Across the four counties studied, African American voter registration rates vary from 0 to 61%. The authors find that 47% of African American men reported voting, compared to 38% of African American women. Black women also were less likely than their male counterparts to participate in politics more broadly, such as working for a campaign or belonging to a political group; in contrast, there were few or smaller gender differences in political activity more broadly among Southern whites. There were signs of change, however: Matthews and Prothro report almost no gender differences in the likelihood of African American women and men engaging in student-led civil rights protests during the 1950s.[42]

Age. Women in the 1940s and 1950s experienced a range of formative experiences, depending on their age cohort. To examine the effects of age, we divide respondents into three cohorts which capture different political socialization experiences of American women of this period. Women born before 1900 came of political age before the ratification of the Nineteenth Amendment and were, for the most part, disenfranchised until 1920. These women bore the full brunt of social norms that discouraged participation. Women born between 1900 and 1920 had the right to vote by the first election in which they were eligible (the voting age was usually 21 prior to 1972). While they may have observed the struggle for suffrage, they were never personally disenfranchised on the basis of sex. For women born after 1920, women's suffrage was unremarkable in the sense that their own political experience included no period in which women could not vote.

Turnout typically increases with age: Older voters have more experience with the process, more access to information, and more experience to draw on to make choices in elections. *The American Voter* reports that for women, the relationship between age and turnout follow this pattern, except that women who came of age before the extension of suffrage were *less* likely to turn out than women who were slightly younger.[43]

Figure 5.4 reports the average turnout of women and men in each group across the six presidential elections from 1940 to 1960. In every cohort, women are less likely to vote than men. Yet, the gap narrows among the youngest cohort and is largest in the oldest cohort, suggesting that as norms about women in politics faded or changed and women increasingly had access to politically relevant resources (such as employment), women's turnout was becoming similar to men's. While many older women turned out to vote, powerful social norms that operated to reduce women's turnout continued to impact turnout in elections 20 to 40 years after the extension of the right to vote.

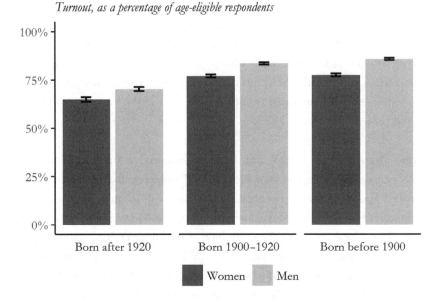

Turnout, as a percentage of age-eligible respondents

Figure 5.4 The turnout gap is smaller for younger women and larger for women born before 1900 (Gallup), 1940–60

Education. One of the strongest and most consistent findings in voting research is that education is associated with higher voter turnout. Education offers a range of politically relevant resources, including familiarity with political concepts and actors, norms of civic duty, and politically informed and active social and professional networks.[44] The authors of *The American Voter* noted that greater political interest, attention, and sophistication were associated with higher educational attainment, and also emphasized that those with higher status jobs (made possible by higher education) were more likely to participate due to "motivation to protect status position" rather than advantages in cognitive skills or political interest.[45] Notably, however, more recent research suggests that the visible effects of education may be a function of selection rather than the effects of schooling per se. Citizens who choose, or who have the opportunity to, pursue educational opportunities may already have the tools for political engagement, rather than developing them through education.[46]

Is education associated with higher turnout for women as it is for men? Education is not consistently recorded in Gallup surveys during this period, so

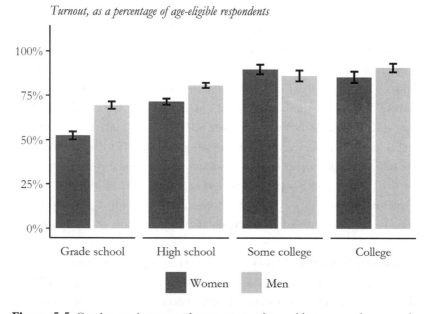

Figure 5.5 Gender gap in turnout largest among those with no more than a grade school education (ANES), 1948–60

in Figure 5.5 we rely on the American National Election Studies (ANES) data, which begins in 1948, and show the average turnout of men and women at various levels of educational attainment.

Both women and men became more likely, in general, to turn out to vote as their educational attainment rises. Less education had a particularly demobilizing effect on women, however. Over 90% of college-educated men turn out to vote, which falls to a rate of approximately 70% of men who only finished grade school, about a 20-point drop. For women, on the other hand, 90% with at least some college report voting, compared to just about half of women without a high school diploma, a drop of nearly 40 percentage points. A woman without a high school diploma had a 50/50 chance of being a voter, but a college-educated woman had a nearly 90% probability of voting, indistinguishable from college-educated men. This distinction has a significant impact on women's turnout overall, as 30% of women (and men) did not attain more than a grade school education as late as the 1950s, compared to fewer than 10% receiving college degrees.

The impact of education on turnout offers evidence of a distinctive gender rather than an unequal resources explanation for women's turnout.

Importantly, it is not that men have much more education; while a higher percentage of men have college degrees than women (around 10% compared to 6% for women), the distribution of educational attainment among men and women is not dramatically unequal in the 1940s and 1950s. Rather, poorly educated women are far less likely than similarly situated men to turnout out to vote.[47] Observing similar patterns, the authors of *The American Voter* conclude that the "vestiges of older political sex roles are most apparent ... at lowest social levels."[48] However, they (and we) are unable to offer direct evidence of the differential prevalence of such views among educational groups; it may well be that other factors associated with less education discouraged these women from turning out to vote or that less well-educated men had access to mobilizing resources (e.g., union membership) that similarly situated women did not.

Marriage, family, and work. The type of household you live in influences whether you vote. Are you single or married? Working or not? Caring for children? The greater stability and community embeddedness associated with marriage and family is expected to encourage voter turnout; indeed, simply living with another person is associated with increased political awareness and voter turnout. Similarly, we might expect that the presence of children expands political interest (e.g., schools, security, health care) and mobilizes voters. On the other hand, the obligations of parenting may crowd out political interest and participation. Given traditional gender roles in the home, we also might expect the effects of parenting to be greater for women than men.[49] People who participate in the paid workforce are generally more likely to vote than those who do not, and professional occupations are associated with higher rates of political engagement. Paid work provides opportunities to develop civic skills, gather politically relevant knowledge, and interact with others who may encourage or model political engagement.[50]

Across this two-decade period, women and men occupy remarkably different social positions. Women were unquestionably unequal in terms of access to paid employment in the 1940s and 1950s. In the Gallup surveys, as many as 77% of women report being out of the labor force compared to fewer than 14% of men. To combine work with other household characteristics, we turn to the ANES samples, since Gallup rarely queries marital status and reports occupational status only for the (usually male) head of household. While they often shared lives, women's lived experiences differed from men's. Nearly half

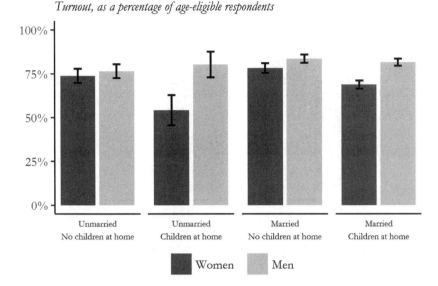

Turnout, as a percentage of age-eligible respondents

Figure 5.6 Women with children at home are the least likely to turn out (ANES), 1956–60

of all men were married, working, and have children in the home in the 1950s. By contrast, nearly 40% of all women were married, with children, but *not* employed outside of the home (the second most common category is married, with no children and no work outside the home, 16%).

What effects do these patterns have on voter turnout? While the multivariate analysis indicates that marriage and participation in the labor force have roughly the same small positive effects on the participation of women and men in the 1950s, the impact of children is quite different. Figure 5.6 shows the rate of turnout for women and men depending on marital status and the presence of children.[51] Women with children in the home were much less likely to turn out to vote than either women without children, or men with children in the home. There was no similar decline in turnout among men who have children (the large confidence intervals around turnout for unmarried men with children at home reflects the extremely small number of respondents in that category). A woman with children was less likely to turn out to vote in the 1950s, but parenting status makes no difference to whether men go to the polls.

Figure 5.7 Women who work are as likely to vote as those who stay home – same as men (ANES), 1952–60

Different responsibility for child care and employment outside of the home were central to the feminine mystique of this period, particularly for women and men in upper- and middle-class white communities. We have just seen how mothers were less likely to turnout than fathers, regardless of marital status. Employment, on the other hand, had only a very small positive impact on the likelihood that women would turn out to vote in this period, as Figure 5.7 indicates. Women turned out at similar rates (and less than men), regardless of their employment status.

Politics and place. The South was characterized by distinctively low turnout for both women and men during this period. Restrictive voting laws and an authoritarian political culture meant few opportunities for African American women and men to vote (68% of whom lived in the South in 1950[52]), and suppressed the turnout of low-income and less-educated Southern whites as well. We have seen in the previous period that restrictive election laws had a bigger impact on women than men. In addition, many expected that Southern gender and racial norms, particularly the ideal of the white Southern lady – charming, gentle, obedient, and utterly feminine – discouraged traditional political participation among white women in particular.[53]

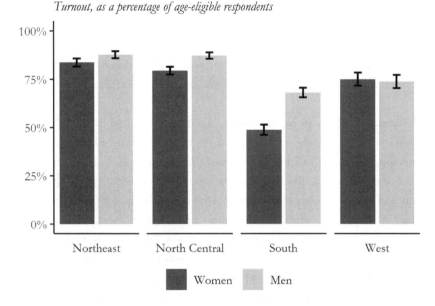

Turnout, as a percentage of age-eligible respondents

Figure 5.8 Substantial turnout gender gap in the South, smaller or nonexistent gaps elsewhere (ANES), 1952–60

Turnout in the South was indeed lower than in any other region (see Figure 5.8). While the turnout gender gap was small or nonexistent in other regions, the difference in turnout between women and men was larger – and to a considerable degree – in the South. As a result, women in the South were the least likely to vote of any group, owing largely to legal and extra-legal barriers to vote for African Americans in a region with a substantial African American population. The fact that Southern women were so much less likely to vote than Southern men, however, suggests the Southern context was particularly demobilizing for women. In the period immediately after suffrage, state-level contexts that discouraged voting (such as the sort of restrictive electoral laws and non-competitive elections which characterized the South during this period) had a particularly strong impact on women. This pattern persists for women in the South in the 1950s.

UNDERSTANDING WOMEN'S TURNOUT

Women remained less likely to vote than men in the 1940s and 1950s, although the extent and presence of the turnout gender gap varies across different groups and locations. Married women without children, college-educated women, younger women, and women outside the South were nearly as likely to turn out to vote as similarly situated men. Despite these variations, most observers and scholars described lower rates of turnout in these decades as applying to women as a whole. How did they explain this greater reluctance to vote?

A woman's place is in the home. That women would turn out less than men was not surprising to observers at the time. The early scholars of public opinion and voting unanimously agreed that gender role socialization, especially the persistent and widespread norm that politics is men's work, explained much of women's reluctance to engage with politics. Lane concludes that more than 20 years after suffrage, a significant percentage of women still "do not include 'voting' in their concept of the things women do, that is, in their image of the female role."[54] He explains: "A major feature of our culture's typing of the two sexes is the assignment of the ascendant, power-possessing role to the man and the dependent, receptive role to the woman ... a woman enters politics only at the risk of tarnishing, to some extent, her femininity."[55] Berelson and his colleagues note differences between the sexes in "socially sanctioned responsibility for political affairs"; men are expected to follow and engage in politics, women are not.[56] While politics is men's work, women's traditional occupations also create a number of "built-in handicaps," including, according to Harris: "the burdens of housework, the self-isolation, the determined tradition of apathy and lack of mobility, the imposed second-class citizenship, and the failure to assume independent thinking."[57] Note that while these scholars rarely make the distinction explicitly, their stereotypical women is clearly a middle-class white woman who does not work outside the home, not a poor or African American woman, many of whom did engage in the paid labor market.

Political efficacy. The turnout gender gap also is attributed to gender differences in political efficacy, the sense that an individual can personally influence the political world. In the ANES surveys of the period, women were less likely to report that they understand the complexities of politics or believe that their participation has an impact. Citizens who do not believe they can understand or influence politics are less likely to be politically active. Once again, gender roles are held responsible: "The man is expected to be dominant in action directed toward the world outside the family; the woman is to accept his leadership passively. She is not expected, therefore, to see herself as an effective agent in politics."[58]

Role models. The absence of political role models during this era also reinforced norms discouraging women's political participation. Consider Lane: "The media, and also the literary heritage reread by every generation, tend to create images of women in domestic, or, perhaps, artistic and literary or even dramatic or even career roles – but not in political roles." He cites analysis showing that public affairs accounts for less than 10% of radio serials aimed at women, far less than other topics like marriage, careers, or crime.[59] Role models in politics were certainly in short supply. In the 1940s and 1950s, no more than two women served in the US Senate (2%) at any one time, and no more than 17 women served in the House concurrently (4%).[60] Later work suggests that the presence of female role models in politics can indeed encourage political engagement among women, especially young women.[61]

Explaining women's turnout. There is good reason to believe that gender roles and gender role socialization contributed to women's lower rates of turnout. We saw in Chapter 4 that, even 20 years after suffrage, at least some women expressed a belief voting was an inappropriate activity for women. However, while the scholars of the 1940s and 1950s generally had far more data on women voters than previously available, their claims about gender role attitudes are largely based on research from an earlier period or their own assumptions.[62] Neither the ANES surveys employed by the authors of *The American Voter* or the community studies examined in *Voting* report direct measures of gender role attitudes or beliefs about women voting. Seeking to explain women's turnout in 1952, Lane cites Merriam and Gosnell's path-breaking work on non-voting, but their survey was conducted in Chicago in 1924, almost 30 years earlier.[63] Given the ubiquity of the "politics-as-men's-work" idea in the mass media and scholarship, it seems likely that cultural norms of socialized disinterest in politics contributed to women's lower rate of turnout but also that assumptions about women and politics (that same socialization) shaped the conclusions observers and scholars reached about women voters.

Or perhaps we are asking the wrong question. Like previous scholars and observers at the time, we have described women's lower turnout as the puzzle to be solved. Yet, by 1960, nearly three of every four women reported turning out to vote in presidential elections, just 7–8 points fewer than men. Perhaps the better question to ask is why and how so many women managed to overcome the barriers to women's voting – both distinctive gender norms proscribing political activity for women and resource disadvantages in terms of work and family – and cast ballots in presidential elections as early as the 1940s and 1950s.

WOMEN'S VOTE CHOICE

The vote choices of women and men were far more similar than different in the 1940s and 1950s. "Why is there not a distinctive women's vote?" ask Berelson and his colleagues, who find "only minor differences in voting between men and women" in the 1948 presidential election.[64] What small differences there were tended to favor Republicans. Harris emphasizes women's greater support of Eisenhower; his polls finds a six-point Republican advantage among women in 1952.[65] *The American Voter* describes partisan vote choice differences as "slight," with women "3–5 percent more Republican" in 1952 and 1956.[66] Gallup highlighted the greater support among women for Nixon over Kennedy in 1960.[67]

A majority of women (and men) voters supported Democrats Roosevelt, Truman, and Kennedy in 1940, 1944, 1948, and 1960, and Republican Eisenhower in 1952 and 1956. Figure 5.9 reports the share of the two-party vote women and men gave to Republican candidates from 1940 to 1960. Despite the fact that both women and men over-report turnout, reported vote choice is both consistent across the two surveys and matches the actual vote. The similarity of female and male vote choice is striking. In the Gallup data, the gender gap (women more likely to vote for Republicans) never exceeds five points, and is usually closer to zero. The ANES data show a slightly larger gap, but in only one case (1956) does the gap (barely) exceed five points.

Women Are Not a Voting Bloc

Survey data also revealed considerable variation in how women voted depending on social position, race, and region. These differences were

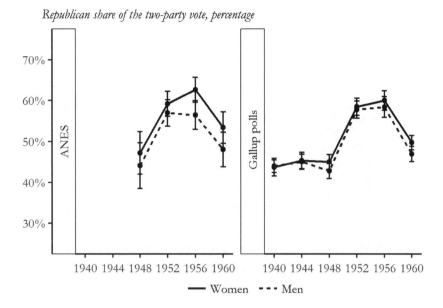

Republican share of the two-party vote, percentage

Figure 5.9 Women and men favor same candidates, only a slight Republican lean among women, 1940–60

highlighted in explanations for overall trends in voting among women. For example, the authors of *The American Voter* attributed the small Republican lean among women to resource inequalities: "much of [this] discrepancy is traceable not to something unique in female political assessments, but to aggregate differences in other social characteristics between the sexes." They claim that "if we take a large variety of other social characteristics into account, there are no residual differences in partisanship between men and women."[68] Yet this conclusion assumes that social characteristics are correlated with political choices in the same way for women as for men. A distinctive gender approach would expect gender differences even when controlling for key demographic differences. As we see in this section, the resource inequality expectation holds in some cases, but not in all.

Race. White women were the most likely to vote Republican among all groups in each of the elections between 1940 and 1960, as Figure 5.10 demonstrates. That said, the partisan gender gap among whites is miniscule. The same pattern (women slightly more Republican) is observed among racial

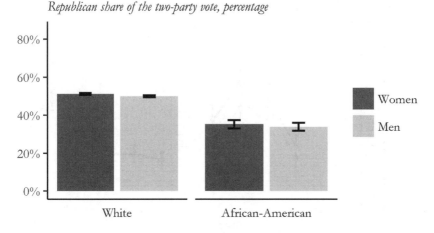

Republican share of the two-party vote, percentage

Figure 5.10 White women are the most likely to vote Republican, but race matters far more than gender (Gallup), 1940–60

and ethnic minorities, but due in part to the small numbers of non-whites in these surveys, the margins of error are wider and differences are not statistically significant.

The meaningful gap was clearly between white and black voters, not between women and men. More than half of white voters of either sex cast ballots for Republicans. A substantial majority of African American voters of either sex vote for Democrats. Race was (and remains) more important than gender for determining vote choice.

Age. The early voting studies reported that Republican identification (and intensity of partisanship) is positively associated with age; younger voters were more likely to be Democrats. Is this conclusion consistent across men and women? In the 1940s and 1950s, the female electorate continued to include women who had come of political age before the enactment of women's suffrage, which may have shaped their partisanship as well as their turnout. Figure 5.11 shows that Republican support does increase in the older compared to younger age cohorts. Older and middle-aged women remain more likely than similarly aged men to cast Republican ballots. Yet, among the youngest voters, we see a weak signal that the Republican advantage among women may be eroding.

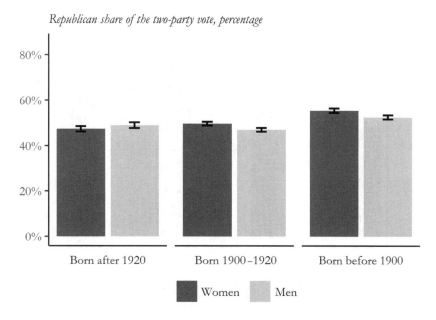

Republican share of the two-party vote, percentage

Figure 5.11 Older women slightly more Republican, but partisan advantage among younger women may be reversing (Gallup), 1940–60

Education. Earlier in this chapter, we learned that not only does turnout increase with educational attainment, but less education is associated with particularly low turnout for women. The turnout gender gap among less-educated women had a significant effect on women's turnout overall: College education was expanding after the Second World War but was not yet widespread. Across the Gallup polls through 1960, slightly more than half (53%) of women voters had no education beyond high school, while slightly less than half (47%) of men were in the same categories, a real but small difference.

Throughout most of the twentieth century, education was associated with the propensity to vote Republican. The ANES data in Figure 5.12 confirms this trend: Both men and women became more likely to vote Republican as their educational attainment increased. Only among high school graduates do we see a meaningful gender gap, with women who graduated high school more likely to vote Republican than similar men. As with the young, we may be seeing the beginnings of the shift to a pro-Democratic gender gap among highly educated voters, although, given the relatively small number of college-educated men or women, differences in this period are not statistically significant. On the whole,

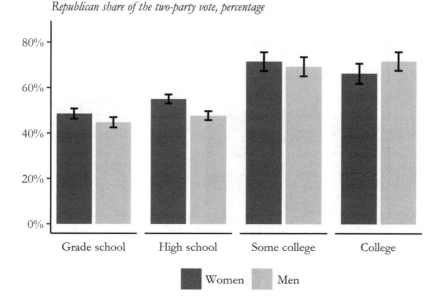

Figure 5.12 Educational attainment associated with voting Republican for both women and men (ANES), 1948–60

college-educated women, like college-educated men, supported Republicans, while those without college degrees voted for Democrats, although women less so than men.

Marriage, family, and work. As we have seen, observers often framed traditional mothers as the default category for women voters, and indeed, married, stay-at-home mothers were the largest group during this period – nearly 40% of women voters fell into that category. Figure 5.13 shows the average Republican vote share among women and men in and out of the labor force.

Women who do not work were more likely to vote Republican than anyone else. While men were roughly equally likely to vote Republican regardless of employment status, women *outside* of the labor force were more likely to vote Republican than were employed women. In this period, women were far less likely to work outside the home than were men, so this is an important source of the broader pro-Republican gender gap in presidential vote choice.

We turn to the effects of family in Figure 5.14. The effects of marriage operate in opposite directions for men and women. Women who were married

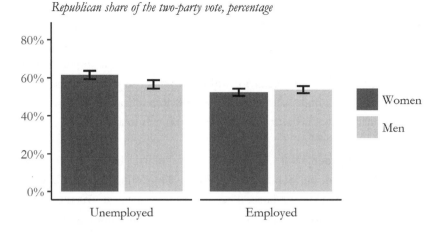

Figure 5.13 Women who don't work are the most Republican (ANES), 1952–60

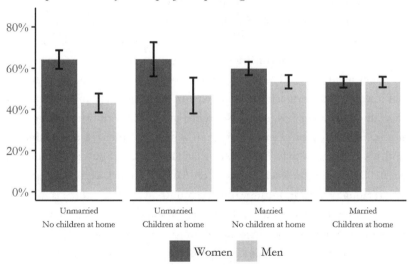

Figure 5.14 Single women are the most Republican (ANES), 1956–60

were somewhat less likely to vote Republican than women who were single. Men who were married were more likely to vote Republican than men who were single. While both effects were small, the net result is that single women were significantly more likely to support a Republican candidate than single men. Parenthood, on the other hand, does not have a significant effect on whether women or men vote Republican in this period. Women with children were less likely to vote, but once they got to the polls, they were generally as Republican as non-mothers. This observation highlights the importance of observing women's voting behavior within specific historical contexts. In the 1940s and 1950s, single women were the most Republican-leaning group of all. This will not be the pattern as the century comes to a close.

Politics and place. Not only was turnout distinctively low in the South during this period, but Southern partisanship was distinctive as well. These two dynamics are closely related: The authoritarian political structure of the Jim Crow South was designed to keep any person who could not be reliably counted upon to support the state and local Democratic political establishment out of polling places. Although Southern states had large African American populations, these communities were systematically disenfranchised, so that the pool of Southern voters was overwhelmingly white.

Figure 5.15 confirms that Southerners were uniquely more Democratic – that is, less likely to vote Republican – in presidential elections in the 1940s and 1950s.[69] The authors of *The American Voter* pointed to Southern women – who they assume would have favored Democrats and were less likely to turn out to vote than Southern men – to explain the national Republican advantage among women. Yet, unlike Southern men, Southern women voters are not significantly more Democratic than women in other regions. Campbell and his colleagues may be correct that Democratic Southern women in particular were most likely to stay home on Election Day, but we observe less regional variation in the women's vote than in men's. This is different from the first elections after suffrage (see Chapter 4), when women tended to be more supportive of the locally dominant Democratic party than men.

This examination of regional differences in voting also helps remind us that all gender differences are not necessarily caused by women. The rate at which women vote Republican was fairly consistent across all four regions, with a small, just barely significant decline in the South. Men in the South and West were substantially less likely to vote Republican, not only compared to women in their own regions, but compared to men in other regions as well. What made Southern and Western men so much more Democratic than other voters in the 1950s?

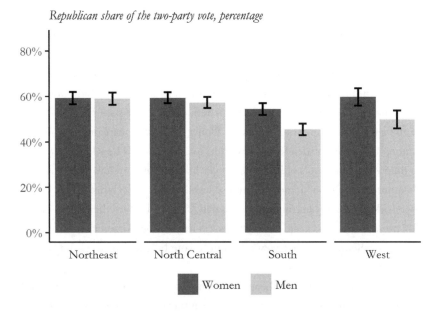

Republican share of the two-party vote, percentage

Figure 5.15 Men in different regions favor different parties, but less regional variation in women's vote (ANES), 1952–60

Explaining Women's Vote Choice

In the 1940s and 1950s, women voters faded from novel to normal. At the same time, a dominant "feminine mystique" promoted conventional conceptions of femininity and clear distinctions between women and men. Women of this period both experienced strong traditional gender norms (distinctive gender) and had access to fewer resources (resource inequality). In this context, how did observers and scholars understand women voters?

(Still) vote like husbands. Why were women's and men's votes so similar? The most prominent and consistent explanation was the assumption that women tend to defer to their husbands in political decision-making. As before, this belief reflects a distinctive gender approach, viewing women as either naturally, or socialized to be, disinterested in politics and willing to defer to male authority and expertise.

The authors of the classic works on voting during this period all echoed this assumption. According to Berelson, Lazarsfeld, and McPhee, "The men discuss politics with their wives – that is, they *tell* them – but they do not particularly respect them. On the side of the wives there is trust; on the side of the husbands, apparently, there is the need to reply or to guide."[70] Campbell, Converse, Miller, and Stokes similarly assert that, "The wife who votes but otherwise pays little attention to politics tends to leave not only the sifting of information up to her husband but abides by his ultimate decision about the direction of the vote as well."[71] In his influential 1964 paper, "The Nature of Belief Systems in Mass Publics," Converse further explains that due to women's lesser sophistication, knowledge, and interest, "The wife is very likely to follow her husband's opinions, however imperfectly she may have absorbed their justifications at a more complex level."[72] Lane declares: "The wife is 'persuaded' rather than the husband partly, at least, because her role is culturally prescribed as less political; she loses less by yielding. An alternative reaction is for the wife to retain her views but not to vote because she does not want to 'cancel her husband's vote.'"[73]

The evidence to support the assumption that women vote as their husbands tell them was largely indirect. In *Voting*, the authors find that women were more likely than men to report that they would go to a family member to discuss a political question and to report discussing politics with a family member. From this Berelson et al. conclude that women trust in their husbands for political direction, and "apparently" the husbands' feel a need to respond or guide, but the authors do not report direct measures of trust or perceived need to reply or guide.[74] Left unstated is whether we should assume that the 41% of men who reported discussing politics with a family member also trusted their wives and if those wives felt a need to reply or guide. Similarly, the authors of *The American Voter "believe* this bias arises largely because of female willingness to leave political matters to men" (emphasis ours). They view observed gender differences in levels of conceptualization (women less likely to explain their preferences in ideological terms) as evidence that "the ultimate behavior of the dependent wife springs from the more sophisticated concepts of her husband."[75] Political scientist C. Everett Ladd described this analysis decades later: "The stereotyping achieved in this 'classic' account has rarely been equaled and never surpassed."[76]

Scholars' conclusions about women voters were both informed by popular stereotypes, and helped to shape these stereotypes. A 1952 *Detroit Free Press* article, "They Vote as Hubby Tells 'Em to Vote," quotes *Voting* coauthor and Columbia sociologist William McPhee as suggesting that while women may have distinctive preferences early on in campaigns, by election day, "the women go to the polls and vote the way their men tell them to."[77] Similarly, a 1960 *New York Times* article claims that a University of Michigan poll (almost certainly the ANES) "showed that women tended to vote as their husbands did."[78]

Not everyone agreed with the vote-like-husbands narrative. Former congresswoman and DNC women's division chair, the "dignified" Mrs. Chase Going Woodhouse, claimed in 1948 that women "no longer follow their husband to the polls. Now they lead the way."[79] One 1956 party leader framed his argument in resource inequality logic, "women cannot be counted on simply to follow the political faith of their husbands. If married couples tend to vote the same way – and they do – it is because their environment gives them the same orientation, rather than because the woman rubberstamps the man's choice."[80] Writing about a 1956 poll, pollster George Gallup concludes that "the political maxim that women voters follow the pattern of male voters appears destined for the scrap heap."[81] That said, the possibility that women vote as instructed by their husbands was sufficiently widely held that the press and other party leaders felt compelled to address it throughout this period.

Distinctive women? In the 1940s and 1950s, scholars generally dismissed the idea that women had distinct policy preferences that led to divergent vote choice. The authors of *The American Voter* acknowledge, "Of course some wives, as well as some women without husbands, do strike out on their own politically," but make it clear that they do not expect this group to be large.[82] Campbell and his colleagues note the possibility of distinctive policy preferences of women and men in certain periods (such as over Prohibition in the past) but claim that in the current moment, "there is no reason to believe that women *as women* are differentially attracted to one of the political parties."[83] The authors of *Voting* similarly conclude that "there are few policy issues persisting over a period of time that affect men and women differently."[84] A 1960 newspaper article entitled "Is She a Wise Voter?" reports that despite conventional wisdom, a University of Michigan survey (ANES) found that women were no more interested in the Korean War, education, health, or pensions than were men.[85]

This matter-of-fact scholarly consensus on the absence of gender differences might have come as a surprise to anyone who followed politics during the 1940s and 1950s. Politicians and the press routinely expressed the belief that women were concerned with specific issues, usually associated with their roles in the home and as wives and mothers. Explained one party leader in 1956, "women are more interested in some issues, the ones that touch their families most closely. I mean school matters, health matters and, right now, the rising cost of living."[86] Rising prices in particular were consistently framed as an important political issue for women in this period due to their expected role in managing the family finances. According to another party leader that same year, "The housewife will be the first person to rebel at the higher cost of living."[87] Some scholars echoed this view. For example, Lane argued that women are more attuned to inflation due to their roles as "the shoppers in the family."[88]

From the Second World War through the Cold War and the Korean conflict, women's particular interest in ensuring that their husbands and sons would not again be called to war or would return soon from current conflicts was another consistent theme.[89] The 1952 Gallup data offer some support for this conclusion: asked what the "next steps" should be in the Korean War, in 1952, only 17% of women supported intensifying the conflict, compared to nearly 25% of men. Women are simply less "hard-boiled about war than men,"[90] explained pollster Louis Harris. The "greatest gift we can give our mothers is world peace" claimed Harry Truman in 1948.[91] Argued one party leader in 1956, "Women are just less warlike than men, and they get pretty emotional about it. That 'I didn't raise my boy to be a solider' cry is pretty potent." The article goes on to note: " 'The whole platform is angled for the women's vote,' remarked a cynical Republican, 'The peace angle I mean.' "[92]

While the parties certainly sought to distinguish themselves from each other on key issues, in a broader historical context what stands out is the rather muted distinctions between the parties in the decades immediately following the Second World War. Activist Phyllis Schlafly would later castigate the Republican party for offering only "an echo" of the Democratic party rather than a clear conservative "choice." Even if women did have distinctive attitudes on education, inflation, or world peace, the choices at the ballot box might not have offered sufficient opportunity or incentive to translate those divergent preferences into divergent partisan choices. Overall, the authors of *The American Voter* and other social scientists of the time voiced considerable skepticism about the extent to which policy views organized voters political choices in the 1940s and 1950s. Thus, even if women *did* have different policy preferences and priorities, we might not be surprised that we observe so little gender difference in partisanship and voting during this era.[93]

Candidate appeal. The appeal of particular candidates to women, and the idea that women were more swayed than men by personalities and appearances, was another repeated theme. According to one columnist, "In other words, where a male voter picks out his candidate and says, 'I agree with him,' a woman picks out hers and says, 'I like him!' "[94] Eisenhower's "special appeal to women" was of particular note to scholars and the press, with some debate over whether his "father image" or "explanations of an even more Freudian nature" were responsible.[95]

Candidate-centered explanations also were popular in 1960, as the press highlighted women's reactions to John Kennedy. One journalist describes the scene of a Kennedy appearance:

> At Pomona Airport near Atlantic City last Monday several hundred moist-eyed women were mauling each other with bargain basement techniques to win positions again the wire retaining fence. Breaking loose from New Jersey's cigar smokers, Senator John F. Kennedy walked over toward the crowd of women and a chorus of squeals reached out to greet him. Silvery haired grandmothers, matrons in the clutch of middle age and young girls who should have been in school contended heatedly for his outstretched hand, or failing that, reached out to touch his shoulders, his sleeve.[96]

At another location, "Enthusiastic women from adolescence to old age literally jumped for joy."[97] Still another: "Many of the women in today's audiences showed a strong desire to get near Senator Kennedy or to touch him. At several places his automobile caravan had to slow down or come to a halt to avoid injury to women who rushed from curbs to try to touch his hand or sleeve."[98]

The tendency of women to be swayed by particular candidates is closely related to the view that women's political decision-making is rooted in emotion, rather than logic, a persistent (distinctive gender) perspective dating from well before suffrage (see Chapter 2). One writer went so far as to warn that women were "so carried away emotionally by handsome young political candidates that they may someday vote demagogues into public office."[99] Others disagreed: "Sure, women are different from men ... but our voting behavior is just as rational as theirs," argued a Republican women's division official in 1960.[100] All that said, it is worth noting that while women were very slightly more likely to vote for Eisenhower in 1952 and 1956, women were actually slightly less likely to vote for Kennedy in 1960, despite all the reported swooning.

Explaining women's vote choice. Given the very small gender differences in candidate preference in the six presidential elections from 1940 to 1960, it is highly unlikely that men and women relied on vastly different calculations or approached evaluation of candidates from vastly different positions. The striking similarity of men's and women's votes is what distinguishes the politics of the 1940s and 1950s. Republicans enjoyed a clear advantage with the largest group of women, women not working outside of the home; while they were the group least likely to vote, their numbers give them a sizeable impact on the voting behavior of women overall. On the whole, however, we see women performing their duty in elections in ways far more similar than not to their male counterparts, both overall and within key groups. The available evidence suggests that women's vote choice was largely determined by the same factors which determined men's in these presidential elections.

CONCLUSION

The stereotypical suburban mother of the 1950s was occupied with her home and family, not politics. In actuality, women voted – almost 75% of them by 1960. Traditionally feminine images define the gender order of this period as the earlier flappers and Rosie the Riveter rapidly gave way to June Cleaver and Leave It to Beaver. Women's and men's lives did diverge in terms of both expectations and reality, and some of those differences had political consequences. While women increasingly entered the workforce, they remained significantly less likely to work outside the home than men, and women who did not work were far less likely to vote. Half of all women had only a high school degree, and nearly 50% of men as well, but women with less educational attainment were far less likely to vote than similarly situated men.

More than 20 years after suffrage, the basic presumption that politics is men's business remained powerful. While women's roles were changing, popular assumptions about women and ideal femininity did not reflect that shifting reality. Women in politics continued to be viewed as an exception rather than the rule. We observe this most strikingly in the widespread popularity of the claim that women were less likely to vote due to the norm that politics is not women's place. Yet in terms of actual electoral behavior, these two decades are distinct from the period prior, in that the turnout gender gap shrank considerably.

Women who did vote overwhelmingly chose the same candidates and parties as men did. Yet, expectations for women voters – among the press, politicians, and scholars – were resistant to updating. Women often were assumed to have distinct political priorities than men, driven largely by their traditional roles in the home; women, in these narratives, were motivated by concerns over rising prices (as the family's shopper), the threat of war (as a wife and mother), and education policy (for her children). On the other hand, those who noted that women and men generally cast ballots for the same parties and candidates during this period often attributed this dynamic to the reliance of women on the political guidance of their husbands and other men.

The emergence of sophisticated public opinion polls transformed the study of voting and made it possible to examine women's electoral behavior as never before. While the available evidence improved dramatically, it remained the case that we can only observe what we measure. Creators of the original public opinion polls did not view women or gender as particularly interesting or political. Given the era, credit is due for the attention these pollsters and scholars did give to women, and the way in which they, appropriately, described gender differences as limited and small. Yet, pollsters generally did not include items that would allow scholars to directly test popular claims about gender role attitudes or the direction of interpersonal influence. In every period, interpretations of the available data are shaped by assumptions about the nature of gendered decision-making, social structure, and interpersonal dynamics. Given the persistence of a gender gap in turnout through 1960, scholars and journalists had little reason to question or challenge ideas that women were fundamentally disinclined to engage with politics.

These questions moved from the background to the foreground in the 1960s and 1970s as the modern women's movement challenged and transformed American assumptions about women, gender, and sex. Women's political power and political interests were debated and defined in new and consequential ways. The conditions of women's lives underwent dramatic changes, contributing to shifts in women's political interests and preferences as well.

Contrary to the period from 1920 to 1960, the 1960s would witness dramatic shifts in women's and men's voting rights. The lines of cleavage between the two major parties were reordered post-1960 as well, with the interconnected issues of the social welfare state and civil rights becoming increasingly central to the partisan divide.

In the next chapter, we examine women voters from 1964 to 1976, a period of remarkable transition for American women and American politics. We enter that period having established two empirical pillars of women's engagement with American elections after suffrage: Women were less inclined to participate, and women's votes largely mirrored those of men. Neither of those pillars would survive these transitions.

CHAPTER 6

Feminism Resurgent

AMERICAN WOMEN BOAST A LONG LEGACY OF POLITICAL ACTIVISM ON issues ranging from the struggle for independence from England to their own political and social rights. In the nineteenth century, women organized an independent social and political movement for women's rights and suffrage. Many of those women also were active in, and learned from, the abolition, temperance, and Progressive movements. Their crowning achievement, the ratification of the Nineteenth Amendment, made gender-equal suffrage in the United States a reality and opened the door to electoral participation for generations of women.

On August 26, 1970, the fiftieth anniversary of the ratification of the Nineteenth Amendment was marked by a nationwide Women's Strike for Equality in which tens of thousands of women in every major US city (and some small ones as well) marched for greater equality and opportunity for women. As with the suffrage movement, the tools and ideas gained in other social movements, as well as the political opportunities offered by electoral politics and new public policies, facilitated women's activism. The first wave of the women's movement coalesced around the narrow goal of suffrage, but the second wave sought a broad restructuring of gender relationships, hierarchies, and opportunity in the United States and around the world. Important shifts in women's work and family arrangements both shaped and were shaped by these efforts.[1]

Despite renewed activism for women's rights, women voters of this period were initially more invisible than they had been at any time since suffrage. In the 1960s, presidential campaigns made few efforts to reach out to women voters as other issues – civil rights, the Great Society, the Vietnam War – dominated presidential elections. Election analyses either failed to examine or gave only the most cursory attention to women voters. Yet, the gender gap in turnout continued to close, making women an increasingly dominant segment of the electorate. And the partisan gender gap was shifting from a very small but persistent Republican advantage among women to an inconsistent and at most very small Democratic advantage. Any advantage Republicans held among women had disappeared by 1964 and began to shift to a Democratic advantage as early as 1972.

By the 1970s, women's rights issues, such as abortion and the Equal Rights Amendment (ERA), were increasingly salient in national politics. For a brief period, bipartisanship on women's rights facilitated policy achievements in areas ranging from education to credit markets. While coverage of and candidate appeals to women voters focused on the new women's rights agenda, it was other dominant issues of the period – social welfare and civil rights – that scholars point to as key explanations for women's behavior in presidential elections in these and later decades.

In this chapter, we review the tumultuous politics of the 1960s and 1970s. We look at the changing conditions of women's lives and the emergence and impact of the second wave of the women's movement. For women voters, this is a transitional era; economic and social disruptions were substantial, but had not yet impacted electoral politics. It is only *after* 1976 that we consistently see women turning out more than men and women turning toward Democratic candidates. Across the four presidential elections from 1964 to 1976, the turnout gender gap narrowed, and the enduring pro-Republican partisan gender gap began to decay. In the conclusion, we look ahead to the momentous 1980 presidential election and the establishment of the gender gap as an important and widely reported new reality of American politics.

AMERICAN ELECTORAL POLITICS, 1964–1976

The 1960s and 1970s were a period of considerable political upheaval and transition in the United States. These four elections feature some of the most dramatic partisan swings in American history, including both Democratic (1964) and Republican (1972) landslides. Social movements – including the civil rights movement, the New Left, the anti-war movement, and the women's movement – disrupted and transformed society and politics. The American electorate, characterized by strong and stable partisan identification in the

1950s, became more issue-oriented, less partisan, and less trusting of govern-ment, across the 1960s and early 1970s.[2]

Long-time Senate leader and vice president Lyndon Johnson assumed the presidency in November of 1963. Johnson claimed the mantle of the martyred Kennedy to push an aggressive policy agenda, particularly with regards to civil rights. Congress broke a three-month filibuster to pass the Civil Rights Act (CRA) of 1964 with bipartisan support from Republicans and northern Democrats. The landmark legislation prohibited discrimination on the basis of race, color, religion, or country of origin in education, employment, and public accommodations. Together with the 1965 Voting Rights Act (VRA), the CRA completed the transformation of the national Democratic party from the defender of segregation to the party of civil rights. As expected, this shift contributed to the eventual realignment of the previously Democratic Solid South, closer party competition at the national level, and increased partisan polarization among elites. These reverberations unfolded over decades, but were initially seen in decreased support among Southern white voters for Democratic presidential candidates.[3]

On the Republican side, moderates and conservatives continued to battle over the direction and leadership of the party. Conservatives wrested control of the GOP in 1964, nominating Arizona Senator Barry Goldwater for president despite considerable intraparty opposition. Goldwater, author of *The Conscience of a Conservative*, supported free markets, opposed the New Deal and most fed-eral taxing and spending, and viewed communism at home and abroad as an urgent threat to the United States. While Goldwater claimed to oppose fed-eral action on civil rights on a states' rights basis, his campaign nonetheless "accepted the support of racists and segregationists of the most extreme sort."[4] The Republican party adopted a deliberate "Southern strategy," seeking to undermine the national Democratic majority by appealing to racially conser-vative white voters, especially in the South.[5]

Johnson was reelected in a landslide. Although too extreme for voters in 1964, Goldwater helped to reorient the Republican party and its electorate in a more fiscally and racially conservative direction, with long-term consequences for the American party system. In the short run, however, a record number of Democrats were elected to Congress, giving Johnson the super-majority he needed to expand his already ambitious legislative agenda to address racism, poverty, and inequality. Congress enacted a range of Great Society programs in the mid-1960s including Medicare and Medicaid, Head Start, environmental and consumer protection, community services programs, and housing reform. Pushed by civil rights leaders convinced the CRA was not sufficient, the Voting Rights Act (VRA) of 1965 not only prohibited voting discrimination but provided federal enforcement of the law, transforming the status of voting rights in the United States. The VRA's impact was enormous; more than a million new African American voters registered to vote by 1970.[6]

Backlash against Great Society programs and civil rights achievements was immediate. Even as the CRA and VRA were signed into law, majorities of white Americans (and super majorities of white Southerners) continued to assert that the civil rights movement was pushing too fast. Riots in major American cities and increases in violent crime spurred calls for law and order which were almost always racially coded. From the New Deal through the 1950s, the issues of social welfare and civil rights had been distinct. Beginning in the mid-1960s, Americans increasingly associated welfare "hand-outs" with African Americans, even as African Americans became more economically equal with whites. The Democrats' shift to advocacy for civil rights and the association of the party with the expanded and racialized social welfare system undermined Democratic identification and electoral support among a number of traditionally Democratic groups, including Southern whites and white ethnics.[7]

By 1968, Americans also were increasingly dissatisfied with the Vietnam War. Faced with revolt within his own party, President Johnson withdrew from the Democratic nomination contest. Both civil rights leader Dr. Martin Luther King, Jr. and presidential candidate Robert F. Kennedy were assassinated in a distinctly tragic and violent year in US history. The Democratic party's convention was marked by chaos and conflict inside and outside the conventional hall, as anti-war protestors clashed with Mayor Daley's police in the streets of Chicago.[8] To many observers, the Democratic party "appeared, quite simply to be coming apart."[9]

Republican nominee Richard Nixon reached out to the "forgotten American" and emphasized his commitment to law and order and to ending the war in Vietnam. Nixon was challenged on the right by the independent candidacy of Alabama governor George Wallace, who campaigned against civil rights, big government, and social change. Wallace won nearly one-third of the Southern popular vote and the Electoral College votes of five Southern states. While Humphrey closed the gap in the final weeks, Nixon was elected president with just 43% of the popular vote but 302 Electoral College votes. Notably, of the eleven states of the former Confederacy, Humphrey won only Texas, signaling the continued erosion of the Democratic Solid South.[10]

In response to the disaster of their 1968 convention, Democrats transformed their presidential nomination process to be more open and representative. As a result, 40% of delegates to the 1972 Democratic National Convention were women, compared to just 13% in 1968. (Women at the Republican national convention increased from 16% in 1968 to almost 30% in 1972.) Feminist activists on the left were highly active at the 1972 convention in particular, helping to associate the Democratic party with the women's movement in the minds of voters.[11]

South Dakota Senator George McGovern, benefitting from the new nomination rules he helped to write, secured the Democratic nomination in 1972. McGovern's support among activists gave him a reputation for liberal positions beyond his actual record or statements, and strengthened the association between the Democratic party and various social movement causes. With the war in Vietnam winding down and continuing conflict over social change, civil rights, and social welfare, Republican president Richard Nixon was reelected with almost 61% of the vote and a near Electoral College sweep just eight years after Johnson's landslide victory.[12]

By 1974, the Watergate scandal had forced the first resignation of a US president in history. In 1976, President Gerald Ford faced a strong intraparty challenge from former actor and California governor Ronald Reagan, widely viewed as the leader of the resurgent conservative forces within the GOP. Ford was able to hold on to the nomination, but his unpopular pardon of Nixon and general anti-Republican sentiment threatened his reelection. The Democratic nominee, Georgia governor Jimmy Carter, was considered a national outsider with a reputation for honesty and narrowly won the 1976 presidential election. While Ford was a relative moderate, the GOP was nonetheless moving in an increasingly conservative direction on economic, racial, and eventually social issues. The final election of this period thus featured a comparatively small ideological divide on the major issues of the day. Ideological moderation would be in short supply in the elections to follow.

AMERICAN WOMEN IN THE 1960s AND 1970s

Women's Lives

The traditional gender roles that defined the 1950s were challenged and transformed in the two decades that followed. In 1960, more babies were born in the United States than in any other year in American history thus far, the apex of the Baby Boom. In a return to the longer-term trend of declining US fertility dating to the 1790s, fertility rates fell consistently after 1960. The decline was particularly sharp between 1964 and 1976, with reported births per 1,000 women aged 16 to 44 declining by nearly one-third (see Figure 6.1). One factor: The Supreme Court's 1965 ruling that the right to privacy included access to contraception. Family structures also shifted profoundly as "for the first time, substantial numbers of women in prime adult years pursued paid work instead of fertility and mother-intensive child-rearing."[13] The average age of first marriage rose, and both women and men increasingly lived alone or in non-family households, largely unheard of arrangements prior to 1960. Growing numbers of households were headed by women. Divorce and extra-marital cohabitation were increasingly common, particularly in the 1970s.[14]

The Civil Rights Revolution

The civil rights victories of the mid-1960s also transformed women's lives. For African American women and men, the 1964 CRA opened up opportunities in education, employment, and public life. African American women were especially likely to take advantage of these opportunities; from 1964 to 1976, the percentage of African American women with a college degree grew at a rate exceeding that of African American men or white men or women.[15]

Together with the elimination of the white primary and the concerted efforts of the civil rights movement to register African American voters throughout the South, the 1965 VRA brought about a stunning increase in African American registration and turnout. In the eleven states of the former Confederacy, the registration of African American voters increased from 12% in 1947 to 43% in 1964 to 63% by 1976. The impact in specific states was often dramatic: In Alabama, African American registration increased from only 1% in 1947 to 58% in 1976. The consequences for the political power and representation of the African American community were wide-ranging. As we will see, the

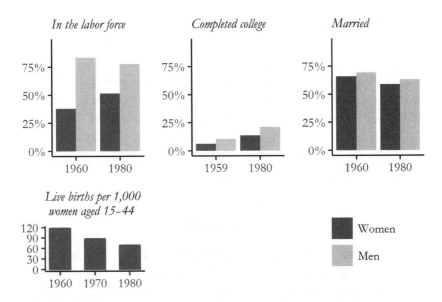

Figure 6.1 Women are less likely to marry or have children, but more likely to work in the 1960s and 1970s.

impact on the composition of the female electorate was substantial as well; the rate at which African American women's turnout increased across the 1960s exceeded that of African American men, as well as white men and women.[16]

The CRA had a significant impact on the lives of all American women, regardless of race, as well. At the urging of the National Women's Party, Rep. Howard W. Smith (D, VA) proposed adding sex to Title VII of the bill, which prohibited employment discrimination. While Smith appears to have opposed sex discrimination, it is likely he also believed the addition of sex would help kill the bill. The laughter and jokes that greeted his amendment confirmed that intuition. Yet, women members of Congress, eventually aided by President Johnson, advocated for the sex clause, and it was signed into law. Only with significant pressure from the women's movement did the agency charged with enacting Title VII, the Equal Employment Opportunity Commission (EEOC), eventually enforce the sex provision, providing a substantial tool for greater gender equality in the workplace.[17]

With the help of Title VII, the female workforce experienced the largest increase in American history between 1960 and 1980. Married women and women with children entered the workforce in unprecedented numbers: the labor force participation rate for women exceeded 50% by 1980. Women increasingly worked for reasons other than economic necessity, as work became "more attractive and hospitable" to them. At the same time, occupations remained stubbornly sex-segregated and women's wages continued to lag those of men. Nonetheless, in the 1960s and 1970s, spending at least part of one's adult life in the paid workforce became the norm for women of nearly every class, age, race, and family condition for the first time in American history. (Men's labor force participation, by contrast, continued a long-term decline, dropping below 80% for the first time in 1972.)[18]

The Second Wave

The second wave of the women's movement developed along two tracks during this period. The so-called "older branch" was associated with professional women in business and government. Despite the many stories about the frenzied response to Kennedy on the campaign trail, Nixon had secured a slightly higher percentage of votes from women in 1960. Following his narrow victory, the Kennedy administration took a number of steps to consolidate his support in advance of what was expected to be a very close contest in 1964. In an effort to reach out to women, Kennedy established a Presidential Commission on the Status of Women in 1961. The Kennedy Commission brought together women who were already active in traditional politics. The Commission's report, issued in 1963, documented the unequal status of women in economics, politics, and society and offered more than twenty far-reaching policy recommendations. That same year, Kennedy signed the Equal Pay Act into law. By 1967, governors in all fifty states had established similar state-level commissions.[19]

In 1963 – the same year that the Kennedy Commission released its report – labor activist Betty Friedan published *The Feminine Mystique*, documenting deep dissatisfaction among college-educated women with the traditional role of mother and housewife. The best-selling book set off a national conversation about the status of women. At a 1966 national meeting of members of state commissions on the status of women, activists failed to get support for a demand that the EEOC enforce Title VII's sex provisions. Frustrated with inaction, activists formed a new advocacy group, the National Organization for Women (NOW), with Friedan as the first president. By the early 1970s, a variety of organizations had been created to advocate for women's interests, including the Women's Equity Action League (WEAL) and the National Women's Political Caucus (NWPC).[20]

At the same time, the so-called "younger branch" of the women's movement emerged among activists in the social movements transforming American politics and society. Beginning in the 1950s, sit-ins, school desegregation battles, Freedom Rides, and bus boycotts focused the nation's attention on the injustice of racial segregation throughout the United States and especially in the South. The 1963 March on Washington and 1964 Freedom Summer only intensified this effort. On college campuses across the country, the free speech movement challenged conservative status quo values in the early 1960s. The institution of the draft and the stalemate in Vietnam inspired the anti-war movement in the second half of the 1960s. Many activists moved across and participated in multiple movements, forming a vibrant activist community by the mid-1960s.[21]

Women in these movements found themselves, more often than not, relegated to traditional gender roles of clerical support and housework. When they spoke up about gender inequality in movements, they were ridiculed and silenced. In response to demands for a hearing for women's caucus resolutions at a 1967 conference for young activists, for example, the chair told activist Shulamith Firestone, "Cool down, little girl, we have more important things to talk about than women's problems." Firestone did not follow this advice, but rather went on to write *The Dialectic of Sex* (1971), a classic feminist treatise.[22] A number of activist women took the skills, rhetoric, and ideology they had developed and used in prior movement activism and put these resources to use for women's liberation, the common term for the younger branch of the women's movement.[23] Women formed consciousness-raising groups to share and explore how gender inequality shaped their own lives and politics. Rather than traditional interest organizations like NOW, women's liberation activists formed local groups around both general women's rights and specific concerns, such as sexual violence, women's health, and employment discrimination. Many engaged in radical and attention-grabbing protest tactics.[24]

In 1970, NOW called for a Women's Strike for Equality to take place on August 26, the fiftieth anniversary of the ratification of the Nineteenth Amendment. Tens of thousands of women took to the streets in every major US city and many smaller towns, in the largest public demonstrations for women's rights since suffrage. The second wave became a truly mass movement. The two branches increasingly merged into one varied and influential movement in the 1970s. Activists at every level worked on a range of issues and effectuated real change in the social, economic, political, and legal status of women.[25]

For women of color, this second wave provided both opportunities and challenges. Women from underrepresented racial and ethnic groups were important intellectual and organizational leaders in the second wave. The original steering committee of the NWPC, for example, included Native American activist LaDonna Harris, welfare rights activist Beulah Sanders, and civil rights pioneer Fannie Lou Hamer. Aileen Hernandez was elected president of NOW in 1970. Shirley Chisholm became the first woman to receive presidential nomination votes at a major party convention in 1972. Polls revealed that African American women were more likely than white women to express support for feminist goals and the political advancement of women.[26]

On the whole, however, the women's movement was often dominated by a white and middle-class base to the exclusion of women of color, poor women, and lesbians, among others. While the rhetoric of the women's movement often presumed a universal female reality, women of color in particular highlighted the diversity of women's experiences, challenges, and interests. Activists and authors pointed out the ways in which race and sex interacted to create bias that was not additive but multiplicative for African American women. The tendency of the women's movement to focus on educational and professional opportunity, for example, failed to recognize that the achievement of those goals often necessitated the labor of other women in the childcare, cleaning, retail, and service sectors – work characterized by low pay, few benefits, and employment insecurity and often performed by poor women, women of color, and immigrant women. As a result, black women organized a number of important separate women's movement organizations and initiatives. Building a diverse and representative movement would remain an on-going challenge for the women's movement.[27]

Women, Feminism, and Politics

The political response to the second wave evolved over time. Most politicians in both parties initially treated women's demands as unserious and unimportant. By the late 1960s, however, the general idea of women's equality increasingly received at least rhetorical support from political elites. From the end of the Second World War until the mid-1960s, neither political party had been particularly attentive to women's rights issues. To the extent that parties took positions, Republicans were slightly more favorable to women's rights proposals such as the ERA and equal pay legislation before the mid-1960s. As late as 1968, the parties' platforms were very nearly silent on women's rights.[28]

By the early 1970s, however, Democrats had become increasingly favorable to the cause for women's rights. Democrats' change of heart can be attributed to the association of women's rights with civil rights, the labor movement's shift to women's rights support, and the activism of many feminists within the Democratic party. For a brief period in the early 1970s, both Democrats and Republicans took positions in support of women's rights proposals. Both parties featured entire sections on women's rights in their 1972 platforms, endorsing the ERA, equal pay, child care, and the appointment of women to the federal government.[29]

Bipartisan support translated into legislative success. Among numerous anti-sex discrimination provisions, Congress passed Title IX of the Education Amendments in 1972, prohibiting sex discrimination in all aspects of education, and the Equal Credit Opportunity Act of 1974, ending the legal practice of sex discrimination in credit markets. After more than 50 years, Congress passed the ERA with a bipartisan vote and sent the amendment to the states for ratification in 1972. In 1973, the Supreme Court ruled in *Roe v. Wade* that the Constitution protected the right to abortion. These legal victories signaled not only the increasingly widespread support for women's rights but represented real, consequential changes in the opportunities and conditions of women's lives.[30]

Bipartisanship was short-lived. By the mid-1970s, opposition to feminism and other social change emerged as an organized and vocal movement. The charge against feminism was led most prominently by Phyllis Schlafly, a long-time conservative activist and author of *A Choice, Not an Echo*, which had been a rallying crying for Goldwater activists in 1964. When Congress passed the ERA in 1972, Schlafly shifted her focus from anti-communism to opposing feminism in general and the ERA and abortion rights in particular. Schlafly and others on the right organized and articulated a backlash to the women's movement and social change. Encouraged by Republican activists, religious and social conservatives were increasingly politically active through evangelical churches and explicitly religious political organizations, such as the Moral Majority. In 1976, moderates within the GOP were able to maintain the party's long-standing endorsement of the ERA and equivocate on abortion. In 1980, however, Republicans established a new stance on women's rights issues that would define the party for decades to come.[31]

Like the parties, presidential campaigns were slow to adjust to the rapidly changing political and social context for women. In both 1964 and 1968, the major party candidates made few targeted appeals to women voters, and the media paid little attention to the potential behavior or impact of women in these presidential elections. Civil rights, social welfare, and Vietnam dominated political debate. The very few references to women voters often continued the pattern of assuming the influence of husbands, the appeal of attractive candidates, and a concern with issues related to the home and family.[32] Then California Republican Party chair Caspar Weinberger (Secretary of Defense in the Reagan administration) recounted in a *Los Angeles Times* column a televised panel "featuring some lady politicians and campaign experts" who concluded that "far fewer women take the trouble to vote than men, and usually when they do vote, they follow the pattern set by their husbands or their families." The panel, he explained, believed women had less time to vote and that "many women are primarily interested in their homes and families, and feel that out-side events are better left in the hands of their husbands," a number which Weinberger describes as "diminishing" but still representing a "substantial portion" of women. Moreover, "Most panel members conceded that physical attractiveness or glamor in male candidates was always helpful" and that the divorces of some recent candidates had hurt their chances.[33]

The content of presidential campaigns shifted dramatically in the 1970s. American foreign policy (especially in Vietnam), the economy, and political scandal dominated these elections. The nature of the appeals to and discussion of women voters shifted noticeably. While stereotypical framing still occurred (the first ever female co-chair of the RNC is described as "super-stylish" and "vivacious" in 1971[34]), there is far more substantive discussion about the parties' and candidates' positions on the issues the women's movement had put on the political agenda, such as the ERA, abortion, sex discrimination, and the representation of women. While not a major focus for either the McGovern or Nixon campaigns in 1972, both candidates took steps to appeal to women voters. In a substantial shift, the candidates did not talk about policies expected to be of interest to women as mothers and wives, but rather emphasized their commitment to appointing women to political office. The increased number of women delegates at the 1972 Democratic National Convention also garnered considerable attention. While the parties' platforms were not dramatically different in 1972, Nixon's public statements criticizing the women's movement and McGovern's endorsement by prominent feminists such as Gloria Steinem provided increasingly clear images to the public of which party was associated with the feminist cause.[35]

In 1976, both candidates supported the ERA and other feminist issues, but differences between the parties on women's rights were increasingly apparent. As the Republican party struggled to resolve its internal conflict over women's rights, the Ford campaign devoted little attention to women voters as women in 1976. The Carter campaign, on the other hand, viewed women as a key mobilization target, claiming to have established coordinators for women's issues in all fifty states and pledging to appoint women to federal offices. The content of political appeals had clearly shifted from framing women in traditional terms to emphasizing equality and opportunity for women.[36]

OBSERVING WOMEN VOTERS

Opportunities to observe women voters expanded in the 1960s and 1970s. Two new sources of data in particular help us to overcome some of the data limitations of the earlier period: the exit poll and the Current Population Survey (CPS) November Voting Supplement. Exit polls are large samples of actual voters canvassed as they visit polling places. This survey tool has the advantage of sampling only actual voters, rather than respondents in later national surveys who may claim to have voted, but did not. Today a number of news outlets collectively sponsor a large exit poll, the National Exit Pool, but in the 1970s and 1980s, individual media outlets – CBS News, the *Washington Post*, and the *Los Angeles Times* – conducted extensive exit polls. We rely on two exit polls in this chapter, a 1972 and 1976 exit poll commissioned by CBS News. The primary advantage of exit polls is scale. The large samples (typically 50,000 or more) can provide reliable estimates of the vote choice of relatively small groups – single, white, college-educated, women under 30, for instance. State-level estimates also permit media outlets to project the Electoral College winner. The challenge and drawback of exit polls include the possibility of interviewer effects, non-response, and the challenges to selecting a limited number of polling places to generate a representative statewide or national sample.[37] We revisit the problems with exit polls in later chapters and never use exclusively exit polls to support our conclusions.

The second data innovation in this period is the November Voting Supplement to the CPS. The Census Bureau samples all residents of the United States in a monthly survey, with the primary objective to determine the official unemployment rate published by the Bureau of Labor Statistics. Each presidential election year, the large CPS survey asks respondents if they voted in the recent federal election. There is no information recorded about vote choice or attitudes and preferences, only turnout. These CPS data provide an incredibly clear picture of the demographic makeup of the electorate – by race, marital status, employment, education, presence of children in the home, and, after 1980, by immigration status (first-generation, second-generation, third-generation or later).[38] The disadvantage is we can only use CPS data to understand turnout, not vote choice.

Changes in the scholarly community greatly facilitated our understanding of women voters as well. Along with the social and political changes we described above, increasing numbers of women entered the political science profession (and the academy more broadly) in the late 1960s, 1970s, and beyond. In 1972, only 9% of full-time political science faculty were women; by 2000, this number would still be only 24%. While important research about women as voters was conducted (by women and men) prior to the 1970s, many of these path-breaking women political scientists generated landmark work on women in politics broadly, and about women voters specifically, much of which we rely on throughout this book.[39]

TURNOUT

Candidates, parties, and groups (most notably the League of Women Voters) continued to urge women to fulfill their civic duty by voting in the 1960s and 1970s, although women were less emphasized as targets for traditional electoral mobilization during the 1960s.[40] At the same time, press reports highlighted the increasing turnout of women voters, the narrowing turnout gender gap, and the fact that women often constituted more than half of all voters in elections.[41]

Turnout in presidential elections from 1964 to 1976 is summarized for three different data sources in Figure 6.2. Women's turnout was about 5 percentage points behind men's in the 1960s, but the large sample surveys (CPS and Gallup)

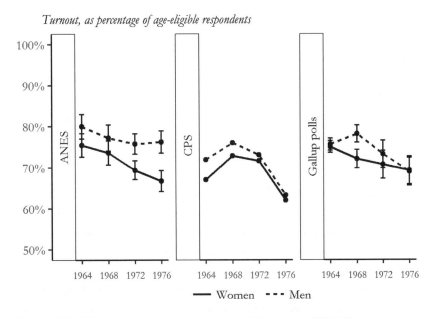

Figure 6.2 The turnout gender gap narrows and disappears, 1964–76

suggest that the gap had closed entirely in 1972 and 1976. The ANES obviously diverges significantly from the other polling data in 1976. While 1980 is generally recognized as the first year in which the rate at which women voted exceed that of men (based on CPS data), the ANES does not show women's turnout exceeding men until 2004. At minimum, even by 1972, we can reject, on empirical grounds, the basic idea that women were discouraged by nature or socialization in a way that kept them from polling places. Moreover, while the rate at which women voted still lagged slightly behind men's early in this period, it was sufficiently high that, by 1964, more women cast ballots in presidential elections than did men due to the greater numbers of voting-aged women in the population.[42] By the 1960s and 1970s, women were very nearly as integrated into the electorate as were men.

Women Are Not a Voting Bloc

In the 1960s and 1970s, the truly eligible female electorate became more diverse thanks to the Voting Rights Act, and women increasingly had access to the resources, including education and employment, that have long been associated with political participation. How did these changes shape the turnout of women in this period? As in the previous chapter, we rely on logistic regression to determine the impact of various factors on both turnout and vote choice for women and men. The relationships we report in the figures and our discussion below is informed by that analysis; that is, we highlight and describe the effects of demographic factors that are persistent when we introduce statistical controls.

Race. The removal or weakening of structural barriers transformed African American political participation during this period. While African American women and men continued to experience racial discrimination and have access to fewer of the resources (such as education and income) associated with electoral participation, the elimination of the white primary in 1944, the prohibition against the poll tax in 1964, and particularly the passage of the VRA in 1965 – combined with the persistent activism of the civil rights movement – led to substantially increased levels of African American registration and turnout over time.[43]

How did African American women respond to these changes? Previous chapters described how legal barriers, such as those which hampered African American electoral participation prior to 1965, had a disproportionate impact on women immediately after suffrage.[44] This pattern persisted in the South. In their 1961 survey of black and white Southerners, Matthews and Prothro found a larger turnout gender gap among African Americans than among white Southerners. The authors' blunt conclusion: "Negro [sic] women tend to be frozen out of southern politics."[45]

As key barriers fell, African American women's political participation, in general and relative to African American men, increased substantially. Figure 6.3 summarizes the average self-reported turnout of African American men and women from 1964 to 1976. Similar to findings from the 1940s and 1950s, turnout gaps are small among both whites and racial and ethnic minorities. By 1976, over 10% of Gallup poll respondents who reported voting are African American and there is no turnout gender gap in participation for minorities.

The dramatic shift in African American turnout meant greater political power, influence, and representation for the African American community

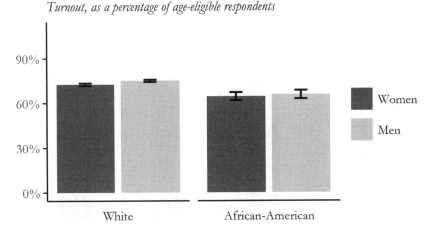

Figure 6.3 African American women and men turn out at roughly similar rates after 1960 (Gallup), 1964–76

and for African American women in particular. The enfranchisement of African American women also transformed the female electorate as a whole by adding a significant segment of voters who were increasingly supportive of the Democratic party. The impact of African American women only begins to be felt in this period, but becomes increasingly consequential for understanding women voters as a whole and the gender gap after 1976.

Age. Both women and men continued to follow the pattern of increasing turnout with age, followed by a decline in the later years of life. The decline in turnout among voters born before 1900 was basically nonexistent among men, but dramatic among women. Women born before 1900 were not only reaching old age, but had been socialized politically during a period in which women were disenfranchised. The effect appears to be lifelong, as women of that generation continued to lag behind men of their age, and their sisters of nearly every age, in using their right to vote.

For those who came of political age after the Nineteenth Amendment was ratified, gender is increasingly irrelevant to electoral participation. Both ANES and Gallup data suggest that, for the voters born after 1920, the turnout gender gap is indistinguishable from zero. In their classic study of turnout in the early 1970s, *Who Votes?*, Wolfinger and Rosenstone argue that "the shrinking

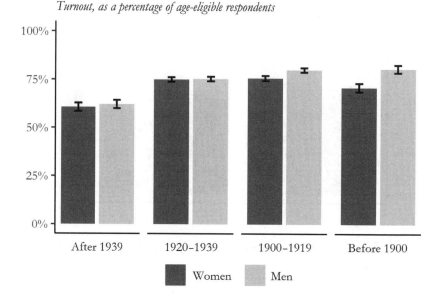

Turnout, as a percentage of age-eligible respondents

Figure 6.4 Turnout gender gaps found only among the oldest voters (Gallup), 1964–76

difference between the sexes in turnout stems from the dwindling number of women socialized to political roles that assign predominant influence to men." In other words, and consistent with distinctive gender, gender socialization is what distinguishes older women from younger and explains the persistent gender gap in turnout among the oldest cohorts (see Figure 6.4). The authors specifically reject other explanations rooted in resource inequality: "the closing gap is not an artifact of narrowing sex differences in education," as it persists when education is controlled for.[46]

Education. Education continues to be a crucial predictor of turnout for women and men. As Wolfinger and Rosenstone note, the gender gap in turnout narrows across all education groups in this period (see Figure 6.5). Women with only a grade school education continue to report the lowest turnout, both relative to similarly educated men and to all other women and men, suggesting the persistence of particular gender dynamics among the poorly educated. As in the 1940s and 1950s, the turnout gender gap is basically eliminated among the more highly educated groups. While only about

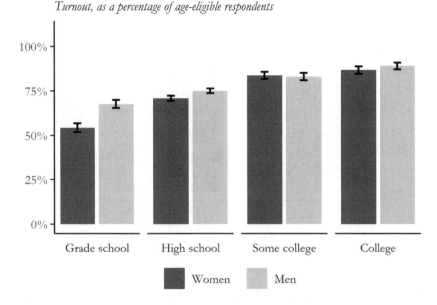

Turnout, as a percentage of age-eligible respondents

Figure 6.5 Small gender gaps among those with similar educational attainment (ANES), 1964–76

half of women without a high school education voted, about 80% of women with college degrees cast ballots on Election Day. As the percentage of women with college degrees marches upward (and closer to men) in this period, it is not surprising that the overall turnout gap becomes smaller, consistent with resource inequality explanations that pin gender differences on differences in resources, like education, and not on gender per se.

Marriage, family, and work. The Nineteenth Amendment prohibited discrimination on the basis of sex in the application of voting rights but did little to directly confront sex bias in other aspects of politics and society. Women continued to be less likely to be employed, and, when employed, paid less and concentrated in lower status occupations. However, in the 1960s and 1970s, work for at least part of their adult lives became the norm for most American women. This shift had consequences for the participation of women in elections. Figure 6.6 shows the average turnout for women and men based on workforce participation. Women who did not work outside the home continued to have the lowest turnout of all groups. Employed women, on the other hand, are more

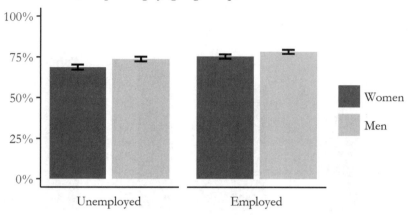

Turnout, as a percentage of age-eligible respondents

Figure 6.6 Women who work as likely to turn out as men who work (ANES), 1964–76

likely to vote than women who stay home, and just about as likely to vote as men in or out of the labor force. This is a different pattern from the 1940s and 1950s, when women who worked and those who stayed home voted at the same rate, and both were less likely to vote than employed and unemployed men. As the composition of the female workforce changed, work became a factor – albeit a small one–in the turnout of women.

Marriage and the presence of children, on the other hand, operate in exactly the same way on men and women (see Figure 6.7). Single parents are the least likely to turn out, by far, and interestingly, single fathers even more so than single mothers. In general, married people – both women and men – are more likely to turn out to vote than unmarried. The most important change from the 1940s and 1950s is an increase in turnout among married women with children: the presence of children no longer decreases turnout for married women. Women's lives were changing, and so were the relationships between household arrangements and voting.

Politics and place. While formal barriers to voting in the South came under federal challenge in the 1960s, the South's long legacy of low turnout and one-party politics persisted at first. Figure 6.8 shows the rate of women's and men's turnout across regions in the United States. Women in the South continued to be uniquely less likely to use their right to vote, both compared

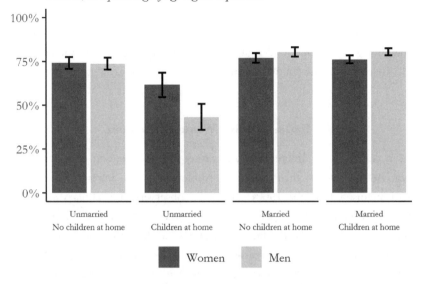

Figure 6.7 Single parents the least likely to vote, having children no longer dampens turnout among married women (ANES), 1964–76

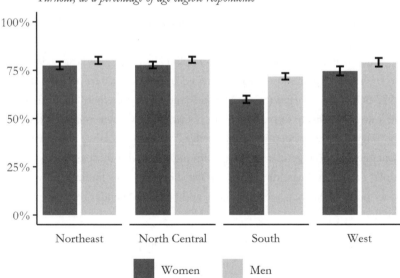

Figure 6.8 Turnout remains distinctively low in the South, especially among women (ANES), 1964–76

to Southern men and to men and women in the rest of the country. Southern men also remain significantly less likely to vote than citizens in other regions, but the effect of Southern context is considerably greater for women. Indeed, the only clear turnout gender gap across these four regions is in the South; in all other parts of the country, women were as likely to turn out as were men.

Understanding Women's Turnout

As a general rule, difference attracts interest and attention, similarity does not. As the rate of turnout among women and men became increasingly indistinguishable in the 1960s and 1970s, observers and scholars no longer perceived the need for explanation. As we note above, press coverage during this period highlighted the fact that women had become more numerous as voters than were men, but a reason for this change was rarely suggested. Many scholars were similarly disinterested. The "enlarged" (430 page) version of *The Changing American Voter* (an update to *The American Voter*, covering 1952 to 1972) contains virtually no information or analysis of women as voters. The women's movement receives passing reference, as does the electoral behavior of women after suffrage, but the authors of this careful study of electoral and party change in the 1960s and 1970s do not view women as a politically relevant group.[47]

Scholars who did look at gender and political engagement largely depended on the same explanations they had relied upon in previous periods. In their 1977 book, *Political Participation*, Milbrath and Goel note that "the finding that men are more likely to participate in politics than women is one of the most thoroughly substantiated in social science." They note, as we do as well, that the largest turnout gender gaps were among those with the least education. To explain these findings, they point to *The American Voter's* findings on women's lesser political efficacy (see Chapter 5) and persistent gender role norms about politics:

> The traditional division of labor which assigns the political role to men rather than women has not vanished. The survey interviewer seeking respondents for a political study discovers after only a few house calls that there are significant remnants of the tradition in modern society. A favorite excuse for not wishing to be interviewed is to claim that the husbands takes care of the family politics.[48]

For these authors, then, distinctive gender explanations – due to either nature or nurture, women were less interested in politics – continue to dominate thinking about women's political participation even as the gender gap narrows.

Others take a more resource inequality approach, emphasizing the dramatic changes in women's resources and position in American society. In her classic paper on "Working Women and Political Participation, 1952–1972," political scientist Kristi Andersen highlights how the growth of women in the paid workforce, and especially of women in professional occupations, provides a key explanation for the increasingly similar participation in campaigns among women and men. At the same time, she attributes some of the high levels of participation among employed women, as well as young women, to changing gender norms that were initially most strongly felt among these groups, another example of how resource inequality (access to employment) and distinctive gender (beliefs about women's equality) interact in producing voting patterns.[49]

VOTE CHOICE

In the 1960s and 1970s, scholars and journalists generally concluded that women voters differed little from men in their political preferences. As we have seen, women voters were viewed as slightly distinctive in the 1950s, often described as more conservative and/or Republican than men (the "traditional gender gap"). By the 1960s, scattered accounts of women supporting Democrats begin to appear: George Gallup, for instance, reported that Kennedy was polling higher among women than men in 1963 "trial heat" polls against Arizona Senator Barry Goldwater and early polls in 1964 picked up the same result favoring Lyndon Johnson.[50] But this emerging Democratic advantage was both inconsistent and small.

The Republican vote share (percentage of the major party vote) for women and men across three different polling organizations are reported in Figure 6.9 for presidential elections from 1964 through 1976. As the consistently overlapping confidence intervals indicate, all of our data sources confirm the absence of meaningful gender differences in presidential vote choice. (The exception is the Gallup data in 1972 – women more Democratic than men – but the other data do not show a difference.) In a period eventually defined by vigorous public debate over gender roles and sex equality, there is little evidence that

Republican share of the two-party vote, percentage

Figure 6.9 No difference in the vote choice of women and men, 1964–76

women, on average, have distinctive preferences for either major party in the 1960s and 1970s.

Women Are Not a Voting Bloc

Women's lives were undergoing dramatic shifts in the 1960s and especially the 1970s. What was the impact of the resulting changes in the composition of the female electorate – increasingly racially diverse, educated, and employed – on women's political preferences? A resource inequality perspective would predict substantial change, as women's and men's resources and experiences became increasingly equitable. A distinctive gender approach, on the other hand, might expect that fundamental gender differences would persist regardless of such transitions, or that perhaps greater autonomy and independence would give women more opportunity to know and speak their minds.[51]

In each of the figures that follow, we report the average Republican vote share of various groups of women and men across these four presidential

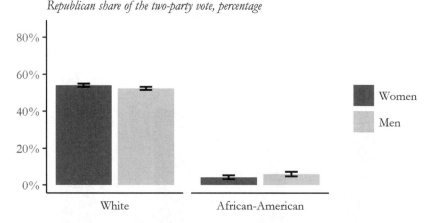

Republican share of the two-party vote, percentage

Figure 6.10 Racial differences are profound and there is no difference in Republican support between African American women and men (Gallup), 1964–76

elections. We focus on percent Republican for consistency throughout this book. Keep in mind that lower percentages for Republicans indicate higher relative Democratic support.

Race. Differences in the partisan preferences of white and black Americans in the late 1960s and 1970s were stark (Figure 6.10). More than half of whites, regardless of sex, voted for Republican candidates. More than 90% of African Americans, regardless of sex, voted for Democrats. This is far and away one of the largest partisan cleavages of the time, and swamps any tiny gender differences we observe. Said another way, black women were far more similar to black men (and white women to white men) at the ballot box than black and white women were to each other.

The effective enfranchisement of African American women in the 1960s diversified the women's vote and added a key group to the female electorate that was increasingly favorable to the Democratic party. However, the votes of African American women received little attention from candidates, the press, or political scientists, including those studying African American voters, in the 1960s and 1970s.[52] Black women, many newly enfranchised and registered, were overwhelmingly Democratic during this period, but so were black men. We saw in Figure 6.3 that African American women and

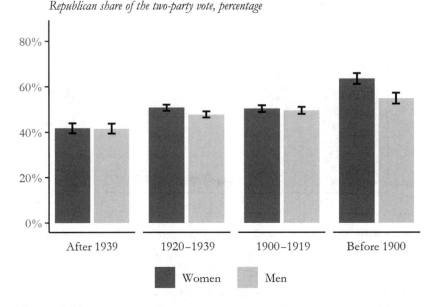

Republican share of the two-party vote, percentage

Figure 6.11 Republican advantage among women disappears among all but the oldest women (Gallup), 1964–76

men also were equally likely to vote. As a result, the vote choice of women of color is not sufficiently distinct from men of color in a way that would lead us to expect a more diverse electorate will lead to a larger partisan gender gap in this period.

Age. Women born before 1900 remained more likely to vote Republican than older men, and indeed, significantly more Republican than any other age-gender group. We report the Republican vote share of women and men of different age cohorts in Figure 6.11. As new issues moved on to the agenda in the late 1960s and early 1970s, the Republican advantage among women largely disappeared among all but the oldest voters, but the modern gender gap in favor of the Democratic party had not yet emerged among any of the younger cohorts. Differences in partisan preference across cohorts are fairly muted among men, but sharper among women. A woman who came of political age before suffrage was highly likely to vote Republican (more than 60%). A woman in the youngest cohort, however, was more likely than not to cast a ballot for Democrats.

Marriage, family, and work. In the 1960s and 1970s, women entered the paid workforce in unprecedented numbers. Employment has long been recognized as providing many resources – skills, knowledge, experience, income – that both facilitate electoral participation and shape partisan vote choice. In particular, an important line of previous research argues that employment outside the home was important for women's political views during this era. The workplace exposes women to non-traditional gender roles and to gender-based discrimination, provides an opportunity for women to develop politically relevant skills, and helps women gain political knowledge through social interactions. In particular, Susan Carroll has argued that by helping women gain greater autonomy, higher-status employment in particular assisted women in identifying their independent, gendered interests. Those interests are typically understood to include various policies to counter gender bias and assist working parents.[53] On the one hand, the Democrats had clearly allied themselves with civil rights and an active federal government by the mid-1960s. On the other hand, the clear identification of the Democratic party with the cause of women's rights was still emerging in the 1970s.

Figure 6.12 suggests that the impact of employment on women voters' preferences changed in the 1960s and 1970s. In the previous period, women who did *not* work were distinctly Republican, compared to women who worked, as well as compared to all men. In this period, the dynamic has shifted: There is no longer a partisan gender gap among the unemployed; women and men outside of the labor market favor the same parties at the same rates. Unemployed men and women also are as likely to vote Republican as employed men. The growing numbers of working women, however, are now distinctively Democratic. In other words, the modern gender gap emerges particularly early among employed women, consistent with resource inequality perspectives that emphasize the importance of work for the development of women's independent political preferences. The changing place of work in women's lives is reflected with a changing impact of work on women's political choices.

The effects of marriage and the presence of children also shift in this era. In the 1940s and 1950s, single women were the group most likely to support the Republican presidential candidate, whether or not there were children in the home. By the 1970s, the presence of children becomes key: Single women are now distinctively Democratic – compared to both single women without children and married women overall (see Figure 6.13). Single women without

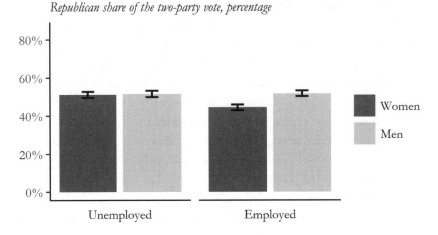

Figure 6.12 Women who work are more likely to vote Democratic (ANES), 1964–76

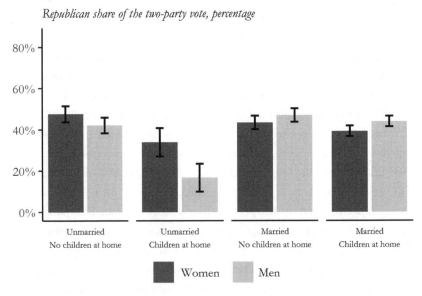

Figure 6.13 Single parents are more likely to vote Democratic (ANES), 1964–76

children, however, continued to be distinctively Republican, as they had been in the 1950s. Marriage is associated with a greater likelihood of voting Democratic for women, but marriage has no impact on the vote choice of men. The association of marriage with greater Democratic support for women will be a short-lived phenomenon, but the distinctive political preferences of single parents, and especially single mothers, will be increasingly consequential in the decades that follow.

Education. Educational attainment has long been recognized as a key determinant of political participation and preferences in part due to its association with greater political interest, knowledge, and engagement.[54] Recent research using Gallup data shows the partisan gender gap appearing earlier – in the 1960s and 1970s – among more educated citizens who presumably had more awareness and comprehension of the emerging polarization between the parties on many issues in American politics, including on social welfare and civil rights issues.[55] In the ANES data, however, the presidential vote still reflects the patterns observed in earlier periods. Figure 6.14 shows that both women and men became more likely to vote Republican as their educational attainment increased. Women with a high school level of education were very slightly more likely to cast Democratic ballots than similarly educated men, but there were no significant differences among any other educational group; differences are particularly slight or nonexistent among those with any exposure to college. Importantly, education remains a key predictor of partisan choice for both women and men. Fewer than half of those without exposure to college vote Republican compared to more than half of those who attended college. We see in future chapters that as educational attainment continues to expand over time, this long-standing relationship between education and Republican voting deteriorates sharply among women.

Politics and place. The 1960 election was the last in which Democrats managed to secure a majority of white southern voters. The enfranchisement of black voters in the South provided a new source of support for Democrats, but Southern whites were increasingly dependable voters for Republicans. As a result, the partisan distinctiveness of the South that we observed in the previous four decades is fading in the 1960s and 1970s. Figure 6.15 shows the Republican vote share across the United States, on average, from 1964 to 1976. Among men, there are virtually no differences in support for the GOP across all four regions, a stunning transformation.

The regional sources for the gender gap shifted as well. While region did not affect men's Republican support in presidential elections from 1964 to 1976,

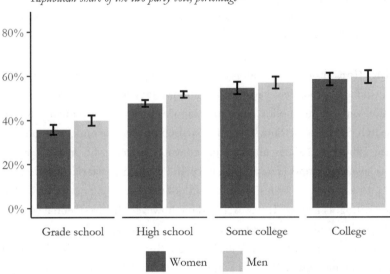

Figure 6.14 Republican preference rises with education, with the smallest gender gaps among the highest educated (ANES), 1964–76

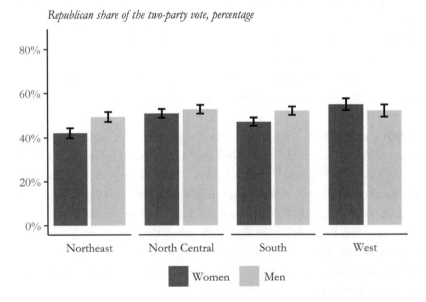

Figure 6.15 The "modern" gender gap emerges earliest in the Northeast (ANES), 1964–76

women's support for Republicans was significantly lower in the South and the Northeast. Overall, the regional gender dynamics of partisanship were shifting. The gender gap favoring Republicans observed in the West in the 1940s and 1950s disappeared in the 1960s and 1970s, while in the Northeast, where women and men had been equally Republican in the previous period, there was now a pro-Democratic gender gap. The largest shift occurs in the South, where Republicans had had an advantage among women in the immediate postwar period. Not only does that pro-Republican gender gap disappear but it completely flipped to a pro-Democratic gap in the 1960s and 1970. We discuss the racial dimensions of these changes in Chapter 7.

Understanding Women's Vote Choice

On the whole, we see few differences in the vote choice of women and men during the 1960s and 1970s. While the social movements of the period, particularly the women's movement, were transforming politics and lives, men and women remained overwhelmingly similar in their vote choices. As we have seen, the voting behavior of women attracts little scholarly attention in this period, but the emergence of feminism contributed to a great deal of public speculation as to the changing political attitudes and priorities of American women.

Women's issues. As press and public attention to feminism grew in the 1970s, contemporary observers increasingly speculated on whether and how women's rights issues would affect women voters. "What Role Will Women's Issues Play?" asked the *Los Angeles Times* in 1976.[56] The association of Democrats with civil rights and other social movements, and the activism of prominent feminists within the Democratic party (especially in 1972) helped associate Democrats with the women's rights cause in the 1970s. However, parties' and candidates' official stances on women's rights issues were generally similar in the late 1960s and early 1970s and there is little evidence that women and men held distinct opinions on these issues. The ANES began including a generic question on women's role in 1972, asking respondents to place themselves along a range of opinion from "women should have an equal role with men in running business, industry and government" to "women's place is in the home." In Figure 6.16, we report the percent

Percentage in each category

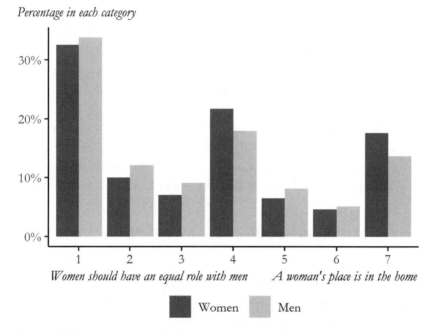

Women should have an equal role with men   *A woman's place is in the home*

■ Women   ▨ Men

Figure 6.16 Support for equal roles for women generally similar among women and men (ANES), 1972–76

of women and men placing themselves at each of the seven places on the seven-point scale in the 1972 and 1976 elections combined.

The distribution of responses is remarkably similar for women and men in the 1970s. Women and men are equally likely to say that women and men should have an equal role, and if anything, women were more willing than men to favor traditional gender roles for women on the other end of the spectrum. These attitudes were linked to partisanship in the same way for women and men as well. Women who agree most strongly with the "equal role" response are no more likely to vote Democratic (47%) than men who respond in the same way (45%). As the overall data on vote choice suggested, the public debate over women's roles had neither polarized men and women on the narrower issue of women's rights or translated into broader partisan differences in presidential votes during this period.

Social welfare. Later scholars seeking to explain the eventual emergence of the gender gap have highlighted the greater support for social welfare programs among women in a period in which Republicans became increasingly hostile to such policies.[57] As the social welfare state expanded in the 1960s and 1970s, women were increasingly dependent on social welfare as both beneficiaries and providers. Much of the growth in women's employment in this period came from the expanding social welfare sector and related occupations in education and health. From 1960 to 1973, human services employment accounted for more than 60% of the growth in white women's employment and almost 80% of African American women's, compared to much smaller growth among both white and African American men. Women also were increasingly likely to be direct beneficiaries of social welfare programs or – due in part to rising marital instability – able to imagine that they might be in need of assistance someday.[58]

Did women and men diverge on social welfare issues in the 1960s and 1970s? The evidence suggests yes. For example, in 1968, the November Gallup poll asked about a negative income tax, a government payment to increase family income of all families to a certain minimum level ($3,200 in 1968 dollars). Women were more likely than men to favor a negative income tax, 35% of women versus 29% of men. In General Social Survey (GSS) data, women were less likely than men to say that government spends too much on social welfare in the 1970s. That said, gender differences on social welfare issues are generally small in the 1960s and 1970s, particularly compared to larger gender gaps on the use of force, both foreign and domestic.[59]

Did divergence on social welfare issues shape the partisan gender gap – or lack thereof – in this period? In an important article, political scientists Karen Kaufmann and John Petrocik note that men have been less supportive than women of social welfare since the early 1950s. It is not until the mid-1960s, however, that views on social welfare spending began to track with party identification. They also point out that the Democratic Great Society programs of the 1960s and the conservative reaction against them made social welfare issues increasingly salient by the late 1960s. Partisanship at the individual level is extremely resistant to change, however, and these effects unfold over many years. In the 1960s and 1970s, any Republican advantage among women is eliminated as women voters select the same parties and candidates as men, or become slightly more Democratic. A reasonable explanation for this shift would be that women's distinct social welfare preferences have become more salient (and eventually more distinctive) and those attitudes are slowly pushing some men away from the Democratic party while keeping some women in the Democratic fold.[60]

CONCLUSION

The second wave of the women's movement (following up on the first wave, the suffrage movement) challenged and transformed gender roles and expectations. The passage of the Voting Rights Act in 1965 and other civil rights accomplishments made access to the ballot a reality for more millions of American citizens, female and male. In the language of political development, then, the 1960s and 1970s were defined by major transformations in both gender order and legal order, making this period distinct in terms of social and legal disruption and warranting treatment as an unique era.

The times they were a-changing, but the electoral behavior of women and men in the 1960s and 1970s shows more similarity than difference. The turnout gap narrowed to nothing, and women and men overwhelmingly cast ballots for the same candidates and parties in presidential elections. Starting in 1964, more than half of voters in presidential elections were women. Given the changes in women's roles and the salience of civil and women's rights in politics, it is perhaps unsurprising that women's turnout edged upwards to match men's by the 1970s. At the same time, the small Republican advantage among women before 1964 declined to the point where differences between men and women were negligible. John Kennedy's narrow victory in 1960 was the last election in which women voters on the whole were (very slightly) more likely than men to support the Republican presidential candidate.

The issues that were front and center in these tumultuous decades – race and civil rights, social welfare, the size of government, women's equality – continued to dominate politics in the years that followed. In 1980, the nomination of Ronald Reagan permanently shifted the Republican party in a conservative direction. Feminist activists, seeking political advantage in the face of increasing opposition to equity and equality for women, promoted gender differences in Reagan's 1980 vote totals as the "gender gap." The result was an unprecedented level of attention to and debate over women voters in the 1980s and 1990s – from politicians, the press, and scholars.

CHAPTER 7

The Discovery of the Gender Gap

I N THE WAKE OF THE PRESIDENTIAL ELECTION OF 1980, THE WOMEN'S movement was at a crossroads. The victorious Republican party had removed the Equal Rights Amendment (ERA), the defining feminist issue of the time, from its platform after nearly 40 years of support, and, for the first time, added an unequivocal statement in opposition to abortion rights. New president Ronald Reagan was strongly supported by Phyllis Schlafly, the well-known anti-feminist activist and organizer.[1]

Women's issues and women voters were front and center throughout the 1980 presidential campaign, as many expected that Reagan's positions on women's rights would alienate women at the polls. A *New York Times* story days after the election was initially read as undermining that prediction; 46% of all women had voted for incumbent Jimmy Carter and 47% for the victorious Ronald Reagan, suggesting that, while Reagan narrowly won the women's vote, one candidate was not more appealing to women than the other. Others, however, quickly seized on a different comparison: 47% of women had voted for Reagan compared to 55% of men, an 8-point difference. The National Organization for Women proclaimed "Feminist Bloc Emerges in the 1980 Elections" on the cover of its December/January newspaper (1980–1).[2]

In 1981, activists preparing to present data on the vote choice and opinion of women and men labeled the column showing the differences between the two groups as the "gender gap." With that, a new, politically consequential term was born.[3] Figure 7.1 is a Google ngram, which shows the frequency in which the term "gender gap" appears in books published each year since 1920, when the Nineteenth Amendment was ratified. The phrase is extremely rare or nonexistent prior to its introduction by feminist activists after the 1980 election. As its use expanded, the "gender gap" quickly became popular shorthand for political (and other) differences between women and men.

Percentage of American English books, E Notation

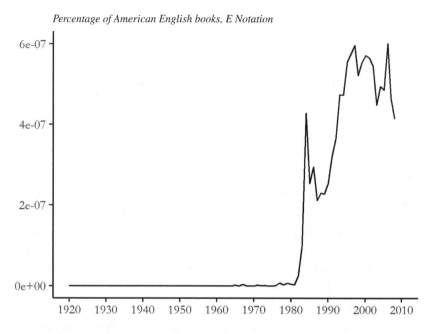

Figure 7.1 The appearance of the "gender gap" in published books, 1920–2008.
Source: Google Ngram Viewer (books.google.com/ngrams)

The discovery of the gender gap directed an historic level of attention to women voters in the 1980s and 1990s. Parties and candidates sought to explain and exploit the gender gap to their own advantage. The press and activists highlighted the Reagan administration's insensitive comments about women and the Republican party's hostility to feminism. Scholars also quickly took note of this phenomenon, but from the start, they tended to find that other issues – social welfare, foreign policy and conflict, and the economy – were key to understanding the gender gap rather than women's rights issues per se. Women voters continued to be center stage in the 1990s as the so-called "culture wars" kept issues of gender equality, reproductive rights, and work-life balance at the forefront of political debate.

This chapter examines the five presidential elections from 1980, when the gender gap was discovered and named, through 1996, an election which featured a record-setting gender gap and the rise of the "soccer mom" as a target of press and political attention. We trace changes in women's lives, the debate over women's rights, and the persistence of partisan difference over these issues throughout this period. Parties and candidates sought to appeal to women voters in new, different, and consequential ways, as the partisan gender gap became an established feature of American elections.

AMERICAN ELECTORAL POLITICS, 1980–1996

In the wake of the Watergate scandal and the resignation of President Richard Nixon in 1974, Democrat Jimmy Carter was elected to the White House in 1976. The victory was short-lived, however. In 1980, Carter faced crises at home (high inflation, unemployment, and gas prices) and abroad (the Iranian hostage crisis, the Soviet invasion of Afghanistan) that undermined his approval and put his reelection at risk. On the Republican side, the conservative wing of the GOP was ascendant as former actor and California governor Ronald Reagan was chosen as the party's standard bearer. Reagan had a long association with Republican conservatives, including delivering a popular speech, "A Time for Choosing," in support of Barry Goldwater in 1964.[4]

The Republican party retook both the White House and the US Senate (for the first time in almost 25 years) in 1980, in what was widely described as a Conservative Revolution. With the Iranian hostages returned on the day of his inauguration and the economy steadily improving, Reagan was reelected in 1984, defeating Carter's vice president Walter Mondale. Reagan's popularity was sufficient to aid his own vice president, George Bush, in winning the Republican nomination and presidency in 1988, against the Democratic nominee, Massachusetts governor Michael Dukakis. Throughout the 1980s, issues of both fiscal conservatism (taxes, regulation, size of government) and social conservatism (women's rights, prayer in schools, homosexuality) dominated political debate, as the Republican party melded economic and social conservatism together.[5]

Democrats struggled to compete in the Reagan era. The Southern Democratic base of the party continued to erode, helping to undermine Democrats' long-standing majority status in the electorate and in Congress. The Democratic Leadership Council (DLC), created in 1985, pushed the Democratic party to moderate its positions and image to better compete with the resurgent Republican party. In 1992, former DLC chair and Arkansas governor Bill Clinton secured the Democratic nomination, despite multiple accusations of sexual impropriety. Clinton ran as a "new kind of Democrat," emphasizing welfare reform and a tough stance on crime, as well as more traditional Democratic issues like health care. With the economy in recession, the Clinton-Gore ticket returned Democrats to the White House in 1992 for the first time in 12 years. Due in large part to the independent presidential campaign of Texas billionaire Ross Perot, however, Clinton won with just 43% of the popular vote.[6]

Democratic control of both the executive and the legislative branches lasted only two years. In 1994, Republicans became the majority party in the US House for the first time in more than 40 years, and Newt Gingrich (R, GA) became Speaker of the House. Gingrich and his supporters in the House represented the newly dominant conservative wing of the GOP and in many cases, the rise of Southern Republicans in Congress. Clinton shifted in a moderate direction in response, most notably in the welfare reform bill passed in 1996. Congressional Republicans had a number of policy successes, but also some missteps; most notably, the GOP shouldered most of the blame for the 1995 government shutdown, which contributed to the party's reputation for extremism. On the whole, the partisan fights of the 1990s foreshadowed the widening polarization, close party competition, and intense partisanship in Washington and within the electorate which would define the next two decades.[7]

AMERICAN WOMEN IN THE 1980s AND 1990s

Women's Lives

Women's roles continued to expand and evolve in the 1980s and 1990s. In Figure 7.2, we again present key demographic markers across this period. The percentage of women in the labor force continued to expand, as men's employment rate fell slightly. The percentage of households with children under 18 where both parents worked outside the home increased from 25% in 1960 to nearly 60% by 1990. While 70% of households were defined by a male-only breadwinner in 1960, only one-third of households with children fit that traditional model by 1990. Female-headed households also continued to increase; in 1960, approximately 7% of households with children were headed by a single mother, compared to a full 20% by the 1990s.[8] Family size was changing as well: the number of women with four or more children fell almost 70% from the mid-1970s to the mid-1990s.[9] Women continued to advance in higher

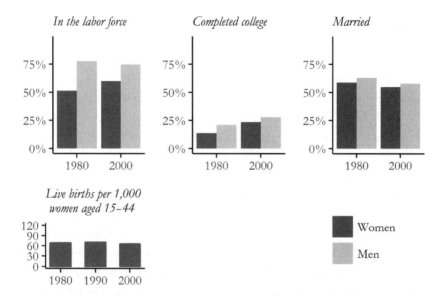

Figure 7.2 Women complete college and enter the labor force at rates close to men in the 1980s and 1990s

education; in 1970, only 36% of college graduates were women, by the 1990s, women comprised half of all students graduating from college. The combination of these factors suggests that it increasingly did not make sense to think about the typical woman voter as married, out of the labor force, and without a college degree, an image of the modal woman voter that informed earlier scholarship and continued to persist as an ideal.

Women in Politics

As women's roles were changing, women's place in politics was changing as well. The women's movement became an institutionalized force by the 1980s, with a host of revived or new organizations, on the left and also on the right, mobilizing women, advancing women's political careers, and advocating for women's interests. With the publicity surrounding the gender gap after the 1980 election, observers, politicians, and parties debated the interests of and sought to appeal to women voters as never before.

The majority party candidates staked out opposing positions on most women's rights issues during the 1980 presidential campaign. Reagan helped move the Republican party to strong opposition to abortion rights and was generally viewed as preferring women's traditional roles in the family. In part to counter this view, Reagan also made the appointment of a woman to the Supreme Court a central campaign promise. Carter, on the other hand, highlighted working women and his commitment to gender equality, including the ERA. At the same time, other issues – the place of the United States in the global order, the economy, taxes, and the role of government – dominated much of the campaign.[10]

The discovery and naming of the gender gap in the wake of the 1980 presidential elections transformed discourse about women voters. Feminist activists promoted the term, and it was quickly adopted by the press. The phrase "gender gap" first appeared in an American newspaper (the *Washington Post*) on October 13, 1981. Coverage was partly driven by a conscious strategy of feminist organizations and activists, as well as Democratic elites, to keep women voters in the public eye as a way to advance their causes and gain votes.[11]

Reagan himself was often identified as a central reason for women's supposed dissatisfaction with the Republican party. Reagan and his surrogates did not help the situation by making a number of high-profile gaffes. In 1981, for example, a senior presidential aide attributed Reagan's lesser support among women to his emphasis on economic issues: "Economic leadership appeals to men while women don't understand interest rates as well as men."[12] Press stories in the early 1980s repeatedly inquired into "Reagan's woman problem."[13] Yet, the gender gap was clearly bigger than just Reagan, as Republican candidates for other offices and presidential nominees after Reagan continued to face an electorate in which men were more likely to vote for the Republican candidate than were women.[14]

The heightened attention to women voters after 1980 had important consequences. Both journalists and scholars portrayed the gender gap as creating a more friendly climate for women candidates in terms of party and group support and press coverage.[15] Promoting issue stances and new legislation viewed as benefiting women, as well as promising to appoint more women to office, became common campaign refrains from candidates at every level.[16] The parties' rhetorical responses to the gender gap diverged. In the 1984 presidential campaign, Democrats emphasized women's changing roles, portrayed women as holding distinct views on issues of war and peace, the economy, and the social safety net, and criticized Reagan's inattentiveness to women's interests. The Republican campaign, on the other hand, highlighted women professionals and business owners, but also traditional family values, religious ideals, and opposition to abortion.[17]

The most consequential short-term response to the discovery of the gender gap was the selection of Geraldine Ferraro as the Democrats' vice presidential nominee in 1984. Facing a popular president and an improving economy, Democrats were anxious to capitalize on the potential advantage of the emergent gender gap. Feminist activists gathered endorsements for the idea of the first woman vice presidential nominee and for Ferraro specifically, promoted polls that seemed to show the public, and women in particular, would be supportive, negotiated with party leaders, and ultimately threatened to protest from the floor of the Democratic National Convention (but quickly backed off) over the nomination of a woman for vice president. While Ferraro broke an important glass ceiling and attracted considerable attention, there is little evidence her place on the ticket had much, if any, impact on the final outcome; indeed, there is little evidence that vice presidential nominees ever impact election outcomes significantly. Republicans, on the other hand, engaged in careful analysis of women voters, and crafted targeted messages to groups of women considered most persuadable for the Republicans, potentially helping the GOP to ward off a widening gender gap in 1984.[18]

Four years later, Democratic nominee and Massachusetts governor Michael Dukakis emphasized family leave, health care, and child care in his appeals to women, running ads specifically targeted at women voters. Many of these issues recognized women's roles as mothers (in a campaign memo identifying six issues of concern to women, four were specific to mothers), but recognized the challenges created by women's entrance into the paid labor force. Early polls predicted an enormous gender gap in 1988, but Republican nominee George H.W. Bush and his party were credited with taking steps to appeal to women and close that gap. Bush's nomination acceptance speech, for example, called for a "kinder, gentler nation," and was viewed as an appeal to those voters, especially women, alienated by extreme conservatism.[19]

In the 1992 presidential campaign, high-profile incidents came to represent how women's issues were handled by the Republican ticket. President Bush twice vetoed a bill ensuring twelve weeks of unpaid leave for children or family emergencies. Vice President Dan Quayle publicly criticized a TV character, Murphy Brown, who has a child outside of marriage. Pat Buchanan had challenged Bush from the right in the primaries, securing a spot as a keynote speaker at the Republican National Convention. Buchanan used the opportunity to proclaim there was "a religious war ... for the soul of America" and to attack feminism as "not the kind of change we can tolerate in a nation we still call God's country."[20]

Democratic nominee Bill Clinton sought to undermine the perceived Republican advantage on "family values" by claiming to seek "an America that values families." The Family and Medical Leave Act of 1993 was the first law Clinton signed as president. Hillary Clinton also was the subject of much attention during the 1992 campaign. Her image as a professional woman conflicted with traditional notions of the role of political spouses and especially First Ladies. Her dismissive comments about how she could have "stayed home and baked cookies and had teas" and "I'm not sitting here some little woman standing by my man like Tammy Wynette" elicited widespread controversy and critique.[21]

As a result of the 1991 Thomas-Hill hearings, sexual harassment also was at the forefront of American politics in the 1992 election. Lawyer and professor Anita Hill accused Supreme Court nominee Clarence Thomas of inappropriate workplace behavior. The all-white, all-male, Democratic-majority Judiciary Committee questioned Hill aggressively and approved Thomas' nomination, as did the US Senate, which in 1991 had just four women members out of 100 Senate seats. Partly in response to the Thomas hearings, an unprecedented number of women ran for Congress in 1992, earning it the moniker, "The Year of the Woman." The number of women in the Senate tripled, and the number of women in the US House increased from 28 to 47, helped along by a record number of retirements and open seats, due to redistricting, scandals, and an anti-incumbent mood. Importantly, the more accurate label would have been the Year of the Democratic Woman, as all of women's gains in the Senate and most of women's gains in the House were by Democratic women. This was the start of a new pattern; from the early 1990s onward, the percentage of Democratic candidates and office-holders who were women increasingly outpaced the percentage of female Republican candidates and office-holders, another aspect of partisan gender difference.[22]

While the press had declared 1992 the year of the woman, the 1994 midterms earned a different gender descriptor. Republicans won majorities in both the Senate and – for the first time in more than 40 years – the House as well. Press reports, both before and after the election, attributed much of the

GOP's historic success to the "year of the angry white male." Nationally men were six points more likely to vote for Republican candidates than were women in the 1994 midterm elections.[23]

The presidential election of 1996 is perhaps most notable for women for the invention of the phrase "soccer mom." Originally identified by a senior advisor to Republican nominee Bob Dole in describing Clinton's outreach to women, soccer moms were soon described as a sought-after swing vote in hundreds of newspaper and magazine stories. The term itself had clear class and racial connotations; a non-trivial number of articles explicitly described "soccer moms" as married women with children who live in the suburbs, as well as middle-class and white. In a striking return to rhetoric about women voters in the first decades after suffrage, the soccer mom label clearly framed women as making political decisions in large part based on their roles as mothers. Clinton did not mention soccer moms by name, but devoted significant attention to mom-friendly issues, such as education, childcare, and child and maternal health, in the 1996 campaign. Dole, on the other hand, often referenced soccer moms in speeches and spoke about how his policy positions would address their needs. This focus on one, not particularly representative, group of women would continue in the presidential elections which followed.[24]

OBSERVING WOMEN VOTERS

New survey organizations and new survey questions meant continuing improvements in data quality and access after 1980. By 1996, exit polls were regularly conducted by the Voters New Service, funded by a consortium of television networks and newspapers. The Pew Organization also began conducting extensive post-election polling, with data available from 1996 on. Starting in 1976, the CPS includes questions about Hispanic ethnicity, so we can observe the turnout of non-Hispanic whites, African Americans, Hispanics, and other racial and ethnic minorities. Given the important historical, social, and political differences between different racial and ethnic groups, as well as the growing racial diversity of the United States, this is an important advance for understanding American voters. The 1990s also provided a rare opportunity to investigate how women voters responded to relatively successful third-party candidates in the modern era. Ross Perot was the only third-party candidate since 1924 to carry more than 15% of the popular vote.

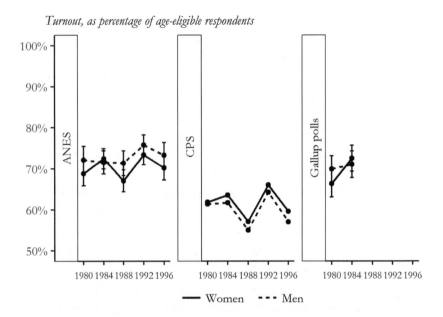

Turnout, as percentage of age-eligible respondents

Figure 7.3 CPS indicates women consistently more likely to vote than men after 1980 but ANES and Gallup less clear, 1980–96

TURNOUT

While the 1980 presidential election is recognized for the emergence of the contemporary gender gap, it was also the first election in which women cast ballots in presidential elections at a higher rate than men; due to the larger number of adult women in the electorate, more women than men had voted in presidential elections since 1964.[25] This trend continued and expanded across these two decades.

Turnout in presidential elections was generally unimpressive in the 1980s and 1990s, falling below 50% in 1996. Women's turnout exceeded men's turnout beginning in 1980, and the large data collection effort by the Census, the Current Population Survey (CPS), suggests that this gap persisted throughout the 1990s (see Figure 7.3). This new gap has profound implications for how we think about women as political actors. For nearly 60 years after suffrage, popular accounts and scholarly understanding rested on the assumption or understanding that women were by nature or by socialization less likely to vote. As we have seen, this claim lacked empirical support even 40 years earlier. The

1970s may not have offered a political breakthrough for women, in the sense that participation remained largely even with men and there was no partisan gender gap. But stereotypes of women's disinterest or lack of capacity for electoral politics become increasingly inconsistent with the reality of women using the vote across the 1980s and 1990s.

Women Are Not a Voting Bloc

As always, these broad trends are not the full story. We continue to highlight the diversity of women and the many ways in which different groups of women (and men) engaged in electoral politics in different ways. As in previous chapters, we rely on logistic regression to determine the impact of various factors on both turnout and vote choice for women and men. The relationships we report in the figures and our discussion below is informed by that analysis; that is, while we present bivariate relationships, we highlight and describe the effects of demographic factors that are persistent when we introduce statistical controls.

Race. Thanks to the large CPS samples and the expansion of questions related to race and ethnicity, we can now reliably examine the turnout of multiple racial and ethnic groups. Turnout data for men and women in four racial categories appear in Figure 7.4. While differences across racial and ethnic groups remained considerable, the turnout gender gap was consistent, at least in direction: Among nearly all groups, women turn out more than men. Turnout gaps among most racial and ethnic groups are quite small, but black women turn out at notably higher levels than black men or other people of color. The particularly large turnout gender gap among African Americans is an emerging phenomenon which has important implications going forward.

Age. Age continues to shape patterns of turnout in important ways. Turnout increases with age, except among the oldest voters, both female and male. Differences between women and men, however, vary across cohorts, as Figure 7.5 indicates. Younger women are clearly more likely to turn out than younger men in the 1980s and 1990s. This pattern narrows as cohorts age and then reverse among the oldest cohort, where women continue to lag men at the ballot box. The numbers of women and men born before 1920 is dwindling, however, and so is their impact on overall turnout trends. Nonetheless, whether

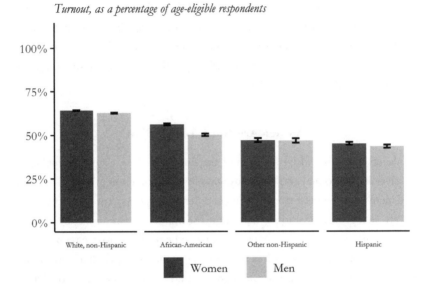

Turnout, as a percentage of age-eligible respondents

Figure 7.4 Considerable turnout gender gap among African Americans, smaller gaps among non-Hispanic whites and Hispanics (CPS), 1980–96

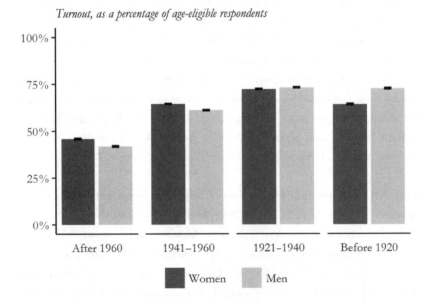

Turnout, as a percentage of age-eligible respondents

Figure 7.5 Women more likely to turn out than men, except among the oldest voters (CPS), 1980–96

one votes remains strongly associated with age (and certainly more so than gender) for both women and men.

Education. Education remains key to understanding patterns of turnout as well. While women were attending college in higher and higher numbers after 1968, the college completion rate for women remained lower than for men until 2015 (see Figure 1.2). The ANES data, which arguably underestimates women's relative turnout (see discussion of Figure 7.3), suggests that women were as likely to turn out as men, except among the poorly educated (women's turnout lower) and the highly educated (women's turnout higher). The lower relative turnout among less well-educated women is a persistent finding since the introduction of the ANES in the 1950s. Turnout gender gaps have always been smallest among the most highly educated and are now reversed, with women more likely to turn out than men (see Figure 7.6). The net effect is that college completion has a more powerful impact on women's turnout: A woman with only a grade school education has a 50% chance of voting, compare to a 92% likelihood among women with college degrees, a 42-point difference. Men's turnout, in contrast, rises only from 57% to 89% as we move from least to most well-educated, a 22-point difference. (Women with college degrees are generally younger, but controlling for age does not eliminate this effect.) In terms of turnout, gender matters a little and education matters a lot, but the two are not unrelated, as women were increasingly catching up to men in terms of educational attainment.

Marriage, family, and work. Women who did not work outside the home had distinctively low turnout in the 1980s and 1990s. Fifty years earlier, women who stayed home were just as likely to vote as women who worked, and both less than men. As increasing numbers of women entered the workforce, that pattern changed. As in the 1960s and 1970s, the rate at which women work outside of the home continued to rise, and women who worked turned out at higher rates than those who did not (see Figure 7.7). Employment status was not associated with differing rates of turnout for men meaning employment continues to signal different things for women and men in terms of political engagement. Note, however, that while women who did not work were less likely to vote than all other groups, this difference is relatively small compared to racial and educational turnout differences.

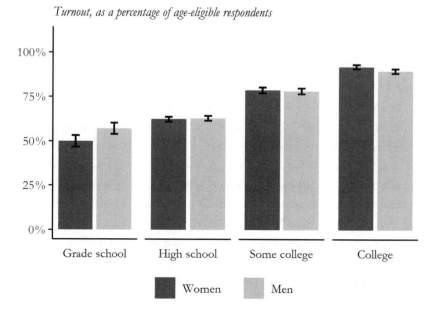

Figure 7.6 College-educated turn out more than poorly educated, and the effect is stronger for women (ANES), 1980–96

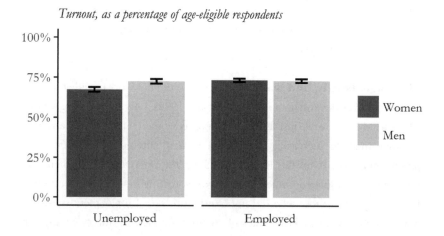

Figure 7.7 People who work are more likely to vote, and the effect is more powerful for women than for men (ANES), 1980–96

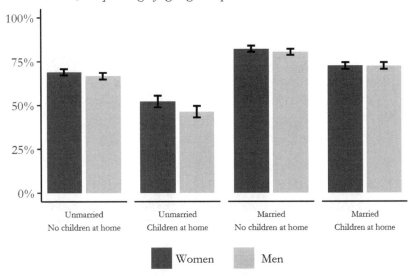

Turnout, as a percentage of age-eligible respondents

Figure 7.8 In contrast to earlier periods, the effects of marriage and children are the same on men and women (ANES), 1980–96

Families were changing and so were turnout patterns, as Figure 7.8 shows. Single parents remained the least likely to turn out to vote, especially the relatively small number of single fathers. Marriage continues to be associated with higher turnout, regardless of sex. Yet the presence of children now depresses the turnout of both women and men, including that of married parents. In the 1940s and 1950s, women who had children in the home were much less likely to turn out than either other women or similarly situated men. This is no longer the case in the 1980s and 1990s. Single mothers are less likely to vote than married mothers, but not less likely to vote than single dads.

Politics and place. Since suffrage, Southern women have consistently been the least likely to turn out, followed by Southern men. Southerners remain the least likely to vote – or reside in contexts less supportive of their electoral participation (see Figure 7.9). However, the gender gap in turnout in the South – consistently the largest in the country – narrows to statistical insignificance in the 1980s and 1990s, and is no longer any larger than what is observed in other

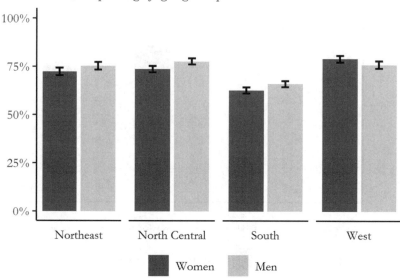

Turnout, as a percentage of age-eligible respondents

Figure 7.9 The turnout gender gap closes in the South (ANES), 1980–96

regions. As the Democratic Solid South collapses, so does the distinctiveness of Southern women compared to Southern men.

Explaining Women's Turnout

In the presidential election immediately following the ratification of the Nineteenth Amendment in 1920, our best estimates are that women were more than thirty points less likely to turn out to vote than were men. The turnout gender gap narrows slowly over the twentieth century until it is completely eliminated and then reversed in 1980. This is an historic achievement for women in American politics.

How can we explain this accomplishment? Interestingly, the discovery of the gender gap as an important electoral phenomenon in the wake of the 1980 presidential election generally took up all the gender-and-politics oxygen and very few explanations for the reversal of the turnout gender gap were offered by observers or scholars. In *The New American Voter* (another update to *The American Voter*), Miller and Shanks simply observe that "[t]he mobilization of women thus joined the mobilization of Black voters to make major socio-political changes in the composition of the active voting electorate during the period of our inquiry." While the reasons for black mobilization gains are rightfully viewed as structural, no similar explanation is given for women's mobilization.[26] The general consensus appears to be that this shift represented the natural advance of women into electoral politics since 1920, and what was more important was the impact women voters might have on outcomes.

The turnout gender gap reversal is, however, a bit of a puzzle. Dominant explanations for voter turnout highlight the importance of resources such as income, education, and employment. Despite gains, women continued to lag behind men on all three dimensions in the 1980s and 1990s, although the education gap was closing quickly. One reading of these facts suggests the failure of resource inequality explanations (women still had fewer resources, but voted more) and an opening for updated distinctive gender explanations that now frame women as particularly dutiful, civic-minded, and participatory, rather than as apolitical and disinterested. On the other hand, women continued to express less interest, engagement, and attention to politics during these decades, all of which suggest women's turnout should be lower, not higher, than men's.

Changing gender norms (distinctive gender) certainly deserve some of the credit. As we see most clearly in the age cohorts, older generations of women socialized to traditional gender roles have been less likely to vote than similar men since suffrage. As these women have aged out of the electorate, women have become as or more likely than men to turn out to vote.[27]

Despite changing gender norms, women still shoulder the greater burden of household work and childcare; the real difference was that by the 1980s, many women worked outside the home in addition to those traditional responsibilities. We might expect those demands to diminish women's likelihood of voting. Evidence suggests, however, that family responsibilities may not have held women back politically to the extent and in the ways that many had long assumed. In a unique study of a range of types of political participation conducted in the late 1980s and early 1990s, political scientists Nancy Burns, Kay Lehman Schlozman, and Sidney Verba find little evidence that factors such as the division of household work, relative control over family time or money, or relative contribution to the household income depress women's participation. This is not to say that gender dynamics in the home and in the workplace do not matter at all. Men do become more active in politics when they

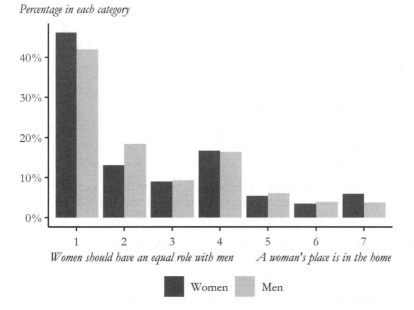

Percentage in each category

Figure 7.10 Large majorities of women and men endorse an equal role for women in business, industry, and government (ANES), 1980–96

have more authority in the home. Men also are more likely to hold jobs that involve the supervision of others, which provides a substantive boost to their political engagement.[28]

While gender stereotypes and bias continued to be found in politics, the previously common view that politics is men's work and home is women's domain was clearly weakening. As we discussed in Chapter 6, since 1972 the ANES has included a 7-point scale of agreement with two statements about women's roles: Women should have equal roles in business, industry, and government or a woman's place is in the home. Figure 7.10 reports responses to this question for men and women in the 1980s and 1990s. As in the 1970s, responses are overwhelmingly similar for women and men. The real shift over time is in the distribution. While the equal role responses are the most common for both women and men in both periods, only about 30% of respondents placed themselves at the most equal position in the 1970s and about 15% still claimed the most traditional response. By the 1980s and 1990s, more than 40% of women and men strongly favor gender equality and the percent of respondents at the least equal end has dropped below 10%. We may expect

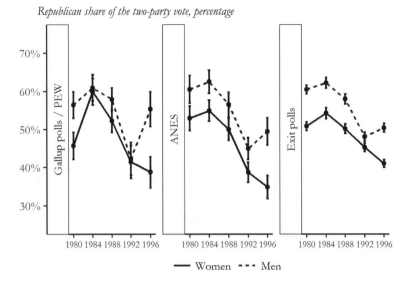

Republican share of the two-party vote, percentage

Figure 7.11 The size of the gender gap varies from election to election, but women remain more likely to cast ballots for Democrats, 1980–96

that social desirability bias is playing a part here – in addition to attitudes about gender roles, what may have changed is the perceived social acceptability of traditional attitudes – but even a shift in perceived norms is consequential for political behavior.

WOMEN'S VOTE CHOICE

The partisan gender gap that emerged in 1980 widened substantially by 1996. Figure 7.11 reveals the size and persistence of the gender gap across three surveys and five presidential elections. After 1980, the gender gap narrowed in 1984 and 1988 as both parties fought to attract newly salient women voters. By 1992, the gender gap narrows to the smallest gap of this period (see discussion of the impact of Ross Perot below). In 1996, however, Clinton's reelection campaign lost ground among men and gained among women, resulting in the largest partisan gender gap recorded thus far.

These data make it clear that gender gap dynamics reflect broader partisan trends and the actions of both women and men. Between 1984 and 1992,

Third party vote share, percentage

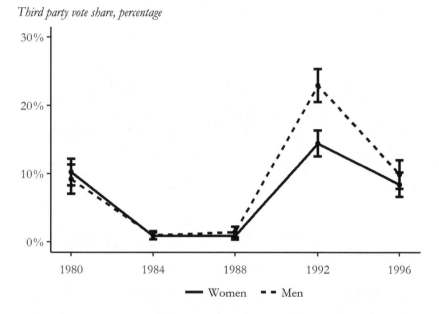

Figure 7.12 Women less likely than men to support Ross Perot (ANES), 1992

Republican support declines among both women and men., even as women remain more Democratic. What accounts for the large gender gap in 1996 is that men move back toward the GOP, while women continue to move toward the Democrats.

What about Ross Perot? The 1992 presidential election included a long-shot independent presidential run by mercurial business executive Ross Perot. Running on a platform of no-nonsense solutions to runaway government spending and protectionist trade policy, Perot managed to capture the largest third-party share of the popular vote since La Follette ran under the Progressive party label in 1924 (see Chapter 4). As in 1924, Perot's support came from both women and men, but men were more likely to defect from the major parties and cast third-party ballots in 1992 (see Figure 7.12). This gender dynamic has been reported in analyses of the Perot phenomenon, but is rarely a major focus.[29] Interestingly, this replicates the pattern we observed in 1924: In most states, women and men supported La Follette at similar levels, but in the states where La Follette did very well, men were more likely than women to defect to the third-party Progressive candidate.

Women Are Not a Voting Bloc

The emergence of the gender gap in 1980 was a widespread phenomenon across a range of identities and characteristics. That said, the pro-Democratic gender gap is certainly clearer and more substantial among some groups, including the better-educated, employed, single parents, Southerners and Westerners. We continue the approach we have taken in previous chapters of analyzing the impact of various population characteristics on the vote choice of women and men. Race is by far the dominant factor in determining vote choice regardless of sex. The effects of education and employment continue to drive up Republican support among men, but are much less powerful predictors of women's vote choice.

Race. Race remains a uniquely powerful predictor of vote choice. The large exit polls of this period permit us to observe not only white and African American vote choice in this period, but generate reliable estimates of Hispanic party preference as well.[30] We present race, gender, and vote choice across the five elections from 1980 to 1996 using exit polls in Figure 7.13. Race and ethnicity remained powerful predictors of partisan vote choice in the United States in the 1980s and 1990s. A third or fewer people of color voted for Republican presidential candidates in the 1980s and 1990s, compared to more than 50% of whites. Approximately one-third of Latino voters casted ballots of Republicans, and only one-fifth of African Americans.

The pro-Democratic gender group characterized all racial and ethnic groups, but was smallest, and statistically insignificant, among Latino voters. Black women emerged as distinctly Democratic in their voting behavior during the 1980s and 1990s, overall and compared to black men. About 12%, on average, of women of color cast Republican ballots in presidential elections, compared to just slightly under 17% of men of color. Recall from Figure 7.4 that black women are more likely to vote than black men (the largest racial turnout gender gap), making black women a particularly potent force in creating the modern gender gap.

The result was that women of color in particular became more reliably Democratic, they also became an increasingly important factor in election outcomes. Between 1980 and 1996, white women shifted from accounting for over 85% of the female electorate to 81%, a dramatic decline given the usual

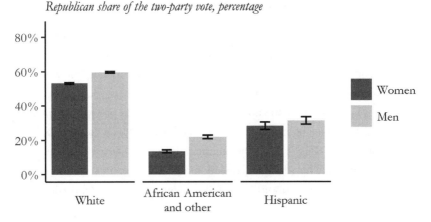

Republican share of the two-party vote, percentage

Figure 7.13 Women of color most Democratic and white men most Republican (exit polls), 1980–96

glacial shift of demographic change. White women were still a much larger group than minority women, but unlike white women, the growing group of minority women voters were overwhelmingly and reliably casting ballots for Democratic presidential candidates. Minority men were neither as large a percentage of the male electorate (84% white in 1996), nor quite as reliable as Democratic partisans.

Age. Women were equally or more likely to vote Democratic regardless of age; in contrast to even the immediate past period, in no age cohort were women more Republican than men in the 1980s and 1990s. Figure 7.14 reports the Republican vote share for women and men in four age cohorts. The emerging gender gap is not confined to young, newly socialized voters, but extends to women born between 1921 and 1940, some of whom are over 75 by the time of the 1996 Clinton victory. On the whole, the share of women's votes that go to Democrats is fairly consistent across cohorts, while the oldest men are more Democratic than other men, perhaps reflecting the lingering impact of New Deal realignment on that cohort.

Education. The Democratic advantage among women also persists across education levels. Indeed, what is striking is that the level of Democratic

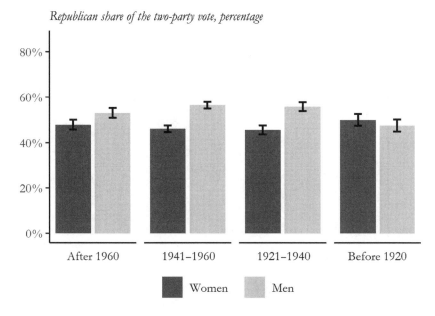

Republican share of the two-party vote, percentage

Figure 7.14 Partisan gender gap persists across age cohorts; only the oldest women are not distinctively Democratic (ANES), 1980–96

support among women is increasingly constant across all levels of educational attainment, as Figure 7.15 demonstrates. What we are witnessing is the long-standing relationship between education and support for the major parties beginning to unravel. For decades, exposure to college was a powerful predictor of support for the Republican presidential candidate. College remained a clear predictor of Republican support among men in the 1980s and 1990s. For women, however, this relationship weakens: College-educated women were only about 10 percentage points more likely to support Republicans than women with only a grade school education. This was a shift: As late as the 1970s, the relationship between education and Republican support was overwhelmingly similar for women and men. There was no partisan gender gap among those with no education beyond grade school (comprising about 10% of the population in the 1980s and 1990s), but declining support over time for Republicans among better-educated women means that the largest pro-Democratic gender gaps emerge at the highest levels of educational attainment.[31]

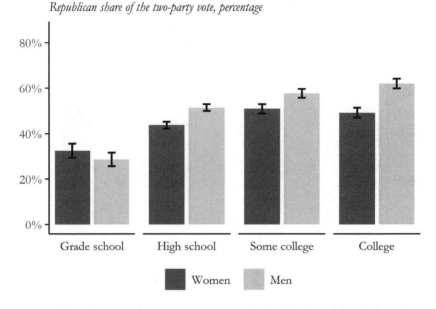

Republican share of the two-party vote, percentage

Figure 7.15 College-educated voters are more Republican than grade school educated voters, but the effect is much weaker for women (ANES), 1980–96

Marriage, family, and work. The most striking change in women's lives leading up to 1980 was arguably their rapid entry into the labor force. This shift persists. By 1996, the gap between men's and women's workforce participation rate was roughly where it is today, with over 60% of women working outside the home (see Figure 7.2). The impact of work on partisan support changes substantially across the twentieth century. In the 1940s and 1950s, women who stayed home were distinctively Republican compared to all men and to women who worked. This pattern begins to erode in the 1960s and 1970s; unemployed women no longer have distinctive partisan patterns, but rather, employed women became the distinctive group, slightly more Democratic than other women and men. In the 1980s and 1990s, employed men were the distinctive group, more likely to support Republican candidates. Women who stay home now were as likely to vote Democratic as employed women (see Figure 7.16). Indeed, in this figure it is the distinctively Republican electoral behavior of (employed) men, not women, that appears to be driving the gender gap, as scholars of this period have

Republican share of the two-party vote, percentage

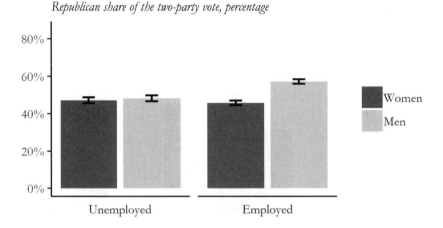

Figure 7.16 Employed men are distinctively Republican in their vote choice (ANES), 1980–96

emphasized.[32] We discuss the impact of work on women's partisanship in greater detail below.

Across household types, women were consistently more Democratic than similarly situated men in the 1980s and 1990s. Figure 7.17 reports the vote choice of married and unmarried women and men, with and without children. For men and especially for women, marriage was associated with a greater likelihood of voting Republican. The effects of parenthood, on the other hand, were largely confined to women. Controlling for marriage, the presence of children does not change men's party choice in a significant way. For women, however, the presence of children makes single women even more likely to vote Democratic. This positive relationship between marriage and Republican vote choice – for women and for men – would continue into the new millennium.

Politics and place. In every region, women were more likely to vote Democratic than were men (Figure 7.18). The pro-Democratic gender gap that was confined to the Northeast and the South in the 1960s and 1970s is now apparent in all regions. It might be somewhat surprising that the Republican vote share was higher in the North Central region, but Reagan's message of economic optimism and recovery resonated particularly well with voters in the rapidly deindustrializing Midwest.

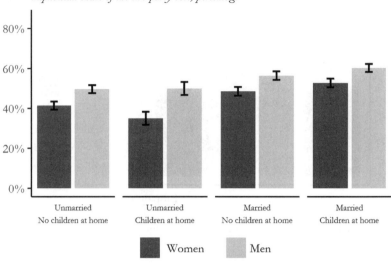

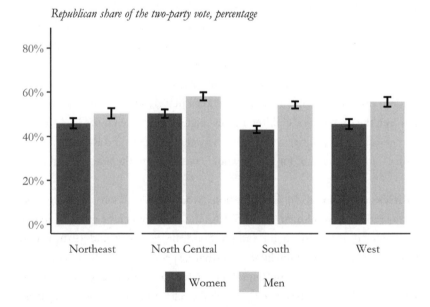

Republican share of the two-party vote, percentage

Figure 7.17 Married moms and dads were the most likely to vote Republican (ANES), 1980–96

Republican share of the two-party vote, percentage

Figure 7.18 The South is no longer distinctive in terms of partisanship and the gender gap is visible in every region (ANES), 1980–96

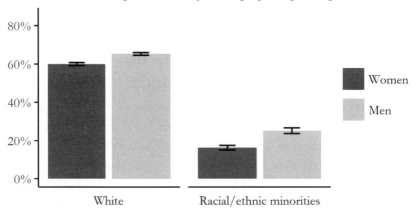

Southern voters, Republican share of the two-party vote, percentage

Figure 7.19 In the South, women – especially women of color – are more Democratic than men (exit polls), 1980–96

In the 1980s and 1990s, the South became increasingly similar to the rest of the country in terms of the relationship between sex and party vote share. The relatively high turnout and strong Democratic support of black Southern women surely played an important part in this shift. This transformation was not strictly a function of increasing mobilization of women of color, however. A partisan gender gap emerged and persisted in the South for both white and minority voters, as we can see in Figure 7.19. Data from exit polls indicate a pro-Democratic but fairly modest partisan difference between Southern white men and women (5 percentage points), and a much larger gap between men and women of color (9 percentage points).

The South is the only region where we observe a shift, over time, from a pro-Republican gender gap in the 1940s and 1950s to a pro-Democratic gender gap in the 1980s and 1990s. In the largely white Southern electorate of the 1940s and 1950s, about 45% of men voted Republican compared to about 55% of women.[33] In the Reagan era, Southern white men jumped to 65% Republican – a 20-point swing! Southern white women increased their likelihood of voting Republican only to 60% – a mere 5-point shift toward the GOP. The sharp movement of men to the GOP clearly was a central factor in generating the pro-Democratic gender gap in the South.[34] Consistent with our findings from the New Deal period, the presence of women stabilized the electorate. The Southern realignment would have been even larger and more dramatic if only men's ballots were counted.

Explaining the Gender Gap

With women voters front and center in the 1980s and 1990s, observers and politicians chimed in with their theories (and sometimes evidence) about what motivated women's distinct partisan preferences. Social scientists jumped in to explain this phenomenon as well. The most popular ideas, however, did not always turn out to be those most supported by empirical evidence.

Women's issues. The identification of the modern gender gap in favor of Democrats is fundamentally intertwined with the expectation that the parties' realignment on policy issues specific to women is the reason. The feminist activists who coined the term "gender gap" did so in a report intended to convince Democrats that Reagan lost women's votes in large part because he opposed the ERA, in contrast to previous Republican candidates, and thus to persuade Democrats to continue the ratification fight. While White House staff in the early 1980s denied that the ERA was relevant to the president's approval numbers, Reagan himself noted, "I have a hunch that part of it's [his lower approval among women] been inspired by the ERA movement."[35]

Similarly, others have assumed that the heated debate over abortion rights contributed to the gender gap. The Republican party not only established new positions in opposition to the ERA in 1980, but in opposition to abortion as well, establishing platform language in support of a constitutional amendment to ban abortion, appointing pro-life judges, and opposing the use of federal funds to pay for abortions. Democrats, on the other hand, adopted a clear pro-choice statement for the first time in 1980. The partisan divide and increased salience of abortion, beginning in the 1980s, remains a popular explanation for the pro-Democratic gender gap.[36]

It is certainly true that in the 1980s and 1990s, Democrats became the party associated with feminism, while Republicans came to be understood as the party of the "family values" opposition. Feminist activists increasingly concentrated their advocacy within the Democratic party, while high-profile Republican women publicly exited the party in protest of the GOP's views on women's rights. Reagan's traditional views of gender roles and patronizing (to many) appeals to women further distanced the party from the cause of women's rights. These patterns continued after Reagan left office; his successor, George H.W. Bush, twice vetoed the Family and Medical Leave Act (FMLA), which was then signed into law when Democrat Bill Clinton became president in 1993. The association of the Republican party with activists such as Phyllis Schlafly and Rush Limbaugh (who coined the term "feminazi") continued this pattern.[37]

The expectation that party differences on women's rights issues explain the gender gap remains popular among the public, politicians, and many observers. Yet as early as 1982 scholars raised serious doubts about such a relationship. Women and men were equally likely to support the ERA, and attitudes toward the amendment had similar impact on the vote choice of both sexes in 1980. Similarly, while more women than men identify or feel "close to" feminists, those attitudes were only weakly associated with vote choice and had similar effects on men. The impact of abortion attitudes on vote choice varied, but in this period were either stronger for men or similar for women and men.[38] Nonetheless, the idea that women were particularly motivated by women's issues remained a consistent theme in press coverage, activist claims, and the strategies of the candidates themselves in the 1980s and 1990s and beyond.

Use of force. Commentators also attributed the new gender gap to women's greater resistance to the use of force both internationally and domestically. As we have seen, the expectation that women are more opposed to war and violence has been a repeated assumption about women voters since before suffrage. Men continued to be viewed as more aggressive, while women's predisposition to care and roles as mothers were understood to make them more sensitive to the costs of conflict. These stereotypes are supported by modern public opinion research: Gender gaps on national defense, foreign policy, and the use of force are among the largest and most consistent sex differences in policy attitudes.[39]

While both parties have been responsible for military actions around the world and domestic conflicts at home, national defense and a strong military, as well as crime, have long been issues "owned" by the GOP. Nixon and Reagan, in particular, were distinguished by an emphasis on "law and order" domestically and a willingness to take a hard line internationally, especially with the Soviet Union. Many speculated at the time that concerns about the possibility of war explained some of women's lesser enthusiasm for Reagan and for the

Republican party. The empirical support for this explanation is mixed, however; attitudes about military spending, the USSR, and the first Gulf War (1991) have inconsistent effects on vote choice among women and men in these elections.[40]

Socioeconomic status, social welfare, and civil rights. A fairly strong consensus among scholars holds that gender differences in social welfare attitudes (and priority) help explain the partisan gender gap in which women were more likely (and men are less likely) to support the party (Democrats) which advocates for social welfare programs and weight social welfare issues more heavily in their political decision-making.[41] Women have been consistently more supportive than men of social welfare programs intended to address the needs of the poor, elderly, disabled, and racial and ethnic minorities.[42] The social welfare state was particularly salient and increasingly polarized in the 1980s. The conservative revolution that Reagan's presidency represented was a direct assault on an active government, including economic regulation, social welfare programs, and environmental controls. Social welfare has been a partisan issue since the New Deal of the 1930s and the Great Society programs of the 1960s, but the Reagan years both heightened and drew attention to partisan cleavages on this issue, likely making it more relevant to political choice.

While women made economic gains in the 1980s and 1990s, the rising rates of divorce and female-headed households, as well as the pay gap, meant that many women were both economically independent and economically vulnerable in this period. As we discuss in Chapter 3, scholars have argued that the increasing independence of women permitted them to identify, express, and act on their own gendered values and preferences (the autonomy hypothesis), explaining this gap in social welfare attitudes with a combination of resource inequality (women's changing access to work) and distinctive gender (unique female perspective). Similarly, women's tendency to be compassionate and other-oriented, an ethic of care, and the experience of motherhood (distinctive gender) potentially help explain women's support for programs which protect those most vulnerable in society.[43] Consistent with resource inequality, others have expected that the greater economic vulnerability of women creates a strong interest in social welfare safety nets and empathy for those who need them (the vulnerability hypothesis). Additionally, much of the growth in women's employment in this period was in the social welfare sector, meaning that women's employment often depended on robust government programs in health, education, and welfare (resource inequality).[44]

Social welfare attitudes might diverge and be associated with the gender gap for other reasons as well. As we discussed in Chapter 6, social welfare programs became increasingly racialized in press coverage and public discourse since the 1960s; this dynamic only expanded in the 1980s and 1990s.[45] Women consistently expressed more egalitarian views, helping to explain their greater relative support for civil rights. These views have been found to help explain the gender gap as well.[46] Here again, the electoral behavior of men was as consequential as that of women. The association of civil rights and (racialized) social welfare with the Democratic party helped move white men, particularly from the South, toward the Republican party to a greater extent than women, a significant factor in the emergence of the gender gap in the 1970s and 1980s.[47]

The behavior of men. As we have seen, the vast majority of discussions of the gender gap (in popular discourse and among scholars) during this period were framed in terms of women voters. Why did *women* tend to support Democrats? Why didn't *women* support Republicans? What were the issues and personalities that motivated *women's* votes? As we have just suggested, there is reason to expect that the behavior of men was as, or in some cases more, responsible for the gender gap than that of women. Indeed, Republicans sometimes tried to emphasize Democrats' problems with men as a way to shift away from discussion of Republicans' problems with women.[48] While the GOP was rarely able to disrupt the dominant narrative focused on women, scholars focusing on party identification confirmed that much of the partisan movement over time was among men, not women, for the reasons – social welfare, civil rights – we have identified above.[49]

CONCLUSION

Women voters in the 1980s and 1990s looked quite different from the women who first entered polling places in the 1920s and 1930s. In an historic reversal, women became more likely to turn out than men. Where there was a slight Republican advantage among women in the first decades after suffrage, women were more likely to support the Democratic presidential candidate than were men in this period.

In terms of our three historical pillars – legal order, gender order, and electoral behavior – it is the actual behavior of women in elections that makes this era distinctive. Women became distinctively more likely to vote and the modern gender gap emerged with a bang. The gender order did increasingly emphasize equality over more traditional norms and structures: Delayed (or no) marriage, fewer (or no) children, and work outside the home characterized the lives of more and more women. At the same time, however, a considerable political backlash against social change highlighted tensions between traditional and egalitarian gender norms and played a powerful role in politics of the period. Finally, the voting rights accomplishments of the 1960s (including the 1982 Voting Rights Act extension) had long-lasting effects as the active electorate, especially women voters, became increasingly racially diverse.

Both distinctive gender and resource inequality continue to inform views and analysis of women voters, but often in different ways than in previous decades. One important line of argument emphasizes how greater independence (economic and otherwise) for women permitted women's distinct values and attitudes (distinctive gender) to be articulated and expressed in politics. Another emphasized that changes in resource inequality (changes in women's employment, marriage, and motherhood) made women both sympathetic to and (potentially) dependent on a strong social welfare state. Women's greater egalitarianism – either inherent (distinctive gender) or a function of a specific economic and social role (resource inequality) – further encouraged women's greater support for social welfare and civil rights. The changing context also is key; as the major American parties moved farther apart on social welfare and civil rights issues, those differences became increasingly salient in presidential elections.

The gender gap was now a persistent feature in American elections, and no presidential contest was free from discussion of the impact of women voters and of that infamous gap on the parties' electoral chances. In our final empirical chapter, we examine the last two decades of the hundred years since the ratification of the Nineteenth Amendment. A defining feature of the twentieth century was the leaps and bounds in gender equality experienced in the United States and around the world. Much has changed for women in a century and we might expect that growing equality would make sex, gender, and women less salient in American elections. As we see in Chapter 8, such an expectation is not supported by evidence or experience in the new millennium.

Women Voters in the New Millennium

PRESIDENTIAL ELECTIONS IN THE TWENTY-FIRST CENTURY BROKE WITH history in many ways, from the Supreme Court's intervention in the 2000 vote count to Barack Obama's barrier-breaking nomination and victory to the unprecedented events of the 2016 campaign. From "W is for Women" to the first major party nomination of a woman candidate for president, women remained front and center in presidential election discourse and debate nearly 100 years after the ratification of the Nineteenth Amendment.

The defining feature of American politics in the first decades of the new millennium was a ramping up of partisan conflict and polarization in government, as well as within the American electorate. Scholarship confirms what many Americans decry: Party elites in Washington increasingly diverged in their policy preferences and prescriptions, and increasingly were unable or unwilling to compromise or even conduct legislative business. Control of the two chambers of Congress shifted frequently, compared to the longer patterns of stability that characterized early decades. Office holders, citizens, journalists, and scholars lamented the apparent inability of government to function in a state of extreme partisan paralysis.[1] By the end of this period, even facts had become partisan, as Republicans and Democrats disagreed sharply about what was, and was not, a problem or reality, as well as on policy solutions.

Women, gender, and women's issues were not exempt from this sharpening partisan divide. The parties disagreed as to whether or not women's equality remained a problem: In the wake of the 2016 election, nearly 70% of Democrats agreed that more work is needed to bring about gender equality compared to just 26% of Republicans. In comparison, the gap between women and men on this item was only 13 points; in this era, women's equality was not a gender divide, but a partisan one.[2] Republican and Democratic party elites diverged on women's rights policies such as equal pay and abortion rights since at least 1980. Since at least the early 1990s, surveys found Republicans to be less supportive of women in non-traditional roles than Democrats.[3] The salience of and polarization around these issues only increased in the twenty-first century. In 2016, scholars found, for the first time, that sexism predicted presidential vote choice (for Trump, against Clinton).[4]

In this final historical chapter, we again review the (recent) electoral context in which women cast their ballots over the five presidential elections from 2000 to 2016. We take stock of the conditions of women's lives and the continuing interplay of gender and politics. We examine how and why women voted in the tumultuous elections of the 2000s and 2010s. On the whole, women continued to be more likely to turn out and more likely to vote Democratic than men regardless of most other group identities. Despite those shared tendencies, women's voting behavior was varied and diverse. In the 2016 presidential election, a majority of white women cast their ballots for Donald Trump, while overwhelming majorities of women who were black, Hispanic, and members of other racial minority groups supported Hillary Clinton.

AMERICAN ELECTORAL POLITICS, 2000–2016

Since the earliest voting studies (see Chapter 5), scholars have observed that party identification is closely related to other forms of identity, such as race, class, and religion. The connections between such social identities and partisanship strengthened dramatically in the early twenty-first century, creating a strong and emotional attachment to party among many Americans. Negative partisanship – party identification driven less by support of one's own party than by opposition to the other – grew considerably. By the end of this period, citizens reported holding strongly negative views about the other party, experiencing high levels of fear, anger, and frustration with opposition identifiers, and preferring not to have other-party partisans as neighbors or potential spouses for their children. The rise of social media and of the partisan press helped encourage personal identification with in-party victory, as well as a strong sense that the out-party was an enemy.[5]

The presidential elections of the 2000s and 2010s took place within this context of heightened partisanship. Controversy over the first presidential election of the twenty-first century did little to reduce partisan rancor. The

Democratic nominee, Vice President Al Gore, sought to both capitalize on the successes of the Clinton administration while distancing himself from the excesses of Clinton himself. The Republican nomination was nearly a lock for Texas Governor and presidential heir George W. Bush, who ran as a "compassionate conservative" and a results-oriented governor who could reach across the partisan aisle. A disputed outcome in Florida required the intervention of the Supreme Court and delayed the selection of the president-elect for more than a month. Despite his narrow Electoral College victory (and losing the popular vote), Bush governed as a partisan, prioritizing income tax cuts and other conservative objectives. The 9/11 terrorist attacks less than a year into his administration transformed American politics, placing terrorism and homeland security at the top of the political agenda.[6]

In 2004, Democrats nominated Senator John Kerry of Massachusetts to challenge Bush. Given the prominence of the War on Terror and increasingly unpopular conflicts in Iran and Afghanistan, Kerry emphasized his status as a veteran of the Vietnam War and his years on the Senate Foreign Relations Committee. Kerry's record of military service was attacked by the 527 group Swift Boat Vets and POWs for Truth, highlighting the growing impact of organizations, ostensibly independent of candidates and parties, on the content and conduct of American elections. Bush defended his record, and his campaign sought to frame Kerry as both too liberal and a flip-flopper. The state of the economy, health care, and moral values were prominent themes in the election of 2004.[7]

While Bush was constitutionally prohibited from running for a third term as president, the election of 2008 was largely a referendum on his presidency, particularly the on-going War on Terror as well as the global financial crisis of 2007 and 2008, the worst economic downturn since the Great Depression. After a drawn-out Democratic nomination contest with Hillary Clinton, Barack Obama became the first African American major party nominee in American history. Arizona Senator John McCain, a Vietnam War POW and a repeat presidential hopeful, wrested the Republican nomination from a crowded Republican field. His running mate, relatively unknown Alaska governor Sarah Palin – only the second female vice presidential nominee in US history – was a media sensation. Her folksy style helped the ticket reach out to the GOP's socially conservative base. Yet war and the economy dominated the election, and an incumbent party faced long odds during an unpopular conflict and a sharp economic slump. Obama's rhetoric of change resonated, and Americans elected the first African American president in history.[8]

In 2012, Republicans nominated businessman and former Massachusetts governor Mitt Romney to challenge incumbent Obama. The political agenda remained largely focused on the state of the economy and recovery, as well as the controversial Affordable Care Act (2010), labeled Obamacare by opponents. In the wake of Obama's 2008 election, frustrated conservatives organized a grassroots movement known as the Tea Party, focused on opposition to taxes, national debt, and government regulation, particularly of health care. Aided by conservative media and donors, the Tea Party promoted their understanding of Constitutional principles and expressed alarm at social and political change in the United States. Drawing largely from those already identifying as Republicans, Tea Party supporters were distinguished by their strongly conservative views on social issues (such as abortion) and on race and immigration. By the 2010 midterms, Tea Party-associated and supported candidates were upending Republican primary races and winning congressional seats. By 2012, Tea Party organization was waning but still active, and many politicians, most notably Romney running mate, Rep. Paul Ryan (R, WI), were linked to the Tea Party movement. Most importantly, the Tea Party movement pushed the Republican party even farther to the right. In Congress in particular, the Tea Party's Freedom Caucus solidified all-or-nothing opposition to President Obama as the Republican party's central strategy.[9]

The last presidential election contest before the centennial of women's suffrage was without precedent in American history. Democrats selected former First Lady, Senator, and Secretary of State Hillary Clinton as the first woman standard bearer for a major American party. On the Republican side, the candidacy of businessman and reality television star Donald Trump attracted massive press attention in a crowded field of contenders. Trump promised to "Make America Great Again" by ending Obamacare, restricting immigration, and ripping up trade deals. Violating American election norms, Trump insulted everyone from his primary and general election opponents to POWs, other Republicans, the press, prominent political leaders, celebrities, and a range of organizations and policies. Trump's populist rhetoric featured patriotism, ethnocentrism, racism, and sexism. Despite initial opposition from many Republican leaders, Trump skillfully attracted news coverage and spoke to widespread fears of social (particularly racial and gender) change, all of which helped him secure the Republican nomination. FBI Director James Comey's revelations about a continuing investigation of Clinton's private e-mail server as Secretary of State late in the general election campaign, and ongoing accusations of Russian interference with the election, cast a long shadow over the 2016 outcome. Nonetheless, Donald Trump was elected president, becoming the first person without military or political experience to assume the office in more than 100 years.[10]

Bookended by the contentious 2000 presidential election outcome and the 2016 victory of Donald Trump, the first elections of the twenty-first century offered drama and disruption. Set against a backdrop of extreme partisan conflict and polarization, elections, and especially presidential elections, became all-or-nothing contests between increasingly divergent partisan coalitions.

AMERICAN WOMEN IN THE NEW MILLENNIUM

Women's Lives

In the first decades of the twenty-first century, women's lives continued to evolve in ways that would be consequential for their politics. Women advanced considerably in terms of educational attainment in the new millennium. By the mid-1990s, the percentage of women aged 25 to 29 with college degrees had exceeded that of men. By 2016, a nearly equal percentage of women and men (more than 30%), regardless of age, had earned a bachelor's degree (see Figure 8.1).[11]

Women's family lives evolved as well. Marriages increasingly occurred later or not at all. The median age for first marriage rose to 27 for women and 29 men for men by 2012; in 1960, those figures were 20 and 23. Cohabitation outside of marriage was increasingly common; about a quarter of adults aged 25 to 34 lived with a partner by the second decade of the twenty-first century.[12]

Families changed in other ways as well. In 1960, nearly three-quarters of children were born into traditional two-parent, first-marriage homes. By 2014, fewer than half were, as children were increasingly born into second marriages (15%), to cohabitating parents (7%), or to single parents (26%), the vast majority of whom were women. Mothers were increasingly the prime breadwinners, not only in single-parent households, but in households with two parents as well. While all racial and ethnic groups experienced similar patterns, these trends

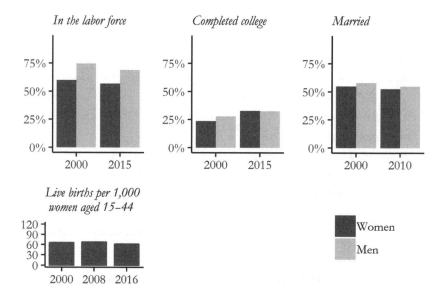

Figure 8.1 Women close the gap in college completion and narrow the gap in labor force participation

were particularly pronounced for black women, who were increasingly likely to be single or single mothers.[13] Women continued to face challenges in balancing work and family, both the demands at home and the costs of motherhood at work, making this tension a perennial campaign topic.[14]

Working outside the home had become the norm for virtually all women. Gender differences in pay continued to narrow, but did not disappear: The earnings ratio between women and men was 64% in 1990 compared to 82% in 2016. Gender segregation in employment persisted, with school teacher, nurse, and secretary the most common occupations for women, compared to truck driver, manager, and retail front-line supervisor for men. Women remained dramatically underrepresented in the top ranks of business, law, and politics.[15]

Overall, women look more similar to men in the 2000s and 2010s, in terms of college completion and labor force participation, than in any previous era. Education and employment were factors that shaped voting behavior in earlier periods, but, despite growing similarity in terms of educational attainment, labor force participation, and household roles, politicians and journalists continued to treat women as voters with distinctive political preferences.

Women and Politics

Candidates and the press viewed women – at least some kinds of women – as a key electoral constituency in the first presidential elections of the twenty-first century. In 2000, Republican standard bearer George W. Bush's claims of "compassionate conservatism" were widely viewed as directed particularly at women voters alienated by conservative extremism. Claiming "W is for Women," the Bush campaign focused on education policy as a way to appeal to women, continuing the long tradition of framing women as primarily mothers committed to nurturing young children. Other themes meant to appeal to women included personal morality and work-family balance.[16]

Democratic nominee Al Gore memorably displayed his commitment to his marriage with a "sustained" kiss with wife Tipper at the Democratic National Convention, visibly distancing himself from Clinton's infidelities. In his convention speech, Gore spoke about how his own mother worked two jobs to support her family, conjuring the "waitress mom" voter stereotype (low-pay, low-education, low-status employment, hard-working mom) which had emerged in the 1998 midterms:

> I've shaken hands in diners and coffee shops all across this country. And some-times when I see a waitress working hard and thanking someone for a tip, I see the face of my mother. And I know, for that waitress carrying trays or a construc-tion worker in the winter cold, I will never agree to raise the retirement age to 70 or threaten the promise of Social Security.[17]

Unlike "soccer moms" who were generally understood as white and relatively privileged, the "waitress mom" frame included low-income and minority women as a target of political appeals and a source of electoral power. While Bush highlighted education, Gore focused on health care, and specifically women's health care, in his appeals to women voters, as well as women-owned businesses, work-family balance, and child safety (e.g., the V-chip, technology designed to restrict children's access to inappropriate television content). Both candidates emphasized the impact on women and families when talking about bread-and-butter campaign issues like jobs and taxes as well.[18]

In the wake of the 9/11 terrorist attacks, "security moms" were the new frame du jour for women voters in 2004. Both candidates sought to assure women voters that they would keep them and their families safe, with Bush pointing to his post-attack leadership and successes, and Kerry critiquing the Republican administration's approach and emphasizing his own foreign policy expertise. Like Gore in 2000, Kerry often framed his rhetoric about the economy in terms of the challenges faced by mothers and families. While ultimately the 2004 gender gap was fairly unremarkable in historic context, many in the press attributed Bush's re-election in part to his success in appealing to the fears of "security moms." Research, however, suggests that women who were parents were no more worried about another terrorist attack than were women who were not parents and married women with children were as likely to vote for Bush as married women without children, casting doubt on the political distinctiveness of security "moms" as commonly framed in the press.[19]

"NASCAR dads" also were highlighted as a political constituency in 2004. First identified in the 2002 midterms, NASCAR dads were described as "small town middle-aged white men, typically from the South, who consider themselves Democrats but lean Republican when it comes to the president."[20] In the same way that political "moms" (soccer, waitress, and otherwise) are defined in ways that reify traditional class, gender, and racial stereotypes, the NASCAR dad was typically framed in terms of masculinity, class, race, patriotism, location, and religion. Unlike "moms," their political interests were rarely conceptualized in terms of fatherhood per se. Analysis of 2004 voting behavior suggested that while mothers as a whole differed from non-mothers on some issues such as social welfare, there were few political distinctions between fathers and non-fathers in that election year.[21]

Women and gender were at the forefront of presidential politics as the historic 2008 Democratic nomination contest came down to a contest between a white woman and a black man. Hillary Clinton initially emphasized her experience and expertise (in contrast to Obama's shorter time on the national stage) more than her gender, but media coverage of the contest highlighted both gender and race. Clinton herself increasingly embraced her ground-breaking candidacy, most famously in a concession speech which highlighted the "18 million cracks" her candidacy made in the "highest, hardest glass ceiling."[22]

Gender continued to be front and center in the 2008 general election when John McCain selected Alaska governor Sarah Palin as his vice presidential running mate. The unconventional choice of Palin helped McCain draw attention away from Obama's historic candidacy and skilled rhetorical style, and her strong social conservative bona fides helped reassure the GOP base about the Republican ticket. The McCain campaign and observers also framed the selection of Palin as an attempt to attract women voters; both Palin and McCain overtly appealed to disaffected Democrats and Republicans angry over the treatment of Clinton in the Democratic primary. Palin often presented herself in gendered terms, from describing herself a "hockey mom" to highlighting her family at campaign events. Her candidacy led to broad discussions of motherhood and work-family balance. Republicans defended the capacity of a woman to govern and parent, despite their record of favoring traditional gender roles. Palin also heightened attention to abortion, as her son with Down Syndrome was presented by the campaign and candidate as evidence of her strong commitment to the pro-life cause.

Press coverage of Palin was widely criticized as sexist and negative. Palin's personal style and her ability to care for her children, especially her four-month-old special needs son, while carrying out her duties drew widespread comment. Palin embodied a number of gendered stereotypes that are rarely found in presidential politics: frontier woman, hockey mom, and beauty queen, among others. Yet despite a widely praised RNC speech and an initial bump in the polls, there is little evidence that Palin helped attract women voters to the Republican ticket. Research has consistently shown women are not particularly likely to vote for women candidates, all else equal, and vice presidential choices are rarely determinative.[23] Anecdotal evidence suggests Palin was appealing to many women voters, but largely conservative and pro-life women unlikely to vote for the Democratic ticket in any case.[24]

In what had become standard operating procedure for presidential campaigns, both Obama and McCain were described as making efforts to appeal particularly to women voters. Both candidates continued to focus on "security moms," emphasizing their ability to end the unpopular war in the Middle East and keep Americans safe at home. Obama was viewed as having to assure women voters of his commitment to women after the contentious primary contest with Hillary Clinton. Both Michelle Obama and Hillary Clinton were frequent surrogates for the Obama campaign. Michelle Obama emphasized work-family balance and her own role as a working mother, while Clinton was viewed as a counter to Sarah Palin's claims as a pioneering woman in politics.[25]

Doubling down on gendered appeals in 2012, Democrats decried a "Republican war on women," highlighting the party's opposition to abortion and contraceptive coverage, as well as the widely reported controversial statements of several prominent Republicans. In Missouri, Republican Senate candidate Todd Akin defended his opposition to abortion even in cases of rape by explaining, "If it's a legitimate rape, the female body has ways to try to shut that whole thing down." Later in the Fall, Indiana Republican Senate candidate Richard Mourdock also defended his strong pro-life position by claiming "even if life begins in that horrible situation of rape, that is something God intended to happen." The Obama campaign countered these contentious claims by emphasizing his support for abortion rights, contraceptive access, and women's health.[26]

Motherhood remained central to the way women voters were framed by the press and appealed to by the campaigns. Both potential First Ladies were highly visible surrogates in 2012. Michelle Obama described herself as "Mom-in-Chief" while Ann Romney and her husband highlighted her role and work as the mother of five sons. Even in the economic messages most central to both campaigns, women voters were again moms; in this case, "waitress moms" and "Wal-Mart moms," lower-income women concerned with supporting their families. Incumbent Obama framed policy debates such as contraception, health care, and pay equity as fundamentally economic issues. Republican nominee and former Massachusetts governor Mitt Romney was mildly rebuked for using the phrase "binders full of women" to describe his efforts to recruit women to high-level government positions. Like Obama, Romney emphasized how his leadership would provide a better economic future for women in particular.[27]

The 2016 presidential election was widely expected to be a milestone for women in American politics. The nomination of Hillary Clinton – the first woman to run for president at the top of a major American party ticket – was indeed ceiling-shattering and historic. Yet, Clinton's presidential nomination was only one of the many exceptional aspects of the 2016 presidential election, and the campaign highlighted sex and gender in ways few could have predicted.

The candidacy of Donald Trump was unprecedented in many ways, including his use of misogynistic rhetoric, his tendency to direct sexist insults at opponents and reporters, and multiple accusations of sexual misconduct and assault. During the Republican primaries, Trump insinuated that Fox News' Megyn Kelly was an erratic debate moderator because of her menstrual cycle. He used a primary debate to assure the American people: "He [Marco Rubio] referred to my hands, if they are small, something else must be small. I guarantee you there is no problem. I guarantee." Trump dismissed Republican contender Carly Fiorina in an interview, saying "Look at that face! Would anyone vote for that? Can you imagine that, the face of our next president?" Trump's behavior toward women during the primaries drew widespread condemnation, but also revealed the apparent willingness of many Republican primary voters to nonetheless select Trump to represent their party.[28]

Facing the first female major party nominee in American history in the general election, Trump continued to use implicitly as well as explicitly sexist language, language which often harkened back to the arguments against women's suffrage (Chapter 2). Echoing the long-standing assumption that women are unfit for political leadership, Trump said of Clinton, "Well, I just don't think she has a presidential look, and you need a presidential look." He further referenced traditional doubts about the capacity of women to meet the physical demands of politics, particularly in national defense, when he claimed that Clinton was "low energy" and lacked "the mental and physical stamina" to confront America's enemies. Trump criticized Clinton's attractiveness, saying "The other day I'm standing at my podium and she walks in front of me ... and when she walked in front of me, believe me, I was not impressed." The rhetoric as well as the T-shirts, buttons, and bumper stickers at Trump campaign events featured overtly sexist slogans and appeals. In the final presidential debate, Trump interrupted Clinton's response to a question about debt and entitlements to dismiss her as "such a nasty woman."[29]

In October a video from a 2005 *Access Hollywood* interview of Trump by host Billy Bush surfaced in which Trump boasted about grabbing, kissing, and attempting to have sex with married women, all of which he claimed he had license to do because he was famous. The tapes added to Trump's pre-election record of insulting women as "disgusting," a "fat pig," or a "dog." The tape and Trump's failure to address these issues satisfactorily set off a storm of controversy, including public critiques from fellow Republicans. By Election Day, more than ten women had accused Donald Trump of sexual misconduct and assault. Trump continued to assure voters, "Nobody has more respect for women than I do. Nobody."[30]

For her part, Clinton embraced her gender identity and status as a pathbreaker in 2016 to a greater extent than she had in her past campaigns. After repeatedly claiming she was not running as a woman in 2008, Clinton took a different tack in 2016: "I'm asking for people to vote for me on the merits," Clinton noted early in the campaign, "I think one of the merits is I am a woman." Clinton made her positions on issues of particular relevance to women, such as paid leave, equal pay, and childcare, central to her policy agenda. Sexist media coverage – ranging from calls for Clinton to smile more, descriptions of her speech as shrill, and questions about her likability – kept attention on how gender operates in politics. Clinton often treated gendered criticism as a badge of honor, such as when she reacted to Trump's disparaging comment that she was playing the "woman's card," by declaring, "If fighting for women's health care and paid family leave and equal pay is playing the woman card, then deal me in!"[31]

OBSERVING WOMEN VOTERS

While the use of exit polls and commercial polling near elections was standard practice by 2000, the practice of polling confronted a number of challenges after the turn of the century. The growing use of cellphones and caller identification made it difficult to reach potential voters before elections. Mistrust of polls and the media also reduced response rates, even for exit polls. The notorious election night exit poll mistake that led the television networks to make a preliminary call for 2000 Democratic presidential candidate Al Gore in Florida led to major changes in the administration of exit polls. Confronted with more absentee and early voting and declining in-person response rates, the major networks hired a new vendor and rebranded the cooperative exit poll effort as the National Exit Pool. We use the earlier Voter News Service (VNS) exit polls for 2000 and NEP data for 2004 to 2012.[32]

Long-standing academic polls had to adjust to the new reality as well. Faced with increasing costs of administering face-to-face surveys, the American National Election Studies discontinued surveys during midterm elections after 2002. A group of universities teamed with what is now known as YouGov to field the Cooperative Congressional Election Study (CCES) in the 2006 midterms, exploiting new web-based strategies to reach voters. With support from the National Science Foundation, the CCES offers a much larger sample of voters than the ANES and conducts these surveys for both presidential and off-year elections, making it possible to study smaller subgroups and obtain better estimates for state-level measures of vote choice. Our discussion of the 2016 election draws on research that exploits the CCES and we use those data to validate exit poll results by race and to estimate some state-level gender gaps in 2016.[33]

Observing women voters remains a challenge, 100 years after women entered polling places. New approaches to polling the public did not, and likely cannot, address all of the modern challenges to survey research. The failure of pre-election polls and exit polls to capture the size of the Trump victory in 2016 led to more scrutiny of the way polls are conducted and how raw polling data are weighted to accurately capture the population of potential or actual voters. One particularly notable problem was the over-representation of college-educated voters and under-representation of working-class voters in exit poll samples. This distorted both the perceived composition of the Democratic base and inflated the likely vote for Hillary Clinton.[34] Nonetheless, well-designed and implemented public opinion polls remain our best resource for understanding American voters.

Turnout

Nearly 100 years after the ratification of the Nineteenth Amendment, women were consistently more likely to cast ballots than men (see Figure 8.2). The turnout gender gap that emerged in 1980 had become the norm. By 2016, women's turnout was consistently at least 3 percentage points higher than men's. While this percentage difference is not large, the greater numbers of age-eligible women in the electorate meant that 127 million women voted in 2016 compared to 118 million men.[35]

Women Are Not a Voting Bloc

Gender was not the only salient identity in the new millennium, not by a long shot. Other forms of identity and experience became only more closely tied to political behavior in the twenty-first century. As in previous chapters, we rely on logistic regression to determine the impact of various factors on both turnout and vote choice for women and men. The relationships we report in the figures and our discussion below is informed by that analysis; that is, we highlight and describe the effects of demographic factors that are persistent when we introduce statistical controls.

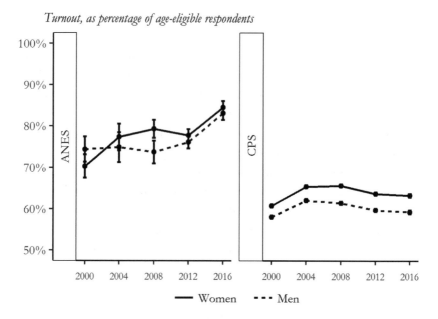

Turnout, as percentage of age-eligible respondents

Figure 8.2 Women consistently more likely to turn out than men, 2000–16

Race and ethnicity. Women are more likely to turn out to vote than men across all racial and ethnic categories across the five elections from 2000 to 2016 (see Figure 8.3). The difference is distinctively large in the African American community. Indeed, the turnout of African American women in the new millennium was truly historic. Just 40-plus years after the passage of the 1965 Voting Rights Act, black women turned out to vote at rates that were not only higher than black men, but also higher than (non-Hispanic) white men. Only (non-Hispanic) white women turned out at slightly higher rates than black women across these five elections. Political scientists for decades have recognized that racial consciousness plays a central role in mobilizing people of color into politics beyond what socio-economic status disadvantages might predict. Political scientist Lisa Nikol Nealy, for example, argues that strong religiosity and a progressive religious tradition helped enhance the electoral participation of African American women in particular.[36] Similarly, political scientist Christina A. Bejarano finds that Latinas were more likely to be involved in community affairs and increasingly responsible for families, both of which may have propelled their electoral engagement.[37]

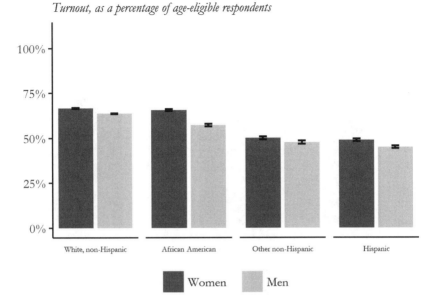

Turnout, as a percentage of age-eligible respondents

Figure 8.3 African American women more likely to turn out to vote than (non-Hispanic) white men (CPS), 2000–16

The candidacy of Barack Obama also played a key role. African American women turned out at the highest rate of *any* group in 2008 and 2012, when Obama was on the presidential ballot. As a result, from 2000 to 2012, the turnout of African American women jumped from 60% to 71%. Black men's turnout increased as well (from 53% to 62%) but not as dramatically.

Turnout gender gaps among people of color have consequences for the active electorate as a whole: Almost 75% of the growth in the number of eligible women voters since 2000 can be attributed to women of color. As the proportion of the electorate which identifies as white declines (from 86% in 2000 to 81% in 2016), and if these patterns persist, we would expect black and Hispanic voters to help drive the turnout gender gap upward. That black women in particular achieved such high turnout in a period in which voting rights were being rolled back at the state and federal level represents a significant achievement.[38]

Starting in 1996, the CPS survey includes questions about the birthplace of both respondents and their parents, so it is possible to categorize people as first-, second-, and third-generation or later immigrants during the presidential

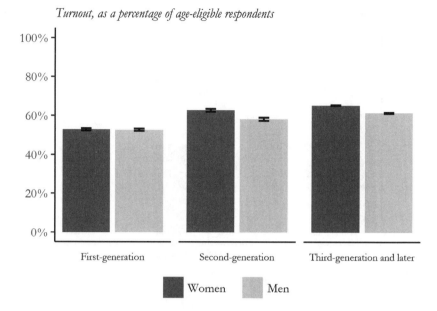

Turnout, as a percentage of age-eligible respondents

Figure 8.4 The turnout gender gap exists among all but first-generation immigrants (CPS), 2000–16

elections from 2000 to 2016. Consistent with previous research, the likelihood of turnout increased across generations, a pattern that holds for both women and men.[39] Interestingly, we find in Figure 8.4 that the turnout gap spans all of these categories, except the most recent immigrants.

Age. The turnout gender gap can be found among all but the oldest voters (see Figure 8.5). The pre-Nineteenth Amendment generation has now passed from the electorate, removing the cohort that has been characterized by the largest turnout gender gap in favor of men since 1920. Yet, men continued to slightly outpace women at the polls among the oldest cohort (now, those born before 1941). We have been attributing the relatively lower turnout of older women largely to socialization; especially in earlier decades, older women were socialized at a time when women's participation in politics was discouraged and political role models were few. Such dynamics may still be at work here, but we would expect such effects to be less potent across the twentieth and into the twenty-first century.

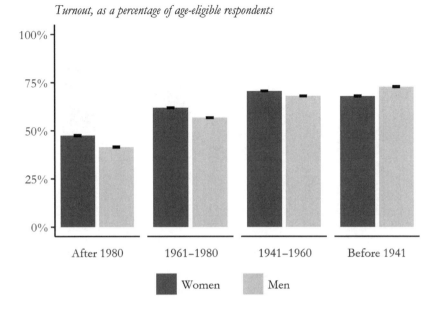

Turnout, as a percentage of age-eligible respondents

Figure 8.5 Women more likely to turn out than men across most age cohorts (CPS), 2000–16

Other gendered dynamics may help explain this pattern. Women on average live longer than men, so we can expect that in the oldest cohort, men are younger, on average, than women. The demobilizing effects of age grow sharply as one moves from their 70s to the 90s, which might explain the lower rate of turnout among the oldest cohort of women. We know that marriage is associated with higher turnout for both women and men (see Figure 8.8); due to women living longer, older women are also more likely to be without a spouse in the home to facilitate turnout. Finally, while younger women of this period are better educated than men, among older women, we still observe a lower rate of educational attainment. Education is, of course, a key predictor of turnout.[40]

There was a relatively large turnout gender gap among younger voters, suggesting women integrated into politics earlier – in terms of cohort – than men in this period, and perhaps others. In previous decades, we consistently observed the greatest (relative) turnout among the youngest women: Younger voters had the smallest turnout gender gaps when men were significantly more

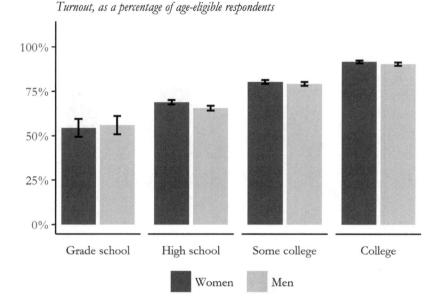

Turnout, as a percentage of age-eligible respondents

Figure 8.6 Turnout gender gaps generally consistent across educational groups (ANES), 2000–16

likely to turn out, and the largest turnout gender gaps when women were more likely to turn out than men.

Education. Where we once observed differences in the turnout gender gap across educational attainment groups, such differences have narrowed considerably by the twenty-first century (see Figure 8.6). At every level, except those with the least education (where there is no difference), women are more likely to turn out than men. We also can see the effects of the changing patterns of education attainment across these ten decades: The large confidence intervals around the turnout rates for the least educated voters reflect that fact that only 5% of men and women failed to complete high school in the 2000s and 2010s, compared to 30% as late as the 1950s. Not only did far more Americans enter college, but women were now more likely to complete a college degree than men: By 2014, 37% of women aged 25–34 had earned a bachelor's degree compared to only 29% of men of the same age.[41]

The most important takeaway from Figure 8.6 is that education continued to have a strong impact on voter turnout, far greater than sex. A woman with

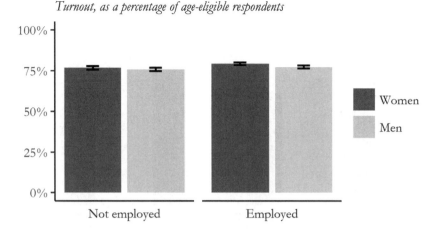

Figure 8.7 Employment has no impact on male or female turnout (ANES), 2000–16

a college degree was 20 points more likely to turn out to vote than a woman who did not finish high school, while the turnout gender gap overall is less than 5 percentage points. In terms of turnout, well-educated women looked far more like well-educated men than they did less-well-educated women. Patterns of educational attainment also help us understand the turnout gender gap: As women increasingly outpaced men in educational attainment, there were simply more women in the electorate with a high propensity to show up to vote in presidential elections.

Marriage, family, and work. Households in the new millennium looked quite different from households in the 1920s or 1950s. Women's patterns of labor force participation were becoming more similar to men's, as was their turnout. Figure 8.7 suggests that employment is not a strong predictor of voting for either women or men, and the small gender gap in turnout can be found in and out of the labor market.

As the rate of marriage declined, marriage remained a strong predictor of turning out to vote; marriage is one of a handful of demographic characteristics (along with age and education) that operate similarly on men and women and persist across the periods. The greater stability, increased social integration, expanded social networks, and opportunities for information-sharing associated with marriage continued to provide both women and men with important resources for voting. For all the talk of

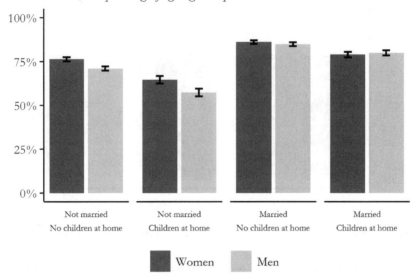

Turnout, as a percentage of age-eligible respondents

Figure 8.8 Marriage provides a turnout boost to women and especially men (ANES), 2000–16

the marriage gap for women in popular discourse in this period, the effect of marriage is essentially the same for women and men, as Figure 8.8 demonstrates. While we observe gender gaps in turnout across all groups, marriage has a substantially larger impact on the propensity to vote, regardless of sex.

Children continued to be associated with depressed turnout, again for both women and men, and especially for those who were unmarried. As with marriage, the effects of parenthood on turnout clearly exceed any small impact of gender on turnout: A married women without children, for example, was more than twenty points more likely to vote than a single father. While the effects of marriage and children remain fairly stable, the distribution of those experiences in the electorate is not. By the twenty-first century, women were more likely to be unmarried (48%) than men (43%) and more likely to have a child at home (36% of women compared to 30% of men), both of which were associated with lower turnout.[42] That women managed to still exceed men in turnout on the whole and among most subgroups is thus a puzzle and one we address below.

Politics and place. The distinctiveness of the South and of Southern women continues to fade. In the first decades of the twenty-first century, turnout remains lower in the South than in other regions but to a far smaller extent than even in the 1980s and 1990s (see Figure 8.9). The turnout gender gap in favor of men had been largest and taken the longest to close in the South. In the 2000s and 2010s, Southern women for the first time exceed Southern men in turnout and to the same extent as women in other regions. Given that the South is the most racially diverse region (34% of Southerners were non-white compared to just 22% in the rest of the country), the persistently high turnout of African American women in particular could go a long way toward explaining how the turnout gap closed and reversed in the South.

Explaining Women's Turnout

Despite incredible gains, women continued to lag in their access to some (but certainly not all) politically relevant resources like high-status occupations, employment, and marriage.[43] Standard models of turnout that focus on resources in particular would predict women to continue to lag behind men in turning out to vote in presidential elections in the twenty-first century. Another important predictor of voter turnout is being encouraged to vote by a friend, candidate, or party, but women were less likely to report being encouraged to vote in these elections.[44] Despite persistent resource and mobilization inequalities, women have exceeded men in casting ballots since the early 1980s. Why?

Gender norms. Many of the same developments that help explain how women came to surpass men in turning out to vote since the early 1980s remained relevant, particularly changing gender roles that no longer discourage women from exercising their right to vote. This is not to say that norms deterring women from politics were entirely a thing of the past. Women continued to lag behind men in terms of running for and holding office and other forms of political engagement, much of which can be explained by gender socialization.[45] More broadly, women continued to express less interest in politics than did men, suggesting (perhaps) that women continued to be less socialized to political engagement than men. In distinctive gender terms, however, these persistent traditional gender norms did not appear to hamper women at the ballot box, or other factors overcame whatever barriers those norms still offered.

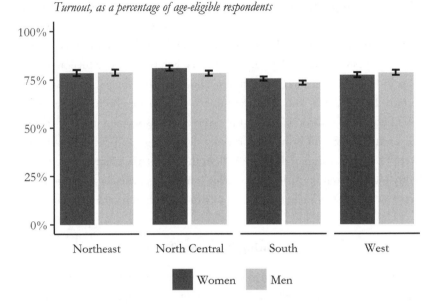

Turnout, as a percentage of age-eligible respondents

Figure 8.9 South continues to lose distinctiveness with regards to gender and turnout (ANES), 2000–16

Education. Educational attainment is consistently one of the strongest predictors of voter turnout, exceeding other standard SES measures like income and employment. While women still lag in the latter in the twenty-first century, women now meet or exceed men in the acquisition of education. As Figure 8.6 shows, educational attainment was positively associated with turnout for both women and men. As women have increasingly met or exceeded men in college attendance and college completion, there were simply more women in the highest educational categories, women who were the most likely to turn out. Here we see a clear resource inequality dynamic: As women became more like men in terms of a key (perhaps even *the* key) resource for voting – education – their turnout met and surpassed men's.[46] Not only have women achieved higher levels of education, but as we saw above, the impact of education appeared to be stronger for women than men in this period, so that the growing numbers of well-educated women likely contributed to the overall turnout gender gap.

Role models. Scholars also have emphasized the impact of the increasing number of visible female role models in politics. Figures 8.10 and 8.11

Figure 8.10 Increasing numbers of women run for and serve in the US Senate (CAWP), 1970–2016

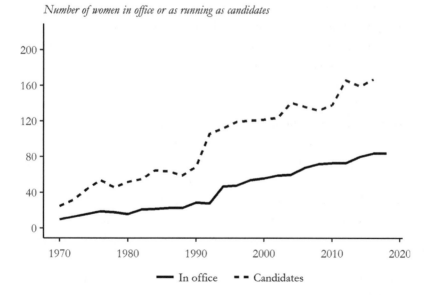

Figure 8.11 Increasing numbers of women run for and serve in the US House of Representatives (CAWP), 1970–2016

trace the growth of women candidates and officeholders in both the House and Senate, using data published by the Center for American Women and Politics.[47] On top of the growth in representation in Congress, women were particularly visible on the national stage in the 2000s and 2010s: In 2007, Nancy Pelosi (D, CA) became the first female Speaker of the House. Hillary Clinton ran a strong campaign for the Democratic presidential nomination in 2008. Sarah Palin became the first woman vice president on a Republican ticket that same year. And of course, in 2016 Clinton secured the Democratic nomination and became the first woman to run for president under a major party banner. The presence of female politicians is associated with women becoming more interested in, attentive to, and engaged in politics. These effects are most consistent among younger women and adolescent girls, suggesting that as women are increasingly socialized into a world where women politicians are visible, women's turnout may continue to exceed that of men.[48]

VOTE CHOICE

The partisan gender gap was fully established and persistently characterized presidential elections in the new millennium. While the size varies, the presence of the gender gap is consistent across various data sources, with the Pew surveys consistently indicating a gender gap in excess of 10% after 2008 (see Figure 8.12). As we will see below, women in the 2000s and 2010s were more likely than men to vote Democratic in every racial category, age group, employment category, education level, and geographic region. This advantage does not translate into *majority* support for Democrats among every group, however; most notably, a majority of white women support the Republican candidate, albeit at a lower rate than white men. The presidential elections from 2000 to 2016 featured three changes to party control of the White House, a contested election decided by the Supreme Court, and the first female presidential nominee. These events hardly registered on the gendered patterns of vote choice: Elections in the 2000s and 2010s were notable for the stability and persistence of the modest Democratic advantage among women across time, space, and groups.

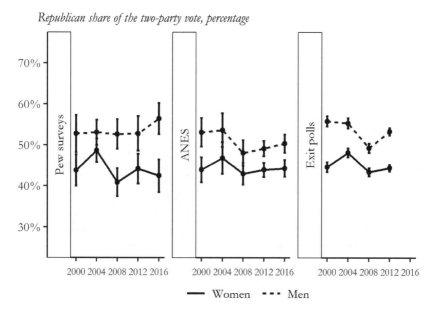

Figure 8.12 Women more likely to vote Democratic than men, 2000–16

Women Are Not a Voting Bloc

A persistent gender gap does not mean that all women voted similarly in the twenty-first century. Rather we find factors such as race, education, and family continued to shape the vote choice of women (and men) in important ways. As in previous chapters, we rely on logistic regression to determine the impact of various factors on vote choice for both women and men. While we present bivariate relationships in the figures, our discussion of the relationships below is informed by that analysis. In other words, we highlight and describe the effects of demographic factors that are persistent when we introduce statistical controls.

Race. The gender gap is impressively consistent across racial groups – roughly 7 percentage points, as we see in Figure 8.13. The far larger and more consequential differences are between racial groups. A majority of white voters – women and men – support GOP candidates across these five elections, on average, about 60% of men and 54% of women for a gender

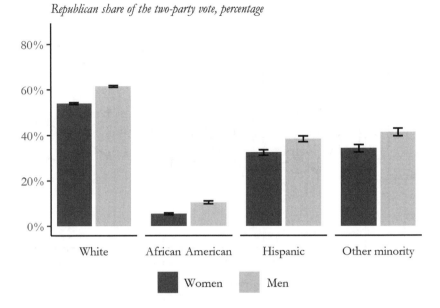

Figure 8.13 Gender gap persists across racial groups, but a majority of white women vote Republican and a super-majority of women of color vote Democratic (exit polls), 2000–12

gap of about 6 points among white voters. The vast majority of voters who identify as racial and ethnic minorities – African American, Hispanic, and others – on the other hand, support the Democratic ticket in every election. The overwhelming support for Democratic presidential candidates by black voters in these elections is stunning. This is especially true among black women, who consistently give less than 10% of their votes to Republicans.[49]

Gender gap rhetoric in the twenty-first century has often made important differences between women invisible, and none more so than race and ethnicity. Talk of a Democratic gender gap gave the impression that most women vote Democratic, a striking example of how comparisons with men can mask important underlying dynamics. Yes, women in every racial group were more likely to vote Democratic than were men. But while the vast majority of women of color cast ballots for the Democratic candidate in presidential elections, white women were more likely than not to vote for Republicans – just less likely than white men. Understanding this reality has significant consequences for our understanding of presidential elections and campaigns.

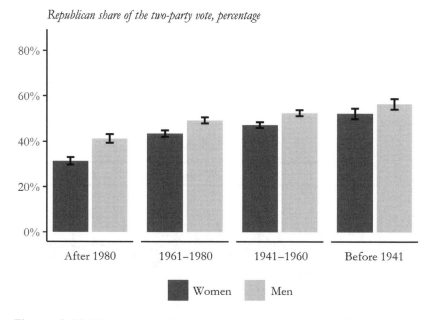

Republican share of the two-party vote, percentage

Figure 8.14 The strongest Democrats are younger women and the strongest Republicans are older men (ANES), 2000–16

Age. The partisan gender gap spans the range of ages, but is weakest among the oldest and strongest for the youngest. Age remains a powerful predictor of vote choice and the likelihood of voting Republican increases with age for both women and men. Younger women were especially reliable Democratic partisans (see Figure 8.14). These patterns may have consequences down the road: Young women socialized into politics in the late 1990s and early 2000s were much more likely than young men to turn out to vote (see Figure 8.5) and much more likely to vote for the Democratic presidential candidate than young men, or any other cohort. Young women will only become more likely to vote over time, and decades of social science research suggests that the vast majority will retain their Democratic preference.

Education. The relationship between educational attainment and vote choice changed dramatically over time, as Figure 8.15 demonstrates. In the 1950s, college education was strongly associated with Republican voting among men, and to a lesser degree among women (see Chapter 5). This

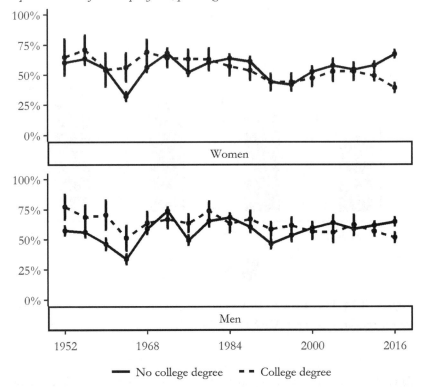

Republican share of the two-party vote, percentage

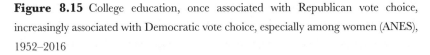

Figure 8.15 College education, once associated with Republican vote choice, increasingly associated with Democratic vote choice, especially among women (ANES), 1952–2016

pattern weakened after 1976: Education no longer sharply differentiated Republicans from Democrats; college attainment had no effect, for instance, on women's vote choice. These trends were now reversing, as education was increasingly associated with Democratic voting, especially for women. The 2016 election in particular saw a dramatic increase in the impact of education on women's vote choice, with college-educated women substantially more likely to support Democrats than non-college-educated women. Figure 8.15, which plots the long-term trend in Republican vote share among men and women with and without college degrees, highlights the novelty of 2016 in historic perspective.

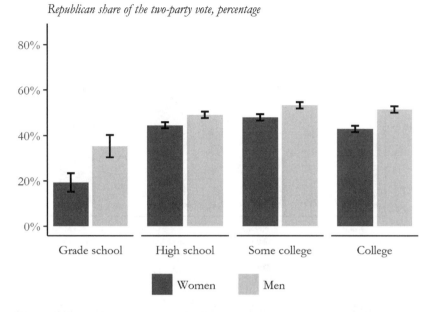

Republican share of the two-party vote, percentage

Figure 8.16 The partisan gender gap spans all education levels (ANES), 2000–16

The partisan gender gap showed up across levels of education in the 2000s and 2010s (see Figure 8.16). In the 1950s, the only education group in which a gender gap appeared (women more Republican) was those with a high school education (Chapter 5). As the small Republican advantage among women disappears in the 1960s, women and men of all education groups became similarly likely to vote for Republicans (Chapter 6). When the pro-Democratic gap emerges in the 1980s, college-educated voters lead the way, with the largest gender gap, by far. In the 2000s and 2010s, the gender gap remained large among the nearly 40% of voters who had college degrees, but also characterized every other group.

Marriage, family, and work. Beginning especially in 2000, strategists and journalists increasingly highlighted the "marriage gap," the tendency for married voters (especially women) to favor Republican candidates while single voters (especially women) voted Democratic. While this gap was hardly new, the growing proportion of unmarried or never married voters made the gap increasingly important to election outcomes.[50] The marriage gap attracted particular attention in the Obama years. For example, *US News & World Report*

Republican share of the two-party vote, percentage

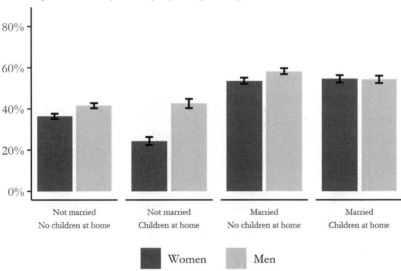

Figure 8.17 Single women especially Democratic, married women with children especially Republican (ANES), 2000–16

observed that "Unmarried women have historically voted for Democrats – in 2004, for example, 62% chose Sen. John Kerry over President Bush – but Obama's performance [in 2008] easily surpasses that of his predecessors."[51]

Our analysis supports these claims. Married women and men were more likely to vote Republican than those who were not married (see Figure 8.17). The effect of marriage was now larger for women than men.[52] Republicans had particular difficulty attracting the votes of single women, just over 30% of whom voted for Republican presidential candidates across these five elections compared to about 40% of single men. On the other hand, Republicans had a real advantage with married women; women were consistently less likely to vote Republican than were men in most social groups we examine here, but married women with children were as Republican in their voting behavior as were married men. Turnout, vote choice, and gender intersect in important ways. Marriage is a more important predictor of turnout for men, but a more important predictor of vote choice for women. Married men were substantially more likely to vote than unmarried men, and more likely to vote Republican. Married women were somewhat more likely to vote, but substantially more

Republican share of the two-party vote, percentage

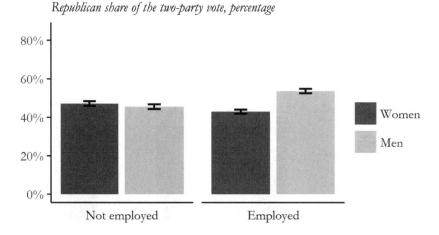

Figure 8.18 Employed men more Republican than all other voters (ANES), 2000–16

likely to vote Republican. The presence of children, however, does not have a significant impact on vote choice for either women or men in multivariate models.

As with other population characteristics, the impact of employment on women's vote varies over time. In the 1950s, women who stayed home (66% of the population) were distinctively more likely to vote Republican and there was no partisan gap between employed women and men. Differences across employment status narrowed in the 1960s and 1970s, as more and more women entered the paid workforce. At that time, employed women were distinctively *less* Republican than employed men or voters of either sex who did not work, but differences were small. By the 1980s and 1990s, whether or not women worked no longer affected their vote choice, but employed men had become substantially more Republican than all other categories of voters.

That pattern persists in this period. Men who worked were far more likely to vote Republican than those who did not (see Figure 8.18). On the other hand, employed women are no more likely to vote Republican than are women who did not work, as we also found in the 1980s and 1990s. The gender gap among working women and men is quite substantial. For men outside of the labor force – retirees, students, stay-at-home dads, or the unemployed – the falloff in Republican votes cast by employed men translates into no significant differences with unemployed women.

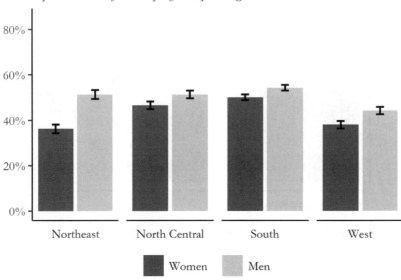

Republican share of the two-party vote, percentage

Figure 8.19 The partisan gender gap is everywhere (ANES), 2000–16

Politics and place. The regional bases for American politics were transformed in the twentieth and into the twenty-first century with consequences for women's vote choice. In the 1980s and 1990s, the gender gap in favor of Democrats characterized every region of the country. In the new millennium, this pattern persists: Women were more Democratic than men in every region (see Figure 8.19). The size of the gender gap varied considerably, however, and in different ways than in the past. Women in the Northeast were particularly likely to cast Democratic ballots, giving that region the largest gender gap in this period, while in the 1980s and 1990s, the gap there was insignificant. In the South, on the other hand, the gender gap in the 1980s and 1990s was substantial; it remains significant, but has narrowed in the 2000s and 2010s. The narrowing of the gender gap in the South was particularly consequential. While Southern women were more Democratic than Southern men through 2000, the gap narrowed to virtually nothing in 2004, helping to close the gender gap for George Bush in that election.[53]

The consistency of the gender gap across regions is striking. Recent research and political discourse has called attention to the ways in which geography – from neighborhoods to states – shapes political preferences. Regional

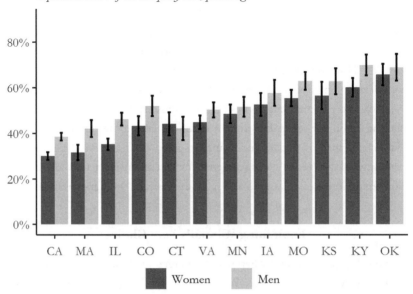

Republican share of the two-party vote, percentage

Figure 8.20 Partisan gender gaps vary across states (CCES), 2016

differences have dominated American politics for decades, but seem increasingly similar in terms of gender dynamics in the new millennium. Despite the gender gap, much as we observed in the 1920s and 1930s, women were more similar to men in the same region (average gap about 7 points) than they were to women in different regions (average difference across regions about 9 points).

These across-place differences were even more dramatic relative to gender if we were to compare men and women's voting at the state level. In Figure 8.20 we use 2016 CCES data (which permits reliable state-level estimates) to examine women's and men's vote choice in the ten states we examined in the 1920s and 1930s (see Chapter 4), as well as two additional western states, Wyoming (the first state to enfranchise women in 1869) and California (adding Western states to the sample).

The first thing to notice – then and now – is that women's and men's partisan preferences move together: In states where women tend to vote Democratic, so do men, and in places were women tend to cast Republican ballots, men do as well. The percentage of women voting Republican varies from 21% in California to 66% in Oklahoma, a 44-point difference. In comparison, the partisan gender gap is 7% overall, with the largest state-level gap of 11 points is observed in Connecticut. Gender mattered, but location – and the many factors associated with location – mattered even more, in 1920 and in 2016.

In every state save one, women are more likely to vote for Democrats than are men. However, the presence and extent of the partisan gender gap varies considerably across states. In general, the pro-Democratic gender gap is largest in states where Democrats do best; men in those states are more Democratic than men in other states, but women in those states are far more Democratic than men in their own states and women in other states. Gender gaps often, but not always, do not reach statistical significance in other states, meaning that the partisan preferences of women and men are basically the same in those states.

Explaining Women's Vote Choice

The pro-Democratic gender gap which emerged in 1980 was now a persistent feature of American elections. Why? As the gender gap became "normal," observers and scholars continued to seek reasons for the distinctive partisan tendencies of American women. Many of the causes first identified in the 1980s and 1990s remained supported by social science research, while others have emerged or been challenged. Indeed, one of the key insights of gender gap scholarship during this period was that the factors which put the gender gap in motion might not necessarily be the same ones that caused it to persist into the twenty-first century.

Compassion and egalitarianism. Women continued to be more likely to express uneasiness or opposition to the use of force and to support social welfare and government action on health care, education, and social problems, policy preferences which were associated with Democratic identity and votes. These findings were and are often attributed to women's greater compassion, to such an extent that gender gap research (but only gender gap research) often refers to social welfare, health care, and education as "compassion issues" (see Chapter 3).[54]

The compassion explanation suggests a distinctive gender explanation: Some fundamental value that women are more likely to hold (due to biology or socialization) explains women's distinct policy and partisan preferences. But what if scholars have been focused on the wrong value? In recent work, political scientists Scott Blinder and Meredith Rolfe analyze a rare survey which includes direct, valid measures of compassion and separate measures of political attitudes. They find little association between compassion and policy preferences of party identification. Rather, they find, as have others, that it is women's greater egalitarianism which drives differences in policy preferences, candidates, and parties.[55] Similarly, Karen Kaufmann finds that as cultural issues such as gay rights became more salient in this period, beliefs about equality became more central to women's and men's policy attitudes and partisanship.[56]

Women's issues. Women's role and the wisdom of policies intended to facilitate greater equality for women continued to be perennial campaign topics. In the twenty-first century, public debate over stem cell research and the Obamacare contraception mandate were the newest battlegrounds over abortion. Lilly Ledbetter helped bring equal pay back to the agenda, while rising child care costs made work-family balance a consistent challenge and campaign issue. Despite the salience of these issues and the repeated use of them in appeals to women voters, there continued to be little evidence that the partisan gender gap was driven by women's issues per se. Research found few gender gaps on whether women ought to have an equal role, the legality of abortion, or support for a woman president. Even where there were differences, there was little evidence women cared more about contraception or abortion than men or relied more heavily on those considerations in their presidential vote choice.[57]

Security moms and the use of force. After the 9/11 terrorist attacks, foreign policy and national defense shifted to the top of the political agenda, and to the front of many voters' minds. Women have been, both stereotypically and in survey research, less supportive of the use of force, which would lead us to expect them to have opposed the retaliatory war in the Middle East launched by Republican George Bush. On the other hand, pundits widely assumed that the nature of the domestic terrorist attacks made women in particular deeply fearful for their family's safety in ways that would benefit the Republican party in the 2004 election. This idea was captured in the "security mom" frame, attributed in 2003 to then-Senator Joe Biden (D, DE) who was quoted as saying, "Soccer moms are security moms now." Writer Joe Klein, who used the Biden quote in a TIME magazine column, argued that women and men experienced the threat of terrorism in different ways; men cared about the war effort, while women were focused on "protection of hearth and home against the next terrorist attack."[58]

Despite the considerable attention given to security moms in 2004, scholars reported that men continued to be more supportive of forceful international responses than women, but that the issue of national security, while highly salient in 2004, did not weigh more heavily on the votes of women than men. Being a mom also did not appear to make women more likely to support the Republican president; there was no difference in the vote choice of women with and without children in 2004.[59]

As with other forms of what political scientist Susan Carroll has termed "momism," the security mom frame reduced attention to other political interests women might have. In her analysis of newspaper coverage of security moms in 2004, Carroll finds that 10% of articles specifically refer to security moms as white, and almost as many as suburban. The emphasis on security moms in 2004 permitted George Bush to largely limit his appeals to women to the issue of homeland security. Carroll writes:

> To the extent the media focused on security moms, they diverted attention away from other women voters and permitted the candidates to overlook their concerns. And women voters did have concerns other than security. In a [November 2004] survey … women identified health care, education, and the economy and jobs as the top issues they wanted the president to address over the next four years. Large proportions of women voters also indicated that they would like to see the administration give priority to violence against women, women's equality under the law, and equal pay.[60]

Gendered parties. The Democratic and Republican parties certainly did not become less gendered in the 2000s and 2010s; if anything, this cleavage sharpened. The parties had diverged on women's issues for more than two decades by 2000, and debates over stem cell research and abortion, paid family leave, women's health, and equal pay kept those issues salient in the 2000 and 2010s. The "face" of the Democratic party was increasingly female as well, particularly compared to the GOP. After the 2016 election, for example, there were 17 Democratic women in the Senate, compared to just 6 Republicans. In the House, 61 women served as Democratic representatives compared to just 23 Republican women. Differences emerged in similar ways among Senate and House candidates. Nancy Pelosi was a visible symbol of the Democratic party as the first female Speaker of the House, and Hillary Clinton's 2008 and 2016 campaigns broke gender barriers in presidential nomination contests. In a period in which mass partisanship was increasingly rooted in group identity, the two parties presented sharply divergent images of what groups were most welcome and central to their party. Political scientist Heather Ondercin has shown how these partisan differences in representation (and, presumably, the images of the parties among the mass public) contribute to the gender gap, from 1980 through 2012.[61]

Femininity and masculinity. As we discuss in Chapter 3, distinctive gender explanations ascribe differences in the electoral behavior of women and men to the divergent values, preferences, and priorities of women and men. Scholars have long recognized, however, that femininity and masculinity are ideal personality types that characterize both women and men to varying degrees; women can be more or less feminine, as well as more or less masculine, as can men. In a sense, distinctive gender explanations that focus on gendered personality types are simply observing that women, on average, are more likely to demonstrate feminine personality traits and less likely to demonstrate masculine traits, and the reverse for men; it is the femininity and masculinity that matter, not sex per se.

Innovative recent research takes these personality dimensions seriously. The assumptions of distinctive gender are often supported: Feminine and masculine traits are associated with different policy preferences and predilections to political engagement. Again, the distribution of these traits is associated with female and male identity, but not entirely correlated with them. In her book, *Masculinity, Femininity, and American Political Behavior*, political scientist Monica McDermott finds that once feminine and masculine traits were controlled for, any differences in political engagement, attitudes, or partisanship were eliminated. That is to say, it is the variation in the presence of these traits between women and men that explains observed differences in the political behavior of women and men.[62]

As McDermott points out, many of the dominant explanations for the gender gap are rooted in some conception of femininity and masculinity (see

Chapter 3). In particular, women's support for social welfare – and thus for the party that advocates for it – is attributed to the feminine qualities of compassion and care, not sex per se. Masculine traits such as toughness and strength help explain the attraction of the Republican party (e.g., tough on terrorism, crime, immigration, social welfare beneficiaries) for men. As party cleavages have sharpened over the past several decades, citizens increasingly describe the Democratic party in feminine terms, and the Republican party with masculine attributes.[63] To the extent that women are more likely to have feminine traits, and men masculine, this pattern may continue to propel the gender gap.

THE UNPRECEDENTED PRESIDENTIAL ELECTION OF 2016

The final presidential election of this book merits particular scrutiny and explanation. In a contest featuring the first female major party nominee and an opponent who expressed misogynist views, many observers expected that women and men would diverge sharply when they cast their votes for president. NPR, for example, predicted in May 2016 that "The Trump-Clinton Gender Gap Could Be the Largest in More than 60 Years."[64] Pollsters, including FiveThirtyEight's Nate Silver in October 2016, reported signs of a "massive gender split," predicting that "if Trump loses the election, it will be because women voted against him."[65]

Yet, the outcome of the 2016 vote was surprisingly normal. In exit polls, the gender gap was 11 points, the highest since 1996 (also an 11-point gap), but only one point larger than in 2012.[66] Commentators expressed particular surprise that more than half (53%) of white women cast ballots for a man who boasted about sexual assault.[67] Why weren't expectations for a groundswell of support for Clinton and an abandonment by Trump among women realized? How could an election be so unusual and the outcome so normal?

Women voting for women. Many apparently expected women to flock to the first woman presidential nominee. From white suits harkening back to the suffrage movement to the "I'm with her" slogan, the Clinton campaign framed her candidacy as a sign of progress for American women and American politics. Yet, the evidence that women give greater support to women candidates is at best mixed. While almost 80% of women who identify with the Democratic party agreed that it is "very important" to elect more women to political office, only 19% of Republican women shared that view.[68] In 2016 Democratic women were already highly likely to vote for Clinton, so gender solidarity was unlikely to push those probabilities much higher. At the same time, there was little reason to expect that gender solidarity encouraged many Republican women to change their minds.

The centrality of gender identity also varies from other identities, such as race, as the distinct in-group responses to the Obama and Clinton campaigns demonstrate. Women are far less likely to report that their gender identity is extremely important to their voting decision compared to the importance that African American voters report for their racial identity. If anything, gender identity seemed to have a bigger impact on men's, not women's, vote in 2016. Women were 12 points more likely to vote for Clinton in 2016, similar to the 13- and 11-point advantages Obama enjoyed in 2008 and 2012. Men, on the other hand, voted for Romney (2012) by a 7-point margin, and McCain (2008) by just one point. Trump's advantage among men in 2016 was a full 12 points, the biggest margin among men since 1988.[69]

Sexism. Many expressed shock and dismay at the willingness of any women to cast their ballots for a candidate who made derogatory comments about women, bragged about sexually assaulting women with impunity, and was accused of sexual harassment and assault by multiple women. Such an expectation assumed, again, that gender was the dominant factor shaping women's voting choice. It also presumed that women do not share Trump's sexist views.

There is strong evidence that the election of 2016 activated sexism as a factor in presidential vote choice. The growing party preference divide between non-college-educated and college-educated whites has been given a great deal of credit for Trump's victory. While much of the narrative focused on economic displacement and anxiety, scholars report that in 2016, the sharp gap in party preference among whites based on education was more attributable to racist and sexist attitudes;[70] in contrast, sexism did not predict vote choice among African American voters.[71]

Social scientists have long recognized that sexist views are not solely the province of men, but are held by many women as well. Modern conceptions of sexism tend to emphasize a belief that women are taking power and privilege away from men, that gender bias is not a real problem or certainly not the problem women have made it out to be, and that women need to be protected.

Not only are women capable of holding sexist beliefs, but those beliefs had a strong and significant impact on their vote choice in 2016. Measures of hostile sexism predicted Trump support in 2016 (but not Romney support in 2012) among white women. Women of color, who the authors hypothesize have less of an interest in defending patriarchal practices or institutions, were less likely to express sexist beliefs or to have their political choices shaped by sexism. These attitudes were related in ways that suggest that the connection between sexism and Republican presidential vote may persist after Trump: In 2016, Republican partisanship became a predictor of sexist attitudes among white women; the two had not previously been correlated.[72]

Race. The 2016 election was ordinary in the sense that race mattered for vote choice in conventional ways. A majority of white voters – women and men – supported the Republican candidate. Overwhelming majorities of black voters – men and especially women – supported the Democratic candidate. Race has long been a powerful factor in vote choice and remained a key determinant in 2016, one that clearly swamps the relatively small impact of sex.[73]

The impact of sex on vote choice also was dependent on or related to race and ethnicity. Figure 8.21 exploits the relatively large samples in the 2016 Cooperative Congressional Election Survey to examine vote choice across categories of race and ethnicity. While majorities of white women voted for Trump, overwhelming majorities of African American women, and strong majorities of Latinas and other racial and ethnic minority women supported Hillary Clinton. For the most part, that observation is true without the "women" qualifier, but we do note that the gender gaps for people of color were generally larger than for white voters, suggesting something of a more significant sex divide among some communities of color. Interestingly, the gender divide (especially among other minorities) is larger in 2016 than we observed across 2000 to 2012 (see Figure 8.13).[74]

Finally, the astonishment over white women voting for Trump highlights the extent to which the social category of woman continues to be implicitly defined as white women. Trump himself later claimed that 52% of women supported him in 2016, a statement that was only true if one limits the definition of women to white women. Turning our attention to women of color tells a very different story about who women preferred for president in 2016.[75]

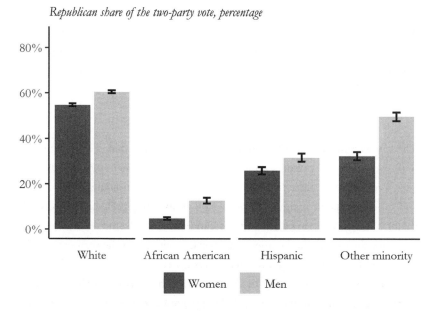

Republican share of the two-party vote, percentage

Figure 8.21 Small gender gap among white voters, strong Democratic support and a larger gender gap among minority voters (CCES), 2016

The power of partisanship. Expressions of dismay over *any* women casting a ballot for Trump reveals the persistence of the expectation that women's gender is the central determinant of women's politics. The 2016 election highlighted what *is* exceptional about the most recent period of mass politics, the extraordinarily potent power of partisan identity within the contemporary electorate. Almost 90% of women who identified as Republicans voted for Trump in 2016, the same rate as Republican men. These figures are entirely consistent with the mobilization of female and male partisans by other recent Democratic and Republican presidential candidates, all of whom were men.[76] Indeed, individual partisanship has become so powerful that there is emerging evidence of voters shifting their views on gender to match their partisan identification, rather than changing their party identification to fit what we might perceive as more fundamental and persistent views on race and sex.[77]

As political scientist Julia Azari has noted, by 2016, the United States was increasingly characterized by weak parties (in which candidates, funders, and others have the upper hand over party organizations) and strong partisanship (in which cross-cutting cleavages are few and party attachments are strong among voters).[78] The parties' presidential nominations in 2016 were unusual – the first woman nominee versus a nominee without political or military experience – but once those nominations were decided, American voters largely fell back on their strongly held partisan loyalties in casting their ballots.

CONCLUSION

The ratification of the Nineteenth Amendment was heralded as a significant step toward greater political and social equality for women. Nearly 100 years later, a major political party nominated a woman as a candidate for the highest and most important political office in the country, and perhaps the world. In rhetoric, dress, and slogans, Clinton's candidacy was framed as evidence of how very far women had come in American politics. Yet the suffrage activists who fought so hard to achieve greater rights, respect, and responsibility for women in politics would likely be dismayed by other aspects of the 2016 campaign. The Trump campaign revealed the persistence of sexist stereotypes, the objectification of women, higher standards for women, and sexual harassment and assault in twenty-first-century America.

Understanding this final period through that lens highlights how much the American gender order has, and have not, changed since 1920. Clinton's and Palin's nominations, Pelosi's speakership, and the growing numbers of (Democratic) women in office are clear and compelling signals of how far norms about women and politics have come in nearly 100 years. Yet, women remained dramatically underrepresented in political leadership – women comprised less than a quarter of seats in the House and Senate after the 2016 election. And 2016 in particular highlighted the remarkable persistence of sexism and misogyny in American politics.

Ultimately, the 2016 campaigns were extraordinary but the outcome mostly ordinary. Neither women nor men were particularly mobilized in 2016. Neither women nor men defected from established partisan preferences. Looking forward to 2020, what we know is that women – regardless of race, region, education, age, marital status, or employment – are more likely to turn out to vote than similarly situated men. In nearly every group and place, women are more likely to support Democratic candidates than similarly situated men. Both of these gaps were remarkably persistent in the 2000s, despite the widely different issues and personalities featured in presidential campaigns.

What has changed, in ways obvious after the 2018 midterm elections, is the number and success of women candidates for federal office. Despite losing the Electoral College, Hillary Clinton garnered three million more votes than Donald Trump. While the outcome of the 2016 election reflected long-held patterns of mobilization and vote choice, the result inspired a record number of women to run for and be elected to Congress, an important reflection of the perception and reality that there is much unfinished business for women in American politics.

CHAPTER 9

A Century of Votes for Women

THE PRESIDENTIAL ELECTION OF 2016 GENERATED A WAVE OF EXPLICITLY gendered protest activism. The post-inauguration Women's Marches in D.C. and around the country are estimated to have involved more than one in every 100 people in the United States and likely represent the largest single-day demonstration in American history.[1] The marches were organized and dominated by women who reclaimed and reworked gender stereotypes with pink hats and feminist slogans. Other organizations which emerged to challenge the Trump administration often were founded by women and/or had an over-whelmingly female membership base.[2] For example, women made up about 70% of members of groups associated with the anti-Trump Indivisible Project. Daily Action, a service that encourages users to call members of Congress, reported that women accounted for 80% of its users after 2016.[3] Women in general were more likely than men to say they have participated in a polit-ical event or protest since the election.[4] The future may well be female: The presidential election of 2016 inspired heightened interest in engaging in protest among (Democratic) adolescent girls.[5]

Other movements which have emerged or resurged during Trump's first fifteen months in office also have been strongly gendered and/or comprised of women. The #MeToo movement has generated historic attention to sexual harassment and assault.[6] The renewed push for gun control in the wake of the Parkland, Florida high school shooting has been supported by – and reveals the latent organizing efforts of – women in such groups as Everytown for Gun Safety and Moms Demand Action.[7] Women made up the vast majority of teachers organizing strikes to demand increased funding for K-12 education in West Virginia, Oklahoma, Arizona, and other states.[8]

The effects of the 2016 election on women and elections writ large may be long-lasting in other ways as well. As we discussed in Chapter 8, research shows that sexism was a factor in determining the Trump vote in 2016 in a way and to an extent not seen for other recent Republican candidates. This effect was limited to Trump in 2016; sexism did not predict voting for Republican House candidates. This may be changing. Early analysis of the 2018 midterm elections shows that sexist attitudes *did* predict votes for Republican House candidates that cycle, and largely by decreasing the likelihood of voting Republican among those with the least sexist views.[9] However gendered parties were in the past, we have reason to expect those linkages to strengthen in the future.

In 2020, Americans will mark the centennial of the Nineteenth Amendment to the US Constitution *and* hold another presidential election. What have we learned about women voters across the previous ten decades? What can we expect of women as they enter their second century as voters?

WHAT WE HAVE LEARNED

In the introduction, we identified four key themes, each of which we return to now. We highlight in particular how women's electoral behavior has changed over time, how popular and scholarly discourse has reflected persistent ideas about women voters, how the diversity of women voters makes it impossible to speak of "the women's vote," and how the changing electoral behavior of American women must be understood within historical context.

There Are Now Persistent Gender Differences in Turnout and Vote Choice

The story of women's turnout is fairly straightforward: Women's turnout has consistently increased relative to that of long-enfranchised men. Immediately after the ratification of the Nineteenth Amendment, women enjoyed fewer of the resources associated with voter turnout and were hampered by persistent gender norms that framed the home, not politics, as the appropriate place for women, norms that had justified women's exclusion from election for more than 100 years. Despite these burdens, women's turnout, relative to men's, steadily increased across the twentieth century. By 1960, women were only ten points less likely to turn out than were long-enfranchised men, and by 1980, the turnout gap had reversed so that women are now more likely than men

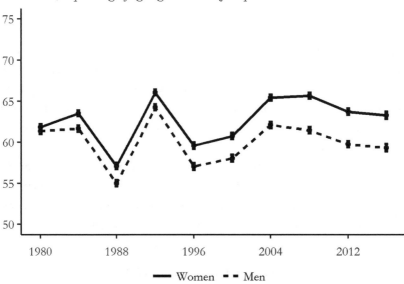

Turnout, as percentage of age-eligible US citizen respondents

Figure 9.1 Women's turnout exceeds men's after 1976 (CPS), 1980–2012

to exercise their voting rights. This turnout gender gap has persisted at about 10 percentage points since 1996 (see Figure 9.1).

While the story of turnout is largely one of increased similarity with men over time, the dynamic for vote choice is one of increasing gender difference. For the first 60 years after the ratification of the Nineteenth Amendment, women tended to give the same share of their votes to Democrats and Republicans as men did. When there was a difference, women were slightly more likely to vote Republican. That small Republican advantage among women disappears in the 1960s and begins to reverse in the 1970s. As with turnout, the 1980 presidential election was a turning point. From 1980 on, a gender gap in favor of the Democrats has been a persistent feature of American presidential elections, as well as elections for other offices as well (see Figure 9.2).

It is not only that the overall trends in voting have varied over time, but the ways in which different groups of women voted have evolved as well. In the 1950s, Southern women, African American women, and mothers (but not fathers) were particularly less likely to use the vote than other women and men. By the new millennium, Southern women were more likely to vote than Southern men, and increasingly close to voting at the same rate as women in

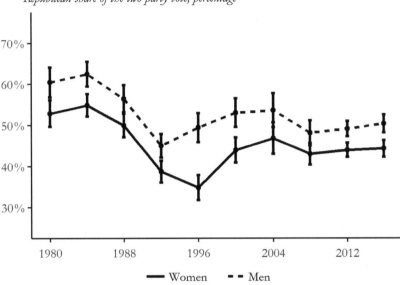

Republican share of the two-party vote, percentage

Figure 9.2 The pro-Democratic gender gap emerges and persists (ANES), 1980–2016

other regions. African American women, in particular, now turned out at very high rates, exceeded only very slightly by white women. The presence of children still depresses turnout, but now both mothers and fathers are more likely to stay home on Election Day. In the 1950s, women who stayed home were the most loyal Republicans; by the 2000s that title belongs to employed men. In the middle of the twentieth century, education was a strong and uniformly positive predictor of Republican vote choice. By the new millennium, that relationship has weakened considerably, somewhat among men and dramatically so among women, with college-educated women increasingly casting Democratic ballots.

Gender Stereotypes Inform How We Understand Women Voters

Women voters have been of perennial interest to political observers since before the Nineteenth Amendment was ratified. The last 100 years has witnessed some of the most dramatic changes in the lived experiences of women in the history of the world. Expectations for women voters have changed as a result. In the 1920s, candidates appealed to women with promises to defend Prohibition, end child labor, and support the League of Nations. In the new millennium, on the other hand, central campaign appeals to women included access to contraception and paid family leave, as well as education and health care policies.

What is most striking over this 100-year period, however, is the remarkable consistency of discourse about and appeals to women voters. In the first presidential election after the ratification of the Nineteenth Amendment, equal pay for women was a central plank in Republican Warren Harding's appeals to new women voters. In 2016, Democrat Hillary Clinton made equal pay for women a prominent campaign issue. In 1920, both parties featured women at their presidential nominating conventions, chose women to serve on party committees, and expanded and highlighted their separate women's organizations. Highlighting women's descriptive representation remained a constant, as candidates ranging from Franklin Roosevelt to Richard Nixon and Ronald Reagan to Bill Clinton have boasted about their records of appointing women to major positions.

Perhaps the most consistent theme has been that women's interests are fundamentally tied to motherhood and the home. That women's place is in the home was the prime rationale for excluding women from electoral politics. The fear that if women could vote, they would abandon their family duties (and even worse, require their husbands to engage in childcare) was prominent in anti-suffrage campaigns. Once the vote was won, the vast majority of appeals to and analyses of women voters have continued to assume – both immediately after suffrage and for nearly 100 years now – that women's interests are primarily derived from home and family.

Women's interests as mothers, in particular, are recurrent themes, from talk of maternity and infant protection in 1920 (what would become the short-lived Sheppard-Towner Act in 1921) through pregnancy discrimination in the 1970s and maternal health and paid family leave in the 1990s through today. From the Second World War and Korea to the Iraq War and "security moms," women's interest in protecting their children from dangerous military service and maintaining the safety of their families are persistent themes as well. Women are assumed to be motivated by the interests of their children more generally as well. Public policy choices related to education and health care are repeatedly cast in terms of the needs of children, not women themselves. Even perennial campaign issues like rising prices are not ordinary economic concerns (as they are described for men), but reflect women's role as the household consumer and money manager.

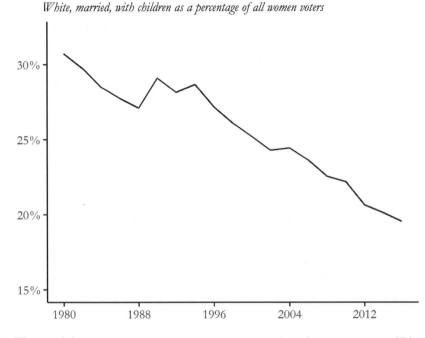

White, married, with children as a percentage of all women voters

Figure 9.3 Stereotypical moms are not representative of women voters (CPS), 1980–2016

Motherhood is certainly a relevant life experience that shapes the political attitudes and behaviors of many women. It is not, however, the only or even the most important factor driving women's political choices. Many women are of course not mothers and all women have identities and concerns that rank at or above motherhood in determining their political engagement and politics. This "momism" discourse has serious costs for the representation of women's interests. As Susan Carroll argued so persuasively, the persistent focus on motherhood redirects attention away from other groups of women, "including feminists, college-age women, older women, women on welfare, women of color, and professional women," and allows candidates to run "without campaigning aggressively on (or, in some cases, even seriously addressing) many of the issues of greatest importance to the majority of women in this country who are [in 2016] not white, middle-class mothers of young children."[10] Indeed, the idea that women voters should be framed as white, married, and with children has become only less accurate over time (see Figure 9.3).

If the stereotypes are problematic, then what do women voters really want? After nearly a century since the Nineteenth Amendment, observers are still not sure. In a recent *New York Times Magazine* article, "16 Ways of Looking at a Female Voter," Linda Hirschman notes: "Both parties have tried a variety of strategies to open or close the gender gap: nominating a woman for vice president (Geraldine Ferraro), pretending there was no difference, collecting women into smaller subgroups (soccer moms, security moms), emphasizing economics (health, welfare, child care) ... Despite these efforts, the gender gap has neither widened nor narrowed much."[11] Discussing the selection of Sarah Palin for the GOP ticket in 2008, *Newsweek* writer Julia Baird similarly summed up the puzzle of women voters: "Since then [1980], the idea of a gender gap – how women vote differently from men – has been fiercely contested: strategists have miscalculated it, pollsters have misinterpreted it and political parties have clumsily attempted to capture it."[12] As we argue in the next section, the reason that we have failed to find that one explanation for understanding women voters is that women are not just one kind of voter and are not mobilized only by their gender per se.

There Is No Such Thing as the "Woman Voter"

The hunt for "the woman voter" was on before the Nineteenth Amendment was even ratified. "Woman Voter Speaks" promised a *New York Times* headline in June 1920, with the subheading, "Feminine Political Interests as Revealed in a Painstaking Eavesdropping Expedition."[13] A clear lesson from the first 100 years since the ratification of the Nineteenth Amendment is that there is no "woman voter." The immigrant woman voting in Boston in 1928 was not the native-born white woman casting her ballot that same year in Minneapolis. The African American woman able to exercise her right to vote in Detroit in 1952 was not the African American woman seeking access to the ballot in Mississippi. In 1976, the activist newly mobilized by feminism was not the activist newly mobilized to defend traditional womanhood. The middle-class black women supporting Hillary Clinton in the 2016 primaries in the South were not the white college-aged women campaigning for Bernie or the rural white women mobilized for Trump or the suburban white women supporting Marco Rubio.

Any attempt to explain the ways in which one identity – gender – matters for politics must contend with how it intersects with other politically salient identities, particularly race.[14] Both black women and men were systematically denied voting rights prior to the voter registration efforts of the Civil Rights Movement and the 1965 Voting Rights Act. Explaining black women's turnout was certainly more a function of race than gender in that period. Since 1965, black women have not only made turnout gains in general, but compared to black men as well. From at least 1980 on, we see the largest turnout gender gaps among African American citizens. By the millennium, black women, long discouraged from voting on the basis of their sex and especially their race, now turn out at levels equal to that of the white men who have enjoyed the franchise the longest. Black women's turnout remains something a puzzle. African American women made important advances in terms of resources, particularly educational attainment, across this period, but communities of color, especially African American and Hispanic, continued to suffer from important resource disadvantages. Women of color are less likely to be mobilized to vote by political parties and interest groups. Recent scholarship demonstrates that the standard resource variables (like income, age, and so on) do not always impact black women's voting behavior as they do white women, suggesting a different process at work. Instead, political scientist Nadia Brown finds that a sense of what social scientists call "linked fate" (a belief that your own future is tied to your racial community's) is a strong mobilizer for African American women, but not for other racial and ethnic groups.[15]

Ultimately, women's turnout and vote choice are determined by a range of characteristics and identities, including, but not limited to, gender. This observation is crucial for how we understand women as voters. When we focus too much on differences between women and men, we risk presenting what political scientists Erin Cassese and Tiffany Barnes identified as an "inflated sense of cohesion among women."[16] As we saw in 2016, observing that women are more likely to vote Democratic than are men (which they are across virtually every demographic category) does not necessarily mean a majority of women vote Democratic in every case. Black and Hispanic women voted overwhelmingly for Democrat Hillary Clinton, even more so than black and Hispanic men, but a majority of white women (and a super-majority of white men) cast their ballots for Republican Donald Trump, consistent with patterns now decades old.

This is not to say that women are not similar to each other in important and notable ways. Women in nearly every social category were less likely to vote than men before 1960 and more likely to vote than men after 1980. Women generally voted for the same candidates and parties as similarly situated men after suffrage and are more likely to vote for Democrats than most similarly situated men from 1980 to today. Gender matters. It is just not the only thing that matters.

History (Also) Matters

Understanding women voters requires attention to historical context and political choice as well. In Chapter 3, we argued that most of the explanations for the electoral behavior of women – both popular and scholarly – can be described in terms of either **distinctive gender** or **resource inequality**. Distinctive gender explanations assume women are in some way a unique social group whose electoral behavior requires group-specific explanations. Whether due to innate differences or gender role socialization, women's personalities, values, and interests are simply different from men's, and those differences explain women's political participation and choice. Resource inequality explanations, on the other hand, attribute distinctive electoral behavior to differences in women's and men's social and economic resources, and the political opportunities and constraints those resources provide. We have long understood that resources and characteristics ranging from educational attainment to religiosity shape political behavior. In the logic of resource inequality, gender differences in political behavior emerge because women are more or less likely to have access to various politically relevant resources.

Across the past ten decades, we have observed both distinctive gender and resource inequality at work as the historical context has shifted and evolved. One of the most important stories of the past century is the dramatic expansion of opportunities and resources available to women, including greater control over their own lives, access to education and income, and changing roles within the family. When the Nineteenth Amendment was ratified in 1920, most adult women did not work outside of the home for pay, were married, and had children. There were important differences, with women of color and poorer women in particular more likely to be in the paid workforce. Strong social norms continued to emphasize that home, not politics, was women's place. By 2020, the vast majority of women will spend a substantial period of their adults lives working outside the home, families are smaller, women exceed men in educational attainment, and the popularity of slogans like "the future is female" and the increasing numbers of women role models in political life suggest that norms about women and politics continue to undergo a revolutionary transformation.

As resource inequality explanations would predict, the changing conditions and opportunities of women's lives have helped transform women's political participation and vote choice. Education in particular has long been a strong predictor of participation in elections; while women never lagged dramatically behind men in educational attainment, their gains across the twentieth and twenty-first centuries have clearly helped facilitate women's expanding turnout in presidential elections, as well as helping to increase women's participation in other forms of political activity, like contributing to or working on campaigns.[17]

The underlying assumption of the resource inequality perspective is that the factors that encourage or discourage turnout and party choice work similarly for women and men. In general, that assumption is supported by the past ten decades of presidential elections: Most factors – education, age, race, employment, and region – often predict turnout and party choice in the same direction and to the same extent among women and men. There are exceptions, often linked to changes in the distribution of those variables and associated shifts in equality. In the 1940s and 1950s, for example, the average family had 3.5 children, and the presence of children depressed the turnout of women, but had no impact on men. Today, families are smaller and generally (but not entirely) more equitable, and parenting reduces turnout for both women and men. Similarly, the relationship between marriage and partisan vote choice has shifted as patterns of marriage have shifted. Married men were consistently more likely to vote Republican from the 1940s to the present day, with a brief exception in the 1960s. For women, on the other hand, marriage was associated with a lower probability of voting Republican (that is, with voting Democratic) from the 1940s through the 1970s. Beginning in the 1980s, however, married women have been, like men, more likely to cast ballots for Republicans than single women. Some of the ways these variables affected women and men differently in the past could be due to resource inequality; as men and women have become more similar in terms of resources, the effects of resources on their voting behavior have become more similar as well.

Yet, there are enough differences in the impact of demographic characteristics over time to suggest that resource inequality explanations are insufficient on their own to explain women's electoral behavior. Gender differences characterize voting behavior across nearly all population groups. That is to say, even when we control for differences in access to key resources such as education, age, and employment, differences between women and men persist. Until recently, Southerners were less likely to turn out than citizens in other regions (owing to the systematic exclusion of African Americans from the right to vote and a general anti-democratic context), but Southern women were far less likely to vote than Southern men, suggesting a context that was particularly demobilizing to women. Old age appears to be particularly demobilizing to women as well, even as women have become more likely to vote at all other ages. In the twenty-first century, employed men are more likely to cast Republican ballots than are men who did not work, but employment status does not predict vote choice for women, suggesting employment may signal something about men that it does not indicate for women.

Distinctive gender and resource inequality approaches have characterized discourse about women as voters since the Nineteenth Amendment was ratified, but the exact form each takes varies with shifting political and social conditions. In terms of distinctive gender, there is a remarkable consistency in the inherent qualities attributed to women throughout American history. Yet, the political meaning that those qualities take on, and how they relate to political choice, is shaped by broader trends and political developments.[18] Women's compassion means opposition to child labor at one time, support for food stamps another. How women's interests as women are defined has been shaped by context as well. Changes in the material conditions of women's lives (e.g., employment status, marital stability), the ways in which the modern women's movement defined and framed issues, and shifts in public policy all influence women's perceived political interests over time. Issues like abortion and sexual harassment have been pointed to as key to women's vote choice one period, for example, but were entirely absent from the political agenda in others.

Changes in the major parties' policy positions have consequences for how women's perceived attitudes and interests map on to electoral choices as well.[19] This is an important point. While many of the characteristics and interests attributed to women are stable over time, the political choices women face are not. Women's greater egalitarianism may be constant over time, but the clear differentiation of the parties and candidates on issues relating to civil rights and equality are not constant, but rather have been transformed over this period.[20]

The impact of social welfare attitudes on the partisan gender gap – one of the strongest and most consistent research findings – illustrates these complexities. Since the 1960s, women have been more supportive than men of social welfare programs. There is consensus among scholars that this divergence in attitudes helps explain the modern partisan gender gap, as women are more likely (and men are less likely) to support the party (Democrats) which advocates for social welfare programs in this period.[21] From a distinctive gender point of view, women's tendency to compassion and an other-oriented ethic of care (perhaps due to women's unique experience of motherhood) all potentially help explain women's support for programs which protect those most vulnerable in society[22] and a tendency to weight social welfare issues more heavily in their political decision-making.[23] Alternatively, or additionally, a resource inequality approach emphasizes women's greater economic vulnerability and dependency on social welfare programs.[24] If women had the same economic resources and opportunities as men, they might share men's social welfare attitudes.

Women's real and perceived economic vulnerability has shifted over time with changes in patterns of marriage, divorce, pregnancy, and employment. The expansion and retraction of the social welfare state over the past ten decades has likewise changed women's interests, both objective and subjective, related to the size and activism of the federal government. Finally, the parties' relative positions on social welfare programs have evolved. Prior to the 1930s, neither party was strongly associated with social welfare, and a social welfare safety net was not a key partisan cleavage. The New Deal programs of the 1930s transformed the American social welfare state and made social welfare a central division between the parties. The link between the Democratic party and social welfare strengthened with the introduction of Great Society programs such as Medicare and Medicaid in the 1960s, while opposition to social welfare and government programs became a more prominent aspect of Republican ideology.[25] Social welfare programs were increasingly associated with people of color in press coverage and public discourse.[26] Thus a strong and salient link between the increasingly racialized issue of social welfare and the Democratic party occurred at the same time that women were experiencing key economic and social changes that made them more dependent of social welfare programs for both employment and benefits.

The 1960s also were the period in which national Democrats became the party of civil rights. Women consistently express more egalitarian views (distinctive gender), contributing to their greater relative support for civil rights and helping to explain the gender gap in partisanship.[27] Unlike men, women were less likely to respond to a newly racialized social welfare agenda by abandoning the Democratic party. Said another way, changes in the parties' issue positions were significant for the partisan gender gap due to their impact on not only women, but men as well. The association of civil rights and (racialized) social welfare with the Democratic party helped move white men, particularly in the South, toward the Republican party, a significant factor in the emergence of the gender gap in the 1970s and 1980s.[28]

The parties' images in terms of gender have shifted in several important ways over time as well, changes that also may help explain the partisan gender gap. Since at least 1980, the parties have established distinct positions on women's rights issues.[29] Since the 1970s, citizens have increasingly described the parties in gendered terms, Democrats as feminine, and Republicans as masculine.[30] Recent research shows that citizens associate the parties with different moral stereotypes, which are also gendered: Democrats are associated with compassion and fairness, while Republicans are considered more patriotic, tough, and wholesome. These stereotypes are rooted in reality: Democratic and Republican identifiers are indeed more likely to prioritize the values associated with their party.[31] Finally, since the 1990s, the parties have diverged sharply in the extent to which women are among the parties' candidates and officeholders (see Figure 9.4). This pattern was stark in the 2018 midterms, as 43% of Democratic nominees to the US House and Senate were women, compared to just 22% (Senate) and 13% (House) of Republican candidates.[32]

Framing parties in gendered terms has become part of the political narrative. As journalist Chris Matthews explained in 1991:

> There is an accepted division of chores in American politics. Republicans protect us with strong national defense. Democrats nourish us with Social Security and Medicare. Republicans worry about our business affairs; Democrats look after our health, nutrition, and welfare. The paradigm for this snug arrangement is familiar. It's the traditional American family. "Daddy" locks the doors at night

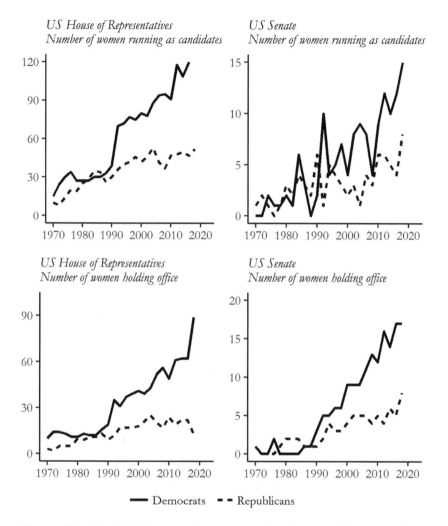

Figure 9.4 After 1990, Democratic women on the rise as candidates and office-holders, but Republican women tend to stagnate (CAWP), 1970–2019

and brings home the bacon. "Mommy" worries when the kids are sick and makes sure everyone gets treated fairly.

These developments may well be creating a partisan context in which voters' group images of the parties are gendered; that is, they view one party as the party for men and one as the party for women. For example, in 2012, 42% of ANES respondents identified the Democratic party as the party that "does a better job for the interests of women" compared to 36% who believed the parties did equally well in this regard, and 13% who believed Republicans were better.[33] Recent research by Heather Ondercin uses the increasing variation in the representation of women in each parties' congressional delegations over time as a measure of the parties' gender images in the late twentieth and early twenty-first century. She finds that as the parties' images became more gendered (as indicated by the increasing relative presence of women among Democratic, but not Republican, congressional delegations), Democratic identification increased among women, but declined among men.[34] There is little evidence that attitudes on women's rights issues (such as abortion or equal pay) explain the gender gap. Rather, the parties' images may have shifted over time in ways that expressed a distinct gender identity. Today, citizens who express more feminine traits tend to vote for Democrats, while those with more masculine traits tend to vote Republican, regardless of the sex of the voter.[35]

Political developments – including evolving party cleavages on social welfare, civil rights, and women's issues – shaped the political choices of women and men. Demographic changes, shifting patterns of work, marriage, and family, and a diversifying electorate further transformed the social categories of women and men. Gender norms – both challenged and defended across this past century – continue to influence how women interact with the political sphere, and how observers understand women as political actors.

THE FUTURE IS FEMALE

Through wars, economic boom and bust, technological revolution, and many presidential contests, the pattern that emerged in the early 1980s has persisted: Women remain more likely to vote and more likely to vote Democratic than similarly situated men. Whereas the first women voters were castigated for their failure to go to the polls or to vote differently from men, today we observe small but important turnout and partisan gender gaps.

Yet, if the first 100 years since the Nineteenth Amendment have taught us anything, it is that we should not necessarily expect these patterns to continue in size or direction. Changes – in politics and party competition, in the economy and world affairs, in women's lives and opportunities – produce changes in the voting behavior of women and men, on average and among particular social groups. Changes in women's political representation, voting rights controversies, and technological and economic change are just a few of the developments we might expect to shape and reshape the turnout and vote choice of both women and men, in both similar and different ways, in the years to come.

Observers continue to both praise and admonish women voters *as women*. After the election of Donald Trump in 2016, white women have come in for particular criticism for voting on the basis of their partisanship, race, socio-economic status, and so on, instead of on the basis of their gender and in solidarity with other women. An even higher level of Republican support among white men does not generate denunciations of how wives, mothers, or daughters have been betrayed by men. Alternatively, black women were credited with the upset of Republican Senate candidate Roy Moore in the 2017 Alabama special election; while two-thirds of White women voters supported the Republican candidate, Democrat Doug Jones secured the Senate seat with 98% of black women voters' ballots. As many have noted, both these criticisms and praise place gender at the center of discourse about women voters.[36] As we have seen repeatedly, however, women are not a cohesive voting bloc. While we cannot predict with certainty what women voters will do next, we expect that reality to remain intact.

"The right of citizens of the United States to vote shall not be denied or abridged by the United States or by any State on account of sex," commanded the Nineteenth Amendment to the US Constitution in 1920. This text transformed women's relationship with the American state and with American elections. In the ten decades since, women have overcome gender norms proscribing political activity and an unequal share of politically relevant resources to expand their participation at the ballot box. Activists have fought to make this right a reality for women still barred from the polls by discriminatory laws and practices. The narrative shifted from the failure of women voters to cast distinctive ballots to the perennial threat of an election-deciding gender gap. While gender is far from the sole factor shaping women's choices at the ballot box, the persistence of this gap across racial, economic, and social lines is just one of the many ways in which women and gender remain important to American elections. We have every reason to expect women voters to be as interesting, diverse, and consequential as we turn to a second century of votes for women.

Notes

1 WOMEN AT THE POLLS

1 "Women's Vote Baffles Politicians' Efforts to Forecast Election." *Bridgeport (CT) Evening Post*, October 29, 1920, p. 1.

2 "How Will the Women Vote?" *Boston Globe*, September 5, 1920, p. 1.

3 Lemons, J. Stanley, *The Woman Citizen: Social Feminism in the 1920s* (Charlottesville, VA: University Press of Virginia, 1973); Greenlee, Jill S., *The Political Consequences of Motherhood* (Ann Arbor, MI: University of Michigan Press, 2014).

4 E.g., Brown, Courtney, *Ballots of Tumult: A Portrait of Volatility in American Voting* (Ann Arbor, MI: University of Michigan Press, 1991); Burner, David, *The Politics of Provincialism: The Democratic Party in Transition, 1918–1932*, Second Edition (Cambridge, MA: Harvard University Press, 1986); Gould, Louis L., *Grand Old Party: A History of the Republicans* (New York: Random House, 2003); Lemons, *The Woman Citizen*; McCoy, Donald R., "Election of 1920." In *History of American Presidential Elections, 1789–1968*, eds. Arthur M. Schlesinger, Jr. and Fred L. Israel (New York: Chelsea House Publishers in Association with McGraw-Hill Book Co., 1971); Pateman, Carole, "Three Questions about Womanhood Suffrage." In *Suffrage and Beyond: International Feminist Perspectives*, eds. Caroline Daley and Melanie Nolan (Washington Square, NY: New York University Press, 1994); Smith, Jean M., "The Voting Women of San Diego, 1920," *The Journal of San Diego History* 26(Spring 1980): 133–54; Bagby, Wesley M., *The Road to Normalcy: The Presidential Campaign and Election of 1920* (Baltimore, MA: Johns Hopkins Press, 1962); Willey, Malcolm, M. and Stuart A. Rice, "A Sex Cleavage in the Presidential Election of 1920," *Journal of the American Statistical Association* 19(1924): 519–20.

5 Rymph, Catherine E., *Republican Women: Feminism and Conservatism from Suffrage Through the Rise of the New Right* (Chapel Hill, NC: University of North Carolina Press, 2006).

6 Kurtzleben, Danielle, "The Trump-Clinton Gender Gap Could Be the Largest in More Than 60 Years," *NPR*, May 26, 2016, www.npr.org/2016/05/26/479319725/the-trump-clinton-gender-gap-could-be-the-largest-in-more-than-60-years [accessed July 9, 2019].

7 Askarinam, Leah, "Women May Decide the Election," *The Atlantic*, November 8, 2016, www.theatlantic.com/politics/archive/2016/11/women-election-clinton-trump/506981/ [accessed July 9, 2019].

8 McCammon, Sarah, "20 Years after Historic Speech, Hillary Clinton Makes Appeal to Female Voters," *NPR*, www.npr.org/sections/itsallpolitics/2015/09/05/437875484/20-years-after-historic-speech-hillary-clinton-makes-appeal-to-female-voters [accessed July 9, 2019].

9 Newton, Small, "Why Donald Trump is Targeting 'Security Moms,'" *Time*, May 17, 2016.

10 See: Bazelon, Emily, "Why Did College-Educated White Women Vote for Trump?" *The New York Times*, November 15, 2016, www.nytimes.com/interactive/2016/11/20/magazine/donald-trumps-america-pennsylvania-women.html?mcubz=0 [accessed August 23, 2017]; Dittmar, Kelly, "No, Women Didn't Abandon Clinton, nor Did She Fail to Win Their Support," *Medium*, 2016, https://medium.com/@kelly.dittmar/no-women-didnt-abandon-clinton-nor-did-she-fail-to-win-their-support-77d41e631fbd [accessed August 24, 2017]; Feldmann, Linda, "Why Hillary Clinton Lost the White Women's Vote," *Christian Science Monitor*, November 22, 2016, www.csmonitor.com/USA/Politics/2016/1122/Why-Hillary-Clinton-lost-the-white-women-s-vote [accessed July 9, 2019]; Foran, Clare, "Women Aren't Responsible for Hillary Clinton's Defeat," *The Atlantic*, November 13, 2016, www.theatlantic.com/politics/archive/2016/11/hillary-clinton-white-women-vote/507422/ [accessed July 9, 2019]; Feldmann, Linda, "Why Hillary Clinton Lost the White Women's Vote," *Christian Science Monitor*, 22 November 2016, www.csmonitor.com/USA/Politics/2016/1122/Why-Hillary-Clinton-lost-the-white-women-s-vote [accessed July 9, 2019]; Malone, Clare, "Clinton Couldn't Win Over White Women," *FiveThirtyEight*, November 9, 2016, https://fivethirtyeight.com/features/clinton-couldnt-win-over-white-women/ [accessed July 9, 2019].

11 Corder, J. Kevin and Christina Wolbrecht, *Counting Women's Ballots: Female Voters from Suffrage Through the New Deal* (New York: Cambridge University Press, 2016); Center for American Women and Politics, "Gender Differences in Voter Turnout," July 20, 2017, www.cawp.rutgers.edu/sites/default/files/resources/genderdiff.pdf [accessed August 28, 2017]; "Exit Polls." *CNN*, November 23, 2016, http://edition.cnn.com/election/results/exit-polls [accessed August 28, 2017].

12 Corder and Wolbrecht, *Counting Women's Ballots*.

13 Center for American Women and Politics, "Gender Differences in Voter Turnout."

14 Kaufmann, Karen M., "The Gender Gap," *PS: Political Science and Politics*, 39 (2006): 447–53; Kaufmann, Karen M. and John R. Petrocik, "The Changing Politics of American Men: Understanding the Sources of the Gender Gap," *American Journal of Political Science*, 43(1999): 864–87.

15 In 1996, due to the presence of third-party candidate Ross Perot, women gave a majority of their votes to Democratic nominee Bill Clinton, but men only gave a plurality of their votes to Republican nominee Bob Dole. Dittmar, Kelly, 2014, "The Gender Gap: Gender Differences in Vote Choice and Political Orientations," Center for American Women and Politics, Rutgers University, www.cawp.rutgers.edu/sites/default/files/resources/closerlook_gender-gap-07-15-14.pdf [accessed September 5, 2017].

16 Campbell, Angus, Philip E. Converse, Warren E. Miller, and Donald E. Stokes, *The American Voter* (New York: John Wiley and Sons, Inc., 1960); Lazarsfeld, Paul F., Bernard Berelson, and Hazel Gaudet, *The People's Choice: How the Voter Makes Up His Mind in a Presidential Campaign* (New York: Columbia University Press, 1948); Berelson, Bernard R., Paul F. Lazarsfeld, and William N. McPhee, *Voting: A Study of Opinion Formation in a Presidential Campaign* (Chicago, IL: University of Chicago Press, 1954).

17 Corder and Wolbrecht, *Counting Women's Ballots*; Silver, Nate, "'Gender Gap' Near Historic Highs," *FiveThirtyEight* blog, October 21, 2012, https://fivethirtyeight.com/features/gender-gap-near-historic-highs/ [accessed September 5, 2017].

18 See Blinder, Scott and Meredith Rolfe, "Rethinking Compassion: Toward a Political Account of the Partisan Gender Gap in the United States," *Political Psychology* 39(2018): 889–906; McCue, Clifford P. and J. David Gopoian, "Dispositional Empathy and the Political Gender Gap," *Women & Politics* 21(2000): 1–20.

19 Native American women and immigrant women also faced legal and other barriers to voting that took years and sometimes decades to overcome; see Keyssar, Alexander, *The Right to Vote: The Contested History of Democracy in the United States* (New York: Basic Books, 2000).

20 Terborg-Penn, Rosalyn, *African American Women in the Struggle for the Vote, 1850–1920* (Bloomington, IN: Indiana University Press, 1998); Lebsock, Suzanne, "Woman Suffrage and White Supremacy: A Virginia Case Study." In *Visible Women: New Essays on American Activism*, eds. Nancy A. Hewitt and Suzanne Lebsock (Urbana, IL: University of Illinois Press, 1993).

21 Cassese, Erin C. and Tiffany D. Barnes, "Reconciling Sexism and Women's Support for Republican Candidates: A Look at Gender, Class, and Whiteness in the 2012 and 2016 Presidential Races," *Political Behavior* https://doi.org/10.1007/s11109-018-9468-2

22 E.g., Klein, Ethel, *Gender Politics: From Consciousness to Mass Politics* (Cambridge, MA: Harvard University Press, 1984).

23 Bonk, Kathy. "The Selling of the 'Gender Gap': The Role of Organized Feminism." In *The Politics of the Gender Gap: The Social Construction of Political Influence*, ed. Carol M. Mueller (Newbury Park, CA: Sage Publications, 1988); Mansbridge, Jane J., "Myth and Reality: The ERA and the Gender Gap in the 1980 Election," *The Public Opinion Quarterly* 49(1985): 164–78.

24 World Economic Forum, *The Global Gender Gap Report 2016*, http://reports.weforum.org/global-gender-gap-report-2016/ [accessed September 7, 2017]; Gershgorn, Dave, "Silent Films? The Gender Gap in American Movie Dialogue," World Economic Forum, March 7, 2017, www.weforum.org/agenda/2017/03/why-women-are-seen-and-not-heard-in-american-movies [accessed September 7, 2017]; Kasdon, Louisa, "It's Time to Do Something about the Chef Gender Gap," *Zester Daily: The Culture of Food and Drink* blog, January 13, 2014, http://zesterdaily.com/people/do-something-about-chef-gender-gap/ [accessed September 7, 2017].

25 For a discussion, see Conroy, Meredith, "Comparing Apples to Oranges? Paying Attention to Measurement in Reporting the Gender Gap in Election 2016," *Presidential Gender Watch 2016* blog, Center for American Women and Politics, October 23, 2017, http://presidentialgenderwatch.org/comparing-apples-oranges-paying-attention-measurement-reporting-gender-gap-election-2016/ [accessed September 7, 2017]; Clark, Cal and Janet Clark, *Women at the Polls: The Gender Gap, Cultural Politics, and Contested Constituencies in the United States* (Newcastle, UK: Cambridge Scholars Publishing, 2008).

26 See Ondercin, Heather L., "Who Is Responsible for the Gender Gap? The Dynamics of Men's and Women's Democratic Macropartisanship, 1950–2012," *Political Research Quarterly* 70(4 2017): 749–61.

27 For a thorough discussion of this problem, see Bourque, Susan C. and Jean Grossholtz, "Politics an Unnatural Practice: Political Science Looks at Female Participation," *Politics & Society* 4(1974): 225–66.

28 Junn, Jane, "The Trump Majority: White Womanhood and the Making of Female Voters in the US," *Politics, Groups, and Identities* 5(2017): 343–52.

29 Burden, Barry C., "The Social Roots of the Partisan Gender Gap," *The Public Opinion Quarterly* 72(2008): 55–75; Kaufmann, Karen M. and John R. Petrocik, "The Changing Politics of American Men: Understanding the Sources of the Gender Gap," *American Journal of Political Science* 43(1999): 864–87; Norrander, Barbara, "The History of the Gender Gaps," in *Voting the Gender Gap*, ed. Lois Duke Whitaker (Urbana, IL: University of Illinois Press, 2008), pp. 9–32; Wirls, Daniel, "Reinterpreting the Gender Gap," *The Public Opinion Quarterly* 50(1986): 316–30.

30 See, for example: Campbell, Angus, Philip E. Converse, Warren E. Miller, and Donald E. Stokes, *The American Voter* (New York: John Wiley and Sons, 1960).

31 Baxter, Sandra and Marjorie Lansing, *Women and Politics: The Visible Majority*, Revised Edition (Ann Arbor, MI: University of Michigan Press, 1983), p. 51.

32 Barabas, Jason, Jennifer Jerit, William Pollock, and Carlisle Rainey, "The Question(s) of Political Knowledge," *American Political Science Review* 108(November 2015): 840–55; Nancy Burns, Kay Lehman Schlozman, and Sidney Verba, *The Private Roots of Public Action: Gender, Equality, and Political Participation* (Cambridge, MA: Harvard University Press, 2001).

33 The phrase is adopted from Banaszak's description of the Seneca Falls Convention as a start date for women's rights activism in the United States; Banaszak, Lee Ann, *Why Movements Succeed or Fail: Opportunity, Culture, and the Struggle for Woman Suffrage* (Princeton, NJ: Princeton University Press, 1996), p. 5.

34 Keyssar, Alexander, *The Right to Vote: The Contested History of Democracy in the United States* (New York: Basic Books, 2000); Klinghoffer, Judith Apter and Lois Elkis, "'The Petticoat Electors': Women's Suffrage in New Jersey, 1776–1807," *Journal of the Early Republic* 12(Summer 1992): 159–93; Young, Louise M., "Women's Place in American Politics: The Historical Perspective," *Journal of Politics* (200 Years of the Republic in Retrospect: A Special Bicentennial Issue) 38(August 1975): 295–335.

35 Andersen, Kristi, *After Suffrage: Women in Partisan and Electoral Politics Before the New Deal* (Chicago, IL: University of Chicago Press, 1996).

36 Gosnell, Harold F., *Why Europe Votes* (Chicago, IL: University of Chicago Press, 1930).

37 Keyssar, *The Right to Vote*.

38 Terborg-Penn, Roslyn, *African American Women in the Struggle for the Vote, 1850–1920* (Bloomington, IN: Indiana University Press, 1998); Lebsock, Suzanne, "Woman Suffrage and White Supremacy: A Virginia Case Study." In *Visible Women: New Essays on American Activism*, eds. Nancy A. Hewitt and Suzanne Lebsock (Urbana, IL: University of Illinois Press, 1993).

39 Keyssar, *The Right to Vote*; Guinier, Lani, "No affirmative right to vote," Room for Debate blog, *New York Times*, June 23, 2009.

40 Population data source: Historical Census Statistics on Population Totals by Race, 1790 to 1990, and by Hispanic Origin, 1970 to 1990, for the United States, Regions, Divisions, and States; US Census Overview of Race and Hispanic Origin: 2010.

41 Lebsock, "Woman Suffrage and White Supremacy," p. 90.

42 Andersen, *After Suffrage*, p. 15.

43 DuBois, Ellen Carol, *Feminism and Suffrage: The Emergence of an Independent Women's Movement in America, 1848–1869* (Ithaca, NY: Cornell University Press, 1978).

44 See Robert C. Lieberman, "Ideas, Institutions, and Political Order: Explaining Political Change," *American Political Science Review* 96 (December 2002): 697–712; King, Desmond S. and Rogers M. Smith, "Racial Orders in American Political Development," *American Political Science Review* 99(February 2005): 75–92.

45 Andersen, *After Suffrage*; Nancy F. Cott, "Across the Great Divide: Women in Politics Before and After 1920." In *Women, Politics, and Change*, eds. Louise Tilly and Patricia Gurin (New York: Russell Sage Foundation, 1990).

46 Here, we are thinking of gender as an order in a similar way that King and Smith describe "racial orders." See King, Desmond S. and Rogers M. Smith, "Racial Orders in American Political Development," *American Political Science Review* 99(February 2005): 75–92.

47 Burns, Schlozman, and Verba, *The Private Roots of Public Action*.

48 Evans, Sara M., *Born for Liberty: A History of Women in America* (New York: Free Press, 1989); Freeman, Jo, *The Politics of Women's Liberation: A Case Study of an Emerging Social Movement and Its Relation to the Policy Process* (New York: David McKay Company, 1975); Klein, *Gender Politics*.

49 Converse, Jean M., *Survey Research in the United States: Roots and Emergence, 1890–1960* (Berkeley, CA: University of California Press, 1987); Herbst, Susan, *Numbered Voices: How Opinion Polling Has Shaped American Politics* (Chicago, IL: University of Chicago Press, 1993); Radcliff, Benjamin, "Exit Polls." In *Polling America: An Encyclopedia of Public Opinion*, eds. Samuel J. Best and Benjamin Radcliff (Westport, CT: Greenwood Press, 2005); see Corder and Wolbrecht, *Counting Women's Ballots*.

50 Center for American Women and Politics (CAWP), "Gender Differences in Voter Turnout (Fact Sheet)," 2015.

51 Corder and Wolbrecht, *Counting Women's Ballots*; The American National Election Studies (www.electionstudies.org), Time Series Cumulative Data File [dataset], 2015.

52 Evans, *Born for Liberty*; Greenlee, *The Political Consequences of Motherhood*; Klein, *Gender Politics*.

53 Corder and Wolbrecht, *Counting Women's Ballots*.

54 Andersen, *After Suffrage*.

55 On the relationship between party identification and voting, see Fiornia, Morris P., "Parties and Partisanship: A 40-Year Retrospective," *Political Behavior* 24(2002): 93–115.

56 Bartels, Larry M., "Partisanship and Voting Behavior, 1952–1996," *American Journal of Political Science* 44(January 2000): 34–50.

57 Mattei, Laura R. Winsky, and Franco Mattei, "If Men Stayed Home … The Gender Gap in Recent Congressional Elections," *Political Research Quarterly* 51(1998): 411–36; Omero, Margie, "Using Exit Polls to Explore the Gender Gap in Campaigns for Senate and Governor." In *Voting the Gender Gap*, ed. Lois Duke Whitaker (Champaign, IL: University of Illinois Press, 2008), pp. 108–18; Richardson, L.E. and P.K. Freeman, "Issue Salience and Gender Differences in Congressional Elections, 1994–1998," *Social Science Journal* 40(2003): 401–17; Ondercin, Heather and Jeffery L. Bernstein, "Gender Gaps in Senate Elections, 1988–2000: The Impact of Campaign Level and State-Level Factors," *Politics & Gender* 3(2007): 33–53.

58 Those distinctions are problematic and complicated for many reasons, including gender identity fluidity and essentialism. For a discussion, see: Beckwith, Karen, "A Common Language of Gender?"; Burns, Nancy, "Finding Gender;" Hawkesworth, Mary, "Engendering Political

Science: An Immodest Proposal;" Htun, Mala, "What It Means to Study Gender and the State," *Gender & Politics* 1(1 2005): 128–66; Sanbonmatsu, Kira, "Representation by Gender and Parties." In *Political Women and American Democracy*, eds. Christina Wolbrecht, Karen Beckwith, and Lisa Baldez (New York: Cambridge University Press, 2008).

59 Sanbonmatsu, Kira, "Representation by Gender and Parties." In *Political Women and American Democracy*, eds. Christina Wolbrecht, Karen Beckwith, and Lisa Baldez (New York: Cambridge University Press, 2008), p. 109.

60 Bureau of Labor Statistics, "Labor Force Statistics from the Current Population Survey," www.bls.gov/cps/ [accessed October 1, 2018].

61 National Center for Health Statistics, *Vital Statistics of the United States*, Volume I, Natality (Hyattsville, MD: US Department of Health and Human Services, 2003).

62 Carroll, Susan, "Women's Autonomy and the Gender Gap: 1980 and 1982." In *The Politics of the Gender Gap: The Social Construction of Political Influence*, ed. Carol M. Mueller (Newbury Park, CA: Sage Publications, 1988).

63 Andersen, Kristi, "The Gender Gap and Experiences with the Welfare State," *PS: Political Science & Politics* 32(1999): 17–19; Erie, Steven P. and Martin Rein, "Women and the Welfare State." In *The Politics of the Gender Gap: The Social Construction of Political Influence* (Newbury Park, CA: Sage Publications, 1988). Manza, Jeff, and Clem Brooks, "The Gender Gap in US Presidential Elections: When? Why? Implications?" *American Journal of Sociology* 103(1998): 1235–66; Schlesinger, Mark, and Caroline Heldman, "Gender Gap or Gender Gaps? New Perspectives on Support for Government Action and Policies," *The Journal of Politics* 63(2001): 59–92.

2 WOMEN WITHOUT THE VOTE

1 Flexner, Eleanor, *Century of Struggle: The Woman's Rights Movement in the United States* (New York: Atheneum, 1970); Jo, Mari and Paul Buhle, eds., *The Concise History of Woman Suffrage: Selections from the Classic Work by Stanton, Anthony, Gage, and Harper* (Urbana, IL: University of Illinois Press, 1978).

2 Rossi, Alice S., ed., *The Feminist Papers: From Adams to de Beauvoir* (New York: Bantam Books, 1973).

3 Flexner, *Century of Struggle*.

4 Epstein, Lee and Thomas G. Walker, *Constitutional Law for a Changing America: Institutional Powers and Constraints*, Second Edition (Washington, DC: CQ Press, 1995); see Keyssar, Alexander, *The Right to Vote: The Contested History of Democracy in the United States* (New York: Basic Books, 2000); Smith, Rogers M., *Civic Ideals: Conflicting Visions of Citizenship in US History* (New Haven, CT: Yale University Press, 1997).

5 *Minor v. Happersett* (1874). See DuBois, Ellen Carol, *Woman Suffrage and Women's Rights* (New York: New York University Press, 1998).

6 Lewis, Jan, "'Of Every Age Sex & Condition': The Representation of Women in the Constitution," *Journal of the Early Republic* 15(Fall 1995): 359–87.

7 Rossi, *The Feminist Papers*.

8 Keyssar, *The Right to Vote*.

9 Pateman, Carole, "Women, Nature, and the Suffrage." *Ethics* 90(July 1980): 564–75.

10 DuBois, *Woman Suffrage and Women's Rights*, p. 84.

11 See Kerber, Linda K., "Separate Spheres, Female Worlds, Woman's Place: The Rhetoric of Women's History." *Journal of American History* 75(June 1988): 9–39; Pateman, "Women, Nature, and the Suffrage."

12 Smith, *Civic Ideals*, p. 131.

13 Kerber, Linda K., "The Republican Mother: Women and the Enlightenment – American Perspective," *American Quarterly* 28(Summer 1976): 187–205; Kerber, Linda K., *Women of the Republic: Intellect and Ideology in Revolutionary America* (Chapel Hill, NC: University of North Carolina Press, 1980); Kerber, Linda K., "The Republican Ideology of the Revolutionary Generation," *American Quarterly* 37(Autumn 1985): 474–95.

14 Andersen, Kristi, *After Suffrage: Women in Partisan and Electoral Politics Before the New Deal* (Chicago, IL: University of Chicago Press, 1996); Marilley, Suzanne M., *Woman Suffrage and the Origins of Liberal Feminism in the United States, 1820–1920* (Cambridge, MA: Harvard University Press, 1996).

15 Keyssar, *The Right to Vote*; Klinghoffer, Judith Apter and Lois Elkis, "'The Petticoat Electors': Women's Suffrage in New Jersey, 1776–1807," *Journal of the Early Republic* 12(Summer 1992): 159–93; Young, Louise M., "Women's Place in American Politics: The Historical Perspective," *Journal of Politics* 38(August 1975): 295–335.

16 Smith, *Civic Ideals*.

17 Kraditor, Aileen S., *Up from the Pedestal: Selected Writings in the History of American Feminism* (Chicago, IL: Quadrangle Books, 1968).

18 Welter, Barbara, "The Cult of True Womanhood: 1820–1860." *American Quarterly* 18(Summer 1966): 151–74.

19 Cott, Nancy F., *The Bonds of Womanhood: Woman's Sphere in New England, 1790–1835* (New Haven, CT: Yale University Press, 1975); Kerber, Linda K., "Separate Spheres, Female Worlds, Woman's Place: The Rhetoric of Women's History." *Journal of American History* 75(June 1988): 9–39; Welter, "The Cult of True Womanhood."

20 There is considerable debate among scholars concerning the uses and misuses of the separate spheres concept. See, for example, Kerber, Linda K., Nancy F. Cott, Robert Gross, Lynn Hunt, Carroll Smith-Rosenberg, and Christine M. Stansell, "Beyond Roles, Beyond Spheres: Thinking about Gender in the Early Republic." *William and Mary Quarterly* 41(July 1989): 565–81; Kerber, "Separate Spheres, Female Worlds, Woman's Place."

21 DuBois, *Woman Suffrage and Women's Rights*; Kerber, "Separate Spheres, Female Worlds, Woman's Place."

22 Pateman, "Women, Nature, and the Suffrage."

23 Lerner, Gerda, "The Lady and the Mill Girl: Changes in the Status of Women in the Age of Jackson." *Midcontinent American Studies Journal* 10(Spring 1969): 5–15, p. 12.

24 Kraditor, Aileen S., *The Ideas of the Woman Suffrage Movement, 1890–1920*, Second edition (New York: W.W. Norton, 1981), p. 16.

25 Advertising image: "Which do you prefer? The home of street corner for women: Vote No on Woman Suffrage" 1915 lithograph, The History Project digital collection, University of

California, Davis. http://marchand.dss.ucdavis.edu/ic/image_details.php?id=2815 [accessed January 30, 2017].

26 Kraditor, *The Ideas of the Woman Suffrage Movement*.

27 Kraditor, *The Ideas of the Woman Suffrage Movement*, p. 16

28 Kraditor, *The Ideas of the Woman Suffrage Movement*.

29 DuBois, *Woman Suffrage and Women's Rights*; Kraditor, *The Ideas of the Woman Suffrage Movement*.

30 Kraditor, *The Ideas of the Woman Suffrage Movement*; Evans, *Born for Liberty*.

31 Welter, "The Cult of True Womanhood," p. 174.

32 Siegel, Reva B., "She the People: The Nineteenth Amendment, Sex Equality, Federalism, and the Family." *Harvard Law Review* 115(February 2002): 947–1046.

33 Keyssar, *The Right to Vote*, p. 196.

34 See: MacKinnon, Catharine A., *Feminism Unmodified* (Cambridge, MA: Harvard University Press, 1987).

35 Blinder, Scott, and Meredith Rolfe, "Rethinking Compassion: Toward a Political Account of the Partisan Gender Gap in the United States," *Political Psychology* 39(2018): 889–906; Erie, Steven P. and Martin Rein. "Women and the Welfare State." In *The Politics of the Gender Gap: The Social Construction of Political Influence* (Newbury Park, CA: Sage Publications, 1988). Huddy, Leonie, Erin Cassese, and Mary-Kate Lizotte, "Gender, Public Opinion, and Political Reasoning." In *Political Women and American Democracy*, eds. Christina Wolbrecht, Karen Beckwith, and Lisa Baldez (New York: Cambridge University Press, 2008).

36 Evans, Sara M., *Born for Liberty: A History of Women in America* (New York: Free Press, 1989).

37 DuBois, *Woman Suffrage and Women's Rights*; Evans, *Born for Liberty*.

38 Baker, "The Domestication of Politics."

39 Spain, Daphne, *How Women Saved the City* (Minneapolis, MN: University of Minnesota Press, 2001).

40 Skocpol, Theda, *Protecting Soldiers and Mothers: The Political Origins of Social Policy in the United States* (Cambridge, MA: Belknap Press of Harvard University Press, 1992).

41 Baker, "The Domestication of Politics."

42 Kraditor, *Century of Struggle*; DuBois, *Woman Suffrage and Women's Rights*.

43 Chatfield, Sara, "Married Women's Economic Rights Reform in State Legislatures and Courts, 1839–1920," *Studies in American Political Development* 32(October 2018): 326–56; Smith, *Civic Ideals*.

44 Flexner, *Century of Struggle*; Rossi, *The Feminist Papers*.

45 Banaszak, Lee Ann, *Why Movements Succeed or Fail: Opportunity, Culture, and the Struggle for Woman Suffrage* (Princeton, NJ: Princeton University Press, 1996).

46 Edwards, Rebecca B., *Angels in the Machinery: Gender in American Party Politics from the Civil War to the Progressive Era* (New York: Oxford University Press, 1997); Evans, *Born for Liberty*.

47 Evans, *Born for Liberty*.

48 Banaszak, *Why Movements Succeed or Fail*; Evans, *Born for Liberty*.

49 Terborg-Penn, Rosalyn, "Discrimination Against Afro-American Woman in the Woman's Movement, 1830–1920." In *The Afro-American Woman: Struggles and Images*, eds. Sharon Harley and Rosalyn Terborg-Penn (Port Washington, NY: Kennikat Press, 1978); Terborg-Penn, Rosalyn, *African American Women in the Struggle for the Vote, 1850–1920* (Bloomington, IN: Indiana University Press, 1998).

50 See Keyssar, *The Right to Vote*; Beeton, Beverly, *Women Vote in the West: The Woman Suffrage Movement, 1869–1896* (New York: Garland Publishing, 1986); McCammon, Holly J. and Karen Campbell, "Winning the Vote in the West: The Political Successes of the Women's Suffrage Movements, 1866–1919," *Gender and Society* 15(2001): 55–82.

51 Young, "Woman's Place in Politics."

52 Erwin, Marie H., *Wyoming Historical Blue Book: A Legal and Political History of Wyoming, 1868–1943* (Denver, CO: Bradford-Robinson Printing Co., 1946), p. 528.

53 Women were enfranchised in the territory of Utah in 1870, but the women's suffrage was later revoked as part of the political struggle between the Church of Latter Day Saints (Mormons) and the federal government over polygamy. Women's suffrage was reinstated in 1896 when Utah achieved statehood. See Keyssar, *The Right to Vote*.

54 Banaszak, *Why Movements Succeed or Fail*.

55 Banaszak, *Why Movements Succeed or Fail*; Kraditor, *Up from the Pedestal*.

56 Ford, Linda, "Alice Paul and the Triumph of Militancy" in *One Woman, One Vote: Rediscovering the Woman Suffrage Movement*, ed. Marjorie Spruill Wheeler (Troutdale, OR: NewSage Press, 1995), pp. 277–94.

57 Evans, *Born for Liberty*.

58 Wheeler, Marjorie Spruill, ed., *One Woman, One Vote: Rediscovering the Woman Suffrage Movement* (Troutdale, OR: NewSage Press, 1995).

59 Evans, *Born for Liberty*; Flexner, *Century of Struggle*.

60 "Women and the Vote," *New Zealand History*, Archives New Zealand, https://nzhistory.govt.nz/politics/womens-suffrage [accessed September 21, 2017].

61 Banaszak, *Why Movements Succeed or Fail*.

62 McConnaughy, Corrine M., *The Woman Suffrage Movement in America: A Reassessment* (New York: Cambridge University Press, 2013).

63 Banaszak, *Why Movements Succeed or Fail*; McConnaughy, *The Woman Suffrage Movement in America*; Evans, *Born for Liberty*; Marilley, *Woman Suffrage and the Origins of Liberal Feminism in the United States*; Buechler, Steven, *The Transformation of the Woman Suffrage Movement: The Case of Illinois, 1850–1920*. (New Brunswick, NJ: Rutgers University Press, 1986); Pateman, "Women, Nature, and the Suffrage;" Baker, "The Domestication of Politics;" Grimes, Alan P., *The Puritan Ethic and Woman Suffrage* (New York: Oxford University Press, 1967); Mead, Rebecca J., *How the Vote Was Won: Woman Suffrage in the United States, 1868–1914* (New York: New York University Press, 2004); McGammon, Holly J., Karen E. Campbell, Ellen M. Granberg, and Christine Mowery, "How Movements Win: Gendered Opportunity Structures and US Women's Suffrage Movements, 1866 to 1919," *American Sociological Review* 66(February 2001): 49–70; Teele, Dawn Langan, *Forging the Franchise: The Political Origins of the Women's Vote* (Princeton, NJ: Princeton University Press, 2018).

64 Gosnell, Harold F., *Why Europe Votes* (Chicago, IL: University of Chicago Press, 1930).

65 For example, Illinois provided one extra registration day, August 25, for women (and men) before the state primary on Sept. 15 ("Wednesday Only Day for Women to Get Votes," *Chicago Tribune*, August 20, 1920, p. 3). The Boston Election Board permitted women to register in early August in anticipation of ratification ("Women May Register as Voters from August 12 to 18," *Boston Globe*, July 16, 1920, p. 1). See also: "Mayor Extends Time for Registration," *Boston Globe*, 19 August 1920, p. 4; "Women Now Registered Stay on Lists," *Bridgeport (CT) Post*, September 22, 1920, p. 1.

66 "Drive Women From Polls in South: Southerners Threat to Use Gun and Rope on Race Leaders," *The Chicago Defender*, October 30, 1920, p. 1.

67 Lebsock, Suzanne, "Woman Suffrage and White Supremacy: A Virginia Case Study." In *Visible Women: New Essays on American Activism*, eds. Nancy A. Hewitt and Suzanne Lebsock (Urbana, IL: University of Illinois Press, 1993); Mickey, Robert, *Paths Out of Dixie: The Democratization of Authoritarian Enclaves in America's Deep South, 1944–1972* (Princeton, NJ: Princeton University Press, 2015); Nealy, Lisa Nikol, *African American Women Voters: Racializing Religiosity, Political Consciousness and Progressive Political Action in US Presidential Elections from 1964 through 2008* (Lanham, MD: University Press of American, Inc.); Vallely, Richard M. *The Two Reconstructions: The Struggle for Black Enfranchisement* (Chicago, IL: University of Chicago Press, 2004).

68 DuBois, *Woman Suffrage and Women's Rights*, p. 46.

69 "Wimmin Are from Mars, Women Are from Venus," *The Economist* (June 21, 1997): 87–89.

3 EXPLAINING WOMEN VOTERS

1 Corder, J. Kevin and Christina Wolbrecht, *Counting Women's Ballots: Female Voters from Suffrage Through the New Deal* (New York: Cambridge University Press, 2016). These estimated averages are based on a nine-state sample from 1936.

2 Center for American Women and Politics, "Gender Differences in Voter Turnout," July 20, 2017, www.cawp.rutgers.edu/sites/default/files/resources/genderdiff.pdf [accessed August 28, 2017]; Center for American Women and Politics, "The Gender Gap: Voting Choice in Presidential Election," 2017, www.cawp.rutgers.edu/sites/default/files/resources/ggpresvote.pdf [accessed September 20, 2017].

3 Carroll identified similar categories in 1988, describing the "major explanations" for the gender gap as falling into "two general types. The first stresses women's unique economic position; the second emphasizes unique, gender-based differences between women and men." See: Carroll, Susan, "Women's Autonomy and the Gender Gap: 1980 and 1982." In *The Politics of the Gender Gap: The Social Construction of Political Influence*, ed. Carol M. Mueller (Newbury Park, CA: Sage Publications, 1988), p. 237. We consider the fact that we settled on similar categories as pioneering scholar Sue Carroll to constitute significant external validity of our framework.

4 For example: Kraditor, Aileen S., *The Ideas of the Woman Suffrage Movement, 1890–1920*, Second edition (New York: W.W. Norton, 1981).

5 *Bradwell v. State of Illinois* 83 U.S. 130 (1873).

6 Schlafly, Phyllis, *The Power of the Positive Woman* (New York: Jove Publications, 1978), p. 12.

7 Jantz, Gregory L., "Brain Differences Between Genders," *Psychology Today*, February 27, 2015.

8 Inglehart, Ronald and Pippa Norris, "The Developmental Theory of the Gender Gap: Women's and Men's Voting Behavior in Global Perspective," *International Political Science Review / Revue Internationale de Science Politique* 2(2000): 441–63; Preece, Jessica Robinson, "Mind the Gender Gap: An Experiment on the Influence of Self-Efficacy on Political Interest," *Politics & Gender* 12(2016): 198–217.

9 Hatemi, Peter K., Sarah E. Medland and Lindon J. Eaves, "Do Genes Contribute to the 'Gender Gap'?" *The Journal of Politics* 71(2009): 262–76.

10 Eagly, Alice H. *Sex Differences in Social Behavior: A Social-Role Interpretation* (Mahwah, NJ: Lawrence Erlbaum, 1987); Eagly, Alice H. and Maureen Crowley, "Gender and Helping Behavior: A Meta-Analytic Review of the Social Psychological Literature," *Psychological Bulletin* 100(1986): 283–308; Reskin, Barbara F., Debra B. McBrier, and Julie A. Kmec, "The Determinants and Consequences of Workplace Sex and Race Composition," *Annual Review of Sociology* 25(1999): 335–61; Diekman, Amanda B. and Monica C. Schneider, "A Social Role Theory Perspective on Gender Gaps in Political Attitudes," *Psychology of Women Quarterly* 34 (2010): 486–97.

11 For example, Ruddick, Sara, *Maternal Thinking: Toward a Politics of Peace* (Boston, MA: Beacon Press, 1989); Elshtain, Jean Bethke, *Public Man, Private Woman* (Princeton, NJ: Princeton University Press, 1981); for empirical analysis of the impact of parenting on political attitudes, see Elder, Laurel, and Steven Greene, "Parenthood and the Gender Gap." In *Voting the Gender Gap*, ed. Lois Duke Whitaker (Urbana, IL: University of Illinois Press, 2008), pp. 119–40; Greenlee, Jill S., *The Political Consequences of Motherhood* (Ann Arbor, MI: University of Michigan Press, 2014).

12 Diekman and Schneider, "A Social Role Theory Perspective on Gender Gaps in Political Attitudes"; Iversen, Torben, and Frances Rosenbluth, "The Political Economy of Gender: Explaining Cross-National Variation in the Gender Division of Labor and the Gender Voting Gap," *American Journal of Political Science* 50 (1 2006): 1–19; Howell, Susan E. and Christine L. Day, "Complexities of the Gender Gap," *The Journal of Politics* 62(2000): 858–74.

13 See, e.g., MacKinnon, Catharein A., *Feminism Unmodified* (Cambridge, MA: Harvard University Press, 1987).

14 See Lizotte, Mary-Kate, "The Gender Gap in Public Opinion: Exploring Social Role Theory as an Explanation." In *The Political Psychology of Women in US Politics*, eds. Angela L Box and Monica Schneider (New York: Routledge, 2017).

15 McDermott, Monica L. *Masculinity, Femininity, and American Political Behavior* (New York: Oxford University Press, 2016).

16 Gilligan, Carol, *In a Different Voice: Psychological Theory and Women's Development* (Cambridge, MA: Harvard University Press, 1982).

17 Examples of work that draws in part from Gilligan: Clark and Clark, *Women at the Polls*; Gilens, Martin, "Gender and Support for Reagan: A Comprehensive Model of Presidential Approval," *American Journal of Political Science* 32(1988): 19–49; Howell, Susan E. and Christine L. Day, "Complexities of the Gender Gap," *The Journal of Politics* 62(2000): 858–74; Kam, Cindy D., "Gender and Economic Voting, Revisited," *Electoral Studies*, Special issue on The American Voter Revisited, 28(2009): 615–24; Norrander, Barbara, "The Independence Gap and the Gender Gap," *The Public Opinion Quarterly* 61(1997): 464–76; Trevor, Margaret C., "Political Socialization, Party Identification, and the Gender Gap," *The Public Opinion Quarterly* 63(1999): 62–89; Welch, Susan and John Hibbing, "Financial Conditions, Gender, and Voting in American National Elections," *The Journal of Politics* 54(1992): 197–213.

18 For example: Chaney, Carole Kennedy, R. Michael Alvarez and Jonathan Nagler, "Explaining the Gender Gap in U.S. Presidential Elections, 1980–1992," *Political Research Quarterly* 51(1998): 311–39; Clark and Clark, *Women at the Polls*; Kaufmann, Karen M. and John R. Petrocik, "The Changing Politics of American Men: Understanding the Sources of the Gender

Gap," *American Journal of Political Science* 43(1999): 864–87; Norrander, Barbara, and Clyde Wilcox, "The Gender Gap in Ideology," *Political Behavior* 30(2008): 503–23; Fox, Richard L. and Zoe Oxley, "Women's Support for an Active Government." In *Minority Voting in the United States* Volume I, eds. Kyle L. Kreider and Thomas J. Baldino (Santa Barbara, CA: Praeger, 2016).

19 Blinder, Scott, and Meredith Rolfe, "Rethinking Compassion: Toward a Political Account of the Partisan Gender Gap in the United States," *Political Psychology* 39(2017): 889–906; but see McCue, Clifford P. and J. David Gopoian, "Dispositional Empathy and the Political Gender Gap," *Women & Politics* 21(2000): 1–20.

20 DuBois, Ellen Carol, *Woman Suffrage and Women's Rights* (New York: New York University Press, 1998); Kerber, Linda K. "Separate Spheres, Female Worlds, Woman's Place: The Rhetoric of Women's History," *Journal of American History* 75(June 1988): 9–39.

21 On the socialization of women out of politics, see the discussion of the classic socialization studies in Andersen, "Working Women and Political Participation, 1952–1972."

22 Preece, Jessica Robinson, "Mind the Gender Gap: An Experiment on the Influence of Self-Efficacy on Political Interest," *Politics & Gender* 12(2016): 198–217; Jennifer L. Lawless, and Richard L. Fox, *It Still Takes A Candidate: Why Women Don't Run for Office* (Cambridge: Cambridge University Press, 2010); Kanthak, Kristin, and Jonathan Woon, "Women Don't Run? Election Aversion and Candidate Entry." *American Journal of Political Science* 59(2015): 595–612; Gidengil, Elisabeth, Janine Giles, and Melanee Thomas, "The Gender Gap in Self-Perceived Understanding of Politics in Canada and the United States." *Politics & Gender* 4(2008): 535–61; Karp, Jeffrey A. and Susan A. Banducci, "When Politics Is Not Just a Man's Game: Women's Representation and Political Engagement," *Electoral Studies* 27(2008): 105–15; Karpowitz, Christopher F. and Tali Mendelberg, *The Silent Sex: Gender, Deliberation, and Institutions* (Princeton, NJ: Princeton University Press, 2014).

23 Preece, "Mind the Gender Gap," p. 213.

24 Atkeson, Lonna Rae, "Not All Cues Are Created Equal: The Conditional Impact of Female Candidates on Political Engagement," *The Journal of Politics* 65(2003): 1040–61; Burns, Nancy, Kay Lehman Schlozman, and Sidney Verba, *The Private Roots of Public Action: Gender, Equality, and Political Participation* (Cambridge, MA: Harvard University Press, 2001); Wolbrecht, Christina and David E. Campbell, "Role Models Revisited: Youth, Novelty, and the Impact of Female Candidates," *Politics, Groups, & Identities* 5(2017): 418–34; Campbell, David E. and Christina Wolbrecht, "See Jane Run: Women Politicians as Role Models for Adolescents," *Journal of Politics* 68(May 2006): 233–47; Hansen, Susan B., "Talking About Politics: Gender and Contextual Effects on Political Proselytizing," *The Journal of Politics* 59(1997): 73–103; Karp, Jeffrey A. and Susan A. Banducci, "When Politics Is Not Just a Man's Game: Women's Representation and Political Engagement," *Electoral Studies* 27(2008): 105–15; but see: Dolan, Kathleen, "Symbolic Mobilization? The Impact of Candidate Sex in American Elections," *American Politics Research* 34(2006): 687–704; Lawless, Jennifer L., "Politics of Presence? Congresswomen and Symbolic Representation," *Political Research Quarterly* 57(2004): 81–99. Even where a positive association between the presence of female role models and women's engagement exists, the mechanism for this effect is less clear. Women politicians may challenge stereotypes about the appropriateness of women in politics. They may also, or alternatively, raise issues of interest to women, signal an open and responsive political system, or generate interest based on their uniqueness,

all of which could potentially stimulate political engagement among women (for a discussion, see Wolbrecht and Campbell, "Role Models Revisited").

25 See discussion in Corder and Wolbrecht, *Counting Women's Ballots*.

26 Kerber, Linda K., "The Republican Mother: Women and the Enlightenment – American Perspective," *American Quarterly* 28(Summer 1976): 187–205; Kerber, Linda K., *Women of the Republic: Intellect and Ideology in Revolutionary America* (Chapel Hill, NC: University of North Carolina Press, 1980); Kraditor, *The Ideas of the Woman Suffrage Movement*.

27 Spain, Daphne, *How Women Saved the City* (Minneapolis, MN: University of Minnesota Press, 2001).

28 Horowitz, Juliana Menasce, Ruth Igielnik, and Kim Parker, "Women and Leadership 2018," Pew Research Center, September 20, 2018 www.pewsocialtrends.org/2018/09/20/women-and-leadership-2018/ [accessed October 4, 2018].

29 See Corder and Wolbrecht, *Counting Women's Ballots*.

30 Bonk, Kathy, "The Selling of the 'Gender Gap': The Role of Organized Feminism." In *The Politics of the Gender Gap: The Social Construction of Political Influence*, ed. Carol M. Mueller (Newbury Park, CA: Sage Publications, 1988); Mansbridge, Jane J., "Myth and Reality: The ERA and the Gender Gap in the 1980 Election," *Public Opinion Quarterly* 49 (1985): 164–78; Wirls, Daniel, "Reinterpreting the Gender Gap," *Public Opinion Quarterly* 50(1986): 316–30.

31 "Exit Polls." *CNN Politics*, April 13, 2017, www.cnn.com/election/results/exit-polls [accessed July 9, 2019]; Lett, Pheobe, "White Women Voted for Trump. Now What?" *New York Times* Taking Note blog, www.nytimes.com/2016/11/10/opinion/white-women-voted-trump-now-what.html?_r=0 [accessed April 13, 2017].

32 Lizotte, Mary-Kate, "Gender, Voting, and Reproductive Rights Attitudes." In *Minority Voting in the United States*, Volume I, eds. Kyle L. Kreider and Thomas J. Baldino (Santa Barbara, CA: Praeger, 2016).

33 Kaufmann, Karen M., "Culture Wars, Secular Realignment, and the Gender Gap in Party Identification," *Political Behavior* 24(2002): 283–307.

34 See, for example, Swers, Michele L. *The Difference Women Make: The Policy Impact of Women in Congress* (Chicago, IL: University of Chicago Press, 2002). Note that many of these scholars are not themselves presuming that women's interests are defined by caregiving, but rather noting that female politicians and women's interests groups often define women's interests in such ways.

35 Kerber, Linda K., "The Republican Mother: Women and the Enlightenment – American Perspective," *American Quarterly* 28(Summer 1976): 187–205; Kerber, Linda K., *Women of the Republic: Intellect and Ideology in Revolutionary America* (Chapel Hill, NC: University of North Carolina Press, 1980); Kerber, Linda K., "The Republican Ideology of the Revolutionary Generation," *American Quarterly* 37(Autumn 1985): 474–95.

36 See: Ruddick, Sara, *Maternal Thinking: Toward a Politics of Peace* (Boston, MA: Beacon Press, 1989); Elshtain, Jean Bethke, *Public Man, Private Woman* (Princeton, NJ: Princeton University Press, 1981).

37 Elder, Laurel and Steven Greene, "Parenthood and the Gender Gap." In *Voting the Gender Gap*, ed. Lois Duke Whitaker (Champaign, IL: University of Illinois Press, 2008), pp. 119–40; Eagly, Alice H., Amanda Diekman, Mary Johannesen-Schmidt, and Anne Koenig, "Gender

Gaps in Sociopolitical Attitudes: A Social Psychological Analysis," *Journal of Personality and Social Psychology* 87(2004): 796–816; Greenlee, Jill S., "Soccer Moms, Hockey Moms and the Question of 'Transformative' Motherhood," *Politics & Gender* 6(2010): 405–31; Kaufmann, Karen M., "The Gender Gap," *PS: Political Science and Politics* 39(2006): 447–53; Norrander, Barbara, "The History of the Gender Gaps." In *Voting the Gender Gap*, ed. Lois Duke Whitaker (Champaign, IL: University of Illinois Press, 2008), pp. 9–32; Schlesinger, Mark, and Caroline Heldman, "Gender Gap or Gender Gaps? New Perspectives on Support for Government Action and Policies," *The Journal of Politics* 63(2001): 59–92; Lizotte, "The Gender Gap in Public Opinion."

38 Carroll, Susan J., "The Disempowerment of the Gender Gap: Soccer Moms and the 1996 Elections," *PS: Political Science and Politics* 32(1999): 7–11; Carroll, Susan J., "Security Moms and Presidential Politics: Women Voters in the 2004 Election." In *Voting the Gender Gap*, ed. Lois Duke Whitaker (Champaign, IL: University of Illinois Press, 2008), pp. 75–90; Greenberg, Anna, "Year of the Woman: Private Parts and Political Parties," *Huffington Post* blog, February 18, 2013, www.huffingtonpost.com/anna-greenberg/womens-vote_b_2330928.html [accessed October 23, 2017].

39 Important early work in this vein includes Baxter, Sandra and Marjorie Lansing, *Women and Politics: The Visible Majority*, Revised Edition (Ann Arbor, MI: University of Michigan Press, 1983); Beckwith, Karen, *American Women and Political Participation: The Impacts of Work, Generation, and Feminism* (Westport, CT: Greenwood Press, 1986).

40 For example: Andersen, Kristi, "Working Women and Political Participation, 1952–1972," *American Journal of Political Science* 19(1975): 439–53.

41 Fuchs, Lawrence H., "American Jews and the Presidential Vote," *American Political Science Review* 49(June 1955): 385–401.

42 Erie, Steven P. and Martin Rein, "Women and the Welfare State." In *The Politics of the Gender Gap: The Social Construction of Political Influence* (Newbury Park, CA: Sage Publications, 1988); Iversen and Rosenbluth, "The Political Economy of Gender"; Carroll, Susan, "Women's Autonomy and the Gender Gap: 1980 and 1982." In *The Politics of the Gender Gap: The Social Construction of Political Influence*, ed. Carol Mueller (London: Sage Press, 1988), pp. 236–57.

43 Berelson, Bernard, and Paul F. Lazarsfeld, "Women: A Major Problem for the Pac," *The Public Opinion Quarterly* 9(1945): 79–82.

44 Evans, Sara M., *Born for Liberty: A History of Women in America* (New York: Free Press, 1989).

45 Andersen, "Working Women and Political Participation, 1952–1972."

46 Ford, Lynne E. *Women & Politics: The Pursuit of Equality*, Third Edition (Boston, MA: Wadsworth, 2011).

47 Andersen, Kristi, "The Gender Gap and Experiences with the Welfare State," *PS: Political Science & Politics* 32(3 1999): 17–19; Erie, Steven P. and Martin Rein, "Women and the Welfare State." In *The Politics of the Gender Gap: The Social Construction of Political Influence* (Newbury Park, CA: Sage Publications, 1988); Manza, Jeff, and Clem Brooks, "The Gender Gap in US Presidential Elections: When? Why? Implications?" *American Journal of Sociology* 103(1998): 1235–66; Schlesinger, Mark, and Caroline Heldman, "Gender Gap or Gender

Gaps? New Perspectives on Support for Government Action and Policies," *The Journal of Politics* 63(2001): 59–92.

48 Manza, Jeff, and Clem Brooks, "The Gender Gap in US Presidential Elections: When? Why? Implications?" *American Journal of Sociology* 103(1998): 1235–66.

49 Carroll, Susan, "Women's Autonomy and the Gender Gap: 1980 and 1982." In *The Politics of the Gender Gap: The Social Construction of Political Influence*, ed. Carol M. Mueller (Newbury Park, CA: Sage Publications, 1988); Huddy, Leonie, Erin Cassese, and Mary-Kate Lizotte, "Sources of Political Unity and Disunity among Women: Placing the Gender Gap in Perspective." In *Voting the Gender Gap*, ed. Lois Duke Whitaker (Champaign, IL: University of Illinois Press, 2008), pp. 141–69; Klein, Ethel, "The Gender Gap: Different Issues, Different Answers," *The Brookings Review*, 3(1985): 33–37.

50 Howell, Susan E. and Christine L. Day, "Complexities of the Gender Gap," *The Journal of Politics*, 62(2000): 858–74.

51 Edlund, Lena, and Rohini Pande, "Why Have Women Become Left-Wing? The Political Gender Gap and the Decline in Marriage," *The Quarterly Journal of Economics* 117(2002): 917–61.

52 Iversen, Torben, and Frances Rosenbluth, "The Political Economy of Gender: Explaining Cross-National Variation in the Gender Division of Labor and the Gender Voting Gap," *American Journal of Political Science* 50(2006): 1–19, p. 12.

53 Huddy, Leonie, Erin Cassese, and Mary-Kate Lizotte, "Sources of Political Unity and Disunity among Women:: Placing the Gender Gap in Perspective." In *Voting the Gender Gap*, ed. Lois Duke Whitaker (Champaign, IL: University of Illinois Press, 2008), pp. 141–69.

54 Burns, Schlozman, and Verba, *The Private Roots of Public Action*.

55 See, e.g., Carroll, "Women's Autonomy and the Gender Gap."

56 E.g., Jackson, John E., "Issues, Party Choice, and Presidential Votes," *American Journal of Political Science* 19(1975): 161–85; Franklin, Charles H. and John E. Jackson, "The Dynamics of Party Identification," *American Political Science Review* 77(1983): 957–73; Fiorina, Morris P., *Retrospective Voting in American National Elections* (New Haven, CT: Yale University Press, 1981); Erikson, Robert S., Michael B. MacKuen, and James A. Stimson, *The Macro Polity* (New York: Cambridge University Press, 2002).

57 Campbell, Converse, Miller, and Stokes, *The American Voter*; see, e.g., Niemi, Richard G. and Herbert F. Weisberg, "How Much Does Politics Affect Party Identification?" In *Controversies in Voting Behavior*, Fourth Edition (Washington, DC: CQ Press, 2001).

58 Green, Donald P., Bradley Palmquist, and Eric Shickler. *Partisan Hearts and Minds: Political Parties and the Social Identity of Voters* (New Haven, CT: Yale University Press, 2002).

59 Ondercin, Heather L., "Who Is Responsible for the Gender Gap? The Dynamics of Men's and Women's Democratic Macropartisanship, 1950–2012," *Political Research Quarterly* 70(2017): 749–61.

60 Men who identify as feminists also are more likely to identify as Democrats, but to a lesser extent than women. Huddy, Leonie and Johanna Willmann, "Partisan Sorting and the Feminist Gender Gap in American Politics." Working paper, 2017, www.researchgate.net/project/The-Feminist-Gap-in-American-Politics [accessed February 15, 2018]; see also Conover, Pamela Johnston, "Feminists and the Gender Gap," *The Journal of Politics* 50(1988): 985–1010; Cook, Elizabeth Adell, and Clyde Wilcox, "Feminism and the Gender Gap – A Second Look," *The Journal of*

Politics 53(1991): 1111–22; Cook, Elizabeth Adell, "Feminist Consciousness and Candidate Preference among American Women, 1972–1988," *Political Behavior* 15(1993): 227–46.

61 Wolbrecht, Christina, *The Politics of Women's Rights: Parties, Positions, and Change* (Princeton, NJ: Princeton University Press, 2000).

62 Preece, Jessica Robinson, "Mind the Gender Gap: An Experiment on the Influence of Self-Efficacy on Political Interest," *Politics & Gender* 12(2016): 198–217.

63 See, e.g., Blinder, Scott, and Meredith Rolfe, "Rethinking Compassion: Toward a Political Account of the Partisan Gender Gap in the United States," *Political Psychology* 39(2017): 889–906; Preece, Jessica Robinson, "Mind the Gender Gap: An Experiment on the Influence of Self-Efficacy on Political Interest," *Politics & Gender* 12(2016): 198–217; Kanthak, Kristin, and Jonathan Woon, "Women Don't Run? Election Aversion and Candidate Entry," *American Journal of Political Science* 59(2015): 595–612.

64 For example: Diekman, Amanda B. and Monica C. Schneider, "A Social Role Theory Perspective on Gender Gaps in Political Attitudes," *Psychology of Women Quarterly* 34(2010): 486–97; Manza, Jeff, and Clem Brooks, "The Gender Gap in US Presidential Elections: When? Why? Implications?" *American Journal of Sociology* 103(1998): 1235–66; Howell, Susan E. and Christine L. Day, "Complexities of the Gender Gap," *The Journal of Politics* 62(August 2000): 858–74.

4 ENTER THE WOMEN VOTERS

1 "Women's Vote Will be a Vital Factor," *Los Angeles Times* April 15, 1920, p. 11.

2 "Women Transforming Polls, Says Mrs. Catt After Vote for Cox," *Minneapolis Morning Tribune*, November 3, 1920, p. 3.

3 Allen, Frederick Lewis, *Only Yesterday: An Informal History of the Nineteen-Twenties* (New York: Harper & Row, Publishers, 1957), pp. 95–96.

4 Burnham, Walter Dean, "Those High Nineteenth-Century American Voting Turnouts: Fact or Fiction?" *Journal of Interdisciplinary History* XVI(Spring 1986): 613–44; Hofstadter, Richard, *The Age of Reform: From Bryan to F.D.R.* (New York: Alfred A. Knopf, 1955); Fuchs, Lawrence H., "Election of 1928." In *History of American Presidential Elections, 1789–1968*, eds. Arthur M. Schlesinger, Jr. and Fred L. Israel (New York: Chelsea House Publishers in Association with McGraw-Hill Book Co., 1971); Evans, Sara M., *Born for Liberty: A History of Women in America* (New York: Free Press, 1989); Sundquist, James L., *Dynamics of the Party System: Alignment and Realignment in the United States*, Revised Edition (Washington, DC: The Brookings Institution, 1983).

5 Hicks, John D., *Republican Ascendancy, 1921–1933* (New York: Harper & Row, 1960); McCoy, Donald R., "Election of 1920." In *History of American Presidential Elections, 1789–1968*, eds. Arthur M. Schlesinger, Jr. and Fred L. Israel (New York: Chelsea House Publishers in Association with McGraw-Hill Book Co., 1971); Degler, Carl N., "American Political Parties and the Rise of the City: An Interpretation," *Journal of American History* 51(June 1964): 41–59; Bagby, Wesley M., *The Road to Normalcy: The Presidential Campaign and Election of 1920* (Baltimore, MA: The Johns Hopkins Press, 1962); Burner, David, "Election of 1924." In *History of American Presidential*

Elections, 1789–1968, eds. Arthur M. Schlesinger, Jr. and Fred L. Israel (New York: Chelsea House Publishers in Association with McGraw-Hill Book Co., 1971); Burner, David, *The Politics of Provincialism: The Democratic Party in Transition, 1918–1932*, Second Edition (Cambridge, MA: Harvard University Press, 1986) Hofstadter, Richard, *The Age of Reform: From Bryan to F.D.R.* (New York: Alfred A. Knopf, 1955); Rosenstone, Steven J., Roy L. Behr, and Edward H. Lazarus, *Third Parties in America: Citizen Response to Major Party Failure*, Second Edition (Princeton, NJ: Princeton University Press, 1996); Scammon, Richard M., ed. *America at the Polls: A Handbook of Presidential Election Statistics, 1920–1964* (Pittsburgh, PA: University of Pittsburgh Press, 1965).

6 Silva, Ruth C. *Rum, Religion, and Votes: 1928 Re-examined* (University Park, PA: Pennsylvania State University Press, 1962).

7 Fuchs, Lawrence H., "American Jews and the Presidential Vote," *American Political Science Review* 49(June 1955): 385–401; Peel, Roy V. and Thomas C. Donnelly, *The 1928 Campaign: An Analysis* (New York: Richard R. Smith, Inc., 1931).

8 Hicks, John D., *Republican Ascendancy, 1921–1933* (New York: Harper & Row, 1960); see also Harris, Louis, *Is There a Republican Majority? Political Trends, 1952–1956* (New York: Harper & Brothers, 1954); MacRae, Duncan Jr. and James A. Meldrum, "Critical Elections in Illinois: 1888–1958," *American Political Science Review* 54(September 1960): 669–83.

9 Degler, "American Political Parties and the Rise of the City: An Interpretation;" Harris, *Is There a Republican Majority?*; Hicks, *Republican Ascendancy.*

10 Burner, *The Politics of Provincialism*; Hicks, *Republican Ascendancy*; Scammon, *America at the Polls*; Sundquist, *Dynamics of the Party System*; Freidel, Frank, "Election of 1932." In *History of American Presidential Elections, 1789–1968*, eds. Arthur M. Schlesinger, Jr. and Fred L. Israel (New York: Chelsea House Publishers in Association with McGraw-Hill Book Co., 1971).

11 Jensen, Richard J. "The Causes and Cures of Unemployment in the Great Depression," *The Journal of Interdisciplinary History* 19(1989): 553–83; Sundquist, *Dynamics of the Party System*; Evans, *Born for Liberty*; Leuchtenburg, William E.,. "Election of 1936." In *History of American Presidential Elections, 1789–1968*, eds. Arthur M. Schlesinger, Jr. and Fred L. Israel (New York: Chelsea House Publishers in Association with McGraw-Hill Book Co., 1971); Scammon, *America at the Polls.*

12 Evans, *Born for Liberty*; Klein, Ethel, *Gender Politics: From Consciousness to Mass Politics* (Cambridge, MA: Harvard University Press, 1984); Van Horn, Susan Householder, *Women, Work, and Fertility, 1900–1986* (New York: New York University Press, 1988).

13 Evans, *Born for Liberty*; Klein, *Gender Politics*; Goss, Kirstin A., *The Paradox of Gender Equality: How American Women's Groups Gained and Lost Their Public Voice* (Ann Arbor, MI: University of Michigan Press, 2013); Cott, Nancy F., "Across the Great Divide: Women in Politics Before and After 1920." In *Women, Politics, and Change*, eds. Louise Tilly and Patricia Gurin (New York: Russell Sage Foundation, 1990); Freedman, Estelle, "Separatism as Strategy: Female Institution Building and American Feminism, 1870–1930," *Feminist Studies* 5(Fall 1979): 512–29; Sarvasy, Wendy, "Beyond the Difference versus Equality Policy Debate: Postsuffrage Feminism, Citizenship, and the Quest for a Feminist Welfare State," *Signs: Journal of Women in Culture and Society* 17(Winter 1992): 329–62.; Young, Louise M., *In the Public Interest: The League of Women Voters, 1920–1970* (New York: Greenwood Press, 1989); see., e.g., "Women Will Oppose Equal Rights Plan," *New York Times*, May 1, 1924, p. 11; Bent, Silas, "The Women's War,"

New York Times, January 14, 1923, p. SM4; Smith, Ethel M., "Women Working for New Laws," *New York Times*, November 29, 1925, p. XX8; "'Equal Rights' Plan Assailed as Futile," *New York Times*, November 23, 1930, p. 6; "Fight 'Equal Rights' Act," *New York Times*, June 2, 1936; McLaughlin, Kathleen, "Women Push Fight for Full Equality," *New York Times*, July 24, 1937, p. 17.

14 Evans, *Born for Liberty*; Klein, *Gender Politics*; Van Horn, *Women, Work, and Fertility, 1900–1986*.

15 Drexel, Constance, "Women Political Chiefs Lay Plans," *Washington Post*, February 25, 1922.

16 Lemons, J. Stanley, *The Woman Citizen: Social Feminism in the 1920s* (Charlottesville, VA: University Press of Virginia, 1973); Greenlee, Jill S., *The Political Consequences of Motherhood* (Ann Arbor, MI: University of Michigan Press, 2014); Brown, George Rothwell, "Aim to Win Johnson," *Washington Post*, June 24, 1920, p. 1.

17 Andersen, Kristi, *After Suffrage: Women in Partisan and Electoral Politics Before the New Deal* (Chicago, IL: University of Chicago Press, 1996); Sainsbury, Diane, "Beyond the 'Great Divide': Women in Partisan Politics Before and After the Federal Suffrage Amendment," *Women & Politics* 20(1999): 59–80; "Party Chairmen Tell of Woman's Political Role," *Washington Post*, May 20, 1923, p. 72; Brown, "Aim to Win Johnson."

18 "Tariff Easy, Say Women; Will Show Men With Vote," *Washington Post*, June 11, 1922.

19 "To Train Women Speakers," *New York Times*, September 8, 1924; "Maine Democrats Organize Women," *New York Times*, September 5, 1924; "Both Old Parties Woo Women Voters." *New York Times*, October 10, 1924, p. 5; "Appeals to Women to Vote for Davis," *New York Times*, November 2, 1924, p. 6; "Three Women Debate Campaign Issues," *New York Times*, November 2, 1924, p. 7; "Women's Vote Will Win 1924 Campaign, G.O.P. Office Says," *Duluth (MN) News Tribune*, September 14, 1924; "Club Prepares Rooms as Headquarters," *Duluth (MN) News Tribune*, September 17, 1924; "G.O.P. Women of State Are Now Organized," *The Duluth (MN) News Tribune*, October 6, 1924; "Davis and Smith at Women's Rally," *Hartford (CT) Daily Courant*, October 26, 1924; see Corder, J. Kevin and Christina Wolbrecht, *Counting Women's Ballots: Female Voters from Suffrage Through the New Deal* (New York: Cambridge University Press, 2016).

20 E.g., "Service to Party Keynote of Talk by Mrs. Fosseen," *Duluth (MN) News Tribune*, September 18, 1924; "Coolidge Club Plans to Hold Precinct Teas; Women Voters to Hear Speakers at a Series of Meetings," *Duluth (MN) News Tribune*, September 25, 1924; "Meriden Women Hear Mrs. Merritt; Hartford Speaker Praises National and State Tickets," *Hartford (CT) Daily Courant*, September 24, 1924. See Corder and Wolbrecht, *Counting Women's Ballots*.

21 Greenlee, *The Political Consequences of Motherhood*.

22 MacKay, Kenneth Campbell, *The Progressive Movement of 1924* (New York: Columbia University Press, 1947); Thelen, David P., *Robert M. La Follette and the Insurgent Spirit* (Boston, MA: Little, Brown, and Company, 1976).

23 Quoted in Harvey, Anna L., *Votes Without Leverage: Women in Electoral Politics, 1920–1970* (Cambridge: Cambridge University Press, 1991), p. 132.

24 Greenlee, *The Political Consequences of Motherhood*; Harvey, *Votes Without Leverage*.

25 Quoted in Peel and Donnelly, *The 1928 Campaign*, p. 100.

26 Peel and Donnelly, *The 1928 Campaign*, p. 84.

27 Quoted in Harvey, *Votes Without Leverage*, p. 134.

28 Greenlee, *The Political Consequences of Motherhood*; Peel and Donnelly, *The 1928 Campaign*.

29 Freeman, *A Room at a Time*; Freidel, Frank, "Election of 1932"; Leuchtenburg, William E., "Election of 1936." In *History of American Presidential Elections, 1789–1968*, eds. Arthur M. Schlesinger, Jr. and Fred L. Israel (New York: Chelsea House Publishers in Association with McGraw-Hill Book Co., 1971).

30 Greenlee, *The Political Consequences of Motherhood*.

31 Evans, *Born for Liberty*; see Adams, Mildred, "To the Woman in Politics Comes Also a New Deal," *New York Times*, April 30, 1933, p. SM4.

32 Evans, *Born for Liberty*, p. 210.

33 Ware, Susan, *Beyond Suffrage: Women in the New Deal* (Cambridge, MA: Harvard University Press, 1981).

34 Ogburn, William F. and Inez Goltra, "How Women Vote: A Study of an Election in Portland, Oregon," *Political Science Quarterly* 34 (1919): 413–33, p. 413.

35 "The Women's Vote," *New York Times*, October 25, 1932, p. 18.

36 For details on the statistical methodology, data, and a detailed analysis of the findings, see Corder and Wolbrecht, *Counting Women's Ballots*.

37 Huckfeldt, R. Robert and John Sprague, *Citizens, Politics, and Social Communication: Information and Influence in an Election Campaign* (New York: Cambridge University Press, 1995).

38 See, e.g., "To Teach Women Politics," *Washington Post*, August 1, 1920, p. 31; "Play Election Devised to Teach Women How to Vote," *Boston Globe*, August 10, 1920, p. 2; "Registration Week Begins Tomorrow," *New York Times*, October 3, 1920, p. 4; "Women Learn How to Vote at Fair," *St. Paul Dispatch*, 6 September 1920, p. 5; "Registration Week Begins Tomorrow," *New York Times*, October 3, 1920, p. 4; see Gordon, Felice D., *After Winning: The Legacy of the New Jersey Suffragists, 1920–1947* (New Brunswick, NJ: Rutgers University Press, 1986); Scott, Anne Firor, *The Southern Lady: From Pedestal to Politics, 1830–1930* (Chicago, IL: University of Chicago Press, 1972).

39 See Harvey, *Votes Without Leverage*; e.g., "Women May Control," *Washington Post*, May 12, 1920.

40 Greenlee, *The Political Consequences of Motherhood*; for example: "Kentucky White Women Urged to Cast Ballots," *Washington Post*, November 7, 1922, p. 1.

41 See, e.g., "Party Chairmen Tell of Woman's Political Role," *Washington Post*, May 20, 1923, p. 72; "Miss Connelly Advises Women to Use the Ballot," *Chicago Defender*, February 2, 1924, p. A1; "Using Plattsburg Idea to Reach Women Voters," *New York Times*, March 16, 1924, p. XX18; "Thirty Million Women to Vote in November Elections: Leaders at Work: Move to Get Rural Vote Out," *Houston Press*, September 3, 1924; "Rallies to Urge Vote of Women," *Los Angeles Times*, September 30, 1924, p. 2; "W.C.T.U. Plans Campaign to Get Voters to Polls," *The Duluth (MN) News Tribune*, September 11, 1924; "Sixth Annual Convention of Voters Called; Get-Out-Vote Campaign Stressed by Women," *Duluth (MN) New Tribune*, September 21, 1924; "Republican Women told to Get Votes," *Washington Post*, June 13, 1924; Lamar, Nancy, "Women Play Important Part in Big Convention," *Washington Post*, June 24, 1924; "Women Politicians Educating Sisters: League of Women Voters Opens Information Booths in Department Stores," *New York Times*, October 6, 1926; Breckinridge, Sophonisba P., *Women in the Twentieth Century: A Study of their Political, Social and Economic Activities* (New York: MGraw-Hill Book Company, Inc., 1933).

42 Converse, Philip E., "Change in the American Electorate." In *The Human Meaning of Social Change*, eds. Angus Campbell and Philip E. Converse (New York: Russell Sage Foundation, 1972); Burnham, Walter Dean, "The Changing Shape of the American Political Universe," *American Political Science Review* 59(March 1965): 7–28; Valelly, Richard M., *The Two Reconstructions: The Struggle for black Enfranchisement* (Chicago, IL: University of Chicago Press, 2004).

43 Blair, Emily Newell, "Are Women a Failure in Politics?" *Harper's Magazine* 151(October 1925): 513–522; Russell, Charles Edward, "Is Woman-Suffrage a Failure?" *The Century Magazine* 35 (1924): 724–30; Tarbell, Ida M., "Is Woman's Suffrage a Failure?" *Good Housekeeping*, October 18, 1924; "Says Women Voters Sidestep Big Issues," *Washington Post*, May 9, 1923, p. 6; "Woman Suffrage Is Failure, World Survey Indicates," *Washington Post*, November 4, 1923, p. 40.

44 Breckinridge, Sophonisba P., *Women in the Twentieth Century: A Study of their Political, Social and Economic Activities* (New York: MGraw-Hill Book Company, Inc., 1933); Young, Louise M., *In the Public Interest: The League of Women Voters, 1920–1970* (New York: Greenwood Press, 1989).

45 Rice, Stuart A. and Malcolm M. Willey, "American Women's Ineffective Use of the Vote," *Current History* 20(July 1924): 641–47.

46 Alpern, Sara and Dale Baum, "Female Ballots: The Impact of the Nineteenth Amendment," *Journal of Interdisciplinary History* 26(Summer 1985): 43–67.

47 See Holbrook, Thomas M. and Emily Van Dunk, "Electoral Competition in the American States," *American Political Science Review* 87(December 1993): 955–62; Patterson, Samuel C. and Gregory Caldeira, "Getting Out the Vote: Participation in Gubernatorial Elections," *American Political Science Review* 77(September 1983): 675–89; Campbell, Angus, Philip E. Converse, Warren E. Miller, and Donald E. Stokes, *The American Voter* (New York: John Wiley and Sons, Inc., 1960); Aldrich, John H., "Rational Choice and Turnout," *American Journal of Political Science* 37(February 1993): 246–278; Rosenstone, Steven J. and John Mark Hansen, *Mobilization, Participation, and Democracy in America* (New York: Macmillan Publishing Company, 1993).

48 Mickey, Robert. *Paths Out of Dixie: The Democratization of Authoritarian Enclaves in America's Deep South, 1944–1972* (Princeton, NJ: Princeton University Press, 2015); Blakey, Gladys C., *A Handy Digest of Election Laws* (Washington, DC: League of Women Voters, 1928); Key, V.O., Jr. 1949. *Southern Politics in State and Nation* (New York: Alfred A. Knopf); Keyssar, Alexander, *The Right to Vote: The Contested History of Democracy in the United States* (New York: Basic Books, 2000).

49 Lebsock, Suzanne, "Woman Suffrage and White Supremacy: A Virginia Case Study." In *Visible Women: New Essays on American Activism*, eds. Nancy A. Hewitt and Suzanne Lebsock (Urbana, IL: University of Illinois Press, 1993); Terborg-Penn, Rosalyn, "Discrimination Against Afro-American Women in the Woman's Movement, 1830–1920." In *The Afro-American Woman: Struggles and Images*, eds. Sharon Harley and Rosalyn Terborg-Penn (Port Washington, NY: Kennikat Press, 1978); Terborg-Penn, Rosalyn, *African American Women in the Struggle for the Vote, 1850–1920* (Bloomington, IN: Indiana University Press, 1998).

50 "Drive Women from Polls in South; Southerners Threaten to Use Gun and Rope on Race Leaders," *Chicago Defender*, October 30, 1920, p. 1; see also "Urged Women to Vote; Almost Killed," *The Chicago Defender*, October 23, 1920, p. 1.

51 US Census, *Fifteenth Census of the United States: 1930. Population*, Volumes I, II, and III (Washington, DC: United States Printing Office, 1932).

52 Wilkerson-Freeman, Sarah, "The Second Battle for Woman Suffrage: Alabama White Women, the Poll Tax, and V.O. Key's Master Narrative of Southern Politics," *The Journal of Southern History* 68(May 2002): 333–74.

53 See Matthews, Glenna, *The Rise of Public Woman: Woman's Power and Woman's Place in the United States, 1630–1970* (New York: Oxford University Press, 1992); Burnham, Walter Dean, "Theory and Voting Research: Some Reflections on Converse's 'Change in the American Electorate'," *American Political Science Review* 68(September 1974): 1002–23; Sundquist, James L., *Dynamics of the Party System: Alignment and Realignment in the United States*, Revised Edition (Washington, DC: The Brookings Institution, 1983); Lichtman. Allan J. *Prejudice and the Old Politics: The Presidential Election of 1928* (Chapel Hill, NC: University of North Carolina Press, 1979).

54 "Forecasts Big Vote by Women of State," *New York Times*, October 7, 1928; "This Year's Woman Vote to Set a High Record," *New York Times*, October 21, 1928, p. 8. Also: "Campaigns to Be Hot: Heaviest Vote in Age Forecast," *Los Angeles Times*, July 1, 1928; "Vox Populi Puts on Petticoat," *Los Angeles Times*, October 21, 1928; "Americans at Fever Pitch for Great Decision Today," *Los Angeles Times*, November 6, 1928.

55 McCormick, Anne O'Hare, "Enter Woman, The New Boss of Politics," *The New York Times Magazine*, October 21, 1928, p. 3; quoted in Greenlee, *The Political Consequences of Motherhood*, p. 27.

56 For example: "43,000,000 Have Qualified for Election Nov. 6. [AP story]," *Hartford (CT) Daily Courant*, October 29, 1928; "Twice as Many Women as Men Register Daily," *The Duluth (MN) News Tribune*, September 20, 1928; "Women Will Decide How Missouri Goes," *New York Times*, October 27, 1928; "Women Play an Important Part in Presidential Campaign," *Santa Fe New Mexican*, October 20, 1928; "What'll Women Do? Is Chicago Election Enigma," *Chicago Daily Tribune*, October 4, 1928.

57 Andersen, Kristi, *The Creation of a Democratic Majority, 1928–1936* (Chicago, IL: University of Chicago Press, 1979); Burner, David, *The Politics of Provincialism: The Democratic Party in Transition, 1918–1932*, Second Edition (Cambridge, MA: Harvard University Press, 1986); Jeffries, John W., *Testing the Roosevelt Coalition: Connecticut Society and Politics in the Era of World War II* (Knoxville, TN: University of Tennessee Press, 1979); Burnham, "Theory and Voting Research;" Lubell, Samuel, *The Future of American Politics* (New York: Harper & Brothers, 1952).

58 Andersen, Kristi, *After Suffrage: Women in Partisan and Electoral Politics before the New Deal* (Chicago, IL: University of Chicago Press, 1996); Burner, *The Politics of Provincialism*.

59 Corder and Wolbrecht, *Counting Women's Ballots*.

60 Contemporary writers worried that women's lack of experience would hamper their transition to being active voters; see Gerould, Katharine Fullerton, "Some American Women and the Vote," *Scribner's Magazine* 127(May 1925): 449–45; Wells, Marguerite M., "Some Effects of Woman Suffrage," *The Annals of the American Academy* 143(1929): 207–16.

61 Gerber, Alan S., Donald P. Green, and Ron Shachar, "Voting May Be Habit-Forming: Evidence from a Randomized Field Experiment," *American Journal of Political Science* 47(July 2003): 540–50; Plutzer, Eric, "Becoming a Habitual Voter: Inertia, Resources, and Growth in Young Adulthood," *American Political Science Review* 96(March 2002): 41–56.

62 Firebaugh, Glenn and Kevin Chen, "Vote Turnout of Nineteenth Century Women: The Enduring Effect of Disenfranchisement," *American Journal of Sociology* 100(January 1995): 972–96; but see Beckwith, Karen, *American Women and Political Participation: The Impacts of Work, Generations, and Feminism* (New York: Greenwood Press, 1986).

63 Kleppner, Paul, *Who Voted? The Dynamics of Electoral Turnout, 1840–1940* (New York: Praeger, 1982); Niemi, Richard G., Harold W. Stanley, and C. Lawrence Evans, "Age and Turnout Among the Newly Enfranchised: Life Cycle versus Experience Effects," *European Journal of Political Research* 12(1984): 371–86.

64 Andersen, *The Creation of the Democratic Majority*, p. 196.

65 Andersen, *After Suffrage*; Baker, Paula, "The Domestication of Politics: Women and American Political Society, 1780–1920," *American Historical Review* 89(June 1984): 620–47.

66 Merriam, Charles E. and Harold F. Gosnell, *Non-voting: Causes and Methods of Control* (Chicago, IL: University of Chicago Press, 1924); see also Gosnell, Harold F., *Getting Out the Vote: An Experiment in the Stimulation of Voting* (Chicago, IL: University of Chicago Press, 1927).

67 Lazarsfeld, Paul R., Bernard R. Berelson and Hazel Gaudet, *The People's Choice* (New York: Columbia University Press, 1948), p. 49.

68 Alpern and Baum, "Female Ballots;" Flanagan, Maureen A., "The Predicament of New Rights: Suffrage and Women's Political Power from a Local Perspective," *Social Politics* 2(Fall 1995): 305–30.

69 Russell, Charles Edward, "Is Woman-Suffrage a Failure?" *The Century Magazine* 35(1924): 724–30., p. 729.

70 Gerould, Katharine Fullerton, "Some American Women and the Vote," *Scribner's Magazine* 127(May 1925): 449–52, p. 450.

71 E.g., Chafe, William H., *The American Woman: Her Changing Social, Economic, and Political Roles, 1920–1970* (New York: Oxford University Press, 1972); Goldstein, Joel H., *The Effects of the Adoption of Woman Suffrage: Sex Differences in Voting Behavior – Illinois, 1914–21* (New York: Praeger, 1984).

72 Harvey, *Votes Without Leverage*; Brown, Courtney, *Ballots of Tumult: A Portrait of Volatility in American Voting* (Ann Arbor, MI: University of Michigan Press, 1991); Burner, *The Politics of Provincialism*; Gould, Louis L., *Grand Old Party: A History of the Republicans* (New York: Random House, 2003); Lemons, *The Woman Citizen*; McCoy, "Election of 1920;" Pateman, Carole, "Three Questions about Womanhood Suffrage." In *Suffrage and Beyond: International Feminist Perspectives*, eds. Caroline Daley and Melanie Nolan (Washington Square, NY: New York University Press, 1994); Smith, Jean M., "The Voting Women of San Diego, 1920," *The Journal of San Diego History* 26(Spring 1980): 133–54; Bagby, Wesley M., *The Road to Normalcy: The Presidential Campaign and Election of 1920* (Baltimore, MA: Johns Hopkins Press, 1962); Willey, Malcolm, M. and Stuart A. Rice, "A Sex Cleavage in the Presidential Election of 1920," *Journal of the American Statistical Association* 19(1924): 519–20; Huthmacher, J. Joseph, *Massachusetts People and Politics, 1919–1933* (Cambridge: The Belknap Press of Harvard University Press, 1959); Goldstein, Joel H., *The Effects of the Adoption of Woman Suffrage: Sex Differences in Voting Behavior – Illinois, 1914–21* (New York: Praeger, 1984). For example: "Recapitulation of Straw Ballot," *Boston Globe*, 16 October 1920, p. 1; "500,000 Illinois Women to Vote on Wednesday," *Chicago Tribune*, September 12, 1920, p. 2; Crawford, William H., "Analyzes Power of Woman's Vote," *New York Times*, October 10, 1920, p. II, 10; "Women Help Win State by Record Vote," *Minneapolis Morning Tribune*, September 14, 1920, p. 1.

73 Rymph, Catherine E., *Republican Women: Feminism and Conservatism from Suffrage Through the Rise of the New Right* (Chapel Hill, NC: University of North Carolina Press, 2006).

74 Harvey, *Votes Without Leverage.*

75 Fuchs, Lawrence H., "American Jews and the Presidential Vote," *American Political Science Review* 49(June 1955): 385–401; Berelson, Bernard R., Paul F. Lazarsfeld, and William N. McPhee, *Voting: A Study of Opinion Formation in a Presidential Election* (Chicago, IL: University of Chicago Press, 1954); Huckfeldt, Robert, Paul Allen Beck, Russell J. Dalton, and Jeffrey Levine, "Political Environments, Cohesive Social Groups, and the Communication of Public Opinion," *American Journal of Political Science* 29(November 1995): 1025–54.

76 Evans, Sara M., *Born for Liberty: A History of Women in America* (New York: Free Press, 1989); Baker, "The Domestication of Politics;" O'Neill, William L., *Everyone Was Brave: A History of Feminism in America* (New York: Quadrangle, 1971); Flexner, Eleanor, *Century of Struggle: The Women's Rights Movement in the United States* (Cambridge, MA: Harvard University Press, 1959); Allen, Florence E., "The First Ten Years," *The Woman's Journal* August(1930): 5; Toombs, Elizabeth O., "Politicians, Take Notice," *Good Housekeeping* March(1929): 14–15: Wells, "Some Effects of Woman Suffrage;" McCormick, Anne O'Hare, "Enter Woman, The New Boss of Politics," *The New York Times Magazine*, October 21, 1928, p. 3; Willey and Rice, "A Sex Cleavage in the Presidential Election of 1920"; Rice and Willey, "Women's Ineffective Use of the Vote;" Russell, "Is Women's Suffrage a Failure?"; Tarbell, "Is Woman's Suffrage a Failure?"; Ogburn, William F. and Inez Goltra, "How Women Vote: A Study of An Election in Portland, Oregon," *Political Science Quarterly* 34(1919): 413–33.

77 McDonagh, Eileen L. and H. Douglas Price, "Woman Suffrage in the Progressive Era: Patterns of Opposition and Support in Referenda Voting, 1910–1918," *American Political Science Review* 79(1985): 415–35; Flexner, *Century of Struggle.*

78 The estimates are support for all third parties (Prohibition, Socialist, and Miscellaneous Independent), but we refer to this as Progressive support since over 96% of the third-party ballots are for La Follette. Due to difficulties with ballot access, La Follette was listed as the candidate for four different parties, depending on the state; Rosenstone, Steven J., Roy L. Behr, and Edward H. Lazarus, *Third Parties in America: Citizen Response to Major Party Failure*, Second Edition (Princeton, NJ: Princeton University Press, 1996); Sundquist, James L., *Dynamics of the Party System: Alignment and Realignment in the United States*, Revised Edition (Washington, DC: The Brookings Institution, 1983).

79 Andersen, *The Creation of the Democratic Majority*; Campbell, Converse, Miller, and Stokes, *The American Voter*; Campbell, James E., "Sources of the New Deal Realignment: The Contributions of Conversion and Mobilization to Partisan Change," *Western Political Quarterly* 38(September 1985): 357–76; Prindle, David F., "Voter Turnout, Critical Elections, and the New Deal Realignment," *Social Science History* III(Winter 1979): 144–70; Wanat, John, "The Application of Non-Analytic, Most Possible Estimation Technique: The Relative Impact of Mobilization and Conversion of Votes in the New Deal," *Political Methodology* 6(1979): 357–74; Burnham, Walter Dean, *Critical Elections and the Mainsprings of American Politics* (New York: Norton, 1970); Erikson, Robert S. and Kent L. Tedin, "The 1928–1936 Partisan Realignment: The Case for the Conversion Hypothesis," *American Political Science Review* 75(1981): 951–62; Hawley, George and Inaki Sagarazu, "Where Did the Votes Go? Reassessing American Party Realignments via Vote Transfers between Major Parties from 1860 to 2008," *Electoral Studies* 31(2012): 726–39; Ladd, Everett C. and Charles D. Hadley, *Transformation of the American Party System: Political*

Coalitions from the New Deal to the 1970's (New York: Norton, 1975); Sundquist, *Dynamics of the Party System.*

80 McPhee, William N. and Jack Ferguson, "Political Immunization." In *Public Opinion and Congressional Elections*, eds. William N. McPhee and William A. Glaser (New York: Free Press of Glencoe, 1962).

81 Burnham, *Critical Elections and the Mainspring of American Politics*; Sundquist, *Dynamics of the Party System*; Kleppner, *Who Voted*; Gosnell, Harold F., *Grassroots Politics: National Voting Behavior of Typical States* (Washington, DC: American Council on Public Affairs, 1942); Campbell, Converse, Miller, and Stokes, *The American Voter*; Andersen, *The Creation of the New Deal Democrats*; Burnham, "Theory and Voting Research;" Gamm, Gerald, *The Making of the New Deal Democrats: Voting Behavior and Realignment in Boston, 1920–1940* (Chicago, IL: University of Chicago Press, 1989).

82 E.g., Box-Steffensmeier, Jan, Suzanna De Boef, and Tse-Min Lin, "The Dynamics of the Partisan Gender Gap," *American Political Science Review* 98(August 2004): 515–28.

83 Roosevelt, Eleanor, "Women in Politics" (second of three articles), *Good Housekeeping* 110 (March 1940), p. 45.

5 FEMININE MYSTIQUE AND THE AMERICAN VOTER

1 See, for example, Goss, Kirstin A., *The Paradox of Gender Equality: How American Women's Groups Gained and Lost Their Public Voice* (Ann Arbor, MI: University of Michigan Press, 2013); Rupp, Leila J. and Verta Taylor, *Survival in the Doldrums: The American Women's Rights Movement, 1945 to the 1960s* (New York: Oxford University Press, 1987).

2 Loper, Mary Lou, "Femme Bloc Could Run US," *Los Angeles Times*, June 27, 1960, p. A1.

3 Friedman, Leon, "Election of 1944." In *History of American Presidential Elections, 1789–1968*, Volume IV, ed. Arthur M. Schlesinger (New York: McGraw-Hill Book Co., 1971); Greenlee, Jill S., *The Political Consequences of Motherhood* (Ann Arbor, MI: University of Michigan Press, 2014).

4 Schickler, Eric, *Racial Realignment: The Transformation of American Liberalism, 1932–1965* (Princeton, NJ: Princeton University Press, 2016); Carmines, Edward G. and James A. Stimson, *Issue Evolution: Race and the Transformation of American Politics* (Princeton, NJ: Princeton University Press, 1989); Mickey, Robert, *Paths Out of Dixie: The Democratization of Authoritarian Enclaves in America's Deep South, 1944–1972* (Princeton, NJ: Princeton University Press, 2015); Brewer, Mark D. and Jeffrey M. Stonecash, *Dynamics of American Political Parties* (New York: Cambridge University Press, 2009); Black, Earl and Merle Black, *The Rise of Southern Republicans* (Cambridge, MA: The Belknap Press of Harvard University Press, 2002); Kirkendall, Richard S., "Election of 1948." In *History of American Presidential Elections, 1789–1968*, Volume IV, ed. Arthur M. Schlesinger (New York: McGraw-Hill Book Co., 1971). On the South and the gender gap, see Norrander, Barbara, "The Intraparty Gender Gap: Differences between Male and Female Voters in the 1980–2000 Presidential Primaries," *PS: Political Science and Politics* 36(2003): 181–86; Schreckhise, William D. and Todd G. Shields, "Ideological Realignment in the Contemporary US Electorate Revisited," *Social Science Quarterly* 84(2003): 596–612.

5 Brewer and Stonecash, *Dynamics of the American Political Parties*; Bernstein, Barton J., "Election of 1952." In *History of American Presidential Elections, 1789–1968*, Volume IV, ed. Arthur M. Schlesinger (New York: McGraw-Hill Book Co., 1971); Moos, Malcom, "Election of 1956." In *History of American Presidential Elections, 1789–1968*, Volume IV, ed. Arthur M. Schlesinger (New York: McGraw-Hill Book Co., 1971); Sorenson, Theordore C., "Election of 1960." In *History of American Presidential Elections, 1789–1968*, Volume IV, ed. Arthur M. Schlesinger (New York: McGraw-Hill Book Co., 1971).

6 Poole, Keith T. and Howard Rosenthal, *Congress: A Political-Economic History of Roll Call Voting* (New York: Oxford University Press, 1997); Schickler, *Racial Realignment*; Brewer and Stonecash, *Dynamics of American Political Parties*; Carmines and Stimson, *Issue Evolution*; Baylor, Christopher, *First to the Party: The Group Origins of Political Transformations* (Philadelphia, PA: University of Pennsylvania Press, 2017).

7 Baxter and Lansing, *Women and Politics*; Klein, *Gender Politics*; Evans, *Born for Liberty*; Rupp and Taylor, *Survival in the Doldrums*; Van Horn, *Women, Work, and Fertility, 1900–1986*.

8 Evans, *Born for Liberty*; Van Horn, *Women, Work, and Fertility, 1900–1986*.

9 Klein, *Gender Politics*; Van Horn, *Women, Work, and Fertility, 1900–1986*.

10 Brown, "Women's Vote."

11 "Topics of the Times," *New York Times*, October 30, 1944, p. 18.

12 Loper, Mary Lou, "A Feminine Bloc? None, Experts Say," *Los Angeles Times*, June 14, 1960, p. A1.

13 For example: "Franchise Education Group Lead by Kaiser Starts Drive for Big Registration and Vote," *New York Times*, October 1, 1944, p. 40; "President Appeals for Women's Vote," *New York Times*, October 4, 1952, p. 9; Furman, Bess, "Six G.O.P. Women Keep House Posts," *New York Times*, November 6, 1952, p. 34; Loper, Mary Lou, "Is She a Wise Voter?" *Los Angeles Times*, August 3, 1960, p. A1.

14 Knowles, Clayton, "Stevenson Says His Rivals Recoil from 'New Ideas,'" *New York Times*, October 25, 1956.

15 Braestrup, Peter, "Both Parties Aim at Women's Vote," *New York Times*, October 17, 1960, p. 21.

16 Leimert, "Increased Governmental Activity by Women Urged for Postwar Era," *Los Angeles Times*, November 5, 1944, p. E1.

17 The cookbooks were produced by the Department of Agriculture, and featured recipes that accommodated wartime rationing. "Candidate Boils Over in a Political Stew As Rival Mails Cook Books to 10,000 Voters," *New York Times*, October 25, 1944, p. 23.

18 "President Appeals for Women's Vote."

19 Brown, "Women's Vote."

20 Loper, Mary Lou, "Six Throw Bonnets in the Ring," *Los Angeles Times*, September 28, 1960, p. A1.

21 Leimert, "Increased Governmental Activity by Women Urged for Postwar Era."

22 Leimert, Lucille, "Rep. Clare Booth Luce Sees Women Taking Leading Role in Postwar Politics," *Los Angeles Times*, January 9, 1944, p. B1.

23 Harrison, Emma, "Mrs. Johnson Campaigns Here, Giving Praise to Mrs. Kennedy," *New York Times*, October 5, 1960.

24 Loper, Mary Lou, "Femme Bloc Could Run US," *Los Angeles Times*, June 27, 1960, p. A1.

25 Harris, Louis, *Is There a Republican Majority? Political Trends, 1952–1956* (New York: Harper & Brothers Publishers, 1954); Lane, Robert E., *Political Life: Why People Get Involved in Politics* (Glencoe, IL: The Free Press, 1959).

26 Converse, Jean M., *Survey Research in the United States: Roots and Emergence, 1890–1960* (Berkeley, CA: University of California Press, 1987).

27 Lazarsfeld, Paul F., Bernard Berelson, and Hazel Gaudet, *The People's Choice: How the Voter Makes Up His Mind in a Presidential Campaign* (New York: Columbia University Press, 1948); Berelson, Bernard R., Paul F. Lazarsfeld, and William N. McPhee, *Voting: A Study of Opinion Formation in a Presidential Campaign* (Chicago, IL: University of Chicago Press, 1954).

28 Burns, Nancy, "The Michigan, then National, then American National Election Studies," American National Election Studies, www.electionstudies.org/history/20060815Burns_ ANES_history.pdf [accessed October 11, 2017]; Converse, *Survey Research in the United States*.

29 Quoted in Berinsky, Adam J., "American Public Opinion in the 1930s and 1940s: The Analysis of Quota-Controlled Sample Survey Data," *Public Opinion Quarterly* 70(2006): 499–526.

30 Bourque and Grossholtz, "Politics as Unnatural Practice;" Poole, Keith T. and L. Harmon Zeigler, *Women: Public Opinion, and Politics: The Changing Political Attitudes of American Women* (New York: Longman, 1985).

31 Malone, Clare, "From 1937 to Hillary Clinton, How Americans Have Felt About a Woman President," *FiveThirtyEight* blog, https://fivethirtyeight.com/features/from-1937-to-hillary-clinton-how-americans-have-felt-about-a-female-president/ [accessed October 11, 2017].

32 Berinsky, "American Public Opinion in the 1930s and 1940s.

33 Walton, Hanes Jr., *Invisible Politics: Black Political Behavior* (Albany, NY: State University of New York Press, 1985).

34 Matthews, Donald R. and James W. Prothro, *Negroes and the New Southern Politics* (New York: Harcourt, Brace, & World, Inc., 1966).

35 Berinsky, Adam J. and Eric Schickler, "Gallup Data, 1936–1945: Guide to Coding & Weighting," The American Mass Public in the 1930s and 1940s [Computer file]. Individual surveys conducted by the Gallup Organization [producers], 1936–1945 (Roper Center for Public Opinion Research, University of Connecticut [distributor], 2011); Berinsky, "American Public Opinion in the 1930s and 1940s. Berinsky, Adam J., Eleanor Neff Powell, Eric Schickler, and Ian Brett Yohai, "Revisiting Public Opinion in the 1930s and 1940s," *PS: Political Science and Politics* 44(2011): 515–20.

36 Caughey, Devin, Adam J. Berinsky, Sara Chatfield, Erin Hartman, Eric Schickler, and Jasjeet S. Sekhon, "Population Estimation and Calibration Weighting for Nonresponse and Sampling Bias: An Application to Quota-Sampled Opinion Polls, 1936–1953." Working paper, May 1, 2017. We are grateful to the authors for sharing these weights with us.

37 https://ropercenter.cornell.edu/ [accessed July 9, 2019].

38 Campbell, Converse, Miller and Stokes, *The American Voter*; Baxter and Lansing, *Women and Politics*.

39 Schickler, *Racial Realignment*; Hobbs, Frank and Nicole Stoops, *Demographic Trends in the 20th Century: Census 2000 Special Reports* (Washington, DC: US Census Bureau, US Department of Commerce, 2002), www.census.gov/prod/2002pubs/censr-5.pdf [accessed October 17, 2017].

40 See Schickler, Eric and Devin Caughey, "Public Opinion, Organized Labor, and the Limits of New Deal Liberalism, 1936–1945," *Studies in American Political Development* 25(October

2011): 162–89. From 1940 to 1952, Gallup racial identity response choices were "White" and "Colored." In 1956, the choices were "White" and "Non-white." Gallup first includes "Other" as a category in 1960, but there are a total of 4 (0.1%) "Other" responses out of 3,123 respondents in the 1960 Gallup poll. As the numbers were so small, we exclude "Other" from our calculations, and treat "Colored" and "Non-white" as African American in Chapters 5 and 6.

41 Walton, Hanes Jr., *Invisible Politics: Black Political Behavior* (Albany, NY: State University of New York Press, 1985); Nealy, Lisa Nikol, *African-American Women Voters: Racializing Religiosity, Political Consciousness, and Progressive Political Action in US Presidential Elections from 1964 through 2008* (Lanham, MD: University Press of America, 2009).

42 Matthews and Prothro, *Negroes and the New Southern Politics*; Lansing, Marjorie, "The Voting Patterns of American Black Women." In *A Portrait of Marginality: The Political Behavior of American Women*, eds. Marianne Githens and Jewel L. Prestage (New York: David McKay Company, Inc., 1977), pp. 379–94; Nie, Norman H., Sidney Verba, and John R. Petrocik, *The Changing American Voter* (Cambridge, MA: Harvard University Press, 1979).

43 Campbell, Converse, Miller, and Stokes, *The American Voter*.

44 See Verba, Sidney, Kay Lehman Schlozman, and Henry E. Brady, *Voice and Equality: Civic Voluntarism in American Politics* (Cambridge, MA: Harvard University Press, 1995); more recent research suggests the impact of education may be less about the experience of college per se, and more about the social and economic processes that produce young people who select into college; see Kam, Cindy D. and Carl L. Palmer, "Reconsidering the Effects of Education on Political Participation," *Journal of Politics* 70(July 2008): 612–31.

45 Campbell, Converse, Miller, and Stokes, *The American Voter*, p. 476.

46 Kam and Palmer, "Reconsidering the Effects of Education on Political Participation."

47 On the potential consequences of the large turnout gender gap amongst less-educated voters, see Berelson and Lazarsfeld, "Women: A Major Problem for the Pac."

48 Campbell, Converse, Miller, and Stokes, *The American Voter*, p. 485.

49 Wolfinger, Raymond E. and Steven J. Rosenstone, *Who Votes?* (New Haven, CT: Yale University Press, 1980); Burns, Nancy, Kay Lehman Schlozman, and Sidney Verba, *The Private Roots of Public Action: Gender, Equality, and Political Participation* (Cambridge, MA: Harvard University Press, 2001); Nickerson, David W., "Is Voting Contagious? Evidence from Two Field Experiments," *American Political Science Review* 102(February 2008): 49–57; Greenlee, *The Political Consequences of Motherhood.*

50 Burns, Schlozman, and Verba, *The Private Roots of Public Action*; Andersen, Kristi, "Working Women and Political Participation, 1952–1972," *American Journal of Political Science* 19 (1975): 439–453; Verba, Schlozman, and Brady, *Voice and Equality.*

51 The American National Election Studies (ANES) queried respondent race and education beginning with the first survey in 1948. Questions about region and employment were added in 1952, and marriage and children items in 1956.

52 Hobbs and Stoops, *Demographic Trends in the 20th Century.*

53 Scott, Anne Firor, "After Suffrage: Southern Women in the Twenties," *Journal of Southern History* 30(1964): 298–318; Scott, Anne Firor, *The Southern Lady: From Pedestal to Politics, 1830–1930* (Chicago, IL: University of Chicago Press, 1972).

54 Lane, *Political Life*, p. 210.

55 Lane, *Political Life*, p. 213.

56 Berelson, Lazarsfeld, and McPhee, *Voting*, p. 241.

57 Harris, *Is There a Republican Majority?*, p. 107.

58 Campbell, Converse, Miller, and Stokes, *The American Voter*, p. 490; see also, Lane, *Political Life*.

59 Lane, *Political Life*, p. 212.

60 History of Women in the US Congress, Center for American Women and Politics, www.cawp.rutgers.edu/history-women-us-congress [accessed November 8, 2018].

61 Campbell, David E. and Christina Wolbrecht. "The Resistance as Role Model: Disillusionment and Protest Among American Adolescents After 2016," *Political Behavior* (2019) DOI 10.1007/s11109-019-09537-w; Wolbrecht, Christina and David E. Campbell. "Role models revisited: youth, novelty, and the impact of female candidates," *Politics, Groups, and Identities* 5(2017): 418–34; Campbell, David E. and Christina Wolbrecht. "See Jane Run: Women Politicians as Role Models for Adolescents," *Journal of Politics* 68(2006): 233–47.

62 The "Equal Role for Women" item first appears on the ANES in 1972. See Bourque and Grossholtz, "Politics as Unnatural Practice."

63 Lane, *Political Life*; see Merriam, Charles E. and Harold F. Gosnell, *Non-voting: Causes and Methods of Control* (Chicago, IL: University of Chicago Press, 1925). Lane also reports three responses from open-ended questions in Berelson, Lazarsfeld, and McPhee's study of the 1940 presidential election in Eric County, Ohio.

64 Berelson, Lazarsfeld, and McPhee, *Voting*, p. 73.

65 Harris, *Is There a Republican Majority?*, p. 116.

66 Campbell, Converse, Miller, and Stokes, *The American Voter*, p. 493.

67 Gallup, George, "Kennedy Gains Among Women Voters," *Los Angeles Times*, November 17, 1963, p. M2.

68 Campbell, Converse, Miller, and Stokes, *The American Voter*, p. 493.

69 Note that there was still significant – and growing – GOP support in the South during this period; see Trende, Sean, "Misunderstanding the Southern Realignment," *Real Clear Politics*, September 9, 2010, www.realclearpolitics.com/articles/2010/09/09/misunderstanding_the_southern_realignment_107084.html [accessed July 9, 2019]. In addition, our analysis focuses on the two-party vote, which means that the significant vote for the Dixiecrats in 1948 is not included in our analyses.

70 Berelson, Lazarsfeld, and McPhee, *Voting*, p. 102.

71 Campbell, Converse, Miller, and Stokes, *The American Voter*, p. 492.

72 Converse, Phillip E., "The Nature of Belief Systems in Mass Publics." In *Ideology and Discontent*, ed. David Apter (New York: Free Press, 1964), p. 233.

73 Lane, *Political Life*, p. 208.

74 Berelson, Lazarsfeld, and McPhee, *Voting*, p. 102–103.

75 Campbell, Converse, Miller, and Stokes, *The American Voter*, p. 492. Bourque and Grossholtz, "Politics as Unnatural Practice" raises questions about the coding of sophistication in these open-ended items.

76 Ladd, Everett C., "Media Framing of the Gender Gap." In *Women, Media, and Politics*, ed. Pippa Norris (New York: Oxford University Press. 1997), p. 118.

77 "They Vote as Hubby Tells 'Em to Vote," *Detroit Free Press*, October 5, 1952, p.B7.

78 Braestrup, Peter, "Both Parties Aim At Women's Vote," *New York Times*, October 17, 1960, p. 21.

79 "They Compete For the Votes of US Women," *Parade* magazine, March 7, 1948, p. 6.

80 Brown, Nona B., "Women's Vote: The Bigger Half?" *New York Times*, October 21, 1956, p. 237.

81 Gallup, George, "65% of Women Choose Eisenhower, Poll Shows," *Los Angeles Times*, June 13, 1956, p. 22.

82 Campbell, Converse, Miller, and Stokes, *The American Voter*, p. 492.

83 Campbell, Converse, Miller, and Stokes, *The American Voter*, p. 493.

84 Berelson, Lazarsfeld, and McPhee, *Voting*, p. 75.

85 Loper, Mary Lou, "Is She A Wise Voter?" *Los Angeles Times*, August 3, 1960, p. A1.

86 Brown, "Women's Vote: The Bigger Half?"

87 "Living Cost Rise Called Top Issue," *New York Times*, September 14, 1956, p. 10

88 Harris, *Is There a Republican Majority?*, p. 109.

89 For example: "Says War Is Issue Deciding Women," *New York Times*, November 1, 1944, p. 26; "38 Women United in 4th Term Plea," *New York Times*, November 2, 1944, p. 15; "Ives Tells Women Here That Eisenhower Is the One Who Can Do Most to Bring Peace," *New York Times*, September 26, 1952, p. 16; "Vote of Women Assayed," *New York Times*, October 14, 1956.

90 Harris, *Is There a Republican Majority?*, p. 111.

91 Greenlee, *The Political Consequences of Motherhood*, p. 42.

92 Brown, "Women's Vote: The Bigger Half?"

93 Poole, Keith T. and Howard Rosenthal, *Congress: A Political-Economic History of Roll Call Voting* (New York: Oxford University Press, 1997); Schickler, *Racial Realignment*; Brewer and Stonecash, *Dynamics of American Political Parties*; Campbell, Converse, Miller, and Stokes, *The American Voter*; Nie, Verba, and Petrocik, *The Changing American Voter*.

94 "Why Women Vote the Way They Do," *Los Angeles Times*, August 21, 1960, p. TW12.

95 Harris, *Is There a Republican Majority?*, p. 113; also Brown, "Women's Vote: The Bigger Half?"; Baestrup, "Both Parties Aim at Women's Vote."

96 Baker, Russell, "Nixon and Kennedy Campaigns A Contrast of Methods and Men," *New York Times*, September 25, 1960, p. 59.

97 Baker, Russell, "Crowds Acclaim Kennedy in Ohio," *New York Times*, September 28, 1960, p. 30.

98 Egan, Leo, "Independents to Fore," *New York Times*, September 16, 1960, p. 17.

99 "Toynbee Says Emotions Rules Women's Vote," *Los Angeles Times*, May 17, 1956, p. 29.

100 Baestrup, "Both Parties Aim at Women's Vote."

6 FEMINISM RESURGENT

1 Davis, Flora, *Moving the Mountain: The Women's Movement in America Since 1960* (New York: Simon & Schuster, 1991).

2 Nie, Norman, Sidney Verba, and John R. Petrocik, *The Changing American Voter*, Expanded Edition (Boston, MA: Harvard University Press, 1979).

3 Black, Earl and Merle Black, *The Rise of Southern Republicans* (Cambridge, MA: The Belknap Press of Harvard University Press, 2002); Schickler, Eric, *Racial Realignment: The Transformation of American Liberalism, 1932–1965* (Princeton, NJ: Princeton University Press, 2016).

4 Martin, John Bartlow, "Election of 1964." In *History of American Presidential Elections, 1789–1968*, ed. Arthur M. Schlesinger (New York: McGraw-Hill Book Co., 1971), p. 3585.

5 Brewer, Mark D. and Jeffrey M. Stonecash, *Dynamics of American Political Parties* (New York: Cambridge University Press, 2009); Martin, "Election of 1964."

6 Brewer and Stonecash, *Dynamics of American Political Parties*; Alt, James E., "The Impact of the Voting Rights Act on Black and White Voter Registration in the South." In *Quiet Revolution in the South: The Impact of the Voting Rights Act, 1965–1990*, eds. Chandler Davidson and Bernard Grofman (Princeton, NJ: Princeton University Press, 1994); "Partisanship, Sectionalism, and Race: Civil Rights and Party Development From the 1950s Through the 1970s." In *CQ Press Guide to US Political Parties*, eds. Marjorie Randon Hershey, Barry C. Burden, and Christina Wolbrecht (Washington, DC: CQ Press, 2014).

7 Kellstedt, Paul M., *The Mass Media and the Dynamics of American Racial Attitudes* (New York: Cambridge University Press, 2003); Gilens, Martin, *Why Americans Hate Welfare: Race, Media, and the Politics of Anti-Poverty Policy* (Chicago, IL: University of Chicago Press, 1999); Nie, Verba, and Petrocik, *The Changing American Voter*; Miller, Warren E. and J. Merrill Shanks, *The New American Voter* (Boston, MA: Harvard University Press, 1996); Brewer and Stonecash, *Dynamics of American Political Parties*; Masket, Seth, "For Most, There's Never a Right Time to Protest," *Pacific Standard*, December 8, 2015, https://psmag.com/news/for-most-theres-never-a-right-time-to-protest-ferguson-missouri-staten-island-grand-jury-96006 [accessed November 1, 2017]; Norrander, Barbara, "The Intraparty Gender Gap: Differences between Male and Female Voters in the 1980–2000 Presidential Primaries," *PS: Political Science and Politics* 36(2003): 181–86; Hutchings, Vincent L., Nicholas A. Valentino, Tasha S. Philpot, and Ismail K. White, "The Compassion Strategy: Race and the Gender Gap in Campaign 2000," *The Public Opinion Quarterly* 68(2004): 512–41; see, e.g., Lubell, Samuel, "Civil Rights and Welfare Stir Voters," *Los Angeles Times*, September 18, 1968, p. 16; MacPherson, Myra, "Women Hold Power Balance at the Polls," *Los Angeles Times*, November 3, 1968, p. H12.

8 Broder, David S., "Election of 1968." In *History of American Presidential Elections, 1789–1968*, ed. Arthur M. Schlesinger (New York: McGraw-Hill Book Co., 1971); Brewer and Stonecash, *Dynamics of American Political Parties*.

9 Broder, David S., "Election of 1968," p. 3715.

10 Brewer and Stonecash, *Dynamics of American Political Parties*; Broder, "Election of 1968; Black and Black, *The Rise of Southern Republicans*.

11 Wolbrecht, Christina, *The Politics of Women's Rights: Parties, Positions, and Change* (Princeton, NJ: Princeton University Press, 2000).

12 Wolbrecht, *Politics of Women's Rights*.

13 Van Horn, Susan Householder, *Women, Work, and Fertility, 1900–1986* (New York: New York University Press, 1986), p. 151.

14 Van Horn, *Women, Work, and Fertility, 1900–1986*.

15 US Census, CPS Historical Time Series Tables, 2015, www.census.gov/data/tables/time-series/demo/educational-attainment/cps-historical-time-series.html [accessed November 1, 2017].

16 Alt, James E., "The Impact of the Voting Rights Act on Black and White Voter Registration in the South." In *Quiet Revolution in the South: The Impact of the Voting Rights Act, 1965–1990*, eds. Chandler Davidson and Bernard Grofman (Princeton, NJ: Princeton University Press, 1994); Matthews, Donald R. and James W. Prothro, *Negroes and the New Southern Politics* (New York: Harcourt, Brace, & World, Inc., 1966); Lansing, Marjorie, "The Voting Patterns of American Black Women." In *A Portrait of Marginality: The Political Behavior of the American Woman*, eds. Marianne Githens and Jewel L. Prestage (New York: David McKay Company, Inc., 1977).

17 Evans, Sara M., *Born for Liberty: A History of Women in America* (New York: Free Press, 1989); Wolbrecht, *The Politics of Women's Rights*; Davis, *Moving the Mountain*.

18 Van Horn, *Women, Work, and Fertility, 1900–1986*.

19 Freeman, Jo, *The Politics of Women's Liberation: A Case Study of an Emerging Social Movement and Its Relation to the Policy Process* (New York: David McKay Company, 1975); Evans, *Born for Liberty*; Davis, *Moving the Mountain*; see, e.g., McGuinness, Liz, "Improve Status, Women Urged," *Los Angeles Times*, October 21, 1965, p. SG1.

20 Evans, *Born for Liberty*; Wolbrecht, *The Politics of Women's Rights*; Davis, *Moving the Mountain*; Freeman, *The Politics of Women's Liberation*; Crimons, Marlene, "Women Mobilize for '72 Campaign," *Los Angeles Times*, July 13, 1971, p. D1.

21 Viorst, Milton, *Fire in the Streets: America in the 1960s* (New York: Simon and Schuster, 1979).

22 Freeman, *The Politics of Women's Liberation*, p. 60.

23 Evans, Sara, *Personal Politics: The Roots of Women's Liberation in the Civil Rights Movement and the New Left* (New York: Vintage Books, 1979); Robnett, Belinda, *How Long? How Long? African-American Women in the Struggle for Civil Rights* (New York: Oxford University Press, 1997).

24 Freeman, *The Politics of Women's Liberation*; Davis, *Moving the Mountain*.

25 Evans, Sara, *Tidal Wave: How Women Changed America at Century's End* (New York: Simon & Schuster, 2003); Davis, *Moving the Mountain*; Evans, *Born for Liberty*.

26 "Women's opinion poll taken," *Chicago Daily Defender*, July 10, 1972, p. 18.

27 King, Mae C., "Oppression and Power: The Unique Status of the Black Woman in the American Political System," *Social Science Quarterly* 56(June 1975): 116–28; hooks, bell, *Feminist Theory: From Margin to Center* (Boston, MA: South End Press, 1984); Harris, Duchess, "From the Kennedy Commission to the Combahee Collective: Black Feminist Organizing, 1960–80." In *Sisters in the Struggle: African American Women in the Civil Rights-Black Power Movement*, eds. Bettye Collier-Thomas and V.P. Franklin (New York: New York University Press, 2001); Davis, *Moving the Mountain*.

28 Wolbrecht, *The Politics of Women's Rights*.

29 Wolbrecht, *The Politics of Women's Rights*.

30 Wolbrecht, *The Politics of Women's Rights*; Davis, *Moving the Mountain*.

31 Wolbrecht, *The Politics of Women's Rights*; Davis, *Moving the Mountain*; Mansbridge, *How We Lost the ERA*; Baylor, Christopher, *First to the Party: The Group Origins of Political Transformation* (Philadelphia, PA: University of Pennsylvania Press, 2018).

32 Greenlee, Jill S., *The Political Consequences of Motherhood* (Ann Arbor, MI: University of Michigan Press, 2014); Wolbrecht, *The Politics of Women's Rights*. See, for example: "GOP Planning to Win

with Womanpower," *Los Angeles Times*, March 10, 1963, p. G9; "Women's Votes Termed of Utmost Importance," *Los Angeles Times*, October 24, 1964, p. 5; Ehinger, Vi, "Women Control County Vote by More than 25,000," *Los Angeles Times*, June 3, 1965, p. OC9; Vils, Ursula, "Women Fight Ballot Box Dropouts," *Los Angeles Times*, October 24, 1966, p. C15; Henry, Bill, "Women For Nixon," *Los Angeles Times*, February 27, 1968, p. SG1

33 Weinberger, Caspar W., "Women as Voters Considered Important to All Candidates," *Los Angeles Times*, August 19, 1966, p. A5.

34 Stumbo, Bella, "Texan Puts GOP Brand on Women Voters," *Los Angeles Times*, September 21, 1971, p. E1.

35 Green, Emma, "How the Nixon Administration Tried to Woo Women," *The Atlantic Monthly*, August 22, 2013; Fasteau, Brenda Feigen and Bonnie Lobel, "Rating the Candidates: Feminists Vote the Rascals In or Out," *New York*, December 20, 1971, pp. 78–84; "Women Voters," *CQ Researcher*, October 11, 1972; Lydon, Christopher, "Gloria Steinem Aids McGovern's Cause," *New York Times*, February 12, 1972; Smith, Sarah, "Advancing the Cause of Women," Nixon Foundation, January 19, 2017 www.nixonfoundation.org/exhibit/advancing-women/ [accessed August 24, 2017].

36 Greenlee, *The Political Consequences of Motherhood*; Hartmann, Susan M., *From Margin to Mainstream: American Women in Politics Since 1960* (New York: Knopf, 1989); Wolbrecht, *The Politics of Women's Rights*; Melich, Tanya, *The Republican War Against Women: An Insider's Report from Behind the Lines* (New York: Bantam Books, 1996); Cimons, Marlene, "Exploding the Myth of Charisma," *Los Angeles Times*, October 1, 1971, p. F1; Cimons, Marlene, "Women's Coalition to Press for Rights," *Los Angeles Times*, December 8, 1975, p. F1; DeWitt, Karen, "What Role Will Women's Issues Play?" *Los Angeles Times*, August 29, 1976, p. D1.

37 See, e.g., Barreto, Matt A., Fernando Guerra, Mara Marks, Stephen A. Nuno, and Nathan D. Woods, "Controversies in Exit Polling: Implementing a Racially Stratified Homogenous Precinct Approach," *PS: Political Science & Politics* 39(July 2006): 477–83.

38 Sarah Flood, Miriam King, Steven Ruggles, and J. Robert Warren. Integrated Public Use Microdata Series, Current Population Survey: Version 5.0 [dataset]. Minneapolis, MN: University of Minnesota, 2017, https://doi.org/10.18128/D030.V5.0

39 Wolbrecht, Christina, "Introduction: What We Saw at the Revolution: Women in American Politics and Political Science." In *Political Women and American Democracy*, eds. Christina Wolbrecht, Karen Beckwith, and Lisa Baldez (New York: Cambridge University Press, 2008); Committee on the Status of Women in the Profession, "The Status of Women in Political Science: Female Participation in the Professoriate and the Study of Women and Politics in the Discipline," *PS: Political Science & Politics* 34(June 2001): 319–26; Tolleson-Rinehart, Sue and Susan J. Carroll, "'Far From Ideal:' The Gender Politics in Political Science," *American Political Science Review* 100(November 2006): 507–13; Sarkees, Meredith Reid and Nancy E. McGlen, "Misdirected Backlash: The Evolving Nature of Academia and the Status of Women in Political Science," *PS: Political Science & Politics* 32(March 1999): 100–8; Sapiro, Virginia, "Gender & Empowerment through Social Science," Remarks delivered at the Institute for Social Research/G.R. Ford School of Public Policy Symposium on Impact of Inequality, Panel on Race, Gender, & Empowerment, November 9, 2017, http://blogs.bu.edu/vsapiro/2017/11/16/gender-empowerment-through-social-science/ [accessed July 9, 2019].

40 "GOP Planning to Win With Womanpower," *Los Angeles Times*, May 10, 1963, p. G9; "Mrs. Johnson to Start 'Get Out Vote' Drive," *New York Times*, September 10, 1964, p. 18; "Women Fight Ballot Box Dropouts," *Los Angeles Times*, October 24, 1966, p. C15

41 "Women's Votes Terms of Utmost Importance," *Los Angeles Times*, October 24, 1964, p. 5; Ehinger, Vi, "Women Control County Vote by More than 25,000," *Los Angeles Times*, June 3, 1966, p. OC9; MacPherson, Myra, "Women Hold Power Balance at the Polls," *Los Angeles Times*, November 3, 1968, p. H12.

42 Gender Differences in Voter Turnout, Center for American Women and Politics, July 20, 2017.

43 Walton, Hanes Jr., *Invisible Politics: Black Political Behavior* (Albany, NY: State University of New York Press, 1985); Matthews and Prothro, *Negroes and the New Southern Politics*.

44 Corder, J. Kevin and Christina Wolbrecht, *Counting Women's Ballots: Female Voters from Suffrage Through the New Deal* (New York: Cambridge University Press, 2016).

45 Matthews and Prothro, *Negroes and the New Southern Politics*, p. 68.

46 Wolfinger, Raymond E. and Steven J. Rosenstone, *Who Votes?* (New Haven, CT: Yale University Press, 1980), p. 43.

47 Nie, Verba, and Petrocik, *The Changing American Voter*.

48 Milbrath, Lester W. and M.L. Goel, *Political Participation: How and Why Do People Get Involved in Politics?* Second Edition (Chicago, IL: Rand McNally College Publishing Company, 1977).

49 Andersen, "Working Women and Political Participation, 1952–1972."

50 Inglehart, Ronald and Pippa Norris, "The Developmental Theory of the Gender Gap: Women's and Men's Voting Behavior in Global Perspective," *International Political Science Review / Revue Internationale de Science Politique*, 21(2000): 441–63; Gallup, George, "Kennedy Gains Among Women Voters," *Los Angeles Times*, November 17, 1963, p. M2; "Poll Gives Edge to Johnson: 64% of Women, 60% of Men," *New York Times*, p. 28; Clymer, Adam, "Women's Political Habits Show Sharp Change," *New York Times*, June 30, 1982, p. A1.

51 Carroll, Susan, "Women's Autonomy and the Gender Gap: 1980 and 1982." In *The Politics of the Gender Gap: The Social Construction of Political Influence*, ed. Carol M. Mueller (Newbury Park, CA: Sage Publications, 1988).

52 See Junn, Jane, "The Trump Majority: White Womanhood and the Making of Female Voters in the US," *Politics, Groups, and Identities* 5(2017): 343–52.

53 Carroll, Susan, "Women's Autonomy and the Gender Gap: 1980 and 1982." In *The Politics of the Gender Gap: The Social Construction of Political Influence*, ed. Carol M. Mueller (Newbury Park, CA: Sage Publications, 1988); Huddy, Leonie, Erin Cassese, and Mary-Kate Lizotte, "Sources of Political Unity and Disunity among Women: Placing the Gender Gap in Perspective." In *Voting the Gender Gap*, ed. Lois Duke Whitaker (University of Illinois Press, 2008), pp. 141–69; Klein, Ethel, "The Gender Gap: Different Issues, Different Answers," *The Brookings Review* 3(1985): 33–7; Manza, Jeff and Clem Brooks, "The Gender Gap in US Presidential Elections: When? Why? Implications?" *American Journal of Sociology* 103(1998): 1235–66; Ladd, Jonathan, Daniel Q. Gillion, and Marc Meredith, "Party Polarization, Ideological Sorting and the Emergence of the US Partisan Gender Gap," *British Journal of Political Science*, 1–27 DOI 10.1017/50007123418000285.

54 Verba, Sidney, Kay Lehman Schlozman, and Henry E. Brady, *Voice and Equality: Civic Voluntarism in American Politics* (Cambridge, MA: Harvard University Press, 1995); Burns, Nancy, Kay

Lehman Schlozman, and Sidney Verba, *The Private Roots of Public Action: Gender, Equality, and Political Participation* (Cambridge, MA: Harvard University Press, 2001).

55 Ladd, Gillion, and Meredith, "Party Polarization, Ideological Sorting and the Emergence of the US Partisan Gender Gap."

56 DeWitt, Karen, "What Role Will Women's Issues Play?" *Los Angeles Times*, August 29, 1976, p. D1.

57 Kaufmann, Karen M., "The Gender Gap," *PS: Political Science and Politics* 39(2006): 447–53; Schlesinger, Mark and Caroline Heldman, "Gender Gap or Gender Gaps? New Perspectives on Support for Government Action and Policies," *Journal of Politics* 63(2001): 59–92; Schreckhise, William D. and Todd G. Shields, "Ideological Realignment in the Contemporary US Electorate Revisited," *Social Science Quarterly* 84(2003): 596–612; Kaufmann, Karen M. and John R. Petrocik, "The Changing Politics of American Men: Understanding the Sources of the Gender Gap," *American Journal of Political Science* 43(1999): 864–87.

58 Erie, Steven P. and Martin Rein, "Women and the Welfare State." In *The Politics of the Gender Gap: The Social Construction of Political Influence*, ed. Carol M. Mueller (Newbury Park, CA: Sage Publications, 1988).

59 GSS Data Explorer, https://gssdataexplorer.norc.org/ [accessed July 9, 2019]; Shapiro, Robert Y. and Harpreet Mahajan, "Gender Differences in Policy Preferences: A Summary of Trends From the 1960s to the 1980s," *Public Opinion Quarterly* 50(Spring 1986): 42–61.

60 Kaufmann and Petrocik, "The Changing Politics of American Men."

7 THE DISCOVERY OF THE GENDER GAP

1 Wolbrecht, Christina, *The Politics of Women's Rights: Parties, Positions, and Change* (Princeton, NJ: Princeton University Press, 2000).

2 Bonk, Kathy, "The Selling of the Gender Gap: The Role of Organized Feminism." In *The Politics of the Gender Gap: The Social Construction of Political Influence*, ed. Carol M. Mueller (Newbury Park, CA: Sage Publications, 1988).

3 Bonk, "The Selling of the Gender Gap."

4 Brewer, Mark D. and Jeffrey M. Stonecash, *Dynamics of American Political Parties* (New York: Cambridge University Press, 2009).

5 Layman, Geoffrey C. and Thomas M. Carsey, "Party Polarization and 'Conflict Extension' in the American Electorate," *American Journal of Political Science* 46(October 2002): 786–802; Layman, Geoffrey C., Thomas M. Carsey, John C. Green, and Richard Herrera, "Activists and Conflict Extension in American Party Politics," *American Political Science Review* 104(May 2010): 324–46; Brewer and Stonecash, *Dynamics of American Political Parties*.

6 Brewer and Stonecash, *Dynamics of American Political Parties*.

7 Black, Earl and Merle Black, *The Rise of Southern Republicans* (Cambridge, MA: Belknap Press, 2002); Mason, Lilliana, *Uncivil Agreement: How Politics Became Our Identity* (Chicago, IL: University of Chicago Press, 2018).

8 Wang, Wendy, Kim Parker, and Paul Taylor, "Breadwinner Moms," Pew Research Center, May 29, 2013, www.pewsocialtrends.org/2013/05/29/breadwinner-moms/ [accessed May 14, 2018].

9 Livingston, Gretchen, "Childlessness Falls, Family Size Grows Among Highly Educated Women," Pew Research Center, May 7, 2015 www.pewsocialtrends.org/2015/05/07/childlessness-falls-family-size-grows-among-highly-educated-women/ [accessed May 14, 2018].

10 Greenlee, Jill S., *The Political Consequences of Motherhood* (Ann Arbor, MI: University of Michigan Press, 2014); Brewer and Stonecash, *Dynamics of American Political Parties*.

11 Carroll, Susan J., *Women as Candidates in American Politics* (Bloomington, IN: Indiana University Press, 1985); Bonk, "The Selling of the Gender Gap;" Borquez, Julio, Edie N. Goldenberg, and Kim Fridkin Kahn, "Press Portrayals of the Gender Gap." In *The Politics of the Gender Gap*, ed. Carol M. Mueller.

12 Quoted in Bonk, "The Selling of the Gender Gap."

13 Cimons, Marlene, "Republican Women Take a Second Look at President," *Los Angeles Times*, Feburary 5, 1981, p. F1; Shogan, Robert, "GOP Advised to Woo Minority, Women Voters," *Los Angeles Times*, November 16, 1982, p. B4; Mehren, Elizabeth, "Reagan's 'Caveman Quote' Furor: Angry Women Vot to Campaign Against President," *Los Angeles Times*, August 11, 1983; Mehren, Elizabeth, "Gender Gap Widening, Polls Show: Women's Political Leader Places Blame on Reagan," *Los Angeles Times*, September 29, 1983, p. H1; See: Bonk, "The Selling of the Gender Gap;" Borquez, Julio, Edie N. Goldenberg, and Kim Fridkin Kahn, "Press Portrayals of the Gender Gap." In *The Politics of the Gender Gap: The Social Construct of Political Influence*, ed. Carol M. Mueller (Newbury Park, CA: Sage Publications, 1988); Coste, Françoise, "'Women, Ladies, Girls, Gals …': Ronald Reagan and the Evolution of Gender Roles in the United States," *Miranda. Revue Pluridisciplinaire Du Monde Anglophone / Multidisciplinary Peer-Reviewed Journal on the English-Speaking World*, 2016, doi.org/10.4000/miranda.8602.

14 Bonk, "The Selling of the Gender Gap;" Chaney, Carole Kennedy, R. Michael Alvarez, and Jonathan Nagler, "Explaining the Gender Gap in U. S. Presidential Elections, 1980–1992," *Political Research Quarterly* 51(1998): 311–39; Mattei, Laura R. Winsky, and Franco Mattei, "If Men Stayed Home … The Gender Gap in Recent Congressional Elections," *Political Research Quarterly* 51(1998): 411–36; Richardson, L. E. and P. K. Freeman, "Issue Salience and Gender Differences in Congressional Elections, 1994–1998," *Social Science Journal* 40(2003): 401–17; Seltzer, Richard A., Jody Newman, and Melissa Voorhees Leighton, *Sex as a Political Variable: Women as Candidates & Voters in US Elections* (Boulder, CO: Lynne Reiner, 1997); Decker, Cathleen, "Persistent Gender Gap Stalks Bush Campaign," *Los Angeles Times*, July 3, 1988, p. A1; Morison, Patt, and Elizabeth Mehren, "Closing Gender Gap Considered by Many to Be Crucial for Bush," *Los Angeles Times*, August 17, 1988, p. B4; Meisler, Stanley, "Election Expected to Reflect Persistence of Gender Gap," *Los Angeles Times*, October 29, 1988, p. 25.

15 Borquez, Goldenberg, and Kahn, "Press Portrayals of the Gender Gap."

16 May, Lee and John Balzar, "6 Democrats Vow to Back Abortion Rights and ERA, Blast Reagan Record on Women," *Los Angeles Times*, February 4, 1982, p. A24; Weaver, Peter, "Election Year Brings Women's Legislation," *Los Angeles Times*, March 15, 1984, p. M19; Kills, Kay, "Bush Scares Up a Women's Issue, but Just One of the Many," *Los Angeles Times*, November 13, 1988, p. E5; Shuit, Douglas P., "Democrats Battle for Feminist Vote," *Los Angeles Times*, April 22, 1992, p. WB1.

17 Greenlee, *The Political Consequences of Motherhood.*

18 Peterson, Bill, "Reagan Did Understand Women: While Democrats Slept, the GOP Skillfully Captured Their Votes," *Washington Post*, March 3, 1984, p. C5; Frankovic, Kathleen A., "The 1984 Election: The Irrelevance of the Campaign," *PS: Political Science and Politics* 18(Winter 1985): 39–47; Bonk, "The Selling of the Gender Gap."; Frankovic, Kathleen A., "The Ferraro Factor: The Women's Movement, the Polls, and the Press." In *The Politics of the Gender Gap: The Social Construction of Political Influence,* ed. Carol M. Mueller (Newbury Park, CA: Sage Publications, 1988); Hartmann, Susan M., *From Margin to Mainstream: American Women in Politics Since 1960* (New York: Knopf, 1989); see also: Beyette, Beverly, "NOW's Time, Say Feminists Promoting Vice Presidential Candidate in '84," *Los Angeles Times*, October 3, 1983, p. C1; Mehren, Elizabeth and Betty Cuniberti, "A Woman Vice-Presidential Candidate May Be Just the Ticket," *Los Angeles Times*, November 6, 1983, p. H1; "GOP Has Five Possible Picks in a Varied Field," *Los Angeles Times*, November 6, 1983, p. H1; "NOW Says a Woman's Place Is on Ticket," *Los Angeles Times*, June 29, 1984, p. F1; Fritz, Sara, "A Woman VP: Bold Stroke Carries Risks," *Los Angeles Times*, July 8, 1984, p. A1.

19 Greenlee, *The Political Consequences of Motherhood*; Brewer and Stonecash, *Dynamics of American Political Parties*; Dillin, John, "Party Woos Women, but Has Uphill Fight. Can Republicans Reach Out?" *The Christian Science Monitor*, August 17, 1988; Hendrix, Kathleen, "What Gender Gap? The Women's Vote Was a Deciding Factor in Electing Bush, Feminists and Analysts Now Say," *Los Angeles Times*, January 16, 1989.

20 Greenlee, *The Political Consequences of Motherhood*; Wolbrecht, *The Politics of Women's Rights.*

21 Greenlee, *The Political Consequences of Motherhood*; Wolbrecht, *The Politics of Women's Rights*; Watson, Robert P., "The First Lady Reconsidered: Presidential Partner and Political Institution," *Presidential Studies Quarterly* 27(Fall 1997): 805–18; Williams, Mary Elizabeth, "Hillary Clinton's Decisive Triumph over Cookie Baking and 'Stand By Your Man,'" *Salon*, July 29, 2016 www.salon.com/2016/07/29/hillary_clintons_decisive_triumph_over_cookie_baking_and_stand_by_your_man/ [accessed May 15, 2018].

22 Wilcox, Clyde, "Why Was 1992 the 'Year of the Woman'? Explaining Women's Gains in 1992." In *The Year of the Woman: Myths and Realities*, eds. Elizabeth Adell Cook, Sue Thomas, and Clyde Wilcox (Boulder, CO: Westview Press, 1994); Thomsen, Danielle M., "Why So Few (Republican) Women? Explaining the Partisan Imbalance of Women in the US Congress," *Legislative Studies Quarterly* 40(2015): 295–323.

23 Carroll, Susan J., "The Disempowerment of the Gender Gap: Soccer Moms and the 1996 Elections," *PS: Political Science and Politics* 32(March 1999): 7–11; The American National Election Studies (electionstudies.org), The ANES Guide to Public Opinion and Electoral Behavior (Ann Arbor, MI: University of Michigan, Center for Political Studies [producer and distributor], 2018).

24 Greenlee, *The Political Consequences of Motherhood*; Carroll, Susan J., "The Disempowerment of the Gender Gap: Soccer Moms and the 1996 Elections," *PS: Political Science and Politics* 32(March 1999): 7–11.

25 "Gender Differences in Turnout," Center for American Women and Politics, 2017 www.cawp.rutgers.edu/sites/default/files/resources/genderdiff.pdf> [accessed May 15, 2018].

26 Miller, Warren E. and J. Merrill Shanks, *The New American Voter* (Cambridge, MA: Harvard University Press, 1996), p. 89.

27 Leighley and Nagler, *Who Votes Now?*; Conway, Margaret M., David W. Ahern, and Gertrude Steuernagel, *Women and Political Participation: Cultural Change in the Political Arena*, Second edition (Washington, DC: CQ Press, 2004).

28 Burns, Nancy, Kay Lehman Schlozman, and Sidney Verba, "The Public Consequences of Private Inequality: Family Life and Citizen Participation," *American Political Science Review* 91 (June 1997): 373–89.

29 Gilbert, Christopher P., Timothy R. Johnson, David A.M. Peterson, and Paul A. Djupe, "Structural Constraints on Perot Voting Patterns: The Effects of Religious Adherence." In *Ross for Boss: The Perot Phenomenon and Beyond*, ed. Ted G. Jelen (Albany, NY: State University of New York Press, 2001); Rosenstone, Steven J., Roy L. Behr, and Edward H. Lazarus, *Third Parties in America: Citizen Response to Major Party Failure*, Second Edition, Revised and Expanded (Princeton, NJ: Princeton University Press, 1996).

30 For a note of caution, see Barreto, Matt A., Fernando Guerra, Mara Marks, Stephen A. Nuno, and Nathan D. Woods, "Controversies in Exit Polling: Implementing a Racially Stratified Homogenous Precinct Approach," *PS: Political Science & Politics* 39 (July 2006): 477–83.

31 See Ladd, Gillion, and Meredith, "Party Polarization, Ideological Sorting and the Emergence of the US Partisan Gender Gap."

32 Kaufmann and Petrocik, "The Changing Politics of American Men;" Wirls, Daniel, "Reinterpreting the Gender Gap," *Public Opinion Quarterly* 50(1986): 316–30.

33 These numbers may seem inconsistent with dominant narratives about the Democratic Solid South, for more information on the earlier Southern shift toward Repubilcans, see Trende, Sean, "Misunderstanding the Southern Realignment," *Real Clear Politics*, September 9, 2010, www.realclearpolitics.com/articles/2010/09/09/misunderstanding_the_southern_realignment_107084.html [accessed July 9, 2019].

34 Hutchings, Vincent L., Nicholas A. Valentino, Tasha S. Philpot, and Ismail K. White, "The Compassion Strategy: Race and the Gender Gap in Campaign 2000," *The Public Opinion Quarterly* 68(2004): 512–41; Kaufmann, Karen M. and John R. Petrocik, "The Changing Politics of American Men: Understanding the Sources of the Gender Gap," *American Journal of Political Science* 43(1999): 864–87.

35 Bonk, "The Selling of the 'Gender Gap,'" p. 95.

36 Wolbrecht, *The Politics of Women's Rights*; Silver, Nate, "'Gender Gap' Near Historic Highs," *New York Times*, October 21, 2012, https://fivethirtyeight.blogs.nytimes.com/2012/10/21/gender-gap-near-historic-highs/ [accessed October 18, 2018]; see, e.g., May, Lee and John Balzar, "6 Democrats Vow to Back Abortion Rights and ERA, Blast Reagan Record on Women," *Los Angeles Times*, February 4, 1982, p. A24.

37 Wolbrecht, *The Politics of Women's Rights*.

38 For example: Mansbridge, Jane J., "Myth and Reality: The ERA and the Gender Gap in the 1980 Election," *The Public Opinion Quarterly* 49(1985): 164–78; Wirls, Daniel, "Reinterpreting the Gender Gap," *The Public Opinion Quarterly* 50(1986): 316–30; Gilens, Martin, "The Gender Gap: Psychology, Social Structure, and Support for Reagan," *Berkeley Journal of Sociology* 29(1984): 35–56; Frankovic, Kathleen A. "Sex and Politics – New Alignments, Old Issues," *PS: Political Science & Politics* 15(Summer 1982): 441–44; Chaney, Carole Kennedy, R. Michael

Alvarez, and Jonathan Nagler, "Explaining the Gender Gap in U.S. Presidential Elections, 1980–1992," *Political Research Quarterly* 51(1998): 311–39; Gilens, Martin, "The Gender Gap: Psychology, Social Structure, and Support for Reagan," *Berkeley Journal of Sociology* 29(1984): 35–56.

39 Frankovic, Kathleen A., "Sex and Politics – New Alignments, Old Issues," *PS: Political Science & Politics* 15(1982): 439–48; Smith, Tom W., "The Polls: Gender and Attitudes toward Violence," *Public Opinion Quarterly* 48(1984): 384–96; Wilcox, Clyde, Joseph Ferrara, and Dee Allsop, "Group Differences in Early Support for Military Action in the Gulf: The Effects of Gender, Generation and Ethnicity," *American Politics Quarterly* 21(1993): 343–59; Shapiro and Mahajan, "Gender Differences in Policy Preferences;" Norrander, Barbara, "The History of the Gender Gaps" in *Voting the Gender Gap*, ed. Lois Duke Whitaker (Champaign, IL: University of Illinois Press, 2008), pp. 9–32.

40 Egan, Patrick J. *Partisan Priorities: How Issue Ownership Drives and Distorts American Politics* (New York: Cambridge University Press, 2013); Gilens, "The Gender Gap;" Chaney, Carole Kennedy, R. Michael Alvarez, and Jonathan Nagler, "Explaining the Gender Gap in U.S. Presidential Elections, 1980–1992," *Political Research Quarterly* 51(1998): 311–39; see, e.g., Shogan, Robert, "Prosperity, Risk of War Key Issues of 'Gender Gap,'" *Los Angeles Times*, September 26, 1983, p. A4; Engel, Margaret, "Feminist Issues Alone Not a Magnet to Women Voters," *Los Angeles Times*, September 14, 1984, p. A3; Goodman, Ellen, "What Do Women Voters Want? Whatever Is Best for All," *Los Angeles Times*, September 26, 1986, p. C5; "Women Favor Dukakis," *Los Angeles Times*, June 15, 1988, p. B16.

41 Richardson, L. E. and P. K. Freeman, "Issue Salience and Gender Differences in Congressional Elections, 1994–1998," *Social Science Journal* 40(2003): 401–17; Schreckhise, William D. and Todd G. Shields, "Ideological Realignment in the Contemporary US Electorate Revisited," *Social Science Quarterly* 84(2003): 596–612; Manza, Jeff, and Clem Brooks, "The Gender Gap in US Presidential Elections: When? Why? Implications?" *American Journal of Sociology* 103(1998): 1235–66; Mattei, Franco, "The Gender Gap in Presidential Evaluations: Assessments of Clinton's Performance in 1996," *Polity* 33(2000): 199–228; Studlar, Donley T., Ian McAllister, and Bernadette C. Hayes, "Explaining the Gender Gap in Voting: A Cross-National Analysis," *Social Science Quarterly* 79(1998): 779–98; Fox, Richard L. and Zoe Oxley, "Women's Support for an Active Government." In *Minority Voting in the United States* Volume I, eds. Kyle L. Kreider and Thomas J. Baldino (Santa Barbara, CA: Praeger, 2016), Kaufman and Petrocik, "The Changing Politics of American Men."

42 Shapiro and Mahajan, "Gender Differences in Policy Preferences"; Fox and Oxley, "Women's Support for an Active Government."

43 Carroll, Susan, "Women's Autonomy and the Gender Gap: 1980 and 1982." In *The Politics of the Gender Gap: The Social Construction of Political Influence*, ed. Carol M. Mueller (Newbury Park, CA: Sage Publications, 1988); Gilens, Martin, 'The Gender Gap: Psychology, Social Structure, and Support for Reagan," *Berkeley Journal of Sociology* 29(1984): 35–56.

44 Howell, Susan E. and Christine L. Day, "Complexities of the Gender Gap," *The Journal of Politics* 62(2000): 858–74; Inglehart, Ronald, and Pippa Norris, "The Developmental Theory

of the Gender Gap: Women's and Men's Voting Behavior in Global Perspective," *International Political Science Review / Revue Internationale de Science Politique* 21(2000): 441–63; Edlund, Lena, and Rohini Pande, "Why Have Women Become Left-Wing? The Political Gender Gap and the Decline in Marriage," *The Quarterly Journal of Economics* 117(2002): 917–61; Manza, Jeff, and Clem Brooks, "The Gender Gap in US Presidential Elections: When? Why? Implications?" *American Journal of Sociology* 103(1998): 1235–66; but see: Huddy, Leonie, Erin Cassese, and Mary-Kate Lizotte, "Sources of Political Unity and Disunity among Women: Placing the Gender Gap in Perspective." In *Voting the Gender Gap*, ed. Lois Duke Whitaker (Champaign, IL: University of Illinois Press, 2008), pp. 141–69; Iversen, Torben, and Frances Rosenbluth, "The Political Economy of Gender: Explaining Cross-National Variation in the Gender Division of Labor and the Gender Voting Gap," *American Journal of Political Science* 50 (2006): 1–19.

45 Kellstedt, Paul M., *The Mass Media and the Dynamics of American Racial Attitudes* (New York: Cambridge University Press, 2003).

46 Blinder, Scott and Meredith Rolfe, "Rethinking Compassion: Toward a Political Account of the Partisan Gender Gap in the United States," *Political Psychology* 39(2017): 889–906; Schlesinger, Mark and Caroline Heldman, "Gender Gap or Gender Gaps? New Perspectives on Support for Government Action and Policies," *The Journal of Politics* 63(2001): 59–92; Howell, Susan E. and Christine L. Day, "Complexities of the Gender Gap," *The Journal of Politics* 62(2000): 858–74.

47 Hutchings, Vincent L., Nicholas A. Valentino, Tasha S. Philpot, and Ismail K. White, "The Compassion Strategy: Race and the Gender Gap in Campaign 2000," *The Public Opinion Quarterly* 68(2004): 512–41; Kaufmann, Karen M. and John R. Petrocik, "The Changing Politics of American Men: Understanding the Sources of the Gender Gap," *American Journal of Political Science* 43(1999): 864–87; Norrander, Barbara, "The Intraparty Gender Gap: Differences between Male and Female Voters in the 1980–2000 Presidential Primaries," *PS: Political Science and Politics* 36(2003): 181–86; Norrander, Barbara, "The Evolution of the Gender Gap," *The Public Opinion Quarterly* 63(1999): 566–76; Schreckhise, William D. and Todd G. Shields, "Ideological Realignment in the Contemporary US Electorate Revisited," *Social Science Quarterly* 84(2003): 596–612; Wirls, "Reinterpreting the Gender Gap," *The Public Opinion Quarterly* 50(1986): 316–30.

48 E.g., Meisler, Stanley, "Election Expected to Reflect Persistence of Gender Gap."

49 Kaufmann and Petrocik, "The Changing Politics of American Men," *American Journal of Political Science* 43(1999): 864–87; Wirls, "Reinterpreting the Gender Gap;" Bedyna, Mary E. and Celinda C. Lake, "Gender and Voting in the 1992 Presidential Election." In *The Year of the Woman: Myths and Realities*, eds. Elizabeth Adell Cook, Sue Thomas, and Clyde Wilcox (Boulder, CO: Westview Press, 1994); Miller and Shanks, *The New American Voter*.

8 WOMEN VOTERS IN THE NEW MILLENNIUM

1 Lee, Frances E., *Insecure Majorities: Congress and the Perpetual Campaign* (Chicago, IL: University of Chicago Press, 2016); Sides, John and Daniel J. Hopkins, eds., *Political Polarization in American*

Politics (New York: Bloomsbury Academic, 2015); Theriault, Sean M., *Party Polarization in Congress* (New York: Cambridge University Press, 2008); McCarty, Nolan, Keith T. Poole, and Howard Rosenthal, *Polarized America: The Dance of Ideology and Unequal Riches* (Cambridge, MA: The MIT Press, 2006).

2 Horowitz, Juliana Menasce, Kim Parker, and Renee Stepler, "Wide Partisan Gaps in US Over How Far the Country Has Come on Gender Equality," Pew Research Center, October 18, 2017, www.pewsocialtrends.org/2017/10/18/wide-partisan-gaps-in-u-s-over-how-far-the-country-has-come-on-gender-equality/ [accessed July 9, 2019]; Beinart, Peter, "The Growing Partisan Divide Over Feminism," *The Atlantic*, December 15, 2017.

3 Wolbrecht, Christina, *The Politics of Women's Rights: Parties, Positions, and Change* (Princeton, NJ: Princeton University Press, 2000); General Social Survey Data Explorer, https://gssdataexplorer.norc.org/ [accessed January 29, 2018].

4 Valentino, Nicholas A., Carly Wayne, and Marzia Oceno, "Mobilizing Sexism: The Interaction of Emotion and Gender Attitudes in the 2016 US Presidential Election," *Public Opinion Quarterly* 82(2018): 213–35.

5 Mason, Lilliana, *Uncivil Agreement: How Politics Became Our Identity* (Chicago, IL: University of Chicago Press, 2018); "Partisanship and Political Animosity in 2016," Pew Research Center, June 22, 2016, www.people-press.org/2016/06/22/partisanship-and-political-animosity-in-2016/ [accessed June 21, 2018]; Barthel, Michael and Amy Mitchell, "Americans' Attitudes about the News Media Deeply Divided Along Partisan Lines," Pew Research Center, May 10, 2017, www.journalism.org/2017/05/10/americans-attitudes-about-the-news-media-deeply-divided-along-partisan-lines/ [accessed June 21, 2018]; Martin, Gregory J. and Ali Yurukoglu, "Bias in Cable News: Persuasion and Polarization," *American Economic Review* 107(2017): 2565–2599; Druckman, James N., Matthew S. Levendusky, and Audrey McLain, "No Need to Watch: How the Effects of Partisan Media Can Spread Via Interpersonal Discussions," *American Journal of Political Science* 62(2018): 99–112; Hopkins, Daniel J. and Jonathan McDonald Ladd, "The Consequences of Broader Media Choice: Evidence from the Expansion of Fox News," *Quarterly Journal of Political Science* 9(2012): DOI: 10.2139/ssrn.2070596; "Cable News Fact Sheet," Pew Research Center, June 1, 2017, www.journalism.org/fact-sheet/cable-news/ [accessed June 21, 2018].

6 Brewer, Mark D. and Jeffrey M. Stonecash, *Dynamics of American Political Parties* (New York: Cambridge University Press, 2009); Jacobson, Gary C., *A Divider, Not a Uniter: George W. Bush and the American People*, Second Edition (New York: Pearson, 2010).

7 Abramson, Paul R., John H. Aldrich, and David W. Rohde, *Change and Continuity in the 2004 Elections* (Washington, DC: CQ Press, 2006).

8 Abramson, Paul R., John H. Aldrich, and David W. Rohde, *Change and Continuity in the 2008 Elections* (Washington, DC: CQ Press, 2009); Crotty, William J. "Electing Obama: The 2008 Presidential Campaign." In *Winning the Presidency, 2008*, ed. William J. Crotty (Boulder, CO: Paradigm Publishers, 2009.

9 Sides, John, and Lynn Vavreck, *The Gamble: Choice and Chance in the 2012 Presidential Election* (Princeton, NJ: Princeton University Press, 2013); Burke, Meghan A., *Race, Gender, and Class in the Tea Party* (Lanham, MD: Lexington Books, 2015); Williamson, Vanessa and Theda Skocpol, *The Tea Party and the Remaking of Republican Conservatism* (New York: Oxford University Press, 2012); Williamson, Vanessa, Theda Skocpol, and John Coggin, "The Tea Party and the Remaking of

Republican Conservatism," *Perspectives on Politics* 9(2011): 25–43; Campbell, David E. and Robert D. Putnam, "Crashing the Tea Party," *New York Times*, August 16, 2011, www.nytimes.com/2011/08/17/opinion/crashing-the-tea-party.html [accessed June 18, 2018]; Zernike, Kate, "Tea Party Set to Win Enough Elections for Wide Influence," *New York Times*, October 14, 2010, www.nytimes.com/2010/10/15/us/politics/15teaparty.html?_r=1&hp [accessed June 18, 2018]; Shear, Michael D., "Ryan Brings the Tea Party to the Ticket," *New York Times*, August 12, 2012, https://thecaucus.blogs.nytimes.com/2012/08/12/ryan-brings-the-tea-party-to-the-ticket/?smid=tw-thecaucus&seid=auto [accessed June 18, 2018].

10 Aldrich, John H., Jamie L. Carson, Brad T. Gomez, and David W. Rohde, *Change and Continuity in the 2016 Elections* (Washington, DC: CQ Press, 2019); Lee, Jasmine C. and Kevin Quealy, "The 472 People, Places and Things Donald Trump Has Insulted on Twitter: A Complete List," *New York Times*, June 10, 2018, www.nytimes.com/interactive/2016/01/28/upshot/donald-trump-twitter-insults.html [accessed June 19, 2018]; Silver, Nate, "The Comey Letter Probably Cost Clinton the Election," *FiveThirtyEight* blog, May 3, 2017, https://fivethirtyeight.com/features/the-comey-letter-probably-cost-clinton-the-election/ [accessed June 19, 2018].

11 US Census Bureau, CPS Historical Time Series Visualizations: Figure 6. Percent of People 25 Years and Older, and 25 to 29 Years Old, with Bachelor's Degree or Higher by Sex: 1947–2017, www.census.gov/library/visualizations/time-series/demo/cps-historical-time-series.html [accessed June 20, 2018].

12 Wang, Wendy and Kim Parker, "Record Share of Americans Have Never Married," Pew Research Center, September 24, 2014, www.pewsocialtrends.org/2014/09/24/record-share-of-americans-have-never-married/ [accessed June 30, 2018].

13 Pew Research Center, "Parenting in America: Outlook, Worries, Aspirations Are Strongly Linked to Financial Situation," December 17, 2015, http://assets.pewresearch.org/wp-content/uploads/sites/3/2015/12/2015-12-17_parenting-in-america_FINAL.pdf [accessed June 20, 2018]; Parker, Kim, "Despite Progress, Women Still Bearing Heavier Load than Men in Balancing Work and Family," Pew Research Center, March 10, 2015, www.pewresearch.org/fact-tank/2015/03/10/women-still-bear-heavier-load-than-men-balancing-work-family/ [accessed June 20, 2018].

14 Greenlee, Jill S., *The Political Consequences of Motherhood* (Ann Arbor, MI: University of Michigan Press, 2014).

15 Kochhar, Rakesh, "Two Years of Economic Recovery: Women Lose Jobs, Men Find Them," Pew Research Center, July 6, 2011, www.pewsocialtrends.org/2011/07/06/two-years-of-economic-recovery-women-lose-jobs-men-find-them/ [accessed June 20, 2018]; US Department of Labor Women's Bureau, Facts Over Time, www.dol.gov/wb/stats/NEWSTATS/facts.htm#one [accessed June 20, 2018]; US Department of Labor Women's Bureau, Most Common Occupations for Women, www.dol.gov/wb/stats/most_common_occupations_for_women.htm [accessed June 20, 2018]; DeSilver, Drew, "Women Scarce at Top of US Business – and in the Jobs that Lead There," Pew Research Center, April 30, 2018, www.pewresearch.org/fact-tank/2018/04/30/women-scarce-at-top-of-u-s-business-and-in-the-jobs-that-lead-there/ [accessed June 20, 2018].

16 Greenlee, *The Political Consequences of Motherhood*.

17 Gore, Albert Jr., "Address Accepting the Presidential Nomination at the Democratic National Convention in Los Angeles," August 17, 2000, The American Presidency Project, University

of California, Santa Barbara, www.presidency.ucsb.edu/documents/address-accepting-the-presidential-nomination-the-democratic-national-convention-los [accessed October 23, 2018].

18 Greenlee, *The Political Consequences of Motherhood*.

19 Greenlee, *The Political Consequences of Motherhood*; Carroll, Susan J., "Moms Who Swing, or Why the Promise of the Gender Gap Remains Unfulfilled," *Politics & Gender* 2(2006): 362–74; Carroll, Susan J., "Security Moms and Presidential Politics: Women Voters in the 2004 Election." In *Voting the Gender Gap*, ed. Lois Duke Whitaker (Urbana, IL: University of Illinois, 2008); Roberts, Joel, "John Kerry: Ladies' Man?" *CBS News*, September 23, 2004, www.cbsnews.com/news/john-kerry-ladies-man/ [accessed June 14, 2018]; Seelye, Katharine Q., "Kerry in a Struggle for a Democratic Base: Women," *New York Times*, September 22, 2004, www.nytimes.com/2004/09/22/politics/campaign/kerry-in-a-struggle-for-a-democratic-base-women.html [accessed June 14, 2018]; Allen, Mike, "Bush Makes Pitch to 'Security Moms.'" *Washington Post*, September 18, 2004: A14; Klein, Joe, "How Soccer Moms Became Security Moms, *Time*, February 10, 2003; Greenberg, Anna, "The Security Mom Myth Revisited," *Huffington Post*, November 23, 2014, www.huffingtonpost.com/anna-greenberg/the-security-mom-myth-rev_b_5868306.html [accessed June 14, 2016].

20 Drehs, Wayne, "NASCAR Dads Could Provide Swing Vote," *ESPN*, February 15, 2004 www.espn.com/racing/news/story?id=1735251 [accessed June 14, 2018].

21 Virus, Mary Douglas, "The Politics of NASCAR Dads: Branded Media Paternity," *Critical Studies in Media Communication* 24(2007): 245–61; Elder, Laurel and Steven Greene, "The Myth of 'Security Moms' and 'NASCAR Dads': Parenthood, Political Stereotypes, and the 2004 Election," *Social Science Quarterly* 88(2007): 1–19; Goodman, Ellen, "Racing After 'NASCAR Dads,'" *Washington Post*, November 8, 2003, www.washingtonpost.com/archive/opinions/2003/11/08/racing-after-nascar-dads/1bfbf5ae-4cf7-42cc-b8a5-83a9f2ddd8a5/?utm_term=.c6da577bfb36 [accessed June 14, 2018]; Chinni, Dante, "NASCAR dads – now you see them, now you don't," *Christian Science Monitor*, February 24, 2004, www.csmonitor.com/2004/0225/p09s01-codc.html [accessed June 14, 2018]; Cooper, Marc, "Among the NASCAR Dads," *The Nation*, March 22, 2004, www.thenation.com/article/among-nascar-dads/ [accessed June 14, 2018].

22 Lawrence, Regina G. and Melody Rose, *Hillary Clinton's Race for the White House: Gender Politics and the Media on the Campaign Trail* (Boulder, CO: Lynne Rienner Publishers, 2010); Lawrence, Regina G. and Melody Rose, "Bringing Out the Hook: Exit Talk in Media Coverage of Hillary Clinton and Past Presidential Campaigns," *Political Research Quarterly* 64 (2011): 870–83; Kinder, Donald R. and Allison Dale-Riddle, *The End of Race? Obama, 2008, and Racial Politics in America* (New Haven, CT: Yale University Press, 2012); Crotty, William J. "Electing Obama: The 2008 Presidential Campaign." In *Winning the Presidency, 2008*, ed. William J. Crotty (Boulder, CO: Paradigm Publishers, 2009); Simien, Evelyn M., "Clinton and Obama: The Impact of Race and Sex on the 2008 Democratic Presidential Primaries." In *Winning the Presidency, 2008*, ed. William J. Crotty; "Hillary Clinton Endorses Barack Obama," *New York Times*, June 7, 2008 www.nytimes.com/2008/06/07/us/politics/07text-clinton.html [accessed June 15, 2018].

23 See, e.g., Dolan, Kathleen, "Is There a 'Gender Affinity Effect' in American Politics? Information, Affect, and Candidate Sex in U.S House Elections," *Political Research Quarterly* 61 (March 2008): 79–89.

24 Greenlee, *The Political Consequences of Motherhood*; Baeil, Linda and Rhonda Kinney Longworth, *Framing Sarah Palin: Pit Bulls, Puritans, and Politics* (New York: Routledge, 2013); Miller, Melissa K. and Jeffrey S. Peake, "Press Effects, Public Opinion, and Gender: Coverage of Sarah Palin's Vice-Presidential Campaign," *International Journal of Press/Politics*, 18(2013): 482–507; Abramson, Paul R., John H. Aldrich, and David W. Rohde, "*Change and Continuity in the 2008 Elections* (Washington, DC: CQ Press, 2009); Baird, Julia, "Sarah Palin and Women Voters," *Newsweek*, September 12, 2008, www.newsweek.com/sarah-palin-and-women-voters-88503 [accessed June 15, 2018]; Greenberg Quinlan Rosner Research, "Assessing the Impact of Sarah Palin on the Women's Vote: Unmarried Women have Unanswered Questions," September 4, 2008, www.wvwvaf.org/wp-content/uploads/2012/04/Key-Differences-emerge-from-focus-groups.pdf [accessed June 15, 2018]; Seelye, Katharine Q., "Palin and the Women's Vote," *New York Times*, August 29, 2008, https://thecaucus.blogs.nytimes.com/2008/08/29/palin-and-the-womens-vote/ [accessed June 15, 2018]; Greenberg, Anna, "Angry White Women Revisited," *Huffington Post*, May 25, 2011, www.huffingtonpost.com/anna-greenberg/angry-white-women-revisit_b_126471.html [accessed June 15, 2018]; Newport, Frank, "Did Palin Help McCain Among White Women?" *Gallup*, September 24, 2008, http://news.gallup.com/poll/110638/did-palin-help-mccain-among-white-women.aspx [accessed June 15, 2018].

25 Greenlee, *The Political Consequences of Motherhood*; Eilperin, Juliet, "McCain, Obama Reaching Out to Female Voters," *Washington Post*, June 12, 2008, www.washingtonpost.com/wp-dyn/content/article/2008/06/11/AR2008061103854.html [accessed June 15, 2018].

26 Sides, John and Lynn Vavreck, *The Gamble: Choice and Chance in the 2012 Presidential Election* (Princeton, NJ: Princeton University Press, 2013); Greenlee, *The Political Consequences of Motherhood*.

27 Sides and Vavreck, *The Gamble*; Greenlee, *The Political Consequences of Motherhood*; Madison, Lucy, "In Courting Women, Romney Camp Bets on the Economy," *CBS News*, October 22, 2012, www.cbsnews.com/news/in-courting-women-romney-camp-bets-on-the-economy/ [accessed June 18, 2018]; Greenberg, Anna, "Year of the Woman: Private Parts and Political Parties," *Huffington Post*, February 18, 2013, www.huffingtonpost.com/anna-greenberg/womens-vote_b_2330928.html [accessed June 18, 2018].

28 Rucker, Philip, "Trump says Fox's Megyn Kelly had 'Blood Coming Out of Her Wherever,'" *The Washington Post*, August 8, 2015, www.washingtonpost.com/news/post-politics/wp/2015/08/07/trump-says-foxs-megyn-kelly-had-blood-coming-out-of-her-wherever/ [accessed July 9, 2019]; "The Fox News GOP Debate Transcript, Annotated," *The Washington Post*, March 3, 2016, www.washingtonpost.com/news/the-fix/wp/2016/03/03/the-fox-news-gop-debate-transcript-annotated [accessed July 9, 2019]; Rappeport, Alan, "Donald Trump's Uncomplimentary Comments about Carly Fiorina," *New York Times*, September 10, 2015, www.nytimes.com/politics/first-draft/2015/09/10/donald-trumps-uncomplimentary-comments-about-carly-fiorina/ [accessed June 18, 2018].

29 Dittmar, Kelly, *Finding Gender in Election 2016: Lessons from Presidential Gender Watch*, Center for American Women and Politics, Rutgers University, 2017; Rappeport, Alan, "Donald Trump's Latest Jab at Hillary Clinton: 'No Stamina,'" *New York Times*, August 15, 2016,

www.nytimes.com/2016/08/17/us/politics/donald-trump-hillary-clinton-stamina.html [accessed July 9, 2019]; Parker, Ashley, "Donald Trump Says Hillary Clinton Doesn't Have 'a Presidential Look,'" *New York Times*, September 6, 2016, www.nytimes.com/2016/09/07/us/politics/donald-trump-says-hillary-clinton-doesnt-have-a-presidential-look.html?_r=0 [accessed July 9, 2019]; Sanghani, Radhika, "The Sexist Hillary Clinton Merchandise that Will Make You Cringe," *The Telegraph*, June 9, 2016, www.telegraph.co.uk/women/life/the-sexist-hillary-clinton-merchandise-that-will-make-you-cringe/ [accessed July 9, 2019]; Diaz, Daniella, "Trump Calls Clinton 'a Nasty Woman,'" *CNN*, October 20, 2016, www.cnn.com/2016/10/19/politics/donald-trump-hillary-clinton-nasty-woman/index.html [accessed June 18, 2018].

30 Dittmar, *Finding Gender in Election 2016*; Aldrich, John H., Jamie L. Carson, Brad T. Gomez, and David W. Rohde, *Change and Continuity in the 2016 Elections* (Washington, DC: CQ Press, 2019); Kurtzleben, Danielle, "Here's the List of Women Who Accused Donald Trump of Sexual Misconduct," *NPR*, October 20, 2016, www.npr.org/2016/10/13/497799354/a-list-of-donald-trumps-accusers-of-inappropriate-sexual-conduct [accessed June 18, 2018]; Blake, Aaron, "21 Times Donald Trump Has Assured Us He Respects Women," *The Washington Post*, March 8, 2017, www.washingtonpost.com/news/the-fix/wp/2017/03/08/21-times-donald-trump-has-assured-us-he-respects-women/ [accessed July 9, 2019].

31 Dittmar, Kelly, *Finding Gender in Election 2016: Lessons from Presidential Gender Watch*, Center for American Women and Politics, Rutgers University, 2017; Parker, Kathleen, "Trump Deals Clinton a Winning Card," *Washington Post*, April 29, 2016, www.washingtonpost.com/opinions/trump-deals-clinton-a-winning-card/2016/04/29/7e38d436-0e39-11e6-a6b6-2e6de3695b0e_story.html?utm_term=.d42861fb2774 [accessed July 9, 2019].

32 Sproul, Robin, "Exit Polls: Better or Worse Since the 2000 Election?" Joan Shorenstein Center on the Press, Politics and Public Policy. Cambridge, MA: Harvard University, 2007.

33 Vavreck, Lynn and Douglas Rivers, "The 2006 Cooperative Congressional Election Study," *Journal of Elections, Public Opinion and Parties* 18(2008): 355–66.

34 Edsall, Thomas B., "The 2016 Exit Polls Led Us to Misinterpret the 2016 Election," *The New York Times*, March 29, 2018.

35 US Census Bureau, Voting and Registration in the Election of 2016, May 2017.

36 Nealy, Lisa Nikol, *African-American Women Voters: Racializing Religiosity, Political Consciousness and Progressive Political Action in US Presidential Elections from 1964 Through 2008* (Lanham, MD: University Press of America, 2009).

37 Bejarano, Christina E., *The Latino Gender Gap in US Politics* (New York: Routledge, 2014).

38 Harris, Maya L., "Women of Color: A Growing Force in the American Electorate," Center for American Progress, October 30, 2014, https://cdn.americanprogress.org/wp-content/uploads/2014/10/WOCvoters3.pdf [accessed June 15, 2018]; Montoya, Celeste, "From Seneca to Shelby: Intersectionality and Women's Voting Rights." In *100 Years of the Nineteenth Amendment*, eds. Holly J. McCammon and Lee Ann Banaszak (New York: Oxford University Press, 2018; Junn, Jane and Natalie Musuoka, "Dynamic Women Voters: Race and Voting in US Presidential Elections," Working Paper, December 7, 2017, www.americanprogress.org/issues/race/reports/2014/10/30/99962/women-of-color/ [accessed July 9, 2019].

39 Bejarano, *The Latino Gender Gap in US Politics*.

40 Roberts, Andrew W., Stella U. Ogunwole, Laura Blakeslee, and Megan A. Rabe, "The Population 65 Years and Older in the United States: 2016," American Community Survey Reports, US Census. October 2018.

41 American Community Survey, US Census, 2014.

42 The American National Election Studies (electionstudies.org), The ANES Guide to Public Opinion and Electoral Behavior (Ann Arbor, MI: University of Michigan, Center for Political Studies [producer and distributor], 2018).

43 Brady, Henry E., Sidney Verba, and Kay Lehman Schlozman, "Beyond SES: A Resource Model of Political Participation," *American Political Science Review* 89(June 1995): 271–94.

44 Leighley, Jan E. and Jonathan Nagler, *Who Votes Now? Demographics, Issues, Inequality, and Turnout in the United States* (Princeton, NJ: Princeton University Press, 2014); Rosenstone, Steven J. and John Mark Hansen, *Mobilization, Participation, and Democracy in America* (New York: Macmillan Publishing Company, 1993); Burns, Nancy, Kay Lehman Schlozman, and Sidney Verba, *The Private Roots of Public Action: Gender, Equality, and Political Participation* (Cambridge, MA: Harvard University Press, 2001).

45 Lawless and Fox, *It Still Takes a Candidate*; Kanthak, Kristin and Jonathan Woon, "Women Don't Run? Election Aversion and Candidate Entry," *American Journal of Political Science* 59(July 2015): 595–612.

46 Leighley and Nagler, *Who Votes Now?*; Burns, Nancy, Kay Lehman Schlozman, Ashely Jardina, Shauna Shames, and Sidney Verba, "What Happened to the Gender Gap in Political Participation? How Might We Explain It?" In *100 Years of the Nineteenth Amendment*, eds. Holly J. McCammon and Lee Ann Banaszak (New York: Oxford University Press, 2018).

47 Center for American Women and Politics (CAWP), Summary of Women Candidates for Selected Offices," 2018, www.cawp.rutgers.edu/sites/default/files/resources/can_histsum.pdf [accessed July 14, 2019]; Center for American Women and Politics (CAWP), History of Women in the US Congress, 2019, https://cawp.rutgers.edu/history-women-us-congress [accessed July 14, 2019].

48 Burns, Schlozman, Jardina, Shames, and Verba, "What Happened to the Gender Gap in Political Participation? How Might We Explain It?"; Atkeson, Lonna Rae, "Not All Cues Are Created Equal: The Conditional Impact of Female Candidates on Political Engagement," *The Journal of Politics* 65(2003): 1040–61; Fridkin, Kim L. and Patrick J. Kenney, "How the Gender of US Senators Influences People's Understanding and Engagement in Politics," *The Journal of Politics* 76(October 2014): 1017–1031; Mariani, Mack, Bryan W. Marshall, and A. Lanethea Mathews-Schultz, "See Hillary Clinton, Nancy Pelosi, and Sarah Palin Run? Party, Ideology, and the Influence of Female Role Models on Young Women," *Political Research Quarterly* 68(2015): 716–31; Reingold, Beth and Jessica Harrell, "The Impact of Descriptive Representation on Women's Political Engagement: Does Party Matter?" *Political Research Quarterly* 63(2010): 280–94; Campbell, David E. and Christina Wolbrecht, "See Jane Run: Women Politicians as Role Models for Adolescents," *The Journal of Politics* 68(2006): 233–47; Campbell, David E. and Christina Wolbrecht, "The Resistance as Role Model: Disillusionment and Protest Among American Adolescents After 2016," *Political Behavior* DOI 10.1007/s11109-019-09537-w; but see Dolan, Kathleen, "Symbolic Mobilization? The Impact of Candidate Sex in

American Elections," *American Politics Research* 34 (November 2006): 687–704; Lawless, Jennifer L., "Politics of Presence? Congresswomen and Symbolic Representation," *Political Research Quarterly* 57(2004): 81–99.

49 Sampaio, Anna, "*Trumpeando* Latinas/os: Race, Gender, Immigration, and the Role of Latinas/os." In *Gender and Elections: Shaping the Future of American Politics*, eds. Susan J. Carroll and Richard L. Fox (New York: Cambridge University Press, 2018); Smooth, Wendy, "African American Women and Electoral Politics." In *Gender and Elections: Shaping the Future of American Politics*, eds. Susan J. Carroll and Richard L. Fox (New York: Cambridge University Press, 2018).

50 Greenlee, *The Political Consequences of Motherhood*; Pomper, Gerald, "The 2000 Presidential Election: Why Gore Lost," *Political Research Quarterly* 116(Summer 2001): 201–23; West, Laurel Parker, "Soccer Moms, Welfare Queens, Waitress Moms and Super Moms: Myths of Motherhood in State Media Coverage of Child Care During the 'Welfare Reforms' of the 1990s," *Southern California Interdisciplinary Law Journal* 25(2016): 313–46; Weisberg, Herbert F., "The Demographics of a New Voting Gap: Marital Differences in American Voting," *Public Opinion Quarterly* 51(1987): 335–43; Keen, Judy, "Bush Working to Woo Female Voters," *USA Today*, March 6, 2000 https://usatoday30.usatoday.com/news/e98/e1300.htm [accessed June 14, 2018]; "The Female Vote," *PBS NewsHour*, September 19, 2000, www.pbs.org/newshour/spc/bb/election/july-dec00/woman_9-19a.html [accessed June 14, 2000]; Bevan, Tom, "Al Gore's Women Problems," *RealClear Politics*, May 11, 2000, www.realclearpolitics.com/Commentary/com-5_11_00.html [accessed June 14, 2018]; Marks, Alexandra, "Women's Vote: Elusive Prize in Election 2000," *The Christian Science Monitor*, April 13, 2000, www.csmonitor.com/2000/0413/p3s1.html [accessed June 14, 2018]; "Gore Woos Women Voters," *The Guardian*, September 10, 2000, www.theguardian.com/world/2000/sep/10/uselections2000.usa [accessed June 14, 2018]; Hart, Betsy, "Women Voters Seem to Want a Caretaker" (Scripps Howard News Service), *Deseret News*, November 3, 2000, www.deseretnews.com/article/791271/Women-voters-seem-to-want-a-caretaker.html [accessed June 14, 2018].

51 Garber, Kent, "Behind Obama's Victory: Women Open Up a record Marriage Gap," *US News & World Report*, November 5, 2008, www.usnews.com/news/articles/2008/11/05/behind-obamas-victory-women-open-up-a-record-marriage-gap [accessed June 15, 2018]; see also, Greenberg Quinlan Rosner Research, "Assessing the Impact of Sarah Palin on the Women's Vote: Unmarried Women have Unanswered Questions," September 4, 2008, www.wvwvaf.org/wp-content/uploads/2012/04/Key-Differences-emerge-from-focus-groups.pdf [accessed June 15, 2018].

52 Data used to construct the figures in this chapter are from the individual 2000, 2004, 2008, 2012, and 2016 ANES Time Series Studies. All other chapters rely on the ANES Time Series Cumulative Data file (1948–2016).

53 Kaufmann, Karen M., "The Gender Gap," *PS: Political Science and Politics* 39(2006): 447–53.

54 For example: Carroll, Susan J., "Voting Choices: The Significance of Women Voters and the Gender Gap." In *Gender and Elections: Shaping the Future of American Politics*, eds. Susan J. Carroll and Richard L. Fox (New York: Cambridge University Press, 2018); Chaney, Carole Kennedy, R. Michael Alvarez, and Jonathan Nagler, "Explaining the Gender Gap in U.S. Presidential

Elections, 1980–1992," *Political Research Quarterly* 51(1998): 311–39; Clark and Clark, *Women at the Polls*; Kaufmann, Karen M. and John R. Petrocik, "The Changing Politics of American Men: Understanding the Sources of the Gender Gap," *American Journal of Political Science* 43 (1999): 864–87; Norrander, Barbara and Clyde Wilcox, "The Gender Gap in Ideology," *Political Behavior* 30(2008): 503–23; Fox, Richard L. and Zoe Oxley, "Women's Support for an Active Government." In *Minority Voting in the United States* Volume I, eds. Kyle L. Kreider and Thomas J. Baldino (Santa Barbara, CA: Praeger, 2016); Norrander, Barbara, "The History of the Gender Gaps." In *Voting the Gender Gap*, ed. Lois Duke Whitaker (Champaign, IL: University of Illinois Press, 2008), pp. 9–32.

55 Blinder, Scott and Meredith Rolfe, "Rethinking Compassion: Toward a Political Account of the Partisan Gender Gap in the United States," *Political Psychology* 39(2017): 889–906; Schlesinger and Heldman, "Gender Gap or Gender Gaps?"; Howell and Day, "Complexities of the Gender Gap;" Inglehart and Norris, "The Developmental Theory of the Gender Gap."

56 Kaufmann, Karen M., "Culture Wars, Secular Realignment, and the Gender Gap in Party Identification," *Political Behavior* 24(2002): 283–307.

57 Silver, Nate, "'Gender Gap' Near Historic Highs," *New York Times*, October 21, 2012, https://fivethirtyeight.blogs.nytimes.com/2012/10/21/gender-gap-near-historic-highs/ [accessed October 23, 2018]; Sides and Vavreck, *The Gamble*; Norrander, Barbara, "The History of the Gender Gaps." In *Voting the Gender Gap*, ed. Lois Duke Whitaker (Champaign, IL: University of Illinois Press, 2008), pp. 9–32.

58 Quoted in Carroll, Susan, "Security Moms and Presidential Politics: Women Voters in the 2004 Election." In *Voting the Gender Gap*, ed. Lois Duke Whitaker (Champaign, IL: University of Illinois Press, 2008), p. 77; Klein, Joe, "How Soccer Moms Became Security Moms," *Time*, February 10, 2003.

59 Kaufmann, Karen M., "The Gender Gap," *PS: Political Science and Politics* 39(2006): 447–53; Carroll, "Security Moms and Presidential Politics."

60 Carroll, "Security Moms and Presidential Politics," p. 88.

61 Ondercin, Heather L., "Who Is Responsible for the Gender Gap? The Dynamics of Men's and Women's Democratic Macropartisanship, 1950–2012," *Political Research Quarterly* 70(2017): 749–61; Atkeson, Lonna Rae, "Not All Cues Are Created Equal: The Conditional Impact of Female Candidates on Political Engagement," *The Journal of Politics* 65(2003): 1040–61.

62 McDermott, Monika L., *Masculinity, Femininity, and American Political Behavior* (New York: Oxford University Press, 2016); Bittner, Amanda and Elizabeth Goodyear-Grant, "Sex isn't Gender: Reforming Concepts and Measurements in the Study of Public Opinion," *Political Behavior* 39(December 2017): 1019–41.

63 Winter, Nicholas J.G., "Masculine Republicans and Feminine Democrats: Gender and Americans' Explicit and Implicit Images of the Political Parties," *Political Behavior* 32(2010): 587–618.

64 Kurtzleben, Danielle, "The Trump-Clinton Gender Gap Could Be the Largest in More than 60 Years," *NPR*, www.npr.org/2016/05/26/479319725/the-trump-clinton-gender-gap-could-be-the-largest-in-more-than-60-years [accessed October 24, 2018].

65 Silver, Nate, "Election Update: Women Are Defeating Donald Trump," FiveThirtyEight, October 11, 2016, https://fivethirtyeight.com/features/election-update-women-are-defeating-donald-trump/ [accessed October 24, 2018]; see MacManus, Susan A., "Voter Participation and Turnout: The Political Generation Divide Among Women Deepens." In *Gender and Elections: Shaping the Future of American Politics,* eds. Susan J. Carroll and Richard L. Fox (New York: Cambridge University Press, 2018).

66 "The Gender Gap: Voting Choices in Presidential Elections," Center for the American Women in Politics, 2017.

67 Lett, Phoebe, "White Women Vote for Trump. Now What?" *New York Times,* November 10, 2016, www.nytimes.com/2016/11/10/opinion/white-women-voted-trump-now-what.html [accessed July 9, 2019], "The real 'shy Trump' vote – how 53% of white women pushed him to victory," *The Guardian,* November 10, 2016, www.theguardian.com/us-news/2016/nov/10/white-women-donald-trump-victory [accessed July 9, 2019]; "Clinton Couldn't Win Over White Women," *FiveThirtyEight* blog, November 9, 2016, https://fivethirtyeight.com/features/clinton-couldnt-win-over-white-women/ [accessed July 9, 2019]; Feldman, Linda, "Why Hillary Clinton lost the white women's vote," *The Christian Science Monitor,* November 22, 2016, www.csmonitor.com/USA/Politics/2016/1122/Why-Hillary-Clinton-lost-the-white-women-s-vote [accessed October 24, 2018].

68 De Pinto, Jennifer, "Women Think U.S. Would Be Better Off with More Women in Office – CBS News Poll," *CBSnews,* January 19, 2018, www.cbsnews.com/news/women-think-u-s-would-be-better-off-with-more-women-in-office-cbs-news-poll/ [accessed October 24, 2018].

69 Sides, John, Michael Tesler, and Lynn Vavreck, *Identity Crisis: The 2016 Presidential Campaign and the Battle for the Meaning of America* (Princeton, NJ: Princeton University Press, 2018).

70 Schaffner, Brian, Matthew MacWilliams, and Tatishe Nteta, "Understanding White Polarization in the 2016 Vote for President: The Sobering Role of Racism and Sexism," *Political Research Quarterly* 133(2018): 9–34.

71 Bracic, Ana, Mackenzie Israel-Trummel, and Allyson F. Shortle, "Is Sexism for White People? Gender Stereotypes, Race, and the 2016 Presidential Election," *Political Behavior* 41(2018): 281–307.

72 Cassese and Barnes, "Reconciling Sexism and Women's Support for Republican Candidates."

73 Junn, Jane, "Hiding in Plain Sight: White Women Vote Republican," *Politics of Color* blog, November 13, 2016, http://politicsofcolor.com/white-women-vote-republican/ [accessed July 9, 2019]; Junn, Jane and Natalie Musuoka, "Dynamic Women Voters: Race and Voting in US Presidential Elections," Working Paper, December 7, 2017.

74 See: Sampaio, Anna, "*Trumpeando* Latinas/os: Race, Gender, Immigration, and the Role of Latinas/os." In *Gender and Elections: Shaping the Future of American Politics,* eds. Susan J. Carroll and Richard L. Fox (New York: Cambridge University Press, 2018); Smooth, Wendy "African American Women and Electoral Politics." In *Gender and Elections: Shaping the Future of American Politics,* eds. Susan J. Carroll and Richard L. Fox (New York: Cambridge University Press, 2018).

75 Anapol, Avery, "Trump Inaccurately Claims He Got 52 Percent of the Female Vote," *The Hill,* March 3, 2018, http://thehill.com/homenews/administration/377787-trump-falsely-claims-he-got-52-percent-of-female-vote [accessed July 9, 2019].

76 Sides, Tesler, and Vavreck, *Identity Crisis*; CNN 2016 exit polls, www.cnn.com/election/2016/results/exit-polls [accessed March 14, 2018].

77 Layman, Geoffrey C. and Thomas M. Carsey, "Party Polarization and 'Conflict Extension' in the American Electorate," *American Journal of Political Science* 46(October 2002): 786–802; Layman, Geoffrey C., Thomas M. Carsey, John C. Green, and Richard Herrera, "Activists and Conflict Extension in American Party Politics," *American Political Science Review* 104(May 2010): 324–46.

78 Azari, Julia, "Weak Parties and Strong Partisanship Are a Bad Combination," Mischiefs of Faction blog, *Vox*, November 3, 2016, www.vox.com/mischiefs-of-faction/2016/11/3/13512362/weak-parties-strong-partisanship-bad-combination [accessed October 29, 2018].

9 A CENTURY OF VOTES FOR WOMEN

1 Chenoweth, Erica and Jeremy Pressman, "This is What We Learned by Counting the Women's Marches," *The Monkey Cage* blog, February 7, 2017, www.washingtonpost.com/news/monkey-cage/wp/2017/02/07/this-is-what-we-learned-by-counting-the-womens-marches/ [accessed July 9, 2019].

2 Putnam, Lara and Theda Skocpol, "Middle America Reboots Democracy," *Democracy: A Journal of Ideas*, February 10, 2018, https://democracyjournal.org/arguments/middle-america-reboots-democracy/ [accessed July 9, 2019].

3 Alter, Charlotte, "A Year Ago, They Marched. Now a Record Number of Women are Running for Office," *Time*, January 29, 2018.

4 Pew Research Center, "Since Trump's Election, Increased Attention to Politics – Especially Among Women," July 20, 2017, www.people-press.org/2017/07/20/since-trumps-election-increased-attention-to-politics-especially-among-women/ [accessed July 9, 2019].

5 Campbell, David E. and Christina Wolbrecht, "The Resistance as Role Model: Disillusionment and Protest Among American Adolescents After 2016," *Political Behavior* DOI 10.1007/s11109-019-09537-w.

6 Zacharek, Stephanie, Eliana Dockterman, and Haley Sweetland Edwards, "Person of the Year: The Silence Breakers: The Voices that Launched a Movement," *Time*, December 18, 2017.

7 Goldberg, Barbara, "US Students Turn to Gun-control Group after School Shooting," *Reuters*, February 21, 2018, www.reuters.com/article/us-usa-guns-everytown/u-s-students-turn-to-gun-control-group-after-school-shooting-idUSKCN1G52YX [accessed July 9, 2019].

8 Dastagir, Alia E., "West Virginia Teachers' Victory Shows 'Power of Women' as More Battles Loom," *USA Today*, March 8, 2018, www.usatoday.com/story/news/2018/03/08/west-virginia-teachers-victory-shows-power-women-more-battles-loom/403374002/ [accessed July 9, 2019].

9 Schaffner, Brian, "Republican Candidates are Being Punished for Trump's Sexism," Data for Progress, November 8, 2018, https://wthh.dataforprogress.org/blog/2018/11/8/republican-candidates-are-being-punished-for-trumps-sexism [accessed November 12, 2018].

10 Carroll, "Voting Choices: The Significance of Women Voters and the Gender Gap." In *Gender and Elections: Shaping the Future of American Politics*, eds. Susan J. Carroll and Richard L. Fox (New York: Cambridge University Press, 2018), pp. 141–42.

11 Hirshman, Linda, "16 Ways of Looking at a Female Voter," *The New York Times Magazine*, February 3, 2008 www.nytimes.com/2008/02/03/magazine/03womenvoters-t.html [accessed June 15, 2018].

12 Baird, Julia, "Sarah Palin and Women Voters," *Newsweek*, September 12, 2008, www.newsweek.com/sarah-palin-and-women-voters-88503 [accessed June 15, 2018].

13 "Woman Voter Speaks: Feminine Political Interests as Revealed in a Painstaking Eavesdropping Expedition," *New York Times*, June 13, 1920, p. 87.

14 See Mason, *Uncivil Agreement*.

15 Brown, Nadia E., "Political Participation of Women of Color: An Intersectional Analysis," *Journal of Women, Politics, & Policy* 35(2014): 315–48; see also Smooth, Wendy G., "African American Women and Electoral Politics: The Core of the New American Electorate." In *Gender and Elections: Shaping the Future of American Politics*, 4th Edition (New York: Cambridge University Press, 2018); Holman, Mirya, "The Differential Effect of Resources on Political Participation Across Gender and Racial Groups." In *Distinct Identities: Minority Women in US Politics*, eds. Nadia E. Brown and Sarah Allen Gershon (New York: Routledge, 2016); Nealy, *African American Women Voters*.

16 Cassese, Erin C. and Tiffany D. Barnes, "Reconciling Sexism and Women's Support for Republican Candidates," *Political Behavior* DOI 10.1007/s11109-018-9468-z.

17 Burns, Nancy, Kay Lehman Schlosman, Ashley Jardina, Shauna Shames, and Sidney Verba, "What Happened to the Gender Gap in Political Participation? How Might We Explain It?" In *100 Years of the Nineteenth Amendment*, eds. Holly J. McCammon and Lee Ann Banaszak (New York: Oxford University Press, 2018).

18 See, e.g., Box-Steffensmeier, Janet M., Suzanna De Boef, and Tse-min Lin, "The Dynamics of the Partisan Gender Gap," *American Political Science Review* 98(2004): 515–28; Ondercin, Heather, "Similarities and Differences Across Generations in the Partisan Gender Gap." Working paper, April 2017.

19 Karol, David, *Party Position Change in American Politics: Coalition Management* (New York: Cambridge University Press, 2009).

20 Schickler, Eric, *Racial Realignment: The Transformation of American Liberalism, 1932–1965* (Princeton, NJ: Princeton University Press, 2016).

21 See, for example: Manza, Jeff, and Clem Brooks, "The Gender Gap in US Presidential Elections: When? Why? Implications?" *American Journal of Sociology* 103(1998): 1235–66; Mattei, Franco, "The Gender Gap in Presidential Evaluations: Assessments of Clinton's Performance in 1996," *Polity* 33(2000): 199–228; Studlar, Donley T., Ian McAllister, and Bernadette C. Hayes, "Explaining the Gender Gap in Voting: A Cross-National Analysis," *Social Science Quarterly* 79(1998): 779–98; Fox, Richard L. and Zoe Oxley, "Women's Support for an Active Government." In *Minority Voting in the United States* Volume I, eds. Kyle L. Kreider and Thomas J. Baldino (Santa Barbara, CA: Praeger, 2016).

22 Gilens, Martin, "The Gender Gap: Psychology, Social Structure, and Support for Reagan," *Berkeley Journal of Sociology* 29(1984): 35–56.

23 Richardson, L. E. and P. K. Freeman, "Issue Salience and Gender Differences in Congressional Elections, 1994–1998," *Social Science Journal*, 40(2003): 401–17; Schreckhise, William D. and Todd G. Shields, "Ideological Realignment in the Contemporary US Electorate Revisited," *Social Science Quarterly* 84(2003): 596–612.

24 Howell, Susan E. and Christine L. Day, "Complexities of the Gender Gap," *The Journal of Politics* 62(2000): 858–74; Inglehart, Ronald and Pippa Norris, "The Developmental Theory of the Gender Gap: Women's and Men's Voting Behavior in Global Perspective," *International Political Science Review / Revue Internationale de Science Politique* 21(2000): 441–63; Edlund, Lena and Rohini Pande, "Why Have Women Become Left-Wing? The Political Gender Gap and the Decline in Marriage," *The Quarterly Journal of Economics* 117(2002): 917–61; Manza, Jeff and Clem Brooks, "The Gender Gap in US Presidential Elections: When? Why? Implications?" *American Journal of Sociology* 103(1998): 1235–66; but see: Huddy, Leonie, Erin Cassese, and Mary-Kate Lizotte, "Sources of Political Unity and Disunity among Women: Placing the Gender Gap in Perspective." In *Voting the Gender Gap*, ed. Lois Duke Whitaker (Champaign, IL: University of Illinois Press, 2008), pp. 141–69; Iversen, Torben, and Frances Rosenbluth, "The Political Economy of Gender: Explaining Cross-National Variation in the Gender Division of Labor and the Gender Voting Gap," *American Journal of Political Science* 50(2006): 1–19.

25 Fox, Richard L. and Zoe Oxley, "Women's Support for an Active Government." In *Minority Voting in the United States* Volume I, eds. Kyle L. Kreider and Thomas J. Baldino (Santa Barbara, CA: Praeger, 2016).

26 Kellstedt, Paul M., *The Mass Media and the Dynamics of American Racial Attitudes* (New York: Cambridge University Press, 2003).

27 Blinder, Scott and Meredith Rolfe, "Rethinking Compassion: Toward a Political Account of the Partisan Gender Gap in the United States," *Political Psychology* 39(2017): 889–906; Schlesinger, Mark and Caroline Heldman, "Gender Gap or Gender Gaps? New Perspectives on Support for Government Action and Policies," *The Journal of Politics* 63(2001): 59–92; Howell, Susan E. and Christine L. Day, "Complexities of the Gender Gap," *The Journal of Politics* 62(2000): 858–74.

28 Hutchings, Vincent L., Nicholas A. Valentino, Tasha S. Philpot, and Ismail K. White, "The Compassion Strategy: Race and the Gender Gap in Campaign 2000," *The Public Opinion Quarterly* 68(2004): 512–41; Kaufmann, Karen M. and John R. Petrocik, "The Changing Politics of American Men: Understanding the Sources of the Gender Gap," *American Journal of Political Science* 43(1999): 864–87; Norrander, Barbara, "The Intraparty Gender Gap: Differences between Male and Female Voters in the 1980–2000 Presidential Primaries," *PS: Political Science and Politics* 36 (2003): 181–86; Norrander, Barbara, "The Evolution of the Gender Gap," *The Public Opinion Quarterly* 63(1999): 566–76; Schreckhise, William D. and Todd G. Shields, "Ideological Realignment in the Contemporary US Electorate Revisited," *Social Science Quarterly* 84(2003): 596–612; Wirls, Daniel, "Reinterpreting the Gender Gap," *The Public Opinion Quarterly* 50(1986): 316–30.

29 Wolbrecht, Christina, *The Politics of Women's Rights: Parties, Positions, and Change* (Princeton, NJ: Princeton University Press, 2000).

30 Winter, Nicholas J.G., "Masculine Republicans and Feminine Democrats: Gender and Americans' Explicit and Implicit Images of the Political Parties," *Political Behavior* 32(2010): 587–618.

31 Clifford, Scott, "Compassionate Democrats and Tough Republicans: How Ideology Shapes Partisan Stereotypes," *Political Behavior* (2019): DOI 10.1007/s11109-019-09542-z.

32 Dittmar, Kelly, "By the Numbers: Women Congressional Candidates in 2019," Center for American Womne and Politics, September 12, 2018, http://cawp.rutgers.edu/congressional-candidates-summary-2018 [accessed November 6, 2018].

33 American National Election Studies, Core Utility, www.electionstudies.org/CoreUtility/all.htm [accessed February 23, 2018].

34 Ondercin, Heather L., "Who Is Responsible for the Gender Gap? The Dynamics of Men's and Women's Democratic Macropartisanship, 1950–2012," *Political Research Quarterly* 70(2017).

35 McDermott, Monica L., *Masculinity, Femininity, and American Political Behavior* (New York: Oxford University Press, 2016).

36 Peoples, Angela, "Don't Just Thank Black Women. Follow Us," *New York Times*, December 16, 2017; Gray, Emma, "White Women, Come Get Your People. (But Who Are Your People?)" (interview with political scientist Corrine McConnaughy), *Huffington Post*, November 10, 2018, www.huffingtonpost.com/entry/white-women-voters_us_5be5ceebe4b0dbe871aa9f4f [accessed November 13, 2018].

Index